SUGGESTED PLACES TO BASE YOURSELF

These bases make ideal starting points for exploring localities the Slow way.

KT-382-162

1 **Boscastle (pages 20–3)** Arthurian legend, wild clifftops, lost churches and plunging wooded valleys – meet Cornwall in its most romantic hiding places.

2 **The Camel Estuary (pages 35–43)** Between a rugged coastline ruled by slate and surf, Methodist chapels and hedonist beaches, John Betjeman country rubs up against a (sea)foodie paradise at Padstow.

3 **Bodmin Moor (pages 53–7)** A tangle of tracks and footpaths past rushing rivers and wooded valleys, open moorland with brooding Neolithic stones, remote villages and vintage pubs.

4 **The Inny Valley (pages 79–82)** The Tamar Valley to the south and Bodmin to the west; to the north, a forgotten corner of rural England offers leisurely cycle rides between villages steeped in history.

5 **Looe (pages 95–7)** Fresh crab and fishing boats, seabirds and waders, with grand gardens overlooking the busy Tamar estuary.

6 **Fowey (pages 117–20)** Spectacular biking and hiking in the lunar landscape of the clay mines, and idyllic canoeing and walking in *The Wind in the Willows* territory.

7 **Truro (pages 163–9)** A cathedral city perfect for pottering, with lots going on; explore cycle trails over the mining heartland of Cornwall and take part in the renaissance of Camborne and Redruth.

8 **Falmouth (pages 176–81)** An inspirational river crisscrossed with ferries and dotted with orchards. Art students and eco-culture lead the way to Penryn.

9 **Helston and the Lizard (pages 196–209)** Discover the wooded creeks and tiny fishing villages, iconic gardens and lonely moors in the wild far south of Cornwall.

10 **Penzance (pages 218–25)** The essence of Cornwall is in its toe-tip: artists' colonies and archaeology, brooding moors and crumbling tin-mines, surf, fishing fleets – and a supremely romantic bay.

11 **The Isles of Scilly (pages 251–72)** Choose your favourite island for days spent living the Slow life, surrounded by white beaches and aquamarine waters.

St Agnes Head
St Agnes

Navax Point

Redruth

St Ives

Camborne

PENWITH A30 Hayle

St Just

Hayle

Sennen

Penzance

Helston

10

Mount's Bay

Land's End

Mullion

St Martin's

Tresco

11 ISLES OF SCILLY

Lizard

St Mary's

Lizard Point

Bradt

Slow
Cornwall
& the Isles of Scilly

Local, characterful guides to Britain's special places

Kirsty Fergusson

Edition 1

...dt Travel Guides Ltd, UK
...quot Press Inc, USA

A CORNWALL & ISLES OF SCILLY GALLERY

Slow travel gives you the time to participate in local events like the Port Eliot Festival, and meet the people behind the landscape, the music and the words. (MB)

Accommodation with a difference: cosy yurts with log burners and proper beds are a new addition to the Cornish camping scene. (PF)

Exploring by bike, on foot or on horseback allows you to absorb the landscape one step at a time. (SAR/S)

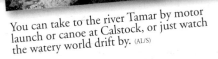

You can take to the river Tamar by motor launch or canoe at Calstock, or just watch the watery world drift by. (AL/S)

You're never far from the coast: Cornwall offers fantastic rambles and bike rides where it's possible to take in both north and south coasts in a single day. (JL)

Taking it Slow

Friendly and unexpected encounters with people, places and wildlife are often the rewards of Slow travel.

There's the opportunity to meet prize-winning farmers and local producers at the Royal Cornwall Show in Wadebridge. (PD)

Shopping for food on Scilly should allow for serendipitous encounters with garden gate stalls or signs like this. (IOSSC)

This may look like a siesta, taken in an impromptu fishing net hammock – but taking time to reflect and absorb the local landscape is all part of the Slow experience. (IOSSC)

Much of Cornwall enjoys a sunnier, milder climate than the rest of England, allowing exotic plants to flourish beside native species against a background of beaches and blue skies. (S/S)

Many of Cornwall's rivers have seen a rise in otter populations in recent years, and there have even been sightings on the river Camel in the centre of Wadebridge. (JP/S)

Nature and nurture

There are plenty of wild places to explore in Cornwall, and an abundance of wildlife to observe on moorland and coastal walks; you'll notice too, how many of Cornwall's gardens have taken on a more relaxed and natural appearance, with colourful perennials extending the season well into autumn.

The chough, which is emblematic of Cornwall, returned to the Lizard in 2000 after an absence of several decades. Increasing numbers now inhabit the cliffs of the south coast. (AH/RSPB)

Many Cornish gardens are famous for their spring flowering trees and shrubs, but at the Hidden Valley gardens near Lostwithiel a gorgeous display of summer perennials lingers late into autumn. (KF)

Some of the finest bluebell woods in England can be enjoyed in early May, at Enys gardens near Falmouth or by the Fowey at Lanhydrock. (JE/S)

Seals are frequently seen around the Cornish coast, bobbing around in the surf or flopped on rocks in the less accessible coves. (ACJ/S)

Spring brings an exhilarating burst of wildflower colour to gardens, cliff tops and fields. (SA/S)

The author was astonished by the quantity and tameness of thrushes on Scilly. (C/S)

As in so many of Cornwall's churches, the gravestones in St Kew are adorned with detailed carvings of angels, thanks to the availability of high quality local slate. (KF)

Tucked away on the outskirts of Gwennap, a crater left by mining activity was used as a preaching pit by John Wesley. The grassy tiers were cut out later by local miners in the early 19th century, as the site grew in status as a place of Methodist pilgrimage. (IW/S)

Hundreds of Celtic crosses stand at places of ancient worship in the Cornish landscape, many of them dating from pre-Norman times. (CRH)

Truro's Victorian masterpiece is the first Anglican cathedral to be built on British soil since Salisbury Cathedral in the 13th century. (LM/S)

Historic Cornwall

The past inhabits the Cornish landscape, investing it with drama. Taking the Slow approach allows you to follow up on your curiosity and discover the history and stories that lie beneath the surface.

The engine houses once contained steam-driven pumping equipment at Wheal Peevor, near Redruth, where copper and tin were extracted during the 18th and 19th centuries. (IW/S)

The Hurlers – a broodingly atmospheric stone circle on Bodmin Moor – lies just a short walk away from the moorland village of Minions. (D/S)

Dolphins are frequently seen off the Cornish coast, and will often accompany the ferry to Scilly for several miles. (IOSSC)

Approached from the coast path, the island fortress of Tintagel appears untouched by tourism. (KF)

Harbour watching is never dull in Falmouth – there's always a lively mix of sailing craft, ferries and commercial shipping to observe on the water. (FM)

Coastal Cornwall

Whatever path you take through Cornwall, the cliffs, the coast and the sea offer breathtaking views.

While artists are drawn to St Ives by the special quality of the light, many more visitors are drawn by the accessible, sandy beaches. (KF)

On the southern shores of the Rame peninsula, there is an almost Mediterranean quality to Kingsand's waterfront. (IW/S)

Nelson, the one-eyed seal, whose friendly presence in the waters around Looe was enjoyed for many years by visitors and locals alike, is commemorated in bronze at the harbour mouth. (BM)

Colourful pilot gigs take to the sea in Scilly, where local teams take on the rest of the world at the annual rowing championships in May. (IOSSC)

On the rugged north coast of the Penwith peninsula, you are seldom far from poignant relics of the tin mining industry. (KF)

The Fal River is the only place in the country where oysters are dredged using traditional methods, by the last oyster fleet working under sail or oar. Rick Stein's Seafood & Oyster Bar in Falmouth serves them up in style. (SJ)

The harbourside pub at Polruan is perfectly placed for walkers crossing the estuary to Fowey. (KF)

Food and drink

Cornish producers occupy a significant position on the Slow Food map; from locally caught fish and seafood, just-picked asparagus, cheeses with a strong regional identity and delicious homemade ice creams to much-admired ciders and ales, you're in for a Slow feast in Cornwall.

Cornish Blue and Yarg have put Cornish cheese on the map in recent years – but there are plenty of other local varieties to discover in farmers' markets. (PD)

Craft ciders are making a strong appearance in Cornwall and a festival celebrating Cornish cider is held each October in Lostwithiel. (SMM)

The paintings of the Newlyn School, evoking the hardships and rewards of life on Cornwall's coast, can be seen at the Penlee Gallery in Penzance. (PRC)

Dame Barbara Hepworth lived and worked in St Ives, where you can visit her studio and wander through the garden filled with her sculptures. (KF)

Artists' and writers' Cornwall

Creative minds have long been drawn to Cornwall, inspired by the sea, the light and the landscape.

Gill Watkiss's windswept figures, seen setting out for blustery walks on the beach or through moorland puddles, epitomise the reality of living with Cornish weather. (KF)

Penwith artist Joe Hemming, who designed the toposcope in the gardens at Trengwainton, at work. Like many Cornish artists, he opens his studio to visitors during Cornwall Open Studios week in early June each year. (KF)

The entire island of Tresco is leased from the Duchy of Cornwall by the Dorrien-Smith family, which explains why it has such a strong and separate identity from the other islands. (AR/S)

Whether you choose to travel by ferry, helicopter or plane, getting to Scilly is always something of an adventure. The Skybus service operates a fleet of six small aircraft to St Mary's from the tiny airport at Land's End throughout the year. (IOSSC)

An elderly passenger on the ferry sighed, 'Bryher. For the solitude and the birds. I have to go every year, even if just for a day.' (SAR/S)

Bursting with plants from across the globe, the Abbey Gardens on Tresco produce a virtuoso display of colour throughout the year. (IOSSC)

The absence of traffic makes walking on Scilly a pleasure. Forget maps – the islands are too small to get lost – and just wander along the many tracks and footpaths each island has to offer. (IOSSC)

The Isles of Scilly

The archipelago of tiny islands and rocks is just a smudge on the horizon from Land's End; at closer quarters the natural, breathtaking beauty of the islands is revealed, inhabited by communities where Slow is not so much a concept as a way of life.

ICE CREAM
Made on St Agnes at Troytown
WHITE CHOCOLATE
VANILLA ROYAL CROWN
RUM & RAISINS
COCONUT
GINGER
STRAWBERRY SORBET
100 mL TUBS   £1.75
Ice cream made with Troytown whole milk & cream

Troytown farm on St Agnes produces its own fabulous ice cream from a small herd of cows. (IOSSC)

When people tell you why St Martin's is their favourite island, they usually mention two things: the empty, white beaches and the concentration of excellent local food produced here. (IOSSC)

Walkers tackling the rugged north coast of Penwith have the opportunity to stay in an authentic gypsy caravan, just a few hundred yards from the coast path close to Trewellard. (HB)

Eccentric Cornwall

Part of the fun of Slow travel is discovering the quirky side of the region you're exploring.

It's not just the planting that surprises at the Potager garden, hidden away in a maze of lanes between Helston and Falmouth. (KF)

Rambling down a back lane on the Lizard peninsula, the author encountered an unexpected welcoming party. (KF)

The Melting Pot café and performance space, next to the Krowji studios on the outskirts of Redruth, is decorated with a gloriously random collection of found objects. (KF)

Author

Kirsty Fergusson lives near St Buryan in the far west of Cornwall. She began work as a freelance garden writer in the 1990s after working as head gardener on a historic Dorset estate and for six years was weekly garden columnist to the *Express*. She continues to write for the gardening press and, having spent some time living and working in southwest France, has branched out into garden tours, in both England and France. She has a website at www.kirstyfergusson.co.uk.

Author's story

Before I came to live in the far west of Cornwall, I remember poring over my OS maps and being enthralled by the dramatic contours of the coastline, the empty moors dotted with archaeological symbols, the deep meandering estuaries and the strange poetry of the place names. The cluster of islands that lay where the sun set on the horizon, as I stood on the cliffs close to my new home near Land's End, fired my imagination, too. I had never been to Cornwall or the Isles of Scilly on holiday and I'd only once crossed the Tamar, in order to write about an artist's garden near Penzance. I didn't have a television and so my knowledge of the region was astonishingly unclouded by TV images, nostalgia, prejudice or the kind of partisan adoration that childhood holidays seem to inspire.

I was fortunate to have time to explore my adopted county out of season, on foot and by bicycle (and occasionally in a canoe): it was an eye-widening, if slightly random immersion, that revealed an exhilarating diversity in local identity. An additional impetus to my travels came from my meandering career in gardening and garden journalism. Cornwall lacks for nothing in horticultural variety and richness and there are few trails I have followed that have not had to include a small wiggle to take in a lush collection of those hardy exotics which thrive in sheltered coombes up and down the peninsula. Without realising it, I had embarked on a Slow exploration of Cornwall. So when Bradt, who had published a piece I'd written years earlier about looking for peonies in Mongolia, announced they were looking for new authors, I jumped at the possibility of more Slow exploring, relishing the opportunity to spend time in the places with which I was less familiar.

I began my research on Bryher, in the Isles of Scilly, and I ended my Slow journey a year later, in bright March sunshine back again on the 'Fortunate Isles', where Slow is not so much a concept as a way of life. Here as in so many parts of rural and coastal Cornwall, I found individuals and communities living well, savouring the special quality of their surroundings and very alert to the growing demand for sustainable tourism having seen their fair share of unsustainable industries. Time after time in conversation, 'Slow', I discovered, proved valuable shorthand for so much that Cornwall and its admirers aspire to in the 21st century.

Reprinted October 2013
First published April 2012
Bradt Travel Guides Ltd
IDC House, The Vale, Chalfont St Peter, Bucks SL9 9RZ, England
www.bradtguides.com
Published in the USA by The Globe Pequot Press Inc,
PO Box 480, Guilford, Connecticut 06437-0480

ISBN: 978 1 84162 392 4

British Library Cataloguing in Publication Data
A catalogue record for this book is available from the British Library

Front cover artwork Neil Gower (*www.neilgower.com*)
Illustrations Gary Long
Photographs Michael Bowles (MB); Helen Buck (HB); Cornish Rail Holidays (CRH);
Percy Robert Craft 1856–1934, *Tucking a School of Pilchards*, 1897, Oil on Canvas, 142
x 212cm, Penlee House Gallery & Museum, Penzance (PRC); Peter Dean/Agripics (PD);
Falmouth/www.falmouth.co.uk (FM); Kirsty Fergusson (KF); Andy Hay/www.rspb-
images.com (AH/RSPB); Isles of Scilly Steamship Company (IOSSC); Shilpa Jain (SJ);
John Lloyd (JL); Sam Morgan Moore Ltd (SMM); Brian Mossemenear (BM); Pencuke
Farm/www.pencukefarm.co.uk (PF); Andrew Roland (AR/S); Shutterstock: catherinka
(C/S), Dubassy (D/S), Julian Elliott (JE/S), A C Jones (ACJ/S), Andrew Longden (AL/S),
Lee Morriss (LM/S), Jacques Palut (JP/S), Stephen Aaron Rees (SAR/S), Samot (SA/S),
Shutterschock (S/S), Ian Woolcock (IW/S)

Maps Chris and Ingrid Lane (*www.artinfusion.co.uk*)

Typeset from the author's disc by Artinfusion
Production managed by Jellyfish Print Solutions; printed in Europe

Acknowledgements

I am hugely grateful to all those who stopped what they were doing in order to chat and answer my questions and show me round their gardens, houses, museums, churches, B&Bs and campsites or point me in the right direction.

These people include, in no particular order, Jake Jackson, Paul Corin, John Harris, Henrietta Boex, Annabelle Read, Carolyn Screech, Laura Richards, Jim Wallwork, David Keast, Steve and Sheila Perry, Reg and Sue Sheppard, Neil and Ruth Burden, Nanette and Anthony Manning, Julie Tamblyn, Jo Craig, Lynda Small, Barry Mays, Sir Richard Carew-Pole, Joy Cheeseman, Jamie Parsons, Mark Camp, Lois Humphrey, John and Dee Watt, Mark Harris, Toby Tobin-Dougan, Mike Nelhams, Michael and Kim Spencer, Sabine Schraudolph, Sioux Dunster, James and Mary St Aubyn, Joe Hemming, Ros and Jim Nixon, Alison Bevan, Celia Randell and many others – volunteer coastguards, church wardens, the ladies in the John Betjeman Centre, dog-walkers, farmers, National Trust car park attendants and volunteers – who all helped along the way.

Sanjay Kumar, Cornwall's best-known Slow chef, deserves applause for spreading the word about Slow through Cornwall, too. He sums up the Slow concept perfectly in remembering his mother's words at the dinner table: 'Chew, don't gulp!' That's the best shorthand description of Slow I've come across yet.

I'd also like to make a special mention of CoaST (Cornwall Sustainable Tourism) – a fantastic social enterprise working hard to ensure that tourism in Cornwall benefits local communities, economies and environments. Thanks to you all, especially Manda, who helped enormously in the initial stages of my research and put me in touch with so many good people across the county.

It's a particular pleasure to thank Tim Locke, who has edited my words with the utmost tact, acuity and patience; Tim's book, *Slow Sussex & South Downs National Park*, has been my model and inspiration.

Finally, a very fond thank you to Hugh Chapman, for asking me to live with him in Cornwall.

Local illustrator: Gary Long Gary Long is an artist and illustrator based in Cornwall and who also has been a part-time lecturer at University College Falmouth. His work is exhibited in the UK and the USA. More information can be found on his website www.garylongart.com.

Attention wildlife enthusiasts

For more on British wildlife in Cornwall, why not check out Bradt's *52 Wildlife Weekends*. Go to www.bradtguides.com and key in 52WW40 at the checkout for your 40% discount.

CONTENTS

Going Slow in Cornwall and the Isles of Scilly

The Slow mindset
Hilary Bradt, Founder, Bradt Travel Guides

We shall not cease from exploration
And the end of all our exploring
Will be to arrive where we started
And know the place for the first time.
T S Eliot, 'Little Gidding', *Four Quartets*

This series evolved, slowly, from a Bradt editorial meeting when we started to explore ideas for guides to our favourite country – Great Britain. We wanted to get away from the usual 'top sights' formula and encourage our authors to bring out the nuances and local differences that make up a sense of place – such things as food, building styles, nature, geology, or local people and what makes them tick. Our aim was to create a series that celebrates the present, focusing on sustainable tourism, rather than taking a nostalgic wallow in the past.

So without our realising it at the time, we had defined 'Slow Travel', or at least our concept of it. For the beauty of the Slow movement is that there is no fixed definition; we adapt the philosophy to fit our individual needs and aspirations. Thus Carl Honoré, author of *In Praise of Slow*, writes: 'The Slow Movement is a cultural revolution against the notion that faster is always better. It's not about doing everything at a snail's pace, it's about seeking to do everything at the right speed. Savouring the hours and minutes rather than just counting them. Doing everything as well as possible, instead of as fast as possible. It's about quality over quantity in everything from work to food to parenting.' And travel.

So take time to explore. Don't rush it, get to know an area – and the people who live there – and you'll be as delighted as the authors by what you find.

Five million people come to Cornwall and the Isles of Scilly each year as visitors, and more ink has been spilt by writers attempting to capture the county than over any other part of Britain. It's not hard to see why: Cornish beaches are astonishingly beautiful, washed by tumbling surf that has travelled the Atlantic, while photogenic fishing villages, squeezed into rocky coves, have long served to define Cornwall at its most picturesque.

But Cornwall is more complex and infinitely more diverse than these images allow; there are the post-industrial, granite-built towns of Redruth and Camborne as well as the whitewash-and-thatch villages of the Roseland peninsula; among the mountains of white china clay spoil there are moments of startling beauty, while the wild moors of Bodmin and Penwith are strewn with the skeletal husks of the tin-mining industry and evidence of prehistoric communities lingers in stone.

Then there's the remarkable heritage of unspoilt country churches, holy wells and pilgrim routes, lying quietly beside busy roads and brash resorts; and colonies of artists, shifting with the times around Lamorna, St Ives, Redruth, Falmouth and Penryn.

The finger-like, almost-island geography of Cornwall means you are rarely more than a few miles from the sea. The variety is seemingly infinite: the rugged north coast with its jutting cliffs of slate and granite, towering sand dunes and windy beaches, where Arthur fought and St Piran landed, or the gentler south coast, with its lush subtropical gardens running down to sheltered coves; busy estuaries, rambling rivers and storm-lashed harbours where old fishing communities still survive.

No wonder then, that dozens of guidebooks exist to help holidaymakers get the most out of their precious week or fortnight, listing Cornwall's 'unmissable' sights, its 'Top Ten Beaches', swankiest celebrity-run restaurants or coolest surf bars and festivals. The Slow concept isn't like that. Slow tourism is about taking the time to get to know a place and what contributes to its uniqueness, rather than encouraging an anxious, superficial lightning tour, aimed at ticking as many cultural, gastronomic or geographical boxes as possible. But it's not about travelling at a snail's pace either; the reward of Slow travel is the understanding that immersion in one place often leads to insights into what makes up the bigger picture.

A Slow approach

In this book, which is one of a series of Slow guides, written by local authors, I've taken a Slow look at both the well-known and the less familiar parts of Cornwall, taking time to chat with local residents and allowing curiosity to get the better of me at every turn. Inevitably, every question answered raised two more; every branching footpath and backroad was an invitation to double back on the chosen route.

I could easily have continued my journey for years and written a book ten times as long. Instead, I must apologise to those special places which did not make it into this book, and to those which did, but deserved more space. But if this line of approach encourages readers – seasoned residents and visitors as well as newcomers – to embark on their own Slow Cornish adventures, then to my mind, this book will be serving its purpose.

It was exciting to meet people tuning into their region in this way. A farming family in the Tamar Valley I spoke to were intrigued by the prospect of going on holiday within their county to unknown Porthcurno; children in their last year at St Buryan primary school were beside themselves with excitement at the prospect of the traditional end-of-year camping trip to the Isles of Scilly, just 30 miles (or a world) away from home. The idea of having an adventure waiting for you on your doorstep, so to speak, is immensely appealing. And a couple who live in Gorran Haven, were inspirational: they had spent their Slow honeymoon staying at a comfortable pub near Zennor and exploring the north coast of west Penwith on the open-topped, double-decker bus that runs along the clifftops between St Ives and Land's End.

Taking the Slow approach and stopping to appreciate what the landscape and the local populations have to say has not always made for comfortable listening. Paddling a canoe up a wooded creek of the Fal, looking for orchards of the Kea plum, I came across a (human) community facing extinction as pressure to cash in on the lucrative holiday rental possibilities of their homes reared its head; on Scilly, where the ideal of sustainable, mixed species fishing is still practised, I discovered that most restaurants serve fish brought over from the mainland. In various parts of the peninsula I discovered head gardeners striving to maintain standards on vastly reduced budgets and museums – including a World Heritage Site mining museum – kept alive by public donation alone.

But independent resilience in the face of adversity and the ability to adapt have long been the signature of both coastal and inland Cornwall. There is much to celebrate in the present determination to support and promote local, sustainable, low-carbon businesses – including tourism – which is rapidly gaining momentum and shaking up our attitudes to how and where we travel, eat, sleep and spend our days. This may be Britain's most popular holiday destination, and provide a second home to thousands, but familiarity can all too often make us blind to what gives a place its unique identity, and deaf to the quieter voices that inform and sometimes change that special sense of place. Tuning in to the Slow concept not only illuminates that uniqueness, it is also creates an awareness of the new, emerging Cornwall of the future.

Further reading

Among the many classic works on Cornwall and Cornish life, the following have been especially helpful in researching this guide and will be enjoyed by readers wanting more specialist information: *The Cornwall Gardens Guide* by Douglas Ellory-Pett, *Secret Beaches of the South West* by Rob Smith, *Gourmet Cornwall* by Carol Trewin and *101 Cornish Lives* by Maurice Smelt.

How this book is arranged

There are ten chapters, starting from the Devon border and travelling west to end at the Isles of Scilly. Each chapter follows the same format.

Note that no charge has been made for the inclusion of any business in this guide.

Maps

Each of the ten chapters begins with a **map**, with places **numbered** as they appear in the text. There are also sketch maps for featured walks. That should be enough to get you started; the pink-covered OS Landranger maps 190 and 200 to 204 cover the county in excellent clarity, at 1:50,000. For walkers, the more detailed and more numerous orange-covered OS Explorer maps at 1:25,000 show more features, such as field boundaries – very handy if you're walking through farmland or trying to locate a Bronze Age burial chamber on the moors (though if you're just following the coast path the Landranger sheets are generally adequate).

Accommodation, eating and drinking

I've listed some **accommodation** – a mixture of bed and breakfast, campsites, self-catering cottages and one or two very special hotels – in places that struck me for their location or friendliness or character, or a mixture of the three. I've not given prices (nothing dates a guide so quickly), but I hope to have given a fair indication of the kind of prices to expect. Under places mentioned in the text I've also added a personal selection of **cafés**, **pubs** and a few **restaurants**, plus anything else involving food and drink that has struck me as being useful. These listings are far from exhaustive; they're simply good (some notably good) pitstops I happen to know about.

Practical information

As far as possible, I've included **telephone numbers** and **websites**, and **opening times** if they're unusual in any way. It's always wise to check opening times before setting out, although in my own experience, discovering a 'Closed' sign has nearly always resulted in another – unexpected – door opening. The main **tourist information centres** (TICs) are listed; the official all-Cornwall **website** is www.visitcornwall.com.

I have also outlined some of the most feasible options for exploring Cornwall using **public transport**; a very handy county-wide map, available free from TICs and online at www.cornwallpublictransport.info, shows all bus and train routes, with bus routes colour-coded according to frequency of services.

Walks and cycle rides
Cornwall is famous for its long- and short-distance **walks**, and there are many references within these pages to the Cornwall section of the South West Coast Path (which follows the entire coastline and is waymarked with an acorn motif; see www.southwestcoastpath.com) as well as lesser-known routes, such as the Copper Trail and Tinners' Way. All these are well documented and easy to find online or in print; the circular walks I have suggested will often make partial use of these longer routes, but will only make sense on the ground if you are equipped with the appropriate OS Explorer map for the area.

I mention a few good **cycle rides** too, following both the Cornish Way (Sustrans route 3), the Clay trails and routes of my own devising. Cornwall is fantastically hilly, which I thought was a curse, until I found myself feeling slightly let down by the flatness of the extremely popular Camel Trail. No uphill struggles, but no downhill, freewheeling exhilaration either. Slow, I realised, does not necessarily mean flat or snail's-pace travel.

Places described within the main text
The first place, numbered 1, is marked on the chapter map with a circled 1, so you can see its location. The numbers are roughly geographical. Food and drink (and occasionally other) listings follow on from some entries.

Feedback request
There are only so many special places and aspects of Cornish life that you can focus on when limited by word counts and book length. Much as we'd like to include them all, it simply isn't possible. We've done our best to include a good mix and to check facts but there are bound to be errors (phone numbers and websites change with alarming frequency) as well as inevitable omissions of really special places. If you send an email to info@bradtguides.com about changes to information in this book we will forward it to the author who may include it in a 'one-off update' on the Bradt website at www.bradtguides.com/guide book-updates.html. You can also visit the website for updates to information in this guide.

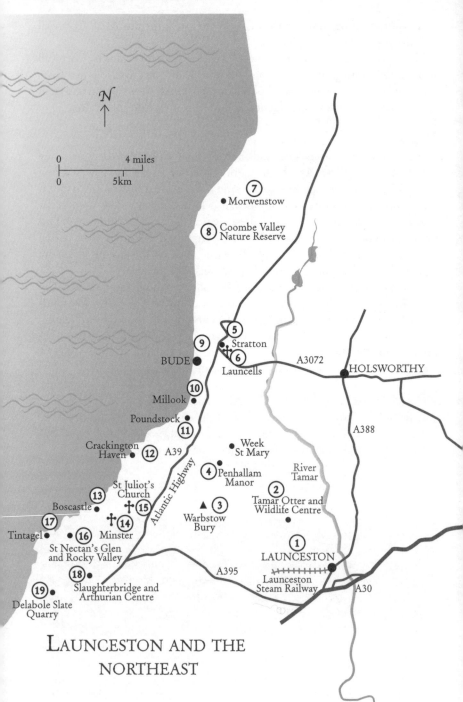

N

0   4 miles
0   5km

⑦ ● Morwenstow

⑧ Coombe Valley
   Nature Reserve

⑤
   ✝ ● Stratton
⑨ ⑥
BUDE ●   Launcells   A3072   HOLSWORTHY

⑩
Millook ●

Poundstock ●
⑪

Crackington   Week
Haven ● ⑫ A39   ● St Mary   River
                                          Tamar
          ④ ● Penhallam
            Manor   ② Tamar Otter and
St Juliot's   Wildlife Centre
Church   A388
⑬   ▲ ③
Boscastle ● ✝ ⑮ Warbstow
⑰   ⑭   Bury
Tintagel ● ✝   ①
        ⑯ Minster   LAUNCESTON
St Nectan's Glen
and Rocky Valley   Launceston
⑱ ●   A395   Steam Railway
Slaughterbridge and   A30
⑲ ● Arthurian Centre
Delabole Slate
Quarry

LAUNCESTON AND THE
NORTHEAST

1. LAUNCESTON AND THE NORTHEAST

Geographically, Cornwall does not lend itself to neat chapter divisions, but **Launceston**, perched with strategic precision, just on the Cornish side of the Tamar, and right beside the main arterial road through the county, is a good place to start exploring the wild northeast coast and its gentler, rural hinterland.

If you exclude the tourist honeypots of Bude, Boscastle and Tintagel, northeast Cornwall is one of the least well-known parts of the county but the rewards for Slow explorers are rich and worth savouring. It's truly a land of contrast: here are some of the most unspoilt rural farmscapes in the West Country, grazed by chubby Ruby Red cattle and dotted about with orchards, woods, and fields bounded by streams and narrow lanes, while the coast, for miles south of the Devon border, is terrifyingly ragged and perilous. Vicious reefs of razor-backed rocks jut into the sea and black beaches emerge at low tide beneath formidable cliffs. The coast path rears and plunges with exhilarating – or daunting – gusto, testing walkers to the extreme; yet I love the fact that a mile or two inland, among the dipping hills, visitors on wheels can meander and potter along sheltered lanes designed for donkey carts, stopping in villages with names that hail from the Anglo-Saxon side of the Tamar – Stratton, Marhamchurch, Week St Mary – or ramble between some of the most leafily sequestered churches in the county, many having carved oak pew ends of exceptional quality.

Travelling westwards, gaps in the cliffs open up and a tiny harbour or beach squeezes in among a scramble of cottages. Experienced boardmasters ride the dangerous surf, their vans and V-Dubs camped along the clifftops. Around **Bude**, where the surf at last rolls safely onto wide, sandy beaches, the natural drama of the coast seems to draw breath before embarking on another roller-coaster ride, rich in appeal to geologists, through **Crackington Haven** and **Boscastle**, rising to a wildly romantic crescendo at **Tintagel**. For me, however, the romantic coastline of Arthurian legend is eclipsed, just a mile short of Tintagel at the head of St Nectan's Glen, where a 60-foot waterfall descends, through a halo of granite and foliage to a sequence of shallow rock pools and falls of staggering beauty and spiritual significance to latter-day Arthurians, pilgrims and healers alike.

Relics of Cornwall's gritty industrial past are never far from view wherever you find yourself on the peninsula, but just inland from Tintagel, Britain's oldest and largest slate quarry at **Delabole** remains in robust health and offers a rival identity to a region stamped everywhere with the image and legend of Arthur.

Getting around

The last **train** from Paddington to Bude ran in 1966 and Launceston station, which connected passengers (including Mrs Simpson and her King) with Waterloo and Padstow, closed in the same year. Today, the nearest you can get by train to this part of Cornwall is Gunnislake, 15 miles south of Launceston, at the end of the branch line from Plymouth. **Driving around** is mostly enjoyable, though you must be prepared for long spells of reversing down narrow country lanes, where large farm machinery and limited passing places make for interesting encounters.

Buses
Pick up Cornwall Council's free guide to north Cornwall buses (or see it online at www.cornwallpublictransport.info) and it's clear that with determination, patience and several changes, you can make your way down most, but not all, of the coast from **Morwenstow to Bude** and on to **Tintagel and Delabole**. A similar degree of bloody-mindedness will get you eventually from **Launceston to Morwenstow**, but not to any of the places mentioned *en route* in this section of the chapter.

Cycling
There is talk that the old **Bude canal towpath** is to be extended in its accessibility as a cycle route which will bring cyclists to within just four miles of Launceston. That's good news, because for the most part, this is not easy cycling country. Nearly every cyclist I came across north of Launceston was fit, lycra-clad, Teutonic and mounted upon the latest carbon-fibre touring machine and powering along this challenging section of the Cornish Way, which links Bude to Wadebridge. The route from Bude east into Devon forms part of the West Country Way, which goes on to Bristol. The online Sustrans shop (*www.sustranshop.co.uk*) sells laminated maps with the routes and other helpful information; even with a map, in the knitwork of tiny lanes around Bude, the clearly signed waymarkers at every junction are invaluable.

Sustrans also supply Goldeneye's North and East Cornwall cycling routes, each map showing 20 circular rides of an average length of about 25 miles.

∽∽∽∾∾∾

Cycle hire
Bude Bike Hire The Bude Cycle Centre, Pethericks Mill, Bude ① 07749 408100 ⓦ www.budebikehire.co.uk. Hires bikes by the day or week and suggests a handful of easy routes around Bude that take in the quieter roads and canal towpath.
Launceston Cycles 6 Southgate St, Launceston ① 01566 776 102 ⓦ www. launcestoncycles.co.uk. Cycle hire on a weekly basis only. Convivial rides of 40–60 miles start here every Sunday.

Accommodation

Coombe ⓣ 01628 825925 ⓦ www.landmarktrust.org.uk ⓔ bookings@ landmarktrust.co.uk. Three miles north of Bude, Coombe (see page 15) is a hamlet cluster owned by the Landmark Trust, consisting of eight whitewashed cottages and a mill mostly dating from the 18th century, clustered around a shallow stream and ford occupying a sheltered valley wedged between a wooded nature reserve and the gloriously unspoilt and pebbly beach at Duckpool. Mostly built of cob and thatch and sensitively restored and furnished by the Trust, the eight cottages sleeping three to six are an absolute treat. Not for the budget-conscious, but last-minute offers are sensibly priced.

Mill House Inn Trebarwith PL34 0HD. ⓣ 01840 770200 ⓦ www.themillhouseinn.co.uk ⓔ management@themillhouseinn.co.uk. Once an 18th-century cornmill, now a small, upmarket hotel that has been given a clean, contemporary makeover: beams, fireplaces and slate floors have been retained, crisp linens and blond wood furniture added. Cooking is 'Contemporary Cornish' and there's often music in the bar: Thursday evenings is folk night with local singers. Not cheap, but ideal as a treat and well placed for exploring Tintagel and the surfing cove at Trebarwith Strand.

The Old Rectory St Juliot, Boscastle ⓣ 01840 250225 ⓦ www.stjuliot.com ⓔ sally@stjuliot.com. Thomas Hardy stayed here while working on the church just down the lane and one of the rooms, named after him, has a splendid Victorian 'thunderbox' in the bathroom. In a leafy, rural spot away from the bustle of Boscastle, this is an average-priced B&B that lives up to its green credentials. Breakfast eggs come from hens in the garden and honey from the newly introduced hives. Rare-breed pigs in the paddock do their bit for the 'eat local' cause too. Evening meals, served in the beautifully restored Victorian greenhouse are bookable and homemade pasties always on offer.

The Old Vicarage Morwenstow ⓣ 01288 331369 ⓦ www.rshawker.co.uk ⓔ jillwellby@hotmail.com. Three rooms, beautifully decorated in Victorian style, with memorable views of the gardens and coast are matched in old country house elegance by a billiards room, library and drawing room straight out of Agatha Christie. A well-priced B&B also offering self-catering for six in the converted stables, this is a house full of history (see page 14) just a field away from the coast path where Morwenstow's legendary vicar scanned the cruel rocks for signs of shipwrecked souls.

Orchard Lodge Gunpool Lane, Boscastle ⓣ 01840 250418 ⓦ www.orchardlodgeboscastle.co.uk ⓔ orchardlodgeboscastle@gmail.com. Boscastle gets pretty jammed with cars in the summer, so Geoff and Shelley Barratt offer discounts to guests arriving by public transport or on foot or by bicycle. A 10-minute stroll from the harbour and just yards from a good local pub, with a pretty garden and log fires in the winter, this is a practical and comfortable base for exploring the region. The five double and two twin rooms are crisply contemporary, and the bathrooms luxurious, but the price remains pleasantly average for a B&B.

Pencuke Farm St Gennys (near Crackington Haven) EX23 0BH ① 01840 230360. ⓔ info@pencukefarm.co.uk. Has three luxury yurts and five self-catering cottages on a small, family-run organic farm adjoining lush meadows. The cottages are cosy, with unfussy, contemporary furnishings, while yurts come elegantly equipped with beds and sofa bed (each yurt can sleep up to six), linen and blankets, table, chairs and logburners. Outside are barbecues and a smart bath and laundry building with a drying room. Prices for weekly rental are very reasonable, and there's a farm shop in the yard. Perfect for families wanting a slice of the Slow life.

Scadghill Farm Stibb, near Bude EX23 9HN ① 01288 352373. Very basic, budget camping in a small, level field, but well placed for the walk on page 15 and those wanting to be close to Bude but outside it.

Wooda Farm Crackington Haven EX23 0LF ① 01840 230129 ⓦ www. woodafarm.co.uk ⓔ max@woodafarm.co.uk. An organic farm, with 20 acres of bluebell woods and pasture, Wooda is a place for creative spirits of all ages. Couples, families, groups of artists and musicians come here to make the most of the barn and stable studios and enjoy the lovely surroundings. Organic lamb and vegetables arrive fresh from the farm, spring water comes from the well and green electricity from the windmill: it's a pretty special place, well off the beaten track. Accommodation is flexible: there's a self-catering cottage which sleeps three in comfort or five with mattresses on the floor and larger groups stay as guests of Max and Gary in the farmhouse. Not expensive, particularly if you bring your own bed linen.

Tourist information centres

Boscastle In the harbour ① 01840 250010 ⓦ www.visitboscastleandtintagel. com.

Bude Crescent Car Park ① 01288 354240 ⓦ www.visitbude.co.uk.

Launceston Market House Arcade, Market St ① 01566 772321 ⓦ www.visit launceston.co.uk.

Tintagel Bossiney Road Car Park ① 01840 779084.

① Launceston

What a thoroughly likeable town this is. From its Norman fortress castle at the top of the hill to the little steam railway at the bottom, from its handsome Georgian terraces and ancient granite churches to its narrow streets and inviting shops, this is a place made for Slow exploration. But for me what clicks about Launceston is its unselfconsciousness and lack of pretension: it enjoys its history and local culture without clobbering you with them. I called in at The Deli for a coffee and told the owner how impressed I was with 'Lanson' (as it is pronounced by those who live here). 'Oh!' she said, politely surprised 'Us locals think so too, but we're never overwhelmed with visitors here. I think most people zoom past on the A30 and don't think to stop.' John Betjeman was pretty taken with Launceston too; Castle Street, he decided, has 'the most perfect collection of 18th-century town houses in Cornwall'.

The quiet prosperity shows in the shops that line the narrow streets off the Town Square: a huge old-fashioned ironmongers, an independent bookshop, antique and quality furnishing shops, three bakers and a butcher that chalks up the local farms and breed of cattle supplying it that week. Glance up above shop doorways and you will see relics of previous trades and crafts, such as a gilded boot, a pair of cherubs and an Art Deco café sign. There was a genuine affability among the shopkeepers that you would be hard pressed to find on a similarly hot July day in a seaside town further on down the peninsula.

Launceston Castle

① 01566 772365 ⑩ www.english-heritage.org.uk/launceston.

The castle dominates the skyline as you approach the town, an archetypal one-pot sandcastle of a fortress, sitting solidly atop its grassy slopes. As you look from high ground to the west, its lonely grandeur is thrown into relief by the gentle, rolling landscape; Turner painted it in 1811 and again in 1851, captivated by its dramatic silhouette, against ferocious skies and flaming sunsets.

A gang of tiny knights in homemade cloaks and chain mail waved their swords as I panted up the steps to the summit of the castle keep, but their threats soon turned to giggles. In fact, Launceston Castle has never seen much in the way of military action and its ruins are testament to neglect rather than battle-scars. When William the Conqueror handed much of Cornwall over to his half-brother, Robert, the Norman chose this natural hill above the hamlet of Dunheved to assert his presence with a wooden motte and bailey fort. It overlooked a thriving Saxon town, Lan-Stephan, with its markets and church dedicated to St Stephen half a mile away, across the River Kensey. Over the next two centuries, as Dunheved and its castle grew in wealth and importance and the balance of power and commerce shifted away from Lan-Stephan, the name shifted too, giving way to the more euphonic 'Lanson'. The older town became known as St Stephens, Launceston's somewhat diminished and forgotten parent.

Stone replaced wood and under Henry III's younger brother, Richard, Earl of Cornwall, the castle acquired its granite walls and a touch of medieval splendour. When Richard died in 1271, his son Edmund fancied a change of scene and moved his seat of power to Restormel, further west. The castle at Launceston remained, functioning as a prison (George Fox, founder of the Quakers, endured a particularly foul incarceration here in 1656) and courtroom for the Assizes, but without the lavish upkeep it had previously enjoyed, fell into slow decay. By the time of the Civil War it offered no real protection and the Battle of Launceston was fought outside its undefended walls. I left my giggling knights to their imagined battles.

The historic centre

Once through the medieval **Southgate arch**, all roads seem to lead to **St Mary Magdalene** in the town centre. Even if you don't go inside (it's mostly a late Victorian restoration) there is plenty to be impressed with on the outside. Every square inch of this grand church is covered in carvings, so fluid and detailed in their execution that they look as though they have been hewn from butter rather than granite. On the entrance porch, look out for St George on the point of impaling a very nasty dragon and St Martin offering half his cloak to Christ disguised as a beggar. The arms on the shields are those of Henry Trecarrel who, it appears, had already commissioned the carved stones for his new manor house at Lezant (see *Chapter 3*), but changed his mind following the awful death of his young son in 1511 and poured his wealth into the building of a new church instead.

On the east gable, the figure of St Mary appears, lying down and surrounded by musicians and choristers. Teenage girls should note that ever since the church's completion, in 1524, local legend has had it that a pebble thrown which lands – and stays – upon her back will bring good luck, specifically in the form of new clothes. If you think the massive square tower at the other end of the church, which is simply ornamented by a clock and the odd gargoyle, looks a little off-centre and mismatched, you would be right: built on the instructions of the Black Prince, the tower pre-dates the rest of the church by almost 150 years.

The construction of this church coincided with the declining fortunes of the splendid 12th-century Augustinian **priory** at the foot of the hill, dissolved on the instructions of Henry VIII in 1539. Precious little remains to be seen today, but the Norman font is to be found in St Thomas's Church, just across the road, while up the hill, in Town Square, the arched entrance to the White Hart Hotel was reputedly plundered from the ruins in the 16th century. The old **Prior's Bridge**, built by the monks to carry them dry-footed across the River Kensey, makes a picturesque detour *en route* to the steam railway station, which occupies much of the priory's former footprint.

The handsome, Georgian brick-built houses on **Castle Street** which impressed Betjeman so much, were largely built on the wealth generated by the quarterly Assizes. (How Launceston's lawyers and landladies must have mourned when, in 1838, the county court was removed to Bodmin.) But the most striking of all the houses was funded by the chance purchase of a winning lottery ticket. In 1760, the Constable of the Castle, one Coryndon Carpenter, bought a lottery ticket and gave it to his girlfriend. The prize was an incredible £10,000. Needless to say, he promptly married her and built the grandest house on the street, which is now the **Eagle House Hotel**.

A schoolmaster poet

Many people will have read – and probably remember – a poem by Charles Causley during their schooldays. *Timothy Winters*, for example, which begins:

Timothy Winters comes to school
With eyes as wide as a football pool,
Ears like bombs and teeth like splinters:
A blitz of a boy is Timothy Winters.

Or *I Saw a Jolly Hunter*, which begins:

I saw a jolly hunter
With a jolly gun
Walking in the country
In the jolly sun.

and ends...

Bang went the jolly gun.
Hunter jolly dead.
Jolly hare got clean away.
Jolly good, I said.

Simple, clear, formal, and read by adults and children alike, Causley's poetry was quite out of tune with British poetry in the second half of the 20th century. He drew endlessly for inspiration on Cornwall and Launceston where he lived by the river, close to the Prior's Bridge, for all but the war years, and a recently launched Charles Causley festival (*www.charlescausleyfestival. co.uk*) is held here in June. The Causley Society has produced a map of Launceston showing buildings and places that Causley wrote about (*www. charlescausleysociety.org*), which is as good a way as any to discover the town. Although a fondly remembered teacher at the local primary school for many years, Causley was far from sentimental about children: 'you walk among them at your peril.'

Causley died in 2003, aged 86, not long after receiving a prestigious literary award. 'My goodness,' he is reported to have said, 'What an encouragement.'

Lawrence House Museum

9 Castle St ⓉＯ 01566 773277 Ⓦ www.lawrencehousemuseum.org.uk.

I met Jake Jackson, the curator of this delightful museum, carrying a painted 13th-century floor tile from the old priory in his hand. 'This is probably my favourite period of Launceston's history,' he smiled, 'when the castle and the priory were at the height of their magnificence and the whole town prospering.' Launceston's long history, from the Bronze Age onwards, is brought to life in this fine Georgian house, with intriguing detours into the particular passions of its inhabitants. The pharmacist and former mayor of Launceston, William Wise, for example, collected and pressed over a thousand wild plants growing around his home town. His herbarium runs to six volumes and a new page is chosen for display each week, appropriate to the season. Down in the basement, next to the Victorian kitchen, local artists from the Gwynngala Group exhibit their paintings and ceramics. It was here that I caught up with the curator again and asked him if he'd known the poet Charles Causley, a much-loved native of the town. 'Actually that's his desk we're standing beside,' he replied, 'and yes, we were schoolmasters together in Launceston.'

Launceston Steam Railway

ⓉＯ 01566 775665 Ⓦ www.launcestonsr.co.uk.

Cornwall is not short of enterprising, energetic (and often eccentric) collectors who have dedicated their lives to the object of their passion. For Nigel Bowman (no surprise to learn that he is an old friend of music machine collector, Paul Corin, whom we meet in *Chapter 4*) it's all about steam locomotives and motor vehicles from the heyday of British engineering. From the moment in 1965 when he decided to give up a teacher training course in order to restore *Lilian*, a steam locomotive he had found languishing in a Welsh slate quarry, Nigel's passion and determination produced remarkable results.

From the station booking office and tearoom, housed in a building first erected at the 1919 Ideal Home Exhibition, the two and a half miles of track runs on the old bed of the North Cornwall Railway, following one of the prettiest stretches of the River Kensey to Newmills, where most people get off for a picnic or go for a walk, before catching a later train back to Launceston for a peep at the railway museum and workshops. The indomitable Mr Bowman is very keen to build his line as far as Egloskerry, three miles on down the valley, to where it is hoped the Camel Trail will one day extend, enabling cyclists and walkers from Launceston to travel off-road to Bodmin and Padstow.

St Stephens

The original heart of Launceston, before the castle was built, is now little more than a cluster of (mostly newish) houses on the road north to the coast. But before the Norman Conquest, it was a town of some importance – there was a mint here, producing coins stamped with the monarch's head and the church tower served as its vault. Practical but profane, and in 1140 the tower was at the centre of a dispute which resulted in its destruction. The whole church was rebuilt in the 13th century, but a further 200 years passed before it received another tower. On the south door, look out for the ring knocker, which was hammered by those seeking 40 days' sanctuary from earthly justice for that brief (1540–1603) period of eccentric generosity to criminals who were able to reach one of the eight English sanctuaries.

Just after crossing the Kensey, you'll see an **octagonal stone building**, built on the instructions of the Duke of Northumberland in 1829 to house the old market cross and act as a place from which election results could be proclaimed. Not that the duke was without political prejudice: a die-hard Tory peer, who never doubted that his man, Sir Henry Hardinge, would win the vote. Even today, after a general election, the winning (Liberal, more often than not) candidate for Cornwall North is driven from the Round House, as it is known, up the hill to Launceston in a Land Rover for the post-electoral celebrations.

∞∞∞

Food and drink

Launceston is well served by local suppliers, but the town tends to be overlooked, eclipsed by Tavistock's plethora of food shops and famous weekly farmers' market, just 11 miles away. But locals know they have a good thing on their doorsteps, and high-quality local produce is easy to come by. Everyone for miles around has heard of **Philip Warren & Sons**, one of Cornwall's most celebrated butchers and graziers. **Bray Farm Shop** provides top competition on its meat counter as well as great picnic food: pasties, pies, pâté and sandwiches. Fish comes fresh from Brixham in **Hamilton's** van in Town Square on Tuesdays (which happens to be market day), Wednesdays and Fridays and fish is brought up daily (apart from Mondays) from Looe to the White Hart Arcade. **Farmers' markets** are held in the Square on the first Saturday of the month and on Fridays local produce is sold in the church hall, next to St Mary Magdalene.

Launceston's **pubs** can be a bit daunting for non-locals and anyone looking for good pub food and real ales is steered towards the **Springer Spaniel** (*01579 370424; www.thespringerspaniel.org.uk*), 6 miles south at Treburley, or the **Eliot Arms** (*01566 772051; www.eliot-arms.co.uk*) at Tregadillet, just a mile or so west of Launceston. Both pubs are child friendly and hot on locally sourced produce as well as Cornish ales: well worth the drive or taxi ride.

The Deli 6-8 Church St ① 01566 779494. Part shop, part easy-going café; eat in at rustic tables and look out for notices of occasional evening openings when there's music, or take away slices of home-cooked frittatas and tarts or scoffins (the house special) as well as sandwiches and salads. Lots of local and Italian deli items on sale too. Closed Sun and Mon.
Food@cowslip, Newlands Farm, St Stephens ① 01566 772654 Ⓦ www.cowslipworkshops.co.uk. A couple of miles out of town and deservedly popular

with locals. Newlands Farm has been farmed by the Colwills for a century and the family are passionately organic in their approach. Home-cooked food from the farm is served in a converted barn or the colourful garden outside and there are exhibitions of paintings or textile art to visit all through the year. Jo Colwill runs textile art workshops here, which have an international following.

Jericho's Brasserie 4 Northgate St ⓣ 01566 770080. On the first floor of Liberty House, formerly the home of the Liberal Club. Ingredients described as 'honest and trusted' are locally sourced – mostly from Bray Farm – and the café plays an important part in welding Launceston's thriving sense of community. Acoustic music nights, held on the last Thursday of every month, are sell-outs, where local youngsters as well as older, more established bands get their chance to strum and sing. Apart from these, evening openings are on Friday and Saturday only.

Shopping

If good, old-fashioned ironmongers are your sort of thing, where you can buy one nail or a gross (not to mention Ronnie Barker's 'fork 'andles') then the **Hardware Centre** is something of a Mecca.

The **Bookshop**, opposite the entrance to St Mary Magdalene, is a gem, particularly if you are looking for anything with a Cornish theme. And lovers of retro memorabilia, from Meccano to biscuit tins, will fall for the **Windmill Coffee Shop**, gloriously unpretentious and stuffed to the gunwales with knick-knackery. It has some seating in a small garden.

A wriggling route to Morwenstow

North of Launceston, the roads soon narrow between high hedges, concealing a rolling, agricultural landscape. The River Ottery is glimpsed, rushing towards the Tamar, beneath ancient granite bridges and old Cornish estates lie hidden among trees and parkland in the valleys. Turn west off the B3254, which runs straight and fast to Bude and Kilkhampton (the most northerly town in Cornwall) and you're in a maze of looping lanes, isolated farms and tiny hamlets, where shops and pubs are few and far between. Village churches and holy wells are rarely disappointing in these parts and the few mentioned in this chapter by no means tell the whole story.

② The Tamar Otter and Wildlife Centre

5 miles northwest of Launceston close to North Petherwin ⓣ 01566 785646
ⓦ www.tamarotters.co.uk.

Nothing could be better than watching wild otters playing unobserved, but here's the next best thing at this centre (previously known as the Otter Sanctuary). Rescued otters as well as home-bred otters from Cornwall and further afield can be seen (and smelled) at close quarters doing ottery things in big pens watered by natural streams and pools. The new name for the centre reflects its growing population of deer (tame enough to be hand fed by children) as well as wild cats, owls, chipmunks and wallabies.

③ Warbstow Bury

Grid reference SX203906.

Travelling westwards, if you feel hemmed in by the narrow lanes, this huge and ancient hillfort is a good place for a pause or picnic. No great climb is involved: a small car park is just a few yards from the summit and the views are stupendous. Look back to Launceston Castle or north for a panoramic view of the coast as far as the glittering satellite dishes of GCHQ Bude on the headland close to Morwenstow. The barrow in the middle is known as the Giant's Grave or King Arthur's Grave, though less romantic souls have decided it is simply a medieval rabbit warren. Kept neatly cropped by sheep, it is best not to bring dogs during lambing in spring.

Thomasine Bonaventura

The extraordinary life of a shepherd's daughter began in Week St Mary where Thomasine Bonaventura was born in or around 1450. She was just a girl, minding her father's flock, when she was spotted by a travelling merchant from London. There was clearly something about Thomasine that impressed John Bunsby, who later returned to her parents' house and invited her to return with him to be his wife's maid. Her acceptance turned out to be one of those life-changing decisions. After several years in London, the wife died and Thomasine became the next Mrs Bunsby. John died soon after and Thomasine inherited his wealth. She remarried, again to an affluent merchant, and when he too died her grief was matched only by the size of her bank account. Her third marriage, to Sir John Percyvall, later Lord Mayor of London, saw Thomasine moving in the highest circles and a favourite at the court of Henry VII. But in 1504, wealthy and childless Thomasine was widowed again.

She sounds like an ambitious, social-climbing adventuress, but nothing could be further from the truth. Right from the start of her unexpected affluence, she set about distributing her wealth in her native parish, helping her parents and the poor, building roads and a much-needed bridge, purchasing woodland to enable a degree of self-sufficiency among local indigents and providing St Stephen's Church at Launceston with a new tower. With no taste for London life after the loss of her third husband, she spent her remaining years back in Week St Mary, overseeing the building of a chantry and a free grammar school. For some very odd reason, the school, which was at first admired and cherished by its local community, lasted only 50 years before it was deemed to be 'yn decaye' and its endowment was transferred to a similar establishment in Launceston. The chantry is long gone, but the school was restored by the Landmark Trust; over the stone-arched doorway, Thomasine's legacy is remembered with a simple carved T.

④ Penhallam Manor

Use the small car park at grid reference SX224979, 1 mile west of Week St Mary.

The half-mile walk through peaceful, airy woodland to the excavated remains of Penhallam Manor is a treat at any time of year, and you are likely – even in high summer – to have the ruins in the leafy clearing to yourself. Discovered when the site was being prepared for tree planting in the 1960s, emergency excavations were carried out and the knee-high remains of a four-square and moated, medieval manor house were exposed. Inhabited from about 1170 until it was abandoned in 1428 and left to decay for over 500 years, there can be few more atmospheric places for a child's imagination to take root and flourish. The footpath continues on, skirting **Ashbury Hill**, to **Week St Mary**, but unless you retrace your steps, you will have to take the road out of the village as there are no footpaths to get back to the car park.

⑤ Stratton

All the road signs point to Bude as you travel north up this last finger of Cornwall, but if the temptation to unpack the surfboard can be resisted, Stratton justifies a generous hour or two, much of which might well be spent in the **Tree Inn** on Fore Street (*01288 352038; www.treeinn.co.uk*) soaking up the history (and Cornish ales). It's always good to find a pub which is still the hub of village life, and this one has a post office and village shop off its ancient courtyard. Formerly Stratton Manor, the building that the pub now occupies, was also at the hub of Civil War history. The Royalist army, under Sir Ralph Hopton and Sir Bevil Grenville, whose house at Stowe Barton lay just outside Kilkhampton, plotted their tactics here as the Parliamentarians closed in and took up position on an Iron Age earthwork close by (now occupied by the Bude Golf Course). But the Royalists won the day at the Battle of Stamford Hill, named after the defeated Earl of Stamford.

The Cornish giant

Anthony Payne was born in Stratton Manor (now the Tree Inn) and served Sir Bevil Grenville as a bodyguard. A giant of a man, standing at seven feet and four inches and with an impressive girth to match, he was not, however, all brawn. Quick-witted, funny and highly intelligent he proved an incredible asset to the Royalist army and survived the battles of Stamford Hill and Lansdowne Hill and went on to serve Sir Bevil's son, Richard, during the Siege of Plymouth. Payne accompanied the body of Sir Bevil, who died at Lansdowne Hill, back to the Grenville family church at Kilkhampton, a few miles up the road from Stratton where his memorial stone can be seen. The giant soldier returned definitively to Stratton when he retired, and when he died, his coffin had to be lowered through a section of ceiling before it could be transported to St Andrew's which, fortunately for all, is just a few steps up the hill.

St Andrew's Church is a fine, 12th-century building, enthusiastically renovated inside during the late 19th century. The Victorian restorers can be forgiven though: they didn't touch the rather battered tomb of the 13th-century knight, who lies cross-legged on the sill of a window in the north aisle, or the stunning Tudor ceilings, which are typically Cornish 'wagon-style', and they handed the design of the east window showing the four evangelists to none other than Edward Burne-Jones and William Morris. In the porch, an old wooden door taken from Stratton's little lock-up, is studded with nails that spell CLINK, an old West Country term for a jail with just one or two cells.

⑥ Launcells

The village of Launcells seems not to exist, but a mile southeast of Stratton, and well tucked away in a leafy coombe beside a trickling holy well, lies the church of St Swithin's, described by Betjeman as 'the least spoilt church in Cornwall'. Inside the 15th-century building are the original floor tiles, made in the Barnstaple potteries and decorated with a raised design of pelicans, lions, griffins and flowers. The finely carved Tudor bench ends are exceptional too, and a further treasure was discovered in 1929, when underneath layers of limewash, fragments of a large painting depicting the sacrifice of Isaac was revealed on the wall of the south aisle. Outside, in the churchyard, is the grave of the Bude inventor, Sir Goldsworthy Gurney (see page 18).

⑦ Morwenstow

Just two miles from the border with Devon at Marsland Mouth, and only a few hundred yards from some of the highest and most treacherous cliffs on the north Cornish coast, Morwenstow lacks nothing in romantic appeal of the most wuthering kind. As you approach from the road (as opposed to the coast path), the excellent **Bush Inn** (see *Food and drink*, below) and working blacksmith's forge (*01288 331160; www.properblacksmith.com*) face each other across a wide and windy sort of village green.

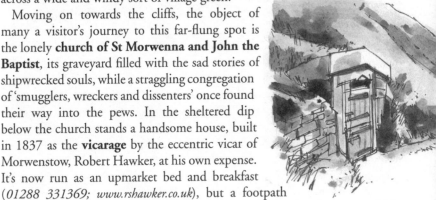

Moving on towards the cliffs, the object of many a visitor's journey to this far-flung spot is the lonely **church of St Morwenna and John the Baptist**, its graveyard filled with the sad stories of shipwrecked souls, while a straggling congregation of 'smugglers, wreckers and dissenters' once found their way into the pews. In the sheltered dip below the church stands a handsome house, built in 1837 as the **vicarage** by the eccentric vicar of Morwenstow, Robert Hawker, at his own expense. It's now run as an upmarket bed and breakfast (*01288 331369; www.rshawker.co.uk*), but a footpath passes close by and you can get a good look at the quirky chimneys, which Hawker designed to reflect the towers of other churches of significance to him.

It's a short step from here to join the coast path, for sublime clifftop views across the sea to Lundy Island and far south along the ragged coast to Bude, far-off Tintagel and the misty beyond. A 30-minute **walk** (well mapped on a board at the field gate between the tearoom and the lychgate to the church), takes you south along the coast path, where a sign indicates a narrow flight of steps, leading down the cliff to a small wooden cabin, hardly bigger than a sentry-box. **Hawker's Hut**, built from planks salvaged from shipwrecks, was a favourite haunt of the vicar, from which he could scan the sea, compose highly-charged verse and smoke his opium pipe. A little further on, turn inland, following the Tidna Valley and you're soon back at the Bush Inn.

Food and drink

Bush Inn ℗ 01288 331242 ⓦ www.bushinn-morwenstow.co.uk. The Bush has stood here since the 13th century, when it was a hostel for pilgrims crossing the peninsula between the north Devon ports and Fowey to the south. In the

The Vicar of Morwenstow

Enough has been written about Robert Stephen Hawker to fill several volumes, and though a Devonian by birth (he was born in Plymouth in 1803) he is one of Cornwall's best-loved eccentrics, not least because he penned the words to 'The Song of the Western Men'. (These rousing verses on the subject of Bishop Trelawney's incarceration in 1687 by James II have become the 'Cornish National Anthem', sung lustily at rugby matches and any other suitable occasion.)

Stories abound of the parson who went about in a sailor's jersey, who was not afraid to climb down the dizzying cliffs to haul up the shredded bodies of the shipwrecked and plied his congregation with gin to give them the courage to lend him a hand, who dressed as a mermaid and sang on a rock at night, who got Tennyson all fired up about King Arthur and who, towards the end of his eventful life, married a 19-year-old Polish governess and converted to Roman Catholicism.

But there was more substance to Hawker than these extreme examples might suggest. When he and his first wife arrived at Morwenstow in 1835, the church had been without a vicar for a century; the vicarage was in ruins and the church decayed. Hawker flung himself into a programme of rebuilding, adding a school and bridge to the parish, as well as the new rectory. He farmed intelligently and with the formidable energy and commitment that characterised everything he set his heart upon, and for good measure, added the Harvest Festival to the church calendar.

Hawker would no doubt have raised a cynical eyebrow to his enduring reputation and popularity; 'Posthumous fame is of little value,' he wrote. 'It is like a favourable wind after a shipwreck.'

main bar you can still see the Celtic fish symbol cut from serpentine stone and a monastic cross is carved into the flagstone floor by the door leading into the garden, while in the middle bar, a tiny window known as a 'Leper's Squint' allowed scraps of food to be passed to beggars. Daphne du Maurier is known to have visited and it's reasonable to think that this building was the model for her *Jamaica Inn*, rather than the eponymous tourist-trap in the middle of Bodmin Moor. History apart, these days the Bush has acquired a well-earned reputation for its food, and the owners, who are also organic farmers, are great supporters of local producers. Line-caught sea bass comes straight from the sea below and game from the surrounding woods and fields is usually on the menu too.

Rectory Farm Tea Room ⓣ 01288 331251 ⓦ www.rectory-tearoom.co.uk. Built in part from beams salvaged from shipwrecks and oozing cottagey charm, this is a great pitstop for walkers looking for a substantial and (I confess, one scone is quite enough) delicious cream tea. The farm next door supplies organic meat and eggs to the kitchen and all the veg is sourced locally too; homemade soups, pasties and tarts make it a popular lunchtime destination.

Along the coast from Morwenstow to Tintagel

Brace yourself if doing this on foot; the coast path is vertiginous in places and the threading clifftop roads take guts and a steady hand for those on two wheels (or four) as well. All traffic seems to be heading for Bude, and south of Bude, Boscastle and Tintagel are the big draw. However, away from the honey-pots, the countryside and beaches are remarkably empty and a happy hunting-ground for naturalists and geologists alike. There are some grand circular walks to be done, taking in small sections of the coast path, wooded, stream-fed valleys and a bit of local history too.

⑧ A wander up Coombe Valley

A moderately demanding six-mile walk, starting between Bude and Morwenstow, which takes in the ruined remains of the Grenville family seat at Stowe Barton, the prettiest of whitewashed hamlets clustered around a working watermill, **Coombe Valley Nature Reserve**, an isolated beach and freshwater pool – and finishes with a blast along the cliffs, if arriving by car. The bus from Bude stops at Kilkhampton (where there are shops and a pub), a good and hilly mile from Stowe Barton.

❶ Park in the **Northcott Mouth** (National Trust) car park and take the bridleway northeast up the sloping field. Follow the waymarkers, climbing for a mile and a half.

❷ You reach the National Trust site of **Stowe Barton**. The remains of the Grenvilles' great manor houses lie here among woodland. The Tudor manor was home to generations of distinguished Grenvilles, including Sir Richard (of

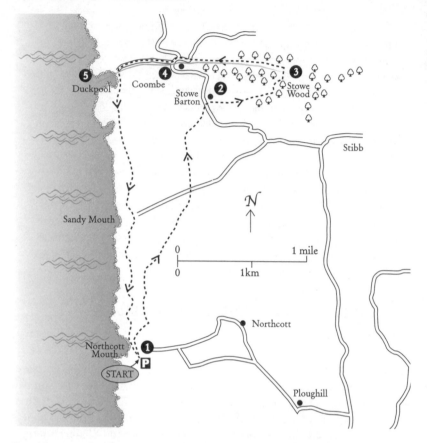

Spanish-trouncing fame), his grandson and hero of the Civil War, Sir Bevil and Bevil's son, Sir John (who we meet on the Isles of Scilly in *Chapter 10*). Sir John, whose Royalist exploits made him a wealthy man under Charles II, demolished the old house and replaced it in 1679 by what was described as 'by far the noblest house in the west of England'. Daniel Defoe passed by and gasped at the quality of the woodcarving in the chapel, which he described as worthy of Grinling Gibbons. John's daughter, however, had other ideas. Less than seventy years after its completion, on her instructions, the house was taken apart and sold off as she relocated the family seat to Stowe in Buckinghamshire.

❸ Follow the footpath signs to Coombe down through the wooded valley nature reserve.

❹ The whitewashed cottages and working watermill at **Coombe** have been pleasingly restored by the Landmark Trust who let the cottages for holidays. Electricity is generated by the watermill. The Hawkers rented a cottage here while waiting for the new rectory at Morwenstow to be completed.

From Coombe, walk on the road beside the stream down to **Duckpool**, where the stream gathers in a natural hollow.

❺ As you arrive at the **beach**, note the lack of swimmers. Duckpool is notoriously unsafe, but attracts a few brave and experienced surfers, regardless of the grasping currents and tides. Turn left to find the coast path back to Northcott Mouth, two miles away. Only two miles, and the views are superb – but it's a daunting stretch for weary legs. If you prefer to start the walk with the clifftop section, there is limited parking space at Duckpool.

⑨ Bude

Bude hit the big time when the railway arrived in 1898 and Edwardian families and grandees alike hastened to its wide sandy beaches and the romance of its unspoilt hinterland. However, the arrival of the trains was bad news for Bude's harbour and canal, which had transported sand and coal inland for over a century. The closure of the railway in 1966 heralded lean times for Bude, and even now, despite the town's vigorous attempts to reinvent itself as a surfing, family-orientated rival to Newquay with a well-established international jazz festival, it is hard to escape the feeling that a loss of substance has occurred somewhere down the line.

Bude is a town of two halves, with the bulk of its hotels, shops and restaurants gathered around the hugely popular, sandy **Summerleaze Beach**. (Surfers tend to gravitate towards **Crooklets Beach**, a little to the north.) Across the River Neet, the canal, wharves and peculiar castle-like building will be more interesting to Slow explorers as well as walkers looking for a good place to stretch their legs.

The **Bude Canal** was an ambitious project, begun during the 18th century 'canal boom', and conceived to link Bude harbour with Plymouth via the River Tamar. By 1820, it was possible to ferry goods to within spitting distance of Launceston, 35 miles away, but given the hilly terrain, barges were only used for the first two miles. Thereafter, as the land rises to a height of 350 feet in six miles, the three-branched canal was constructed on a much smaller scale and without locks. Ingeniously, goods were transferred from the barges into boats with wheels ('tub boats'), winched up on ramps with rails by horses. The whole story is told in the **Bude-Stratton Museum** (*01288 353576; www.bude-stratton.gov.uk/museum*), housed in a wharfside building that used to be the canal company's smithy. Lime-rich sea sand was ferried up the canal for use as fertiliser on farms and the tub boats and barges came back filled with grain or slate where they were transferred to ships in the harbour. Cheaper fertilisers and railways eventually made the canal redundant and it ceased to operate commercially in 1891. There is water still in the first two miles to Helebridge where the barges unloaded into tub boats, but beyond that nearly all trace of the canal's three branches has disappeared.

Sir Goldsworthy Gurney

Gurney was of the same generation of incredibly bright and inventive Cornishmen – Humphrey Davy and Richard Trevithick were his friends – who transformed both industry and daily life with their inventions. Born in Padstow in 1793, Gurney was qualified and running a medical practice in Wadebridge before he was 20. In his youth, and throughout his career as a London surgeon, Gurney was intensely focused on solving scientific problems such as getting steam-driven wagons on the roads. In this he succeeded and his cheap but highly profitable 'buses' were soon running between Cheltenham and Gloucester. He was put out of business by horse-drawn transport companies who, foreseeing their ruin if he was allowed to continue, fixed road tolls so that mechanised transport was severely penalised. Gurney also devised a new bright light, 'the Bude Light', by injecting oxygen into a flame and bouncing the light through crystals and mirrors. At a stroke, London's streets and theatres, and even the House of Commons – which had hitherto been lit by smoky candles – were transformed. Limelight, it was called.

But Gurney never found himself in the limelight and despite a host of other inventions which improved mine safety and launched telegraphy, he remained obscure. His castle, the first building in Britain to be built on sand, stabilised by a concrete raft, and the millennium sculpture at its gates are how Bude remembers him today.

The museum is open from Easter to October, but there is also canal information at the **visitor centre** in the main car park. Here you will find details and maps of long and short circular walks taking in the canal.

Beside the car park stands the decidedly Victorian Bude Castle, overlooking Summerleaze beach. Now the **Bude Castle Heritage Centre** (*01288 353576*) it was once the home of Bude's most inventive son, Sir Goldsworth Gurney, for whom it was built in 1830. Inside are exhibits relating to Gurney's life and numerous inventions, a research library dedicated in the main to the history of Stratton and Bude, an interactive shipwreck map as well as a shop and café.

Outside, in front of the gateway to the castle is a tall and pointy sculpture, striped with bands of colour, representative of sand and sea and sky. This is the **Bude Light 2000**, designed to celebrate Bude, Gurney and the millennium by Carole Vincent and Anthony Fanshawe. You really need to see it at night, when its fibre-optic lights turn it into a brilliant beacon, and not with a parking cone on its nine-foot peak (Bude youth, eh?) in order to be impressed.

Food and drink

Bude has numerous places to eat and drink, catering largely for ravenous surfers and bucket-and-spading families. Milkshakes are really cool these days if you are the surfing type and the best are to be had at **G's Café and Diner** (*15 Queen St;*

01288 353160). Vegetarian and gluten-free menus are always available and the café gets pretty packed at the height of the season, when it opens in the evenings as well as for breakfast and lunch.

Slow foragers will probably want to head up the hill and over the main road to **Stratton** and the Tree Inn (described on page 12) or the **King's Arms** (*Howells Rd; 01288 352396*) which is big on real ales (Doom Bar, Otter and Exmoor) and locally recommended steak and kidney pie.

> **Brendon Arms** Falcon Terrace, EX23 8SD ① 01288 354542 ⓦ www.brendonarms. co.uk. Run by the fifth generation of Brendons, overlooks the canal and is a good place to start or finish a walk. You'll find ales from the St Austell Brewery and Cornish cider, food with a Cornish emphasis and strong sense of community. Child- and dog-friendly.

⑩ Millook

This is a tiny clutch of houses in a deep cleft of the cliffs, with just enough room for a couple of cars to park at the roadside. The stream that tumbles down from the surrounding hills gathers in a sheltered pool above the pebbly beach: perfect for a spot of safe swimming. The sea here, however, is far from safe.

⑪ Poundstock

Poundstock spills over the A39 eastwards, but the core of the village lies in the wooded valley to the west. I was nosing around the 14th-century church of St Winwaloe, when the church warden suggested I might want to look at the **Gildhouse**, normally open only on Wednesdays (*01288 361525; www.poundstockgildhouse.co.uk*). This lovely building was probably constructed to house the masons working on the church and then acquired a new use as a village hall – a function it still serves today, having also done service as a poorhouse and village school. Close to the church a footpath runs over the fields to the coast, dropping down into the tiny cove at Millook. A short, but steep circular walk can be made of it (the church warden's favourite) by returning through oak woods owned by the Woodland Trust, then picking up the lane at Trevoulter Farm which takes you back to Poundstock.

Food and drink

> **Bangors House** Poundstock EX23 0DP ① 01288 361297 ⓦ www.bangorsorganic. co.uk. A 5-acre organic smallholding, luxury B&B and restaurant close to the main road (A39) that chops Poundstock in two. Salads, fruit, vegetables and eggs come fresh to the kitchen where bread is baked daily. Booking is essential.

⑫ Crackington Haven

Paradise for surfers and geologists, with easy parking, a pub and two very good cafés, Crackington Haven's geography makes it unusually good for spectators too. Climb just a short way up the coast path to the village tennis court and you have a close-up view of the action below in the sea, especially on an incoming tide. From the thoughtfully positioned bench there's a good view too of the exposed cliff face on the far side of the beach where you may observe the 'Crackington Formation': compressed folds of sandstone and grey shale. 'Crak' is the onomatopoeic Cornish word for sandstone; you can almost hear the rock fracturing in your mouth. The Haven shop-cum-café in the car park sells a leaflet giving details of a walking trail for the geologically curious. To the south beyond the headland of Cambeak, **High Cliff** is just that – Cornwall's highest cliff at 732 feet; there's easy access from the road that avoids the substantial ascent from Crackington Haven itself.

Food and drink

The Cabin ① 01840 230238 Ⓦ www.cabincafecrackington.co.uk; open all year round. Perched just above the car park, this is justly proud of its locally sourced produce, and the beef in the pasties comes directly from **Dizzard Farm** (which has a good farm shop), three miles north on the coast-hugging road to Bude.
Coombe Barton Inn ① 01840 230345 Ⓦ www.thecoombebartoninn.co.uk. Cornish ales and grand views over the beach.
The Haven Beach Café and Shop ① 01840 230774 On the other side of the car park, and run by a local family who know how to catch a fish or two and which often find their way onto the menu. Local crab is on the menu too, and friendly chat about what's going on in the village and the rest of Cornwall if it's quiet and you're not in a hurry.

⑬ Boscastle

Until 15 August 2004, Boscastle was just a picturesque harbour, its cottages, tea rooms and pubs jostling for space in a narrow valley watered by a small river, the Valency, and its tiny tributaries in the wooded hills above. Then the rain came and by the following morning, everyone had heard of the Boscastle flood. Miraculously, no-one was killed – just two unfortunate dogs in locked cars which were washed away in the torrent. Two hundred people, sheltering in the ground-floor bar of the hotel by the bridge, were warned by a motorist who had just driven down the valley and seen the danger to get out fast; 20 minutes later the ceiling beneath which they had gathered caved in. Fallen trees, higher up the valley, were thought to be responsible for causing the swollen river to burst; then cars, swept along from the village car park jammed against the bridges and the water rose.

Today, the flood and its aftermath are what give Boscastle its strongest identity and help pull in the crowds. Information boards tell you how the new car park (vastly expanded to receive the extra influx of tourists) is porous and that such a thing could never happen again. A native of Boscastle (whose grandmother fought a battle with the MoD who wanted her to dig up her tennis court to grow potatoes during World War II) shook her head and sighed 'so much has been rebuilt, and so authentically restored that it's hard to believe unless you knew the village in its antediluvian days'. The Pixie House by the new harbour footbridge, for example, with a gloriously sagging 300-year-old roof has been entirely rebuilt, saggy roofline and all.

The entrance to the S-shaped harbour is practically invisible from the sea, and given extra concealment by Meachard Rock. Both sides of the harbour offer a good leg stretch: the footpath on the south side leads to a white, castellated watchtower for coastguards, once the site of an Iron Age hillfort, from which you look over the Forrabury Stitches, a medieval 'stitchmeal' field system; to the north of the harbour, the narrow, rocky track climbs to Penally Point. If there is a heavy swell, about an hour before or after low tide, you'll be rewarded with an impressive display of water jetting horizontally into the harbour mouth from a blowhole, known locally as the Devil's Bellows.

Food and drink

Both the **Bottreaux Hotel** and the **Wellington Inn** have good restaurants, well-known for supporting local suppliers and the **Cobweb Inn** does a nice line in locally caught mackerel barbecues during the summer.

Helsett Farm Where organic ice cream is made from a herd of Ayrshire cows, at the head of the valley and sold from a wooden hut beside the harbour. Fantastic. Lush. Sublime.

A walk around Boscastle

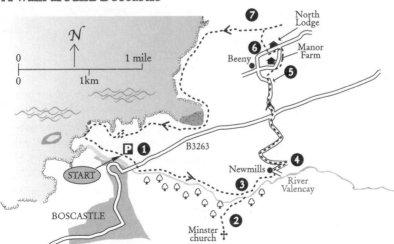

A challenging walk of about seven miles, which takes in both Minster and St Juliot's, a spectacular stretch of coast path, with seals and dizzying cliffs, a waterfall and Boscastle's ancient harbour.

❶ From the main car park in **Boscastle** follow the signed footpath through oak woods uphill along the valley beside the Valency.

❷ A right turning over a bridge to **Minster Church** is a worthwhile detour Return to the footpath by the same track.

❸ Soon after the bridge the path forks. Take the left-hand route with steps.

❹ Reach **New Mills**, a pretty hamlet with a ruined mill. At the junction with a tarmac lane turn left and zigzag up the steep hill to the road at the top (B3263). Turn right and follow the road for 50 yards and then turn left down a narrow lane all the way to the bottom of the hill.

❺ Cross the stile on your right and make your way over fields aiming for the house on the brow of the hill.

❻ To the right of the house, a stile gives onto the lane. Turn right, passing **Manor Farm** and continue up to a junction. Turn left here; then, shortly after the isolated house of **North Lodge**, turn right along a public footpath between hedges. This leads to an open field; continue alongside the hedge ahead.

❼ On reaching the **coast path**, turn left along it south to **Boscastle harbour**.

⑭ Minster

Though Boscastle has changed, its mother church, known simply as Minster, hidden in the wooded hills a mile from the harbour, is seemingly timeless and far from the madding crowds below. A lovely walk from the car park follows the River Valency up into the woods and brings you to the churchyard which in spring is full of daffodils and wild garlic followed by a lush pageant of wild flowers, ferns and grasses – no surprise to learn it is an SSSI (Site of Special Scientific Interest). The church originates from 1150, but was restored and extended in 1507. Look closely and you will see an enigmatic carving of a pair of scissors on the western face of the tower wall which dates from this period or even earlier. A major restoration was carried out again in Victorian times and yet more work was done following the 2004 flood, when water rose to a height of six feet inside the church.

⑮ St Juliot's

Many of Cornwall's medieval churches were in a dismal state of repair by the 19th century and subject to necessary, if occasionally over-enthusiastic Victorian renovation. Thomas Hardy in his younger days worked as an architect and in that capacity came to Boscastle in 1870 to draw up a plan for restoring the church of St Juliot, Victorian style. He stayed in the vicarage and later married the vicar's sister-in-law, Emma Gifford.

> *I found her out there*
> *On a slope few see,*
> *That falls westwardly*
> *To the salt-edged air,*
> *Where the ocean breaks*
> *On the purple strand,*
> *And the hurricane shakes*
> *The solid land.*

Hardy wrote this in 1914, two years after Emma's death, when he came back to Cornwall to revisit the place of their courtship. She had encouraged him to write and his third novel (though the first published under his own name), *A Pair of Blue Eyes*, is all about their early days together. But Hardy, as is well known, was not especially nice to his wife over the 38 years of their marriage and remorse leaks out in his poems.

⑯ St Nectan's Glen and Rocky Valley

On the road from Boscastle to Tintagel a roadside car park, signed 'St Nectan's Glen only', should not be ignored. Nick, a healer from the Midlands, who makes an annual pilgrimage to the **waterfall** at the head of the glen in order to recharge his spiritual batteries, was pulling on his boots in the car park and offered to be my guide. Turning inland, the half-mile walk through ferny oak woods, beside a shallow, splashing river of outstanding loveliness culminated abruptly in a steep flight of steps leading to an unexpected tea garden and Barry, the widowed owner of the glen, who chatted amiably about his decision to sell up and quit what has been his home and business for 27 years. No hermit is Barry, unlike St Nectan, who retreated to this spot in the 6th century. Of the hermitage, only his cell remains, burrowed into the bedrock below the Victorian cottage that incorporates the old chapel walls. But the main reason for coming here is the waterfall, which cascades 60 feet, emerging through a halo of rock to fall into the kieve, a deep hollow, where baptisms of every stripe are regularly performed. Around the pool and the shallow springs and beaches, the trees and rocks are festooned with ribbons, coins and other offerings to the undoubtedly happy spirits of this magical place. Barry, Nick and everyone else locally who knew the glen assured me that the new owners, whoever they were, would have to ensure it remains open to visitors.

The valley of the Trevillet has more surprises to offer on its journey to the sea. On the other side of the B3263, the footpath marked to **Rocky Valley** descends through ruined woollen mill buildings and emerges, twisting above the river, to deliver a breathtaking view of the sea and the rugged, rocky cliffs that frame it. But before hurrying across the wooden bridge below the ruined mill, turn right and there on the rock face are two finely chiselled but entirely enigmatic seven-fold labyrinths, carved for reasons unknown perhaps 1,500 – or just 200 – years ago.

A local woman, out walking her dog, remarked, 'you know, Tintagel is almost a red herring once you know this valley'; I know what she meant: the spirit of the Trevillet from the waterfall to the sea surely inhabits all the myths and legends that have, over the centuries, come to settle a mile away upon Tintagel.

⑰ Tintagel

Drive through Tintagel on a hot summer's day, when the car parks are bursting, the pavements crowded and the gift shops brimming with Arthurian knick-knackery and you might well be tempted to give it a miss, which would be a shame, because if you ditch the car and get out onto the coast path things change dramatically. Standing at a lonely distance from the village, high on the cliff above the sea, **St Materiana's Church** has more than something of the lighthouse about it. Inside the Norman building, a 12th-century granite font carved with crude faces at each of its rounded corners and serpents in between, stands on an oddly decorative plinth of small upright slates. Much of the woodwork in the church is unusual too: the reredos looks as though it was made out of old carved bench ends, depicting the Passion and local coats of arms. In the south transept, a Roman milestone, discovered in the lychgate wall during repair works in 1889, now points the way to heaven; the inscription suggests it was made in the time of Emperor Licinius, who died in AD324.

Tintagel Castle

① 01840 779084 ⑩ www.englishheritage.co.uk.
From the clifftop path, the once fortified island reveals itself in all its natural grandeur. It has been well established that a 5th- or 6th-century monastery and trading post stood here, and relics of Mediterranean oil and wine jars have been found. The **Arthurian connection** is largely due to Geoffrey of Monmouth's 12th-century manuscript, which makes Tintagel the place of Arthur's conception, and a century later Prince Richard – the Earl of Cornwall responsible for building Launceston Castle's stone walls – used the myth to reinforce his own magisterial status in Cornwall.

The ruins seen today are the remnants of the castle Prince Richard built. But Arthur's name remains more potent at Tintagel than Richard's; and when a piece of inscribed slate was discovered during excavations on the island in 1998, pro-Arthurian excitement knew no bounds. In Latin, it read: 'Artognou, father of a descendant of Coll, has had [this] made.' Cynics may shrug, but in the end, the place, in all its wild and windblown glory, is bigger than the academic disputes that surround it. (I reserve my cyncism for the village, which having been known to all and sundry as Trevena for the best part of a millennium, adopted the name of its castle as a marketing ploy in the mid 19th century, when Pre-Raphaelite interest in the Arthurian legend was at its peak and tourism was booming.)

A good morning or afternoon is needed to do justice to the whole site, with its beaches, caves, vantage points and hundreds of steps. The slog uphill back to the village is a hard one after all that, though there are Land Rovers at both ends offering a shuttle service.

King Arthur's Great Halls
Fore St ⓣ 01840 770526.

Abandon all scepticism before entering: the grey, slightly uninviting façade and entrance conceal a splendid secret, revealed within the huge ex-Masonic hall added on to the back of the house. (A very fine coastal garden was destroyed in the process, but you can't make an omelette, etc.) The secret is this: 72 quite simply sublime **stained-glass windows** created in 1930 by Veronica Whall, a gifted pupil of William Morris. There are flowers, jewel-like, along the aisles, while in the Hall a great triptych centres upon Merlin at the darker end and Arthur at the sunlit one. The granite structures and sculpted architectural decoration are genuinely enthralling too. Over 50 Cornish quarries sent their finest granite here, the stones ranging from black or pinky grey to ochre and sparkling white, to be sculpted into wall-mounted shields, canopied throne and Round Table. (Old quarrymen come just to remember the now defunct quarries in the solid craftsmanship.) The Hall is no longer in use as a Masonic lodge, but once a year a terrific banquet is held for members of the Fellowship of the Knights of the Round Table of King Arthur.

As if all that were not enough, a large **antechamber**, hung with ten paintings by the Edwardian artist, William Hatherall, prepares the visitor for the experience in the Great Hall. The paintings show scenes from Mallory's 16th-century telling of the Arthur legend, and the disembodied voice of Robert Powell, as Merlin, is suitably enchanting.

The man with the extraordinary vision and the means to realise it was Frederick Thomas Glasscock, one half of Monk & Glass Custard, upon which the British Empire was nourished. Early in the 20th century the company was sold to Bird's and Glasscock retired to Tintagel to pursue his extravagant dream. It was completed to his exacting satisfaction in 1933, and the following year he embarked on a lecture tour of the States. Sadly, he died on the journey back to Tintagel.

The Old Post Office
Fore St ⓣ 01840 770024; National Trust.

Among the modern shops and houses on Tintagel's main street, this quaint anomaly with its higgledy-piggledy roofs, slumping walls and stumpy chimneys looks like it has been dropped into the present out of a fairy tale. Built in the 14th century for a well-to-do farming family, it served briefly as a post office in Victorian times and is now owned by the National Trust. Best visited out of season.

Food and drink

Tintagel is fairly bursting with cafés, pubs and tea rooms, but it's not all Excaliburgers and Magic Merlin Milkshakes. Ales from **Tintagel Brewery**, brewed at Condolden Farm in the hills behind the village, are a real treat. Look out for Castle Gold, Harbour Special and Cornwall's Pride at the **Cornishman Inn** and the **Tintagel Arms Hotel**.

> **Pengenna Bakery** At the castle end of Fore St and Atlantic Rd. An upmarket bakery, doing a roaring trade in pasties (you can watch them being made from a street window).
>
> **Wylde's Café** Bossiney Rd ① 01840 770007 ⓦ www.wyldestogo.co.uk. At the other end of the village from the bakery, this is the place to go for breakfasts, lunches and teas, all made with carefully sourced local produce and available to take away for picnics too.

⑱ Slaughterbridge

Just north of the hamlet with a gory name, on the B3314, close to the supposed site of Arthur's last battle, the **Arthurian Centre** (*01840 213947; www.arthur-online.co.uk*) sounds like a theme park, but it's probably of more interest to archaeologists and Arthurian scholars than bored children. Behind the hut that serves as a shop and primitive visitor centre, a half-mile walk through fields takes you past the partially excavated site of an **Iron Age village** and round a wooded clearing, which has been identified as Camlann, where Arthur and the evil Mordred fought their last battle in AD542. From here the path drops down to a little river and the recently exhumed cobbled **terrace** that was once part of a 17th-century garden created by Lady Falmouth, who lived at Worthyvale Manor, just out of sight behind the trees. From a wooden platform you look down the steep and muddy riverbank to where the greatest treasure lies, lapped by the rippling water: the **Arthur Stone**. This great stone must have lain here undisturbed for nearly a thousand years until Lady Falmouth identified it as useful material for a footbridge and the historian, Borlase, gently pointed out its significance. Two hundred years later, Tennyson fought through the brambles to gaze at it in wonder. Now scholars and Arthurians wrangle over the meaning of the two inscriptions, one in Latin, one in Ogham (a rare Celtic script which identifies the stone as 6th century). This seems to indicate that the stone was carved around the time of the battle but only wishful thinking can make the almost illegible letters spell out Arthur's name.

Food and drink

Hilltop Farm Shop and Tea Room Slaughterbridge PL32 9TT ℗ 01840 211518
Ⓦ www.hilltopfarmshop.co.uk. Less than a mile from the Arthurian Centre, just
off the B3314 shortly before the junction with the A39, this wonderful place is
open seven days a week, packed with everything you could ever wish for from a
Cornish deli-cum-greengrocer and the home-cooked lunches, cakes and scones
are top drawer. Seriously recommended.

⑲ Delabole Slate Quarry

Pengelly, Delabole PL33 9AZ ℗ 01840 212242 Ⓦ www.delaboleslate.co.uk.

It was a bank holiday and this working quarry, which is open to visitors
from Monday to Friday, was therefore closed the first time I arrived in
Delabole. But the viewing platform from which the vast hole in the ground
(in fact, the biggest manmade hole in the country) can be seen, is next to
the car park at the start of a footpath which follows the mile and a half
circumference of the giant crater. From here peregrine falcons nesting in the
cliffs can be seen soaring on thermals, eyeing the ducklings and baby gulls
foolish enough to venture out into the still, blue pool that fills the bottom of
the quarry. On the brow of the hill where the quarrymen have erected a jokey
'slate-henge' complete with altar ('they're still looking for a sacrificial virgin'
remarked a passing dog-walker from the village) the views to Bodmin and the
west are outstanding.

Delabole slate is top-quality stuff and too expensive to use for everyday
building, so heritage projects account for much of the sales. 'Do you mean to
tell me that when a cottage in the village needs re-roofing, the chances are it'll
be done in cheap Chinese slate?' I asked with some incredulity. But George
Hamilton, who rescued the mine from dereliction in 1999 and whose four
sons all work with him in a workforce of about 30, is unstintingly generous
to the village he grew up in and a community-hearted man through and
through. 'With diversification, this really could be like an Eden Project for
north Cornwall in terms of employment. There are so many other things we
could do that would be of benefit to north Cornwall.' But funding seems to
be a long way off yet, and ironically, the very best-quality slate appears to lie
directly under the village.

Food and drink

The Bettle and Chisel In the centre of Delabole ℗ 01840 211402. Aptly named
after slate-splitting tools, this serves St Austell ales and good, locally sourced,
home-cooked pub grub beneath old photos of the quarry and its workforce.
Child-friendly.

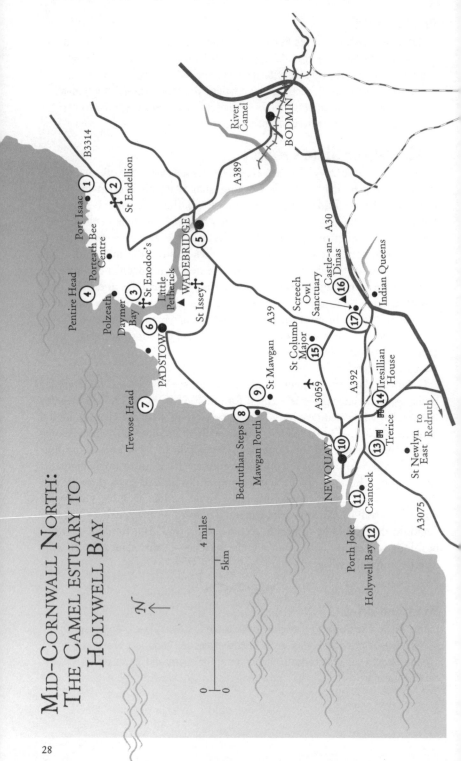

Mid-Cornwall North:
The Camel estuary to
Holywell Bay

2. MID-CORNWALL NORTH: THE CAMEL ESTUARY TO HOLYWELL BAY

The year-round appeal of breaking surf and sandy beaches makes this stretch of the Cornish coast one of the most-visited parts of Cornwall and while Newquay and Rock may not be everybody's idea of paradise (at least everybody of Bermuda shorts-wearing age), Padstow fulfils an alternative vision of Cornish bliss with its pretty houses, working harbour and abundance of upmarket eating establishments where fresh fish and seafood are given celebrity status.

Researching this chapter, I seem to have spent rather more time among the quieter backwaters of the region, looking for angels in the architecture or otters in the Camel, often finding myself ambling in Betjeman's footsteps: pottering about Wadebridge and revisiting his words in quiet churchyards or on windy headlands. I discovered too, that music is particularly strong in these parts. The now famous voices of a group of local men can be heard singing Cornish songs of the sea on the beach at Port Isaac on summer evenings, and the concerts in the lovely church at St Endellion have also found audiences from far beyond the Tamar.

Inland, a landscape of river valleys, woods and fields is crossed by the hugely popular Camel Trail, while the Saints' Way, used by traders and pilgrims for over 1,000 years, offers a superb walkers' route through hidden Cornwall from Padstow to Fowey on the south coast. Off the beaten track, but often just a mile or two away from the big tourist attractions there are unsung valleys and villages to explore, dotted with prehistoric stones, Iron Age hillforts and secluded churches.

Getting around

The A39, or Atlantic Highway as it dubs itself, is the main route across north Cornwall; it's single-carriageway all the way and can be very slow. Inevitably the spur roads off to Newquay and Padstow get very congested too in the high season and the traffic is nose to tail around Wadebridge during the three days of the Royal Cornwall Show in early June.

Trains

Bodmin Parkway station is your best bet for the Camel estuary towns and villages; Newquay fares rather better with its own branch line from Par on the main London – Penzance line, and its station is right in the town centre.

Buses

Wadebridge and Newquay are the hubs. Buses run from Newquay to Crantock and Holywell, making it easy to walk the three-mile stretch of coast path between them, taking in lovely Porth Joke Beach on the way. Frequent, direct buses run from Newquay to Padstow and Wadebridge, where you change for services to Rock, St Endellion and Port Isaac.

Ferries

The *Black Tor* shuttles between Padstow and Rock all through the year, though points of embarkation vary with the tides (*www.padstow-harbour.co.uk*). A summer-only ferry crosses the Gannel from the Fern Pit Landing in Newquay to Crantock Beach (see page 47) when the tide is too high to use the footbridge.

Cycling

The Cornish Way (Sustrans NCN Route 3) splits at Bodmin, offering cyclists the choice of a south- or north-bound coastal route, before joining up at Truro. The northern route makes use of the busy, level Camel Trail (see page 42). Beyond Padstow the route is quieter but hilly, wiggling past St Columb Major, Newquay and Trerice.

Cycle hire

There's no shortage of places to hire bikes along the Camel Trail, but it's wise to book ahead in the summer months – an indication of how popular the trail has become. Padstow and Wadebridge have a number of options; all offer bikes with tag-alongs or trailers for children and/or small dogs.

Bikesmart Eddystone Rd, Wadebridge PL27 7AL ① 01208 814545 ⑩ www.bikesmart.eu. Free car parking for customers.

Bridge Bike Hire/Go By Cycle Camel Trail, Wadebridge PL27 7AL ① 01208 813050 ⑩ www.bridgebikehire.co.uk. One-way trips can be organised with drop-off in Padstow. Part-refund on long-stay car parking charges.

Camel Trail Cycle Hire Eddystone Rd, Wadebridge PL27 7AL ① 01208 814104 ⑩ www.cameltrailcyclehire.co.uk. Free car parking for customers and indoor bike parking available too. Cheaper rates after 15.00 in the summer.

Padstow Cycle Hire South Quay, Padstow ① 01841 533533 ⑩ www.padstowcyclehire.com. Indoor bike parking for small charge (very useful if you've just cycled up from Wadebridge); free car parking and one-way trips possible with drop-off in Wadebridge.

Trail Bike Hire Unit 6, South Quay, Padstow PL28 8BL ① 01841 532594 ⑩ www.trailbikehire.co.uk. New to the bike hire scene and competitively priced. Evening hire from late July to late August at reduced rates.

Accommodation

There are some very swanky places to stay in the region covered by this chapter, which do not really fall within the Slow remit. However, special mention should be given to Mawgan Porth's **Bedruthan Steps Hotel** (*www.bedruthan. com*), much loved by exhausted parents for its terrific programme of morning, afternoon and evening activities for children from babies to teens, and its very grown-up sister hotel next door, the **Scarlet** (*www.scarlethotel.co.uk*) – positively the last word in green luxury and eco-architecture.

Cornish Tipi Holidays Tregeare, Pendoggett, St Kew PL30 3LW ① 01208 880781 Ⓦ www.cornishtipiholidays.co.uk Ⓔ info@cornishtipiholidays.co.uk. A wonderful, wooded spot with its own clearwater lake in a disused quarry, perfect for swimming, fishing or messing about in the boats and canoes provided. Some tipis are grouped together, others are scattered singly or in pairs among the trees, all have their own firepits for outdoor cooking. Tipis come in three sizes, the largest sleeping seven – great fun for a pack of small children, though parents will need deep pockets, as prices are comparable to holiday cottages within equally easy reach of upmarket Rock and Port Isaac.

Molesworth Manor B&B Little Petherick PL27 7QT ① 01841 540292 Ⓦ www. molesworthmanor.co.uk. Ⓔ molesworthmanor@aol.com. A comfortable family home, with a good-sized garden for children to play in, close to Padstow and Wadebridge. Excellent family accommodation at reasonable prices.

Moyles Farm St Minver, Wadebridge, PL27 6QT ① 01208 862331 Ⓦ www. moylesfarm.co.uk Ⓔ mail@moylesfarm.co.uk. Just minutes from Polzeath and Rock, a delightfully kitted-out shepherd's hut (with bathroom at a discreet distance) is the ultimate hideaway for romantics. Two farm buildings and the large mill house have also been stylishly converted to offer up-market self-catering accommodation. Locally cooked meals can be supplied from the freezer on request.

Porteath Barn B&B St Minver PL27 6RA ① 01208 863605 www.britainsfinest. co.uk. Tucked away behind the Bee Centre buildings and just a short walk away from the splendidly isolated Epphaven Beach on the north coast; there are great walks along the coast path to Port Quin or Pentire Head. A B&B in a barn conversion in a lovely garden – bedrooms are downstairs, sitting room with logburner upstairs. Breakfasts are highly rated here – pancakes and homemade jam, kippers and kedgeree are all on the menu. Three twin/double rooms each have their own bathroom; a fourth room is available for members of the same party. Average B&B prices.

Roskear Tregunna, Wadebridge PL27 7HU ① 07748 432013 Ⓦ www.roskear.com Ⓔ accommodation@Roskear.com. Peaceful 18th-century farmhouse off the beaten track, close to the estuary and Camel Trail. Log fires, beamy sitting room and breakfast cooked on the Aga. Two rooms, a double and a twin, share a bathroom; reasonably priced for such an upmarket part of Cornwall.

Woodlands Country House Treator, Padstow PL28 8RU ℗ 01841 532426
Ⓦ www. woodlands-padstow.co.uk Ⓔ enquiries@woodlands-padstow.co.uk.
Luxurious country house ambience 15 minutes' walk from Padstow harbour.
Pretty gardens, croquet lawn, very comfortable rooms with understated décor.
Breakfasts are very special: the buffet table beautifully presented with homemade
muesli, breads and jams and juices; cooked breakfasts are made from locally
sourced ingredients, including their own-recipe sausages. Not for the budget-
conscious, but a top-notch B&B.

Tourist information centres

Newquay Marcus Hill ℗ 01637 854020.
Padstow North Quay ℗ 01841 533449.
Wadebridge Rotunda Building, Eddystone Rd ℗ 0870 122 3337.

Around the Camel estuary

'Heyl' is Cornish for estuary, of which there are just two on the north coast
of Cornwall. There's the Hayle estuary, further to the west and this, the
Cam-heyl or 'crooked estuary', the last before the Taw and the Torridge meet
between Bideford and Barnstaple, way up the coast in Devon. The Camel is
superbly rich in wildlife and is one of the few estuaries in the West Country
where salmon are flourishing, a mark of a healthy river. Birdwatching from
the western shores, where access is made easy by the Camel Trail, is especially
rewarding in winter, when flocks of migrants join the natives dipping their
beaks in the rich estuarine mud.

To the east and west of the wide estuary mouth, strings of fine, sandy beaches
look out towards rocky islets, where seals and seabirds keep a distant eye on
the surfing and seafood-loving crowds who flock here in numbers equal to the
winged migrants.

① Port Isaac

There's not much elbow room in the steep, narrow streets of the photogenic
fishing village (one of the lanes is called Squeeze Belly Alley, which gives a
good indication of the limitations on space) so it's not surprising that cars
are banned in the summer months. Two big car parks on the cliff above the
harbour take the strain and the walk down to 'the Platt' (as it is known locally)
is full of charm and offers a great vantage point over the beach.

Because of the good view and terrific acoustics of the harbour, this spot gets
packed on Friday evenings in the summer (aim for 20.00), when the **Fisherman's
Friends** assemble on the Platt for an unaccompanied concert of shanties and
Cornish folk songs. The ten men, who all grew up in and around Port Isaac,

sang together in the Methodist chapel as
lads, and kept on meeting to sing even
after work claimed them as fishermen,
coastguards, lifeboatmen, builders,
artists, hoteliers and shopkeepers.
There's no leader among them –
each man takes his turn to start
a song and the sound of their
voices builds a full, rich orchestra
of harmonies. These rugged types
have acquired a modestly unexpected fame

over the past few years: I love the story of how they were asked to sing in
the foyer of the Royal Albert Hall for the BBC Folk Awards and found an
unexpected fan: 'David Attenborough came and listened to us and he refused
to go into the Hall until we'd finished our set: "No I'm staying here," he said.'
However, if you catch a glimpse of a film crew in the village, it's more likely to
be Martin Clunes in the limelight, as the village has long been the backdrop to
the popular TV series, *Doc Martin*.

Port Isaac doesn't sound like a Cornish name, but it's a corruption of Issick,
meaning corn, which was exported from here in large quantities from medieval
times onwards. Slate was exported too and Welsh coal landed here. Pilchard
fishing was big business in the 18th and 19th centuries and the old pilchard
cellars have found a wide variety of uses: one of them is now the lifeboat
station. Fish is still landed here and crab and lobster are cooked on the slipway
and sold in the fish market where, if you come in the morning, you'll see the
local chefs in their aprons putting in their orders for the day.

Less than a mile to the east, **Port Gaverne**, a finger-shaped cove, has one
of the safest beaches on the north Cornish coast: pebbly at high tide, but
revealing firm sand and rock pools as the tide retreats.

A fine three-mile walk west along the coast path takes you round Kellan
Head from which there are magnificent views across Port Quin Bay to the
Rumps before dropping down into **Port Quin**, a shingle harbour with a
scattering of houses, tucked away at the sheltered end of a Cornish fjord. This
once busily populated fishing village was able like its bigger neighbour, Port
Isaac, to add substantially to its income by exporting local slate. The railways
stole the trade from the quays and the pilchard industry dried up; almost
overnight it became a ghost village. Now there's just a small cluster of holiday
cottages, including a castellated Victorian folly, Doyden Castle, perched on
the south side of the water, all immaculately restored by the National Trust.
You can make this a circular walk, returning to Port Isaac by a well-signposted,
straightforward inland route across the fields to Roscarrock Manor, one of the
oldest farms in Cornwall. There are Roscarrock family tombs in St Endellion
(see page 34). After Roscarrock there's a plunging coombe to negotiate, and
then Port Isaac appears ahead.

Food and drink

Port Isaac is stuffed with cafés, pubs and restaurants, with cream teas and local fish all over the menus. **The Mote** (*01208 880226*), a restaurant and bar in a cosy little former smuggler's cottage, is particularly good at championing home-grown (or home-fished) food.

② St Endellion

When it came to choosing a middle name for their daughter, the Camerons picked wisely; there's something very special about the village community and the church that stands at its centre, well known these days for its world-class music festivals in spring and summer. There's an Arthurian connection, too: St Endelienta, to whom the church is dedicated, was reputedly the god-daughter of King Arthur (Tintagel, of course, is just a few miles up the coast) who slew the villain that killed the saintly girl's cow. She brought the beast back to life and when she died, it carried her to the place where the first church was built to remember her. There's mention of the church again at the end of the 13th century, when the same bishop who ordered the building of Glasney College in Penryn (see page 174) awarded it collegiate status. Endelienta's shrine, carved in the 15th century by a local sculptor known simply as 'the Master of St Endellion', has been used as an altar since the 1920s, when a very sensitive restoration was started. The darker roof beams date from this period, but the lighter wood, smothered in carved decoration, is early 15th century; the older bench ends can be dated to this period, too.

It must be the lack of stained glass in the windows that makes the building seem so light and airy; it's hard to imagine what it would have been like when a high wooden rood screen separated the nave from the sanctuary. This (like so many) was removed during the Reformation, but there's still a reminder of where it once stood. The narrow stone staircase set into the north wall spirals up to an eight-foot drop, but when the screen was in place, it provided the means by which candles could be placed along its top, or draped with a veil during Lent. In the bell tower an amusingly illustrated 18th-century 'poster' gives rhyming advice to bell-ringers on how they should behave. The tower isn't often open, but there's an identical poster beside the bell-ropes in the equally attractive church in **St Kew**; the little, leafy village a couple of miles to the south makes a rewarding detour for secular reasons too: the pub (see below) does excellent food.

Music at St Endellion

What began in 1958, when a few college friends got together to renovate the old rectory and put on a few concerts in the church, has grown to become what is now one of the most prestigious musical events in Cornwall. Actually, there are two main events: the Easter and summer music festivals, made special by the mixture of amateur and top-flight professionals, rising and established musicians who keep coming back, finding the creative energies and glorious atmosphere of St Endelienta completely irresistible. So irresistible that the summer festival now fields a full symphony orchestra and 75-strong chorus for the annual centrepiece opera. The virtuous circle that generates this kind of passion and energy is in no small part due to the late Richard Hickox, who ran the festival for 40 years; his first wife, Fran, and son, Tom, are still very much involved.

The Easter festival is never without an English-language performance of a Bach Passion, but the intimacy of the church lends itself to more than grand orchestral pieces: there are evening concerts of chamber music, song recitals, jazz and lunchtime proms. Tickets sell out with predictable rapidity, but there are open rehearsals in the mornings and sung Eucharist and evensong. Just before the opening of the festival, confident local musicians are invited to make up a wind or stringed orchestra under the direction of one of Endellion's regulars, and after just three hours' rehearsal, there's an informal performance.

Food and drink

Cornish Arms Pendoggett PL30 3HH ℗ 01208 880263. Free house serving Sharp's Doom Bar and 'PSB' – Pendoggett Special Brew, brewed specially for the pub.
St Kew Harvest Shop St Kew Highway, PL30 3EF ℗ 01208 841818. An excellent farm shop, selling pork from Gloucester Old Spots, local lamb and home-grown fruit and vegetables.
St Kew Inn St Kew PL30 3HB ℗ 01208 841259. A St Austell Brewery pub in a very pretty village; log fires, lovely garden and extremely good food.

③ Daymer Bay and St Enodoc's Church

The poet Sir John Betjeman (1906–84) spent his childhood holidays at Trebetherick and later came to live here by **Daymer Bay**, remembering sunny clifftop picnics and stormy beach walks in his verse. The west-facing beach has lost none of its charm for holidaying families; though the sea is

Cornish angels

Once you start looking for them, churches and churchyards of mid and north Cornwall are a-flap with angels: all smiles and wings, decorating the corners of gravestones or at the base of roof arches, on fonts and bench carvings, windows and brackets. Henrietta Boex, from Falmouth, has made a study of them: 'It's not so much a local preoccupation with angels,' she says, 'as local availability of fine quality slate, which permits fine-line chiselling and doesn't weather like softer stones, which is why they're so noticeable around here. When you start noticing them, you realise that both naive and skilled artists across the centuries had great fun drawing faces and hairdos, trumpets and wings, using their chisels almost like pencils.'

saturated with surfers and windsurfers, there are still the simple pleasures of rockpooling and crabbing at low tide on Trebetherick Point. Brea Hill looms above the beach, creating a 'wind shadow' that keeps the windsurfers on their mettle; footpaths wind around the hill and across the fairways of a golf course to **St Enodoc's Church**, where the Poet Laureate found his final resting place. The granite church, with its squat 13th-century tower nearly suffered the same fate as St Piran's Oratory and church on Penhale Sands (see page 137), disappearing beneath the windblown sand on several occasions over the centuries. A nice (but possibly tall) story relates how, at one point, the vicar and his congregation had to enter the church by a trapdoor in the roof. By the middle of the 19th century 'the sands had blown higher than the eastern gable, the wet came in freely, the high pews were mouldy-green and worm-eaten and bats flew about, living in the belfry'. This was written by the son of the vicar who launched a major effort to remove the sand in the 1860s and oversaw the restoration of the church. A new bell was hung in the tower, claimed from the wreck of an Italian ship that had foundered on the infamous Doom Bar sand spit.

Doom Bar

Padstow's harbour is one of the safest on the north coast, but it's not always easy to approach thanks to the bank of silt and sand that blocks the estuary at low tide and is dangerously invisible at other times. Hundreds of ships have foundered upon it since it started to make its shifting presence felt over 500 years ago. Sharp's Brewery, in Rock, has given its name to its best-selling flagship ale; you'll see Doom Bar in pubs all across Cornwall.

Tresoddit

During the 1980s, *Guardian* cartoonist Posy Simmonds cast her wry gaze over the changing fortunes of neighbouring Rock and Polzeath, both of which have been identified as the model for her fictional Cornish fishing village, Tresoddit.

'The little hamlet holds its breath and gazes out to sea and waits for the safe return of its wayfaring ones,' began one classic strip, suggesting an absent fishing fleet. The streets of Tresoddit are silent, while locals 'eke out a doleful existence'. But then there's a glimpse of a sail: 'They're back up at Crab Pots,' a local reports. 'Car's in the lane ... got their dinghy on the trailer.' In the final frame we see a crowd of London families meeting up at the Jolly Fisherman pub, complaining about traffic jams at Okehampton (the location of the last Waitrose on the A30 route into Cornwall) over gin and tonics. 'The fleet blows into its haven for a sojourn, which must be all too brief. But, for a short while, the streets are full of merry mariners ... and all the tills ring.'

This cliché image of Rock/Tresoddit is a little weatherworn these days, partly overtaken by unsavoury images of well-heeled youth partying on the beach, but more importantly by Rock's emerging identity as a serious sea-foodie destination to rival Padstow, a ferry ride away across the estuary.

Oysters and oystercatchers

On the tidal shores of the Camel, a little south of Rock, Tim Marshall has been farming Pacific oysters for more than two decades. These oysters grow much faster than the native oyster raised in the Helford and Fal – it takes just two years for little 'spats' the size of a fingernail to grow into palm-sized beasts and there's a ready market for them in the upmarket hotels and restaurants that have sprung up around the estuary. Tim rears his oysters in netting sacks, laid out on racks along the shoreline, so they get washed and fed by each returning tide. It's fortunate that one of Tim's favourite birds, the oystercatcher, poses no threat to his business. Using their long, pointed orange bills to stab through shell, they feed on small shore crabs or cockles and mussels in the estuary mud and you'll occasionally see flocks in winter on grassy fields, poking around for worms.

At the time of writing, the Rock Oyster Festival, held over a June weekend in St Minver, is facing an uncertain future. The problem is that since it started in 2010, the arts-food-and-music festival has been more about rock (music) than oysters, and noise levels in St Minver appear to have reached controversial levels.

④ Pentire Head and Rumps Point

A square-headed chunk of land, circumscribed by a sublime section of the coast path, juts out into the sea above Polzeath. It's carpeted with wild flowers – thrift, sea campion, kidney vetch, gorse and – a Cornish rarity – harebells appear in spring. Unbelievably, it was destined for commercial development in the 1930s, but saved by local opposition who raised funds and donated the land to the National Trust. At its westernmost reach is **Pentire Point**, described by Betjeman, looking up from Trebetherick, as having the form of a sleeping lion; it's a grand perch for gazing out over Padstow Bay.

The northeastern knobble of rock is **Rumps Point**, surmounted by an Iron Age cliff-fort, one of three known to have existed on the headland. Binoculars come in really handy here: the lump of rock a few hundred yards out to sea, known as the Mouls, is home to masses of nesting seabirds, including fulmars and a handful of puffins. There used to be many more puffins (tour boat operators in Padstow still refer to it optimistically as Puffin Island), but predation by great black-backed gulls has caused a severe decline in numbers.

Between the two points, a memorial stone beside the cliff path records that the poet Laurence Binyon wrote 'For the Fallen' here in 1914, and quotes the fourth verse, heard each year at Remembrance Day services: 'They shall grow not old, as we that are left grow old ...'

⑤ Wadebridge

Until the late 15th century, two villages faced each other across an unpredictable ford on the River Camel. On the west bank, there was Wade in the parish of St Breock; on the east bank, Egloshayle, with its waterside church dedicated to

St Petroc. The vicar of St Petroc, the Reverend John Lovibond, was also a sheep farmer, and clearly a wealthy one for he paid for a tower to be added to his church and in 1460 decided it was high time his flocks (both woolly and two-legged) were able to cross the Camel to the market in Wade without fear of drowning. The story goes that the piers supporting the 17 arches of the bridge were sunk on foundations made of woolsacks, which is why it's known as the **Bridge on Wool**, but this is likely to be an enthusiastically literal interpretation of the means by which the bridge was funded. Now only 13 arches are visible and it has twice been widened, but it's still an impressive sight and by far the longest medieval bridge in Cornwall. There's a healthy otter population on the Camel, and some have even been seen from the bridge, playing on the muddy shore late in the evening by the light of street lamps; kingfishers too, can sometimes be seen scooting underneath the arches.

Wadebridge is a busy place, servicing scattered communities over a wide rural area and it's full of the 'normal' kind of shops that have no place in swanky Rock and Padstow. But it's no Cinderella – Molesworth Street is wide and paved and home to a good assortment of independent food and clothing shops, as well as **Tristan's Gallery** (*01208 815767*), which exhibits vintage and contemporary images by many internationally familiar names in photography and the much-loved **Wadebridge Bookshop** (*01208 812489*) holds regular talks by local authors and book signings.

The town is also an important access point for cyclists and walkers embarking on the hugely popular Camel Trail, which follows the track of the old railway that once linked Padstow to Bodmin. In 1840, six years after the line opened, 1,100 people crowded onto three specially laid-on trains at Wadebridge for a day trip to Bodmin. The object of the excursion was to see the public execution at Bodmin Gaol of the Lightfoot brothers who had been convicted of murder. Such was the entertainment then: Wadebridge's Regal Cinema, which opened its doors in 1931 (and is still going strong) clearly didn't arrive a minute too soon.

When the line closed in 1967, the Victorian station languished until rescue came in the form of a fund-raising volunteer group. It reopened in 1991 as the **John Betjeman Centre** (*01208 812392*), with additional new buildings to house the activities of the local U3A and over-55s groups. The Poet Laureate would have approved: he loved Victorian railway architecture and the cosy sociability of the tea room seems a fitting tribute to the poet of 'trains and buttered toast'. A single room houses Betjeman memorabilia in a low-key sort of way – you're free to go in and browse among the photos, press cuttings, and glass cases containing notes and first editions. Guided visits can be organised for groups.

Wadebridge's rural hinterland

Immediately south and west of Wadebridge a web of narrow lanes and footpaths takes you into hilly, farming country, dotted with woodland and trickling tributaries of the Camel. There are some idyllic spots by the river, giving opportunities for spotting kingfishers and otters. Thanks to the Camel Trail, it's an easy stroll of just under a mile to Pendarvey footbridge; from here to **Polbrock Bridge** a mile upstream, the river, the surrounding woods and wetland meadows are all rich in wild flowers and outstandingly beautiful. The Conservation Walks branching off the main trail are well marked, bicycle-free and take in peaceful views of woodland and water.

Southwest of Wadebridge, narrow lanes zigzag past **St Breock**, with its pretty church tucked away on wooded slopes, and tiny **Polmorla**, where a handful of houses cluster around an ancient bridge at the bottom of a steep and leafy valley. The contrast with St Breock Downs a mile or two to the south could not be more startling: the exposed hilltops are crowned with wind turbines and an extraordinary collection of **Neolithic standing stones**, best appreciated on foot from the Saints' Way.

Food and drink

Earl of St Vincent Egloshayle PL27 6HT ℗ 01208 814807. A characterful old pub, serving food. Peaceful pints of local ale are interrupted on the hour by an astonishing assortment of chiming, chirping and clanging wall-mounted clocks: over 400 in total.

Relish Food and Drink Foundry Court, Wadebridge ℗ 01208 814214 ⓦ www. relishwadebridge.co.uk. A small, well-stocked deli with a delightful courtyard café, just off Molesworth St. Much applauded for its local and imported cheeses and charcuterie. Hugo, the man behind the expresso machine, has won prizes for his coffee.

Royal Cornwall Show

Wadebridge Showground ⓦ www.royalcornwallshow.org.

For three days in June each year, Cornish farmers and producers rally to their county show in droves. It's a proper, traditional agricultural show, one of the best in the UK and in recent years it's become something of a showcase for Cornish Slow food. In the Food and Farming pavilion, run by farmers Ashley and Hilary Wood, you'll find many of the local producers listed in this guide and have the opportunity to sample the goods, chat to the people involved and leave with a bulging carrier bag. The Woods are passionate and tireless promoters of Cornish food and drink and have set up a very useful website (*www.foodfromcornwall. co.uk*), which lists dozens of Cornish farm shops and producers as well as local events and news.

⑥ Padstow

It is a mean-looking place, of woe-begone aspect ... We imagine no one deliberately visits Padstow for its own sake, but those fond of a fine coast will find it a convenient resting-place for the night.
C S Ward, *Thorough Guide to North Devon and North Cornwall,* 1888

This remote little fishing port ... [which] endures that incessant and often intolerable wind ... faces onto a vast expanse of sand-flats which become at low tide a desert-like wilderness broken only by the inconspicuous trickle of the River Camel.
Roland Roddis, *Cornish Harbours,* 1951

Well, you can't accuse the old guidebooks of over-selling Padstow. Roddis worries that the decline of Padstow's fishing industry will result in the town delivering its soul to tourism, like the harbours he has seen at Volendam and Marken in Holland, where 'worst of all, they sell jellied eels by the dozen' to visitors. The man who saved Padstow from a fate of jellied eels is Rick Stein, whose many establishments now dominate the little town, to the extent that it goes by the sobriquet these days of 'Padstein'. Happily, the fishing fleet is healthy again, the fish market on South Quay lively, and the seafood restaurants along the quay packed throughout the summer. Even on a chilly grey day in February, when I last visited, there was lots of activity in the harbour and lunchtime queues for Stein's fish and chip shop. Battered oysters were on the menu; it's good to see the celebrity chef has retained his sense of humour. Nevertheless, I can't say I was tempted to see if they had survived their battering.

Despite the crowds, the character of old Padstow still reveals itself in its narrow streets and haphazard terraces of old houses and cottages, which even Roddis was forced to admit 'typify all that is best in nautical architecture'. Sir Walter Raleigh, who held the exalted position of Warden of the Stannaries between 1585 and 1603, had a house and adjoining courtroom on Riverside (both private residences now) and older still is the Abbey House, on the far side of the quay, next to the Shipwright's Arms. The small **Padstow Museum** in the Market Place contains a cherished collection of documents, photographs and artefacts relating to Padstow's long history as a seaport. The finds from an archaeological dig that uncovered a Bronze Age cemetery at Harlyn Bay in 1900 are on display along with a slightly creepy post-war 'Obby Oss' mask, used in the pagan festivities which continue – symbolically – to drive out winter from Padstow on May Day each year. And there's a riveting eyewitness account of the staggering bravery and dreadful loss of life when the harbour lifeboats attempted to rescue a stricken trawler on 11 April 1900.

A wander up Church Street, away from the busy harbour, brings you to **St Petroc's Church**, built in the early part of the 15th century on very ancient foundations – the thick base of the tower is a relic of the *second* church, built around 1100. The first, Celtic chapel dates from the 6th century and stood until AD981, when both the church and the monastery Petroc had founded were destroyed in a Viking raid. St Petroc's bones, which were originally buried here, have had a colourful history (see page 67); his equally colourful life is recalled in the (modern) stained-glass window over the main altar, where he is shown with his famously rescued deer, as well as in the beautifully carved emblems of his saintliness in the canopies over the adjoining windows. But my prize for the best carving is on one of the old bench ends, which shows a fox in a pulpit, preaching to a flock of enthusiastic geese. (At least, five of them look interested; the other two have been distracted by something behind them.)

Prideaux Place

PL28 8RP ① 01841 532411 ⓦ www.prideauxplace.co.uk; open summer months Sun–Thu; check website for dates and times.

A short walk up the hill from the church brings you to Prideaux Place, home to the Prideaux-Brunes, who have lived here since it was built (on the site of St Petroc's Monastery) between 1588 and 1592. The Elizabethan house was extended and given a Gothic makeover in 1810, to bring it up to date with prevailing fashion, and the garden too is a palimpsest of various dates and styles, though the layout of the 1730 'Augustan garden' remains remarkably intact.

In *Unwrecked England*, Candida Lycett Green describes Prideaux Place as 'about unwrecked as you can get' and she's right – inside the house, as the current owners, Peter and Elizabeth Prideaux-Brune, will tell you, 'there are 44 bedrooms, of which just six are habitable'. Some of them are just as the American army left them at the end of World War II and throughout the house you find yourself wandering through a microcosm of British history. In the dining room, for example, there's a carving of Elizabeth I trampling on a pig (the pig apparently symbolised vice) and in the drawing room a 'diplomatic' miniature shows a double portrait of Charles I and Oliver Cromwell. (The family sided with the Parliamentarians, but won a pardon – also displayed – for 'past, present and future crimes' by later marrying off a sister to Charles II's Secretary of State.)

Bicycles, Betjeman and Beer

Very much attuned to the Slow concept, Susan and Nick run Cornish Heritage Safaris (*www.cornishheritagesafaris.co.uk*), taking groups of up to six on tailor-made trips to explore the secrets of the Cornish landscape and its history. Standing stones and Arthurian legend provide the theme for some tours, but the 'Bicycles, Betjeman and Beer' tour suggests a day with a bit of a difference. It includes a spot of gentle pedalling along the Camel Trail, fish and chips in Padstow, poems and pottering at St Enodoc where Betjeman is buried and the day ends with a tasting at Sharp's Brewery, best known for its Doom Bar ale.

The gardens, which are currently undergoing a major restoration with the help of Tom Petherick, who was involved in the restoration of Heligan (see page 128), were largely the work of Edmund Prideaux-Brune, who inherited the estate in 1728. Just five years earlier, he had embarked on the Grand Tour, and the gardens he laid out reflect his awareness of Italian style: green formality and fountains prevail. The Deer Park, one of the oldest in the country, is an essay in Arcadian beauty.

National Lobster Hatchery

South Quay ① 01841 533877 ⓦ www.nationallobsterhatchery.co.uk.

I love the straightforward honesty of the name, which tells you exactly what goes on here. Newly hatched baby lobsters don't stand much of a chance in open waters: the survival rate is much less than 1%. (Lobsters are cannibalistic, which doesn't help either.) So a number of designated fishermen around the coast send the hatchery berried (egg-bearing) female lobsters rather than depositing them back in the sea. The eggs are safely hatched and after a few weeks, the baby lobsters are returned to the sea. Result: we can gorge ourselves on lobster without worrying that stocks are in decline. 'And how do you feel about eating lobster?' I asked the young marine biologist working there, among the tiny, semi-transparent babies. 'Can't afford it,' she grinned.

The one room open to the public is small, but well laid out and the first windows into the tanks behind the walls reveal examples of some whopping lobsters and lobster-lookalikes, such as crawfish, displayed in a child-friendly way. Facts and figures come next, aided by a short film. Then there are the babies, tray upon tray of finger-length crustaceans, each in their own cot-like unit, looking vulnerable and rather appealing.

Just a step away are some of Cornwall's most famous seafood restaurants, which you can now visit with your conscience appeased. That's the theory, anyway.

The Camel Trail and Saints' Way

Padstow is the start – or finish – of two important walking routes. The **Camel Trail**, used perhaps by more cyclists than walkers, is a 17-mile level track that follows the route of an old railway, from the South Quay at Padstow along the estuary to Wadebridge (five miles), and on to Dunmere Halt (six miles) through deep, leafy cuttings beside a very picturesque stretch of the Camel. There's a family-friendly pub by the parking space at Dunmere, and from here you can take the mile-long route into Bodmin, or swing north, following the young river upstream to

Wenfordbridge (six miles), just a short hop from the very pretty moorland village of Blisland (see page 64). It's estimated that 400,000 walkers, cyclists, wheelchair users and horseriders use the trail each year, and at peak times in the summer months it does feel like a bit like a healthy, green version of the A30.

The **Saints' Way** starts at the door of St Petroc's in Padstow and follows an ancient overland route taken by Celtic saints and medieval pilgrims travelling between Ireland or Wales and Brittany (where the route continues on to Santiago de Compostella), avoiding the dangers of sailing around Land's End. The 30-mile trail crosses some of Cornwall's most sublime rural landscapes, dividing just south of the A30 to offer two equally enjoyable routes into Fowey.

You can use the first couple of miles of trail to make a decent circular walk up one side of Little Petherick Creek and down the other, following the creekside footpath to Tregonce, where a permissive footpath connects with the Camel Trail and so over the iron bridge back to Padstow.

Food and drink

The whole town of Padstow seems dedicated to producing and selling high-quality food and drink, that might be labelled 'Upmarket Slow'; it's a great place to push the boat out and indulge in some seriously good local cuisine. Among the smaller establishments that might easily be missed, **Margot's Bistro** (*11 Duke St; 01841 533441*) has acquired a loyal and local following, and **The Basement** (*11 Broad St, The Drang; 01841 532846*) looks a little unprepossessing from the outside, but is cosy indoors and deeply committed to seasonal, local produce.

With a preponderance of St Austell Brewery pubs around the quay, there's no problem securing a pint of Tribute, but if you're after a glug of Doom Bar, from Sharp's, the local brewery, look out for the flowery frontage of the **Golden Lion** in Lanadwell St (*01841 532797*).

As it's a little way out of town, you might miss the excellent **Padstow Farm Shop** at Trethillick (*01841 533060; www.padstowfarmshop.co.uk*). It's beyond Prideaux Place (on the lane to Stepper Point), and sells fruit and veg from the old kitchen gardens there as well as home-reared pork, beef and lamb. It's big by any farm shop standards, supplying several Padstow restaurants and offering an online shopping and delivery service too.

From Trevose Head to Holywell Bay

This sublime stretch of west-facing coast is famous for its superb sandy bays – Constantine, Watergate, Lusty Glaze and Fistral: beaches which are legend among the surfing community. The cliffs behind them are pretty special too: battered by winds from the west and sculpted by the sea, a dramatic chaos of deep gorges, collapsed sea caves and colossal, isolated chunks of rock make for spectacular coast path walks.

⑦ Trevose Head

The Doom Bar makes access to Padstow harbour difficult at the best of times, so the lifeboat has been stationed at Mother Ivey's Bay since 1967 and crews must dash the five miles from Padstow by road. It's housed in an impressive piece of contemporary architecture, curved to accommodate the thrust of wind and waves and perched on piers at the far end of a glorious, shallow arc of golden sand – rarely overcrowded, as the nearest parking is a mile away at Harlyn Bay. If you continue by car beyond Mother Ivey's, to Trevose Head, there's a toll of about £3 to pay, which includes all-day parking, close to the lighthouse and a huge blowhole, formed by a collapsed cave.

⑧ Bedruthan Steps

These monumental, flat-topped slabs of slate marching across the sand, like a giant's stepping stones (Bedruthan is the name of a mythical Cornish giant), are so large that in some cases they have individual names. One slab was ironically dubbed Samaritan Island in 1846, when a ship carrying a cargo of silks was wrecked on the unforgiving rock and locals rushed to save the precious cargo, ignoring the crew. Another is called Queen Bess Rock, as the profile of Elizabeth I could be discerned in its contours. It takes some imagination to see her these days.

At low tide, it's possible to walk around the northernmost rock (swimming is not an option in these dangerous waters) to Diggory's Island Sands – a perfect horseshoe of golden beach, edged with rockpools and caves. There's a steep, narrow path back up to the top of the cliffs from the beach, but the first part is a bit of a scramble.

The National Trust has several car parks along the clifftop road between Mawgan Porth and Porthcothan; at Carnewas Point there's a small visitor centre and friendly café.

Food and drink

Bre Pen Farm Shop and Bistro Mawgan Porth TR8 4AL ⓣ 01637 860420 ⓦ www.bre-penfarm.co.uk. The farm shop sells home-reared lamb and local beef as well as farm vegetables and free-range eggs. The bistro uses produce from the farm and includes homemade soups on the menu at lunchtime. Evening meals are French-inspired, using local ingredients.

⑨ St Mawgan

Behind Mawgan Porth, the deep, wooded Vale of Lanherne is a world away from the frantic activity and windy exposure of the beach. St Mawgan is a Miss Marple kind of village, with church fetes, village cricket, a historic pub, pretty gardens open for charity and homemade jams and chutneys on sale at the garden gate. The restored 13th-century church is full of treasures: carved bench ends, a 15th-century rood screen and a superb collection of

Sacred stones

Ed Prynn is a great British eccentric – you need only wander past his bungalow and garden just outside St Merryn (*PL28 8JZ; www.edprynnsstonehenge.com*) to grasp the full extent of the retired quarryman's foibles. The self-appointed Chief Druid of Cornwall has created a granite stone circle (each stone representing an important woman in his life), a giant dolmen ('the Angels' Runway'), an underground fogou (for ritualised re-birthing ceremonies) and other copies or interpretations of Cornish standing stones, and invites the curious – as well as the convinced – to share in the sacred energies of his extraordinary domain. Rites of healing, fertility and handfasting are Prynn's speciality, and he even claimed to have lifted a curse from the England football team in 2010, before the World Cup. For all his eccentricity, Prynn is a man of persuasive charm; in 1987, he convinced Sir Rex Hunt, Governor of the Falkland Islands to send him, free of charge, two massive stones, excavated during the building of the new airport, 'one to remember those who didn't return from the conflict and one to remember those who did'.

Once, he says, his stones were visited by Margaret and Dennis Thatcher, who had been playing golf nearby, though sadly he missed them as he was 'doing the shopping for mother' at the time.

brasses, mostly memorials to the Arundells of Lanherne. In the peaceful churchyard, a timber memorial, shaped like the stern of a rowing boat, remembers the ten sailors who froze to death in their boat and were washed ashore in 1846.

The **Japanese Garden** and bonsai nursery (*01637 860116*) might seem anomalous in such a quintessentially English village idyll, but it turns out to be more about woodland walks, beautifully planted with acers and azaleas, tranquil water and clipped 'cloud trees' – as opposed to acres of Zen gravel.

⑩ Newquay

Newquay is not an obvious destination for Slow travellers, and a sense of place cannot always be guaranteed in its hinterland of backstreets, teeming with – and catering for – an international crowd of party-loving surf-seekers. When Truro's new bronze sculpture of a naked drummer was unveiled, the local twitterati derived much entertainment from suggesting the kind of figure that might similarly symbolise the spirit of Newquay.

'Oh, but it's got that house on an island with a bridge,' say those around me, determined to remain positive. Indeed, there is an Edwardian house on an island with its own suspension footbridge. Lord and Lady Long, who live in it, were instrumental in starting the campaign to clean up Newquay's reputation a few years ago, resulting in the beach being declared an alcohol-free zone; the sustained effort to keep things moving in a positive direction is immediately evident in the highly visible presence throughout the town of the Newquay Safe Partnership.

Problems associated with tourism – albeit high-class tourism – are not new to Newquay. The grand Headland Hotel caused riots when it was built in 1900 on common land used for grazing and drying nets. The victory of tourism over local industry did not bring great happiness to the architect and entrepreneur, Silvanus Trevail (see page 127), but the hotel still stands, a lonely vision of upper-crust grandeur above the teeming surf of Fistral Beach.

It's a longish walk from one side of Newquay to the other, following the coast path along the clifftop seafront, but for much of the way there are gull's-eye views over the beaches and world-class surf activity to admire. If you can time your walk so the tide is in by the time you arrive at Pentire (allow a good hour from the cliffs above Lusty Glaze Beach) there's a delightful opportunity to cross the Gannel to Crantock Beach and return to Newquay by bus from Crantock village. A short detour might take you down to the historic **harbour**, engineered by the great Joseph Treffry (see page 119), once linked by a tunnel and tramway to the railway station. (The tunnel is still used by the pilot gig rowing team for storing their boats and the tramlines remain exposed on the approach to the station in Cliff Road.) High above the harbour, the route passes the Huer's Hut, a stubby whitewashed tower looking more like a Greek island windmill than a Cornish lookout post, from which the news was bawled that shoals of pilchards had arrived.

Beyond the Headland Hotel, a narrow peninsula separates **Fistral Beach** from Newquay's suburban fringes. The coast path cuts across the neck of the peninsula, but a footpath will take you all the way round the rocky promontory if you have the time or inclination and where you may well spot seals flopping on the rocky eastern shore. Looking more like a chapel on the beach than a former lifeboat station is the studio of local artist, Nicholas Williams. On the furthest point the octagonal tower was formerly used by coastguards and the deeply unpopular 'Preventative Men', whose job it was to observe and intercept smugglers.

The wide, grassy expanse of **Pentire Point East**, overlooking the mouth of the Gannel and the white sands of Crantock Beach seems to conclude the east-to-west walking route, but there is a lovely treat ahead: halfway along a lane of suburban bungalows the **Fern Pit Café** is the clifftop base of the Northey family, who have been ferrying passengers across the Gannel for over a century (*www.fernpit.co.uk*). From the café garden, you look down through a canopy of exotic plants to the hundred twisting steps that lead to the Fern Pit landing; I'll never forget that first glimpse of the sapphire water and a little boat ferrying a dog and its family across to dune-flanked Crantock Beach. While you wait for the boat there's a large tank of lobsters and crabs to peer into (beneath a sign that tells you your lobster will be cooked by the time you return) and panels telling the story of the Northey family business. At low tide, the bridge is exposed, but from mid-September to late May, when the Fern Pit is closed, you'll have to head further upstream to find the next bridge at Penpol (which also disappears underwater at high tide). Failing that, the next crossing is the bridleway Laurie Bridge and you'd have to be unlucky and hit a high spring tide to find it closed. A tide timetable takes the uncertainty out of the crossing.

Food and drink

Café Irie Fore St ℗ 01637 859200. Sitting conveniently close to the harbour, this is one of my favourite cafés in Cornwall. Its colourful, teapot-themed exterior looks incongruous among the fast-food outlets, bars and surf shops, and inside there are two small floors, stuffed with squishy sofas and mismatched tables and chairs. The busy staff never fail to make time to rustle up the friendliest of welcomes as well as an inspiring vegetarian menu of smoothies, salads and falafel.

Fern Pit Café Riverside Crescent, Pentire TR7 1PJ ℗ 01637 873181 ⓦ www.fernpit.co.uk. A good old-fashioned café, run by the Northey family since 1910. Strong tea, crab sandwiches and slabs of cake – and breathtaking views to Crantock.

Trevilley Farm Lane TR8 4PX ℗ 01637 872310 ⓦ www.trevilleyfarm.com. On the outskirts of Newquay, just off the road to Trerice is a large farm shop plus kitchen making bread, pasties, soups and cakes, perfect for picking up picnic supplies. It's open all year Mon–Sat and provides a local produce box delivery scheme, handy if you are staying in self-catering accommodation.

⑪ Crantock

Crantock is full of charm though easily overlooked in the headlong rush to the beach. Thatched cottages, a village shop and two pubs cluster about a curious circular walled enclosure, that was once used for corralling stray cattle until their owners could be found, known as the Round Garden. It's like an enclosed village green, with a few benches and fruit trees, much appreciated by walkers looking for somewhere quiet and sheltered to eat their sandwiches.

Crantock Beach is a beauty, backed by steep dunes and separated from Newquay by the Gannel, whose wide, westward sweep makes it difficult to tell where river ends and sea begins. The west end of the beach, furthest from the car park, is safer for swimming (the mouth of the Gannel is treacherous and signs warn against swimming here) and where the dunes give way to cliffs and rocky inlets there's good exploring to be done at low tide. The first deep cleft in the rock is Piper's Hole; look up with care, because the cliff face is a sanctuary for fulmars and jackdaws. Just inside the cave on the right, a slab of rock has been carved with a figure of a woman, a horse and a sentimental verse, unmistakably Victorian in tone.

A few yards on from Piper's Hole, steep steps take you up to the coast path and the short walk to the granite headland, Pentire Point, where there's a collapsed cave, eclipsed in spring by the wild flowers.

Porth (Polly) Joke

I don't suppose adding my voice to the growing numbers of visitors who have 'discovered' this lovely, unspoilt beach, will do it any good at all. In English, it would be Jackdaw Cove, for 'Joke' is a corruption of the 'jack' in jackdaw, and 'chough' is similarly derived. There are plenty of jackdaws around, and since 2012 choughs have at last returned – great news!

What's particularly nice is the way that cattle and sheep are able to wander down from the ancient pastures above, known as 'the Kelseys' to the beach, either looking for shelter or to drink from the trickling stream. It's National Trust land and policy to graze like this, and as they politely say on their notices, 'if the cattle concern you, there are other beaches at Crantock and Holywell'.

⑫ Holywell Bay

When I said I was going to look for the holy well in the cave, the lady at the National Trust car park let me borrow a torch, passed on some rudimentary directions and pointed out that the tide had turned, so not to dawdle. It's not easy to find, but well worth the effort of looking. The cave lies roughly half a mile up the beach, once you've crossed the stream that lies between the car park and the dunes. The dunes give way to cliffs and it's beyond the first small indentation in the rock face and before the deeper crook that marks the end of the beach that you must start looking. It's not easy to find, and impossible if the tide is too far in. But if you see a cluster of rocks, smothered in mussels, you're just about there. Look for a diagonal slit in the cliff and make for the left-hand side. Then you must climb carefully up the slimy 'steps' on your left and peer into the gloom ahead. And there, by torchlight is an amazing sight: a colourful grotto of stepped pools, streaked with red and blue mineral deposits, curving away into the darkest recesses of the roof.

The other holy well, (for Holywell is twice blessed with miraculous water) is less of an adventure to reach. The spring, enclosed by a Gothic arched structure, is in the Holywell Bay Fun Park, behind a newly restored wall. The owner of the fun park permits access provided cars are left at the park's own car park.

Away from the coast

Inland from Newquay the landscape presents itself as a bumpy panorama of windswept hills; wind farms and isolated turbines dominate the exposed horizons. But down the deep lanes, narrow leafy valleys conceal a scattering of hamlets, farms and the long-defunct remains of industrial tram and railways. Nevertheless, in the summer months, you'll still see wisps of steam puffing above the trees below St Newlyn East, where three miniature trains still follow the route through Lappa Valley, a line engineered by Joseph Treffry in 1849 to serve the mine at East Wheal Rose.

⑬ Trerice

Kestle Mill TR8 4PG ① 01637 875404 Ⓦ www.nationaltrust.org.uk; National Trust.

Buried in a green fold of the landscape just three miles south of Newquay, Trerice was clearly not built for commanding views. Shelter from the wind and clear spring water were much more important; when the wind is blowing hard on the north coast – and it's rarely otherwise – you only have to follow the deep lanes to Kestle Mill in order to appreciate the wisdom of building a house here. John Arundell built this devastatingly charming manor in 1570, on the site of a much older ancestral home. One wing has been lost, but what remains is comfortingly domestic, especially when seen from the rear courtyard, and the buildings are wrapped around by intimate gardens and an orchard, in which Elizabethan games of slapcock and skittles have been set out for visitors to play.

The emphasis is very much on hands-on engagement at Trerice, and the National Trust volunteers are keen to help everyone feel they have made some kind of personal contact with the house. It makes for a lively visit – while I was wandering through the great hall, lighted by an astonishing window composed of 576 panes of glass, children were tootling and drumming on Elizabethan instruments upstairs in the minstrels' gallery. Pewter mugs and plates, clothing, weaponry and armour, were laid out to be picked up and handled; there were brasses to be rubbed and – on the day I visited – hats to be made.

Enjoyment is perhaps more important than authenticity at Trerice: it was a surprise to learn that the vast oak table in the Great Hall was the only piece of furniture the Trust had acquired with the house in 1953; everything else had come from other Trust properties. Even the Great Hall was a 19th-century reconstruction of what might have been. And the gardens, with their neat lawns and herbaceous borders are clearly modelled on a 20th-century vision of what a garden should look like, although plans are being made to create an Elizabethan-style garden in a part of the orchard. The new head gardener told me that there's a determined attempt afoot to remove some of the horticultural anachronisms – which explains why the collection of vintage and antique lawn mowers was recently donated to the Trevarno Museum of Garden History: 'it didn't seem appropriate in a Tudor garden'.

⑭ Tresillian House

TR8 4PS Ⓦ www.tresillian-house.co.uk.

Newquay was once ringed by private estates, and a mile along the valley, east of Trerice is Tresillian, an inspiring setting for day and residential courses on cookery (*www.walledgardencookeryschool.com*) as well as yoga and pilates workshops. (The entire house is available as self-catering accommodation for large parties, too.) The organic walled garden, orchards, lake and lawns are models of Edwardian horticultural discipline; the man responsible is John Harris, who learned his craft the old-fashioned way, as an apprentice on a local estate and has been at Tresillian since 1985.

It's not always looked so impressive though. The pale granite manor seen today was built in the first part of the 19th century, on the site of a much older house, the family seat of the Gully Bennets. The 23 acres of garden were landscaped in the prevailing style of lawns and lake, parkland trees and flowering shrubs, laurel hedging and – this being Cornwall – a profusion of camellias. The orchards and walled garden were set a little distance away from the house. Leonard Bennet, who inherited the estate in 1928, undertook the first renovation of the garden, but a further period of decline followed when the property was sold after World War II. Restoring the gardens, woodland and orchards has been a monumental undertaking, which suffered heartbreaking setbacks in 1987 and 1990, when storms ripped through the mature woodland garden. Undaunted, John Harris spent eight years clearing out the fallen debris and uprooted stumps and has planted 15,000 trees, including an orchard of apples which effectively form a library of old Cornish varieties, dating from 1800 or earlier. The cider apples go to Andy Atkinson, a Cornish cider-maker (see page 99), and return appropriately, in liquid form.

⑮ St Columb Major

Built between the 12th and 15th centuries (and partially rebuilt in the 17th century after some local lads blew it up with gunpowder), the parish church seems strikingly large for such a modestly sized town. Modest but certainly ambitious in Victorian times: when Cornwall was campaigning to have its diocese restored in the 19th century (see page 165), William Butterfield, a champion of the Gothic revival, was invited by the town council to draw up plans that would transform the church into a cathedral. (A medieval moated manor house had already been rebuilt as a Bishop's Palace in preparation.) The town's self-confidence was misplaced – it was Truro that eventually won the bid to be Cornwall's cathedral city.

Each year (once on Shrove Tuesday and again 11 days later) the windows get boarded up in the town centre when the whole town turns out to watch a small silver ball being hurled, kicked and wrestled from one end of the parish to the other for the annual hurling match, a game which adheres to its own highly idiosyncratic rules, played here since medieval times. Divided into teams of 'townsmen' and 'countrymen' (the hurler's address determines the team he plays for) the scrabbling, jostling pack can spend hours getting the ball to a predetermined place on the parish boundary. Health and safety take a seemingly low profile. In the library, a helpful librarian drew my attention to a paragraph in an obscure pamphlet: 'throughout the centuries hurling at St Columb has been played without any interference from "outsiders". There is no organising committee, which is probably why the traditions and games have lasted to the present day. Unlike at St Ives, where the tradition is still also upheld, at St Columb the Mayor and Town Council are not involved and the Constabulary merely hold a watching brief and advise impatient motorists that "hurling" is in progress.'

Food and drink

Glebe House ① 01637 880088. Beside the gate to the churchyard, this tea room occupies the oldest building in St Columb, dating from the late 16th century. Everything is homemade and locally sourced, and if you ask nicely, the owners may show you around the historic building.

⑯ Castle-an-Dinas

Confusingly, there are two hills of the same name in Cornwall – the other Castle-an-Dinas is the site of a quarry near Ludgvan in Penwith. This one, a couple of miles east of St Columb Major, is one of the the largest hillforts in Cornwall and easily accessible from the road to Roche. There's a straightforward track from the car park to the summit – which at 700 feet gives fine views in all directions. To the the south, beyond the flat, marshy expanse of Goss Moor Nature Reserve, the church tower of St Dennis rises from the centre of another Iron Age hillfort against a backdrop of the clay mountains. It seems reasonable to think that Dennis is a variation of Dinas (meaning hillfort), conveniently adapted to the name of a saint (albeit a Greek one) when the church was first established on the site.

There's lots of history to mull over while circumnavigating the wide circumference of the ramparts. Excavations of the interior in the 1960s identified two Bronze Age burial barrows dating from 2000BC and the possibility that an even earlier Neolithic causeway ran through the site. The construction of the ramparts came much later – around 1000BC, and there is evidence that people were still living here, thanks to a spring which rises damply against the innermost rampart, long after the withdrawal of the Romans. Romantics like to claim it as the site of King Arthur's hunting lodge. During the Civil War, a losing Royalist army camped here for two nights while Hopton wrangled with other generals over their decision to surrender to the Parliamentarians.

Some pretty nasty stuff took place on the summit in the 18th century, when a St Columb man, convicted of murdering two teenage girls, was imprisoned in a small cage (apparently attached to the stone slab now incised with a surveyor's benchmark) and left to starve to death, and other stories of murder and suicide encourage regular posses of ghost hunters.

Geologically, the hill is unusually rich in wolframite, or tungsten ore. Steam-age tin miners despaired of wolfram because the ore was too hard and too heavy to work; it was only later that it was recognised as an ideal metal for modern weaponry and lightbulb filaments. The relics of Cornwall's only mining operation dedicated exclusively to wolfram, that lasted from 1916 to 1957, can still be still be seen: parts of the southern ramparts were cut away to allow the passage of an aerial ropeway connected to the buildings at the foot of the hill, by the car park.

⑰ Screech Owl Sanctuary

Trewin Farm, St Columb Major TR9 6HP ① 01726 860182 ⑩ www.screechowl sanctuary.co.uk.

Like most people, I imagine, I thought this was a sanctuary for screech owls, but the truth is even more delightful.

Carolyn Screech has been rescuing owls since the age of eight and she and her family (how could she resist marrying someone called Tom Screech?) have been running this rescue and rehabilitation centre for over 20 years, helping an average of 360 owls a year recover from injuries and return to the wild. Baby tawny owls are frequently brought in, but often unnecessarily: 'It's normal for baby tawnies to climb up and down the tree they've hatched in before they can fly – people find them happily scratching about at the foot of the tree and assume they've fallen out and need rescuing.'

The rescue birds are not on display, but Darling is a handsome tawny owl who stayed on after his recovery and clearly enjoys human company. Like many of the resident owls, he'll sit on your wrist and enjoy being stroked, while the helpful young staff explain what goes on at the sanctuary.

There's an impressive resident population of native and foreign owls, all on display in their carefully designed enclosures, from enormous Siberian eagle owls to tiny Indian scops owls (and yes, even a screech owl or two), glaring, peeping and swivelling their necks through 359 degrees as only owls can do. Breeding is part of the conservation work that the Screeches are committed to – and when hatched, some of the baby owls can be visited (and touched) in the crèche. It's hard to tear children away. Meerkats, alpacas and Shetland ponies add more fluffy charm and the entrance to Goss Moor Nature Reserve is right on the doorstep.

3. BODMIN MOOR

'Cornwall is like a frame without a picture', say those who believe that Cornwall's coast is everything. It has to be one of the silliest platitudes ever uttered.

If your only perception of Bodmin Moor is a rather bleak stretch of granite moorland – often obscured by fog – sliced in half from east to west by the A30, then think again. This is where Cornwall hides some of its best treasures, generously revealed to those choosing to take the Slow approach. What I particularly enjoyed when researching this chapter were the exciting contrasts of landscape, culture and people within such a small area. On the east side of the Moor, I camped by the trout-filled River Inny at Tregillis Farm, discussing Steiner agriculture with the new tenant farmers, while just 20-odd miles away, west of Bodmin, I found myself on the sunny slopes of the Camel Valley vineyards, a glass of award-winning Cornish Brut in my hand. Yet just a few minutes before, or so it seemed, I had been stumbling over the rain swept summit of Rough Tor, looking down over the haunting emptiness of Davidstow Moor. There had been a lusty performance of *Twelfth Night* in a tented, outdoor theatre at Upton Cross, and rambling beside the River Fowey, where it rushed and tumbled through beech woods just a half-hour bike ride from the uncanny stillness of Dozmary Pool. There was dazzling stained glass in St Neot, and desolate holy wells in muddy fields; not least, there were two of the best pubs encountered on my travels.

In places, you can't help but be reminded of Dartmoor, whose higher peaks loom on the eastern horizon. Goatish sheep, shaggy cattle and wild ponies graze among gorse and relics of the copper- and tin-mining industry; Neolithic standing stones litter the landscape. Bodmin is perhaps Dartmoor's more condensed cousin, but less visited and most definitely less gentrified. An air of self-sufficient remoteness clings like mist in Bodmin's hidden valleys and to the barren slopes of its highest peaks, Brown Willy and Rough Tor.

Village and farm shops are not a lifestyle option on Bodmin: they are vital lifelines for the rural community, and their precarious existence owes much to the support of visitors.

Getting around

Bodmin Moor is ringed by five towns – Bodmin, Camelford, Launceston, Callington and Liskeard – which are all linked by main roads; the Moor itself is bisected by the fast and furious A30. Once off these main arteries, however,

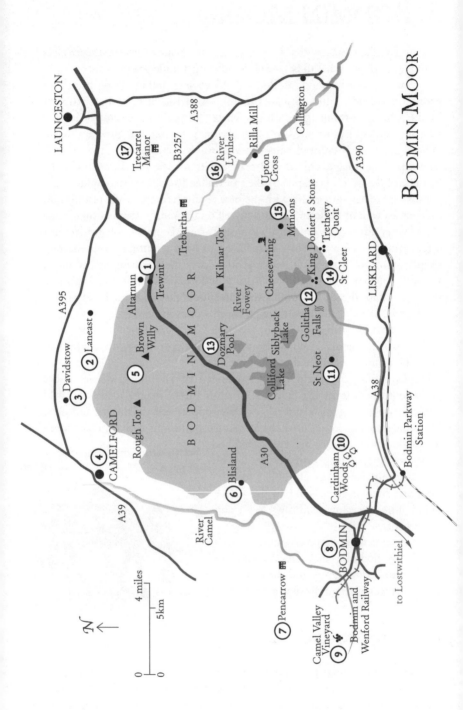

BODMIN MOOR

be prepared for narrow lanes and even narrower medieval bridges or fords, steep gradients and, on the high Moor, animals dozing on the road.

Trains

The mainline from London to Penzance stops at **Bodmin Parkway**, a couple of miles outside the town. The branch line which connected the station to the town centre now operates as a steam railway, which is fun, but not always practical, particularly during the winter months when it is closed. Western Greyhound runs a train-timed bus service (555) between town and mainline station.

Buses

While it is relatively easy to get between the five towns (and to them from Wadebridge), it is not possible to cross the Moor from north to south or east to west by bus. From Liskeard there are spur-like services to Minions and Rilla Mill or St Neot, and the Camelford to Launceston service runs through Davidstow. Despite fierce protest, the western side of the Moor has recently lost its dial-a-ride bus service, leaving villages such as St Breward and Blisland very much in the lurch.

The impressive visitor information centre in Bodmin produces an inspired series of leaflets, titled *Leave the Car at Home Days*. These give you all the information you need to take public transport to various Cornish destinations (including Minions) and suggests a wide range of things to do once you get there.

Cycling

On a sunny, wind-free day one of the nicest rides on Bodmin Moor takes you along the upper reaches of the **River Fowey** for six miles, from Golitha Falls (start in Liskeard if you prefer) right up to the Jamaica Inn at Bolventor, where you make a smart about-turn and head south along a tiny lane that runs between Colliford Lake and Dozmary Pool, all the way to St Neot, from where it's a pretty two-mile ride back to Golitha Falls.

North of the A30, I find the landscape **northwest of Altarnun**, heading towards Davidstow, quite entrancing. Narrow lanes and steep gradients make getting out of Altarnun a bit of a haul, but once on the lane to Bowithick it's all stream-fed moorland, close-cropped by sheep, and too many good places to stop, paddle and picnic to mention. Then, suddenly you're up next to the old Davidstow airfield, which can feel a bit creepy in less than perfect conditions and it's time to turn back through high open farmland to Altarnun.

Families with children may enjoy cycling around **Cardinham Woods** (just east of Bodmin), with gravelled and flattish routes through woodland in the valley bottom, and more challenging tracks on the slopes for mountain bikers. A very pretty section of the Camel Trail is popular with families too, and can be picked up just west of Bodmin at Dunmere Halt. This is a great way to get to Blisland, which lies a mile off the trail close to where it terminates at Poley's Bridge, making a round trip of about 14 miles.

For those wanting a longer mission, you can pick up the thoroughly signposted **Sustrans route 3** across Cornwall at Blisland and follow the western fringe of the Moor to Davidstow and onwards to Bude.

Cycle hire

Bodmin Bikes 3 Hamley Court, Dennison Rd, Bodmin PL31 2LL ⑦ 01208 73192
Ⓦ www.bodminbikes.co.uk.
East Rose Farm St Breward, Bodmin PL30 4NL ⑦ 01208 850674
Ⓦ www.eastrose.co.uk. Between Blisland and St Breward, East Rose is just 15
minutes' ride from the Camel Trail, which links Bodmin, Wadebridge and Padstow.

Horse riding

For many, the Moor is best viewed from between the ears of a friendly horse and several moorland pubs have places where you can leave your mount safely tethered. Escorted rides across moorland or through wooded valleys at a pace you feel comfortable with are offered by:

Hallagenna St Breward Hallagenna Farm, St Breward PL30 4NS ⑦ 01208
851500 Ⓦ www.hallagenna.co.uk Ⓔ riding@hallagenna.co.uk.
Lower Tokenbury Equestrian Centre Caradon Town, Upton Cross PL14 5AR
⑦ 01579 362747 Ⓦ www.lowertokenburyequestriancentre.co.uk
Ⓔ tokenburyriding@hotmail.co.uk.
TM International Sunrising Riding Centre Henwood PL14 5BP ⑦ 01579
362895 Ⓦ www.tminternational.co.uk Ⓔ enquiries@tminternational.co.uk.

The Copper Trail

A century and a half ago, **Bodmin** Moor was alive with industry and criss-crossed with paths trodden by quarrymen, farmers and miners. As the abandoned mines sank back beneath the heather and gorse, many of the footpaths disappeared. Mark Camp, who spent his boyhood years roaming the Moor, had been mulling the idea of 'the best possible' circular walk around it for some time, and the 2005 Countryside Rights of Way Act provided the final impetus to join up the dots on his emerging route. In total the trail covers 60 miles, taking in Minions, St Neot, Bodmin, St Breward, Camelford and Alternun, along with many other good pitstops on the way. To help walkers get the most out of their walk, he has published a pocket-sized book, *The Copper Trail: Once around Bodmin Moor*, available in most TICs, brimming with the kind of information that Slow explorers will welcome. Mark and his guidebook have been of enormous help in planning this chapter.

Walking

Bodmin Moor – on a fine day – is one of the best places in England for walking and exploring. Even a Moor expert like Mark Camp reckons that he never goes out onto the Moor without discovering something new each time.

Accommodation

There are some spectacular camping opportunities around the Moor, ranging from luxury yurts to no-frills wild camping spots. Four of the best are included below. The Best of Bodmin Moor website (*www.bestofbodminmoor.co.uk*) also lists a good selection of hand-picked bed and breakfasts and holiday cottages.

Bedknobs Polgwyn, Castle St, Bodmin PL31 2DX ① 01208 77553
Ⓦ www.bedknobs.co.uk Ⓔ gilly@bedknobs.co.uk. Eco-award winning B&B (recycling, repairing and buying local are the watchwords: even the handmade soaps come from just down the road), and elegantly furnished (check your socks or bring slippers, because shoes are left at the door). Wonderful breakfasts, sandwiches and cream teas served up with lashings of local knowledge. No under-12s or dogs. Grown-up luxury with a conscience doesn't make it the cheapest B&B, but still remarkably good value.

Cabilla Manor Mount, near Warleggan PL30 4DW ① 01208 821224
Ⓦ www.cabilla.co.uk Ⓔ louella@cabilla.co.uk. The explorer, Robin Hanbury-Tennison and his wife, Louella, live in the Georgian farmhouse, which is nicely stashed with books, paintings and rare and lovely things brought back from their travels – and four very comfortable rooms (two of which share a bathroom). Outside on the farm there are sheep and cattle and the white horses they brought back from the Camargue. Bed and breakfast is extraordinary value; dinner (with Robin and Louella) is occasionally available and should be organised well in advance.

Dozmary Pool Barn Dozmary Estate, Bolventor ① 01962 779598
Ⓦ www.dozmary.co.uk Ⓔ lucy@dozmary.co.uk. Just a few feet from the water's edge, high on the Moor, a granite barn has been given a clean, contemporary look with slate floors, lots of light and crisp pale linens. Three bedrooms sleep six. The barn is pretty upmarket and priced accordingly, with a small extra charge for a maximum of two dogs.

East Rose Farm St Breward, Bodmin PL30 4NL ① 01208 850674
Ⓦ www.eastrose.co.uk Ⓔ eastrosefarm@btinternet.com. If camping isn't quite your style, just across a pretty stretch of moorland from South Penquite Farm, by the de Lank River, East Rose Farm offer seven holiday cottages, sleeping from two to six people at a reasonable price. There are bikes for hire and the Camel Trail is close by, but fishing types will want to stay close to the farm's $3^1/_2$ acres of fishing lakes, stocked with bream, roach, tench and rudd.

Luxury Cornish Yurts Little Fursdon, Rosecraddoc, St Cleer, Liskeard PL14 5AG
℗ 01579 343896 or 07962 224285 Ⓦ www.luxurycornishyurts.co.uk Ⓔ relax@
luxurycornishyurts.co.uk. On the south side of the Moor, 'glamping' taken to
the nth degree: each of the three beautifully furnished yurts, side by side in a
crisply mown field, has its own loo and bathroom and outdoor decking. Close
by, a timber shed houses a shared, fully kitted kitchen with decking and seating
outside; a firepit reminds you that you really are supposed to be camping. Open
Easter to end of the October half-term; not that cheap, but very comfortable.

Roscrea 18 St Nicholas St, Bodmin PL31 1AD ℗ 01208 74400
Ⓦ www.roscrea.co.uk Ⓔ rosecrea@btconnect.com. Bang in the centre of
Bodmin, a house with a rich history is now a very comfortable B&B. All rooms
are furnished on a Victorian theme, tea is served on arrival either in the garden
or firelit drawing room; breakfast eggs come from the hens at the bottom of
the garden and excellent evening meals using locally sourced meat, fish and
vegetables can also be cooked on request. Very reasonably priced.

South Penquite Farm Blisland, Bodmin, Cornwall, PL30 4LH ℗ 01208 850491
Ⓦ www.southpenquite.co.uk Ⓔ thefarm@bodminmoor.co.uk. Dominic and
Cathy Fairman and their brood live and farm on this idyllic moorland campsite;
expect free-ranging chickens and ducks, a trickling stream and ecological
sensitivity in the nicely done showers and washrooms. Courses teaching bushcraft
skills are popular with older children; families with young children will love the
safety and freedom the site offers as well as a very pretty slice of moor on the
doorstep. There are three yurts for hire and a VW camper van is available too.
Cheap camping, and the yurts are excellent value. No dogs, but a highly rated
boarding kennels is just next door.

Tregillis Farm South Petherwin PL15 7LL ℗ 01566 782939 Ⓦ www.tregillis.
co.uk Ⓔ laura@tregillis.co.uk. Laura Richards, Jim Wallwork and daughter Mali
farm here following biodynamic principles. They have opened up a lovely field
(sheltered by woodland and bordered by the River Inny) for campers who are
prepared to ditch their vehicles in the farmyard and walk down ferny farm tracks
to the field, half a mile away, past herds of very happy cattle and flocks of Suffolk
sheep, where they have a small number of retro ridge and bell-tents waiting;
Jim's Land Rover can be pressed into service if absolutely necessary. It has basic
showers, loos and campfires, absolute peace and the sense of being a world apart
from mainstream Cornwall. A little more expensive than bringing your own tent,
but well below 'glamping' prices.

Yurtworks Greyhayes, Row Hill, St Breward, Bodmin PL30 4LP ℗ 01208 850670
Ⓦ www.yurtworks.co.uk Ⓔ info@yurtworks.co.uk. Three beautifully kitted-out
yurts in a stunning wooded valley; the biggest has an attached 'pod' for small
children to play and sleep in. All have double beds, crisp linen and logburners
as well as barbecues for outdoor cooking. Each has its own compost loo in a
separate 'yurtlet' and there is a luxururious yurt bathroom complete with roll-top
bath and solar-powered shower, shared by the three yurts. Prices on a par with
holiday cottage accommodation; the largest sleeps six.

The north Moor

North of the A30, the Moor is characterised by craggy granite peaks and marshy flats; woodland is sparse and the sky in all its often brooding glory dominates. Davidstow Moor in the north, with its wartime memories and forgotten history of Formula One racing, has a particularly haunting atmosphere. But follow the infant River Camel, from Camelford southwards along the northwest fringe of the Moor, and it's a different story: wooded, stream-fed valleys, cosy villages and a feeling that civilisation is not too far distant.

① Altarnun and Trewint

Snuggled in a wooded valley, just a stone's throw from the A30, **Altarnun** scores top marks for its photogenic qualities. The church of **St Nonna**, the 'Cathedral of the Moors', with its high tower, sits prettily beside a babbling tributary of the Inny, where a 15th-century packbridge leads to part two of the village. A village green, whitewashed, slate-roofed cottages, village shop, post office and pub complete the picture.

The eighty-odd carved bench ends inside the church are an absolute knockout: there are jesters and jugglers, a piper, fiddler and bagpipe player, a sheaf of corn that is also a face, sheep on the hill and portraits of various characters from the village. They were carved in the early part of the 16th century by one Robert Daye, who proudly added his name to the carvings. You can also visit the holy well, in a field behind the vicarage. Pity the poor 'lunatics', who were immersed here backwards before being marched up to the church for complementary prayers.

The former **Methodist chapel** next to the shop is worth more than a glance, for the bust of John Wesley over the door. **Neville Northy Burnard**, one of Altarnun's most gifted, yet saddest, sons, grew up in the cottage next door, and made this in 1836, at the age of 18.

Once the darling of London society for his portrait busts, Burnard was slowly destroyed by private demons and the bottle. The death of a daughter finally tipped him over the edge and, abandoning work, wife and his other children in the capital, for years he drifted the lanes of Cornwall, ending up in a pauper's grave in Camborne.

So close as to be almost a part of Altarnun, tiny **Trewint** has become something of a Methodist shrine, thanks to the kindness of stonemason Digory Isbell and his wife, Elizabeth, who gave hospitable shelter to Wesley and his companions as they scurried up and down Cornwall on a hectic round of preaching in 1743. The Isbells were so overcome by the Wesleyan style of praying from the heart, without recourse to a prayer book, that although they remained steadfast to St Nonna's in Altarnun (where their graves may still be seen), they became, without contradiction, Wesleyans too. The cottage became the focus of impromptu prayer meetings and Digory built a small extension to his cottage to accommodate them, with a room above for lodging his new-found spiritual mentors. These two rooms and their Wesleyan memorabilia can be visited (*01566 880265; www.wesleycottage.org.uk*) and the pilgrims' garden, outside the front porch, marks the spot where Wesley once preached to a gathering of 300.

Food and drink

Kings Head Altarnun PL15 7RX ℗ 01566 86241. This is a traditional inn with jukebox, local ales such as Skinner's Betty Stoggs and generous helpings of pub grub. Four reasonably priced rooms make this a popular overnight pitstop for walkers.

② Laneast and around

Head north out of Altarnun and immediately you're in a tangle of narrow lanes, dipping and rising at medieval bridges, inviting footpaths (frequently crossing six-foot stone stiles) and isolated farms. There are some lovely walks and bike rides to be done here, for which the OS Explorer map 109 is essential. **St Clether** and **Laneast** are the only settlements of any size – neither have shops or pubs, but they do offer a nice line in holy wells and St Michael's in Laneast has some striking medieval stained glass. The village shop in Altarnun has copies of the *Inny River Trail*, a six-mile circular walk, which takes in the ruined manor at Trethinna, a medieval bridge at Gimblett's Mill and Laneast.

Food and drink

Rising Sun P15 7SN ℗ 01566 86636 ⓦ www.therisingsuninn.co.uk. This stands alone at a rural junction of two lanes, midway between Altarnun and Laneast. A great pub, deservedly popular, both for eating (Slow food is taken very seriously here) and drinking. Real ales come from the **Penpont Brewery**, which is based in an old milking parlour, just a few hundred yards down the lane, above Penpont Water.

The shy astronomer

Not many people can tell you who discovered Neptune, but more than usual know the answer in Laneast. **John Couch Adams**, whose bust – by his exact contemporary, Neville Northy Burnard – can be found in the Lawrence House Museum, was a scholarship boy from a local farming family; a brilliant mathematician and thoroughly decent chap, as modest as he was brainy.

Using mathematics he proved the existence of the most distant planet in the solar system, whose orbit had hitherto been confused with that of Uranus, and in 1845 he passed his findings to the Astronomer Royal, Sir George Airey. In the weeks following, Adams and Airey managed somehow to avoid communicating, which was sad, because seven months after Adams, Urbain Le Verrier, a French astronomer, published a paper in which he came independently to the same conclusion. But Adams had his supporters and eventually an honorable draw was declared. In any case, friendship with Le Verrier was more important to Adams than 'winning'. Later, the gentle polymath was offered the post of Astronomer Royal, and a knighthood, both of which he shyly declined.

③ Davidstow

From miles away you can see (and sometimes smell) the cheese factory; gathered around it are the low buildings of an old pig unit and dairy farm which operated here before they were converted (though possibly not convinced) to become the wartime RAF base. This had always struck me as a sad and lonely part of the Moor, but things have changed, with the opening of two new military museums in the old buildings in 2006. Their deeply knowledgeable and hugely enthusiastic creators have assembled two quite different collections and experiences, which took me pleasantly by surprise.

Davidstow Moor RAF Memorial Museum is curated by David Keast, who spent his boyhood years on the local farm; he and a small band of elderly volunteers are movingly dedicated to keeping the memory alive of those who served here during the war. What you find is an intimate record of the men and women (and carrier pigeons) who lived, worked and, in some cases, died at Davidstow between 1942 and 1945: letters, uniforms, medals, photos ('the photos are the pride of this collection') and lots and lots of model aircraft as well. A nurse and a tail gunner from the base, both in their 90s at the time of writing, have supplied personal memorabilia and still keep in touch. A family spanning three generations at least, the oldest of whom had known the airbase during the war, were visiting while I was there and exchanging stories with the affable Mr Keast. The youngest lad in the party was staring, wide-eyed, at a 1,000-pound bomb, his lips moving as he read the lettering on its side: 'For Display Purposes Only'. Admission is free; donations very much appreciated.

Next door, in a scattering of Nissen huts, air-raid shelters and old accommodation blocks that would not disgrace a film set for *The Avengers*, Steve and Sheila Perry have installed their formidable collection of military memorabilia, from a couple of unsmoked 'Blue Liner' cigarettes to a U-boat bomb, calling it the **Cornwall at War Museum**. 'There are two myths about Davidstow,' grins Steve, ex-army, whose boundless enthusiasm for the place is matched by the kind of knowledge that should see him on *Mastermind;* 'one – it was built by the Americans and two – it was too foggy to be operable. Wrong on both counts. Mind you, I feel sorry for the Canadian 404 squadron, who came here in May '44 after being stationed on Shetland. Cornwall! They must have thought, sunshine and beaches, our luck's in, boys! Then they discovered it was Davidstow ...'

The latest exhibit the Perrys have assembled turns out to be an officers' mess in a restored Nissen hut. A score or more of mannequins in uniform and civvies fill the room – sitting, standing, smoking, drinking, chatting ... their frozen silence was quite unnerving, as though they were all playing musical statues and were waiting for the music to start again. Still more unnerving was the unexpected invitation to join a ghost-hunting party later that week. Investigations into the paranormal are frequent at the airbase; wimpishly I declined.

Every Thursday, Steve drives a minibus on a guided tour around the deserted airfield, bringing it vividly to life with a commentary that blows away the years. He evokes not only the war (when the runways were camouflage-painted green and dotted with painted sheep) but the post-war years too, when for three glorious years in the 1950s, the airfield was home to British Formula One racing, and crowds of 25,000 witnessed the first triumph of Lotus.

The Davidstow starlings

From mid-October to mid-March, at the onset of dusk, up to a million starlings take to the air and perform one of nature's most extraordinary spectacles: swooping and wheeling in perfect synchronicity, the flock resembles a vast black silk scarf being shaken out across the sky. Dozens of spectators drive up to the Moor on fine evenings to follow the performance, which closes with a sudden retreat to the woods around Crowdy where the birds roost for the night.

There were massive objections locally when 20 wind turbines were proposed for Davidstow Moor, chief among which was the effect they would have on the starlings and other moorland birds. To great applause, the proposals were rejected in 2010.

④ Camelford

Despite the golden camel that does weather-vane duty on top of the old town hall's bright green clock tower, everyone locally knows that Camelford and the River Camel takes their name from the old Cornish word cam, meaning a winding stream, and Allan, which means fine-looking.

Steve Perry's injunction not to miss the **Mason's Arms** was ringing in my ears as I freewheeled beneath the uneponymous camel halfway along Camelford's handsome Fore Street. The **North Cornwall Museum & Gallery**, however, turned out to be at the top end of town (*The Clease; 01840 212954*), and it was close to closing time. Twenty minutes was just enough to meet Sally Holden, who curates this delightful, privately owned collection of rural life memorabilia, but not nearly enough time to do proper justice to the exhibition space upstairs in which her extraordinary, nonagenarian mother Bridget Holden was holding her annual exhibition of watercolours, painted in the 1960s. Cornish artists tend to dwell on the sea and the sky, the loveliness and the grandeur of the county, but here was an artist who had found beauty in slate-splitting sheds, quarry rail-trucks and industrial wasteland. Sadly, the museum closed in 2013, but much of the collection is likely to be found a new home thanks to a local initiative.

Food and drink

Four Seasons Café 1 Market Pl ① 01840 211779. Sit outside in the garden by the river if it's sunny and tuck in to breakfast, lunch or tea. Homemade soups and cakes are always on the menu and macaroni cheese is another favourite. Nothing pretentious here, just simple, good food and friendly service.

Mason's Arms ① 01840 213309. Just the job if returning from a leg-stretch over the Moor, with a good, friendly atmosphere, a pretty garden at the back and hearty home cooking. St Austell ales on tap and Cornish cider. Pub grub, much of it sourced as locally as possible.

⑤ The twin peaks: Brown Willy and Rough Tor

From Camelford a ten-mile walk takes in the two highest peaks in Cornwall, or you can drive out along an arrow-straight lane for a couple of miles to the National Trust car park at the foot of **Rough Tor** and take it from there. Rough, by the way, rhymes with cow in these parts (one of the Penpont Brewery's nicest beers is called Rough Tor, but when I asked for a bottle of 'Rowter' in a pub in Wadebridge, I was met with raised eyebrows and had to point; getting your pronunciation not only right, but right in the right place is something of an art in Cornwall). The proximity of the car park to the summit, less than a mile away, means there's usually company on your hike uphill – some walkers have even claimed the company of sad Charlotte Dymond, murdered on the hill in 1844; her lover, a farmhand named Matthew Weeks, was found guilty and hanged at Bodmin.

Brown Willy, whose crook-toothed crown stands across the valley to the east, is the wilder, lonelier place. The views from the summits of the two tors are both revealing and deceiving. Revealed is the buzzard's-eye contextual map of Cornwall: Bristol Channel, English Channel, Camel and Tamar, old farm field systems, new wind turbines, standing stones and claypit spoil. Deceiving, however, is the view east, over the source of the River Fowey. A mere stroll, by the look of it, down to Altarnun ... but the low ground with its too-green grass is treacherous bog and should be avoided. Daphne du Maurier, in *Vanishing Cornwall*, gives a white-knuckle account of an attempt to ride across this seemingly innocuous plateau on a fine November afternoon, which disintegrated rapidly into rain and fog and darkness. 'Bogs, quarries, brooks, boulders, hell on every side ... I had never known greater despondency.' And this was in the days before the Beast of Bodmin appeared. Yes, it's best to keep to the footpaths and walk in daylight up here.

Food and drink

The Old Inn St Breward ⓣ 01208 850711 ⓦ www.theoldinnandrestaurant.co.uk. A lovely and very ancient village pub next to the village church, high on the Moor. A freehouse, serving Cornish ales and cider and good food to a jolly mix of the local football club, walkers and members of the St Breward silver band. Children welcome in the restaurant and garden.

⑥ Blisland

After the bracing wilderness of the north moors, the descent into the wooded valley of the Camel brings a sudden and absolute change of mood and tempo, which reaches its most gratifying moments (for lowland softies at any rate) in Blisland. A huge, tree-fringed village green surrounded on all sides by handsome granite cottages and houses ('it has not one ugly house in it,' wrote Betjeman) and overlooked by one of the best pubs in Cornwall, and a Norman church, the Victorian restoration of which Betjeman said 'could hardly be bettered', are Blisland's high points. But more importantly, perhaps, it's a village with a beating heart that believes in the value of local identity: here's a community that has fought to keep its school, that has raised funds and support to reopen its shop and post office and that is trying to keep its bus service going. If awards were given to Slow village of the year, Blisland would be high on the list of nominees.

A short walk north out of the village takes you back onto the Moor and the **Jubilee Rock** just east of Pendrift. This huge lump of granite was chosen by one Lt John Rogers to celebrate the 1810 golden jubilee of King George III. His elaborately chiselled graffiti has recently been cleaned up to reveal the familiar profile of Britannia, the Royal and Cornish coats of arms as well as those of some local families, together with a plough and the Masonic symbols of compass and square. If you want to walk further, there's a magical spot on the De Lank River less than a mile away, where it rushes over granite boulders through dappled woodland, and there's rarely a soul in sight. To get there, go back to Pendrift and continue due north on the footpath leading down to the river through steeply sloping fields.

Food and drink

Blisland Inn ℗ 01208 850739. Typically there will be seven or eight real ales on tap, all in perfect condition. Decent, basic pub food is served too, but this is a place you go for grown-up drinking with the locals, not for gastronomy, and children are best left outside to entertain themselves on the green. Dogs, however, are given treats if well behaved. 'King Buddha' the larger-than-life landlord (it's tattooed on his tummy) knows what his devoted regulars like, and it has served him well in the form of more CAMRA awards over the years than you can shake a stick at.

⑦ Pencarrow

Washaway, Bodmin PL30 3AG ℗ 01208 841369 ⓦ www.pencarrow.co.uk; garden open Mar–Oct daily, house Apr–Sep Sun–Thu.

Just walk, cycle or drive very slowly up the two-mile drive. It's like woodland in a Tolkein story and at one point the drive actually passes through an Iron Age hillfort. The house, with its grand Palladian façade, and the Italianate gardens are lovely too, but for me, nothing surpasses that magical woodland arrival. The old walled gardens by the car park are now offering pick-your-own soft fruits, which is another good reason to visit.

Despite the external grandeur, there's absolutely nothing stuffy about Pencarrow. Children are encouraged to romp on the lawns, the affable head gardener produces cuttings of favourite plants for sale and the house has a distinctly lived-in atmosphere. The Molesworth St Aubyns have lived here since the time of Elizabeth I and it's still very much a family home. Dogs, toys and family photos are surrounded by Sèvres porcelain, Chinese silk captured from a Spanish treasure ship and family portraits by Sir Joshua Reynolds – and there's a grand piano upon which Sir Arthur Sullivan composed the finale to the first act of *Iolanthe*. Another guest to stay at Pencarrow was Charles Austin, a parliamentary lawyer. He spotted a specimen of *Araucaria imbricata*, recently introduced to Britain from Chile, growing in the park and remarked 'that tree would puzzle a monkey'. And that was how, in 1834, the monkey puzzle tree acquired its popular name.

⑧ Bodmin

Once the county town of Cornwall, poor old Bodmin seems to have lost out over the years to other Cornish towns: Truro won the spiritual and secular prizes of cathedral and county court, Penryn landed the university; the prison closed, the Duke of Cornwall's Regiment moved out, the branch line from

Bodmin Parkway into the town centre was axed and St Lawrence's Hospital, formerly Bodmin Asylum, which posed as a good candidate for Falmouth University's new campus, stands empty. But hats off to the town for making the most of its history. Now it's a town full of museums with interactive visitor experiences, though you might leave feeling you've been to World of Bodmin rather than Bodmin itself. You can be part of the jury at the trial for the murder of Charlotte Dymond in the old courtroom in **Shire Hall**, visit the very nasty pit in **Bodmin Jail** where boyfriend Matthew Weeks was hanged for her murder, and ride on a steam train on the **Bodmin and Wenford Steam Railway**. More soberly, perhaps, the Duke of Cornwall's Light Infantry Museum tells the story of the regiment's involvement in conflict ranging from Waterloo to the American War of Independence to Northern Ireland.

There were no interactive experiences advertised at the tiny **Bodmin Town Museum**, housed in an ancient granite building on the site of an even older Franciscan friary. Instead, I found Reg and Sue Sheppard, passionate volunteer supporters of the museum as well as ardent right-to-roamers, and it was through the very interactive experience of chatting to them that I found out how Bodmin is currently charting its way from an affluent and interesting past to a heritage-laden future. The Sheppards and the excellent **tourist information centre** in the Shire Hall just opposite also pointed me towards some of the best walks in and around the town.

Besides all the museums, Bodmin is good for just pottering: shops are particularly strong on local food and everybody knows the way to **Barnecutts Bakery**, where the bar is set high for pasty aficionados. Granite Georgian buildings sweep up and down the hilly town centre, and although giving an overwhelming impression of greyness, are nearly all worth a second glance. But above all, Bodmin is about its people and the traces they have left for us to read. The victims of Bodmin's macabre gallows are listed in the town museum: Elizabeth Osborne, aged 20, for example: hanged for setting fire to a hayrick. The quality of mercy seems to have been rather strained in Bodmin Assizes. On the other hand, a solid granite **dogs' drinking trough** placed at the entrance to Priory Park, in the town centre, tells a strange, compassionate story. The exiled prince of Siam, Chula Chatrabongse, who lived just outside Bodmin from 1938 until his death in 1965, had a great fondness for his canine companions, and this gift to Bodmin's thirsty dogs is dedicated to his terrier, Joan, and bulldog, Hercules.

Bodmin has its fair share of interesting piles of stones. **Castle Canyke**, clearly visible looking east from Beacon Hill, is Cornwall's largest Iron Age hillfort, and a possible contender for the location of Arthur's stronghold, Killiwig. On the hilly northern fringe of Bodmin, close to the old jail, is **Berry Tower** – all that remains of a fine chapel, built in the early years of the 16th century. Together with the 300-year-old friary, it succumbed to the ravages of the Reformation – after just 30 years of service. But Bodmin's 15th-century church, **St Petroc's**, survives, despite losing its tower to lightning in 1699 and succumbing to the inevitable Victorian restoration. Nevertheless, there are some real treasures inside, including an elaborately carved Norman font and a lectern made from carved bench ends, which in one case shows a man sporting an extra finger. There's a painted German panel dating from 1501 and a fine slate memorial by Neville Northy Burnard. But the biggest treasure lies in a niche in the south aisle wall, where the reliquary casket that once contained the bones of St Petroc can be seen. The 6th-century saint's bones have had a rough time of it over the years. First they were interred at Padstow, but late in the 10th century the Vikings arrived and the relics were hurriedly moved to Bodmin. Then they were stolen by jealous French monks in 1177 and taken to Brittany, where reluctantly (they managed to hang on to a rib) they were handed back to Henry II's justicier, Walter of Coutances, who patched things up by returning them to Bodmin in a fine casket made by Sicilian craftsmen in ivory and gold. Somebody thought it wise to hide the casket during the Reformation, and it was only rediscovered, walled up in the porch, during the 19th century, though empty of all relics. Almost unbelievably it was stolen again in 1994, only to turn up, 40 days later, in a field in Yorkshire. You will notice the improved security surrounding the casket.

The Bodmin and Wenford Steam Railway

Ⓣ 0845 1259 678 or 01208 73555 for passenger enquiries
Ⓦ www.bodminandwenfordrailway.co.uk.

In the 19th century, Bodmin lay between two rival rail companies racing along the south (via Plymouth) and the north (via Launceston) of Cornwall to lay the fastest route from London to Wadebridge and points west. A connecting line, which curled into Bodmin just next to the regimental barracks, was eventually completed in 1895 and for almost 70 years, until Beeching's axe fell, Bodmin's residents could chug across Cornwall without having to walk more than a few hundred yards to their station.

The line and much of its steam and diesel rolling stock were rescued from dereliction in 1986 by a group of local enthusiasts, who formed a trust to preserve this colourful remnant of Cornish train history. Apart from the rides out west to Boscarne Junction (right next to the Camel Trail) and/or east to Bodmin Parkway, one-day courses are offered (over-18s only), giving fellow-enthusiasts the opportunity to work alongside the regular crews and experience the filth, sweat and the glory of the footplate.

Beacon Hill

No prominent hill in Cornwall is complete without a monument of some kind, and Bodmin rises to the occasion with a 144-foot-high spike on a plinth, erected as a monument to Sir Walter Raleigh Gilbert in 1857. Gilbert (whose distinguished lineage is reflected in his hybrid name) was born in Bodmin but spent most of his adult life in India, subduing the Punjab, trouncing the Sikhs, chasing their Afghan allies over the Khyber Pass and generally covering himself in gung-ho glory.

Beacon Hill, on which the monument stands, is now a nature reserve, with a newly planted community woodland and hay meadows where wild flowers are encouraged to self-seed. It makes a good picnic spot and the views over both town and moorland more than reward the (not too strenuous) climb.

Food and drink

Bodmin Market selling 'local produce from local people' takes place on Mount Folly every first and third Thursday of the month.

Bodmin Jail Café Berrycoombe Rd ① 01208 76292 ⓦ www.bodminjail.org; open daily 10.00 to 22.00 Makes a point of using and naming local suppliers and has picked up a good reputation in the town as the place to go for a Sunday roast. The prison gags and puns that adorn each of the courses will have you groaning, but at least porridge isn't on the menu. It's inside the prison walls but outside the museum, so admission to the café is free.

Malcolm Barnecutt's Bakery The Old Guild Hall, Fore St ① 01208 73205. Malcolm's grandfather, Percy, opened the first Barnecutt bakery in Liskeard in 1930, and there are now eight branches scattered across Cornwall. Top-notch pasties sell out faster than you can say 'two pound forty, my 'ansum', but there is a café in the restored 17th-century guildhall rooms, with lunch and tea menus that have happily never heard of the low-carbohydrate Dukan diet.

The Weavers Honey St ① 01208 74511. This is a St Austell pub, serving all the usual suspects. Good bar food; children- and dog-friendly. It's big on footy too, and the weekend sees it packed with big-screen spectators.

⑨ Camel Valley Vineyard

① 01208 77959 ⓦ www.camelvalley.com. Vineyards and shop: open weekdays, also Sat May–Sep; daily tour with either Bob or Sam at 14.30.

Back in the days when English wine was not something you mentioned in polite conversation, Bob Lindo and his wife Annie were rethinking their lives. Bob, a pilot with the RAF, had just emerged barely in one piece from a spectacular crash with no option but to look for another career. 'We were doing a bit of sheep farming in Cornwall already, but it was while trying to repair a fence – lying on my side because of my injuries – that I realised how right this hillside would be for vines,' says Bob. 'Much more appropriate than sheep.' Two decades on, Camel Valley Vineyard is very much established at the top of the English winemakers, league table, a strong Cornish presence in a niche industry so far dominated by producers in Sussex and Kent.

Although the Lindos started with still red and white wines, their runaway success has been the sparkling white 'Cornwall Brut', made by the *méthode champenoise*, but with three grapes particularly suited to the English climate – Seyval Blanc, Reichensteiner and Bacchus. 'It's not champagne; that's what the French make,' says Bob. 'We make Cornish sparkling wine that should be judged on its own merits.' Those in a position to judge have heaped awards and accolades on the product and the Lindos' son, Sam, was recently voted best British winemaker.

The Moor south of the A30

The Moor east of Bodmin is greener, watered by the rivers Fowey and Lynher, their tributaries and lakes where wildfowl gather. Wooded all around its southern fringe from Cardinham to Dobwalls, and dotted with villages linked by threading lanes, this is Bodmin Moor at its most accessible and picturesque. Further east, towards and beyond Minions, the Moor reasserts its wilder, more rugged self, among relics of an industrial mining past and Neolithic standing stones.

⑩ Cardinham Woods

① 01208 78111 (café only) ⑩ www.forestry.gov.uk/cardinham.

I must confess that I didn't get much further than the superb little café in an old woodman's cottage by the river, but this broadleaf forest, owned and immaculately managed by the Forestry Commission, is a wonderful spot for walking, cycling and riding. There are well-kept tracks running all through the woodland, crossing streams and climbing into the hills. Only two miles from Bodmin, the woods are well used by locals and holidaying families who have discovered that trees, water and lots of space make a happy alternative to the beach at any time of the year. David and Lara Spurrell run the café, producing heartening soups, stews and homemade cakes, and keeping the fire going in cold weather. Perfect.

⑪ St Neot

Like Blisland to the north, St Neot has everything going for it – a superb church with staggeringly beautiful stained glass, a thriving community, school and shop – but oh, the shock and surprise when the London Inn, a pub with a fantastic reputation for both eating and drinking that extended far beyond the parish, closed its doors in 2011. (Note to the 2013 edition: the London has re-opened its doors and reinstated itself at the heart of village life with great aplomb. Good news indeed!)

The **church**, dedicated to St Anietus (the Latinised form of Neot), stands on a rise just next to the pub and is the chief glory of the village. On a sunny day, its early 16th-century windows, the subject of a sensitive Victorian restoration, outshine anything else in Cornwall. Bring binoculars if you want to catch all the high-up detail, but there's quite enough visible without them to keep even the idlest visitor completely entranced. It's the human detail (isn't it always?) that makes these windows so special. A respectful Noah doffs his cap as instructions for dealing with the Flood are delivered from on high; a fresh-faced young monk cranes his neck to see the diminutive Anietus (some accounts say he was only two feet tall, but this seems a little exaggerated) being received by the Abbot of Glastonbury; Anietus rescuing a bewildered deer from a suitably grumpy hunter – there are scores of scenes and human faces to be savoured.

A nicely hand-drawn map outside the church suggests a walking route round the village, which clusters around the steep slopes of a tributary of the Fowey, the Loveny. My own map showed the oddly named Romano-British earthworks, Crowpound, just west of the village, where I was lucky enough to come across a family out for a walk whose youngest was able to answer my query. 'It's called Crowpound,' she piped up, 'because the saint made all the crows stay there while the farmers were in church.' There must have been an outcry in the village, when in AD974 the saint's relics, which had been laid to rest in the church a century earlier, were taken to St Neots in Huntingdonshire where a new abbey was being constructed and appropriate saintly relics required. It puts the temporary loss of the pub into perspective, anyway.

⑫ Golitha Falls

This is a popular spot on a sunny day and it's easy to see why: the car park at **Drayne's Bridge** is large and the footpath wide and level, the shallow, rushing river is delightful with the promise of otter-sighting and the beech woods are mossy. Forty minutes is ample time to follow the river to where it disappears, tumbling over granite boulders into the woods, and to return on the higher woodland path. Don't expect a single great fall of water as at St Nectan's Glen; this is a gentle sequence of falls and splashy pools and grand spot for children to lark about. In fact, the happiest people I saw on a wet and chilly August day, when the beaches were empty and the museum queues long, were a family who'd come here in wellies and found they had the streaming woods and water (nearly) all to themselves. If this kind of place is your scene, but find the possibility of crowds a bit off-putting, the wooded falls on the De Lank River just north of Blisland (see page 64) are not so accessible and rarely troubled by visitors, but all the lovelier for that.

On Sundays and Mondays, during June, July, August and September, you can visit **Northwood Gardens** (*01579 320030; www.northwoodgardens.co.uk*), a pleasant walk along lanes of about two miles from either St Neot or Drayne's Bridge. A lush and colourful detour, with an equally inspiring art gallery that hosts visiting exhibitons, with the added bonus of tea and homemade cake.

⑬ Dozmary Pool

From Golitha Falls, a narrow lane follows the River Fowey north the length of its steep-sided valley. If you have brought a bike by car, leave the car in the Drayne's Bridge car park and six miles of easy pedalling, provided the wind is not blowing from the north, brings you to this strangely atmospheric moorland pool. This is where, in the legend, Sir Bedevere came after Arthur's death at Camlan and following instructions, threw Excalibur – only to see the sword rise from the water, held aloft by a lady's hand. Ladies of the Lake aside, the biggest mystery is where the water comes from; nobody seems to have worked this one out yet. Brave swimmers take the plunge here, perhaps hoping to find something more interesting than old beer bottles: on the one occasion when the lake is known to have dried up in the late 19th century, the bottom was found be littered with stone arrowheads.The hills surrounding the pool are rich hunting ground for archaeologists too. Hut circles, standing stones and burial mounds are marked on the map, and getting to them is easier since much of the high moorland became subject to open access. Mark Camp, the man who has done most to clarify the rights of way across the moor and devised the 60-mile circular Copper Trail around it (see box, page 56) is your man for guided walks (*01503 273060; www. walkaboutwest.co.uk*).

⑭ Around St Cleer: King Doniert's Stone and Trethevy Quoit

Around St Cleer (the next good pitstop heading east after St Neot) the Moor rises and trees fall away. King Doniert's Stone and its companion, known simply as the Other Half Stone, stand right next to the road to Minions, just before the turn-off to St Cleer. A bunch of jolly Dutch cyclists were enjoying a break in the little grassy enclosure that surrounds the two stones, both of which are broken chunks of what must have been imposing Cornish crosses. On one of these a Latin inscription begs prayers for the sake of Doniert's soul. Doniert is thought to be the Latinised form of Dumgarth, a 9th-century Cornish king who drowned while crossing the Fowey. Humbler than Shelley's fallen statue of King Ozymandias in the desert perhaps ('Look on my works, ye Mighty, and despair!'), but not lacking in poignancy.

At St Cleer, **Trethevy Quoit** on the east side of the village is the most likely feature to claim your attention. So hidden that it's easy to miss, the massive Neolithic dolmen is thought to date from 4500BC. There are several of these 'quoits' in my part of Penwith, out on the lonely Moor, but finding one so close to a busy village is a rarity, unless you happen to be in France.

⑮ Around Minions

Generous car parks on the outskirts of the village tell you all you need to know about the popularity of this part of the Moor with walkers. This is chiefly due to two spectacular sets of rocks, one a Neolithic stone circle known as

The Hurlers, and the other a naturally formed pile of rocks on Stowe's Hill, called the **Cheesewring**. Coming from a cider-making background, it dawned on me as I stared up at the giant slabs of rock perched one on top of the other, that it resembled nothing so much as a stack of pulp-filled nets, waiting for the press, known in the cider world as a 'cheese'. There's more to discover in this brief amble, though it may be more by accident than design that you come across  the remains of the hillfort that surrounds the Cheesewring, or the Bronze Age track heading north from Stowe's Hill. Easier to locate is the **Rillaton Barrow** (where a Bronze Age gold cup, now in the British Museum, was uncovered), and, with a bit of help, Daniel Gumb's cave. In fact, the excitement of stumbling across the 18th-century cave-home of the enigmatic Gumb – stonemason, mathematician and hermit (if you exclude his three wives and nine children) – is tempered by discovering that it is not Gumb's cave after all, but a replica made using some of the original stone by respectful quarrymen when the original dwelling was undermined by their activities. Close to the car park on the east side of Minions a restored mine building serves as a self-service **heritage centre**, as well as a useful shelter for rain-dodgers.

Food and drink

Crow's Nest Inn Darite PL14 5JG ☎ 01579 345930. A mile south of Minions, surrounded by the ruins of a mining past, this is hard to resist. A log fire welcomes wet walkers – and their children and dogs. There are sheltered tie-ups too, for those wanting to park their horses. St Austell ales and good food.
Minions Post Office ☎ 01579 363386; closed Mon and Fri. Minions can look rather forlorn in the rain, but the tea room behind the post office is a cheerful refuge. Soggy walkers turning up before the official opening time of 10.00 are no rarity here, evidently.

⑯ The Lynher Valley from Upton Cross to Trebartha

Upton Cross is a handsome granite village, which until 2006 was where Yarg, one of Cornwall's best-known cheeses, was made (the business has now been transferred to a larger farm near Truro).

If you don't mind hills, there's a lovely walk down to the valley of the River Lynher at the euphonic **Plushabridge**, where the footpath follows the river north to **Rilla Mill** and back up the hill to Sutton where lanes take you back to Upton Cross.

Liskeard and Caradon Railway

At one time the railway ran right through Minions, transporting ore from Caradon Hill and granite from the quarries down to Moorswater, where it was transferred to barges for the last part of the journey to the dock at Looe on the Liskeard to Looe canal. That was in the mid 19th century, when granite quarrying as well as tin and copper mining were at a peak. But with the closure of the mines in the 1880s, granite was not sufficiently profitable to keep the railway going and the tracks were eventually ripped up and sent to France as part of the World War I effort. Now you will just see the old granite setts which mark its snaking progress across the Moor; lonely trails to nowhere.

Food and drink

Caradon Inn Upton Cross PL14 5AZ ① 01579 364066 ⑩ www.thecaradoninn. co.uk. Popular with drinkers (Doom Bar and guest ales), walkers (child- and dog-friendly too) and theatre-goers (the arts centre is just opposite). Three guest rooms.

Following the River Lynher north, either by the narrow road that wiggles along its eastern banks from Rilla Mill to Trebartha, or on foot, following the Copper Trail, the land is steep and wooded, with scattered villages and settlements hugging the sheltering shoulder of Hawk's Tor and Kilmar Tor. High up, to the west also, looms Twelve Men's Moor, studded with prehistoric remains and fleeting traces of the old mineral railways. **North Hill** has a good old pub, the Racehorse Inn, and some rather fine estate workers' cottages and farm buildings. The estate is **Trebartha**, mentioned in the Doomsday Book and held by the same family until 1940. The 16th-century manor by this time was in ruins and a new one has been built; the gardens are occasionally open in the summer. Timber yards and sawmills are much in evidence; forestry is clearly the estate's main enterprise these days. Footpaths leading up onto the high tops of the Moor start from Trebartha, but are not always clearly marked. It's lonely and desolate on top and you need good visibility to get your bearings, even with a map. It's a very long way to the next village if you keep heading west.

Food and drink

Racehorse Inn North Hill PL15 7PG ① 01566 786916 ⑩ www.theracehorseinn. co.uk ⓔ stay@theracehorseinn.co.uk.
A much-loved locals' pub, with Doom Bar and Tribute on tap as well as 2 guest ales. Good food is sourced from local suppliers. Three smartly done-up rooms are available for B&B; there were appreciative comments in the guest book. Muddy walkers and dogs do not see so much as an eyebrow raised.

⑰ Trecarrel Manor

Trebullet PL15 9QG ① 01566 782286; open by appointment only.

'If you're interested, you'll find your way here,' say Neil and Ruth Burden who farm here and live in the unsignposted Grade I-listed manor house. It is indeed, very hidden, close to the River Inny and lost in a tangle of lanes between Higher Larrick and Trebullett. I am almost tempted to say nothing more and let you make your own Slow discovery of the Great Hall and Lady Chapel which were built early in the 16th century on the site of a much older manor for Henry Trecarrell, mayor of Launceston. Or at least, that was the plan, for Trecarrell never finished his project. Too sad to continue after the death of his wife and child, Trecarrell is better known for flinging himself into the building of St Mary Magdalene in Launceston, which is decorated with all the wonderful carved stone intended originally for the manor. The story of the manor does not end with Trecarrell, however. Guided by Neil, who must be one of the best-informed and generous of local historians, the rich history of this part of Cornwall finds a voice through one of the most interesting buildings in the county. The Burdens are happy to welcome Slow visitors, but theft from the manor some years ago has made them understandably shy of publicity. Do telephone first.

Sterts Theatre

① 01579 362382 ⑩ www.sterts.co.uk.

One of the Moor's happiest surprises is the tented outdoor theatre and gallery at Upton Cross on the eastern edge of the Moor, just a mile east of Minions. The setting may not be quite as spectacular as the cliffside Minack near Land's End, but the canvas canopy means performances, which continue into winter, are never cancelled. Swaddled in blankets and often clutching hot-water bottles, audiences sit on a tiered semicircle of benches, and if the rain beating on the canvas sometimes drowns the actors' voices, nobody minds: it's all part of the Sterts experience.

Conceived in the 1980s by Ewart and Anne Sturrock, who spotted lots of untapped potential in the local community and in the old farm buildings next to their house, a small, community arts centre and outdoor theatre was born. This rapidly grew into an important venue for touring theatre companies, such as Cornwall's home-grown and much-loved Miracle Theatre Company. Ewart continued to direct the community plays, which remain the beating heart of the theatre.

The two-course pre-theatre dinner, cooked by Wendy Thompson (vegetables come from her own garden) and served in the Studio café, is a treat in itself and incredibly good value at £12 at the time of writing. Main courses might include roast chicken or steak pie with, for example, sticky toffee pudding or pavlova to follow. Reservations are essential (*07974 812541*).

4. SOUTHEAST CORNWALL

The bridges that cross the Tamar have a special significance for those whose hearts lie on the western banks – especially for those who regard Cornwall as another country rather than another county. As the historian A L Rowse wrote, 'The Tamar is a decisive boundary such as no other county possesses – but, then, Cornwall is not an ordinary county ...' I've heard of all sorts of odd ritualistic behaviour by travellers on the bridges, but the story I enjoyed most came from a holidaying family where, said the parents, the children breathed out as the car joined the Tamar Bridge on the Devon side and refused to inhale until the Kernow a'gas dynergh (Welcome to Cornwall) sign on the Saltash side had been passed, 'so the air doesn't get mixed up'.

I've no great fondness for the blink-and-you've-missed-it Dunheved Bridge that the A30 rushes over at Launceston, and while I often use the impressively engineered road and rail bridges at **Saltash**, 20 miles to the south, it's the three medieval road bridges that lie in between which give the greatest sense of place. The medieval narrowness of Greystones, Horsebridge and Newbridge allow Slow travellers to savour the moment of arrival, to register the *exactness* of departure. And of these, my favourite is the 15th-century **Greystones Bridge**, three miles southeast of Launceston, so narrow you instinctively breathe in as you cross. Arriving on the Cornish side, a left-hand turn, highly unsuited to heavy vehicles, rises swiftly above river and water meadows and there, on a near-vertical slope is **Howard's Wood**, now in the care of the Woodland Trust, with 'Welcome' written on the gate. That's a good start to a county.

Artists and fruit growers have colonised the gentle banks of the Tamar. Despite Rowse's defiant assertion, I find the boundaries blurred in these parts. The **Tamar Valley** is its own world, neither especially Cornish or Devonish, but happy with its own identity. Many on the Cornish side flit across into Tavistock for shopping or eating out; just as further south, many who work in Plymouth commute via the Torpoint ferry to homes on the **Rame peninsula**. It seems to me that there is less anxiety here than in other parts of rural Cornwall, less edginess; yet also less affluence and security than in the leafy creekside villages of the Helford, Fal and Fowey.

South of the River Lynher, Cornwall's 'forgotten corner' may be linked umbilically to Plymouth, yet in the remote farmland beyond **Torpoint**, its self-proclaimed obscurity is easy to appreciate. There are grand houses at every strategic estuarine juncture, their gardens lush in the mild maritime climate, and in the south, fishing villages with an almost Mediterranean air about them; to the west are desolate, storm-lashed cliffs, shanty-town chalets and long, empty beaches.

Westwards of Seaton, the Channel coast suddenly assumes its Cornish personality; fishing ports, hidden rocky coves and Neolithic stones bear names that speak an older tongue; this is the start of the Pens and Pols, the Lans

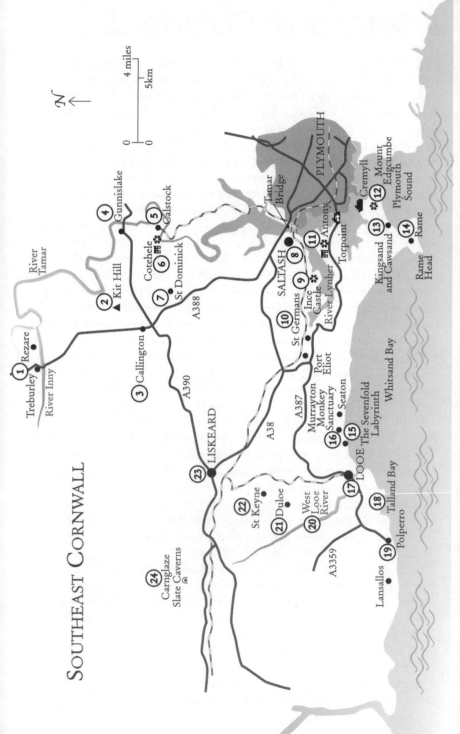

SOUTHEAST CORNWALL

River Tamar

River Inny

1 Rezare
Treburley

2 Kit Hill

3 Callington

4 Gunnislake

5 Calstock

6 Cotehele

7 St Dominick

St Dominick

A388

A390

A387

A38

A3359

LISKEARD

23

24 Carnglaze Slate Caverns

22 St Keyne

21 Duloe

20 West Looe River

19 Polperro

Lansallos

18 Talland Bay

17 LOOE

The Sevenfold Labyrinth

16 Murrayton Monkey Sanctuary

15 Seaton

Whitsand Bay

10 St Germans

Port Eliot

9 Ince Castle

River Lynher

8 SALTASH

11 Antony

Torpoint

Tamar Bridge

PLYMOUTH

Cremyll

12 Mount Edgcumbe

Plymouth Sound

13 Kingsand and Cawsand

14 Rame

Rame Head

4 miles

5km

N

and Looes; instead of Johns and Michaels, churches are dedicated to semi-mythical Celtic saints. Inland, where wooded river valleys rise to meet the southern fringe of Bodmin Moor, there are some of the best walking and camping spots to be enjoyed in Cornwall, a wonderfully eccentric museum of music machines, beech trees that are home to Amazonian woolly monkeys and, in **Liskeard**, the opportunity to discover a handsome market town with an equally engaging identity.

Getting around

One of the great pleasures of visiting southeast Cornwall is the public transport network of trains, buses and ferries that make getting around without a car relatively easy, at least in comparison with other parts of Cornwall that are less well served.

Trains

Two thriving branch lines make travelling by train a real option. The hubs are **Plymouth**, from which you can take the arrestingly lovely ride north to Gunnislake, crossing the Tamar at Calstock, and **Liskeard**, which sees the start of a single-track line down to Looe which follows the route of the old Liskeard to Looe canal. Both lines publish maps and timetables which also give details of 'Rail Ale Trails' (*www.railaletrail.com*) suggesting decent pubs within walking distance of stations along the line.

Buses

Buses connect with many of the stations on the branch lines, giving reasonable cross-country coverage, and connecting with the main hubs at Callington, Saltash, Torpoint, Looe and Liskeard. Coast-path walkers will find the **Rame peninsula** covered by the 81 bus, which loops around the peninsula from Torpoint to Cremyll and connects at Hessenford with buses to Looe and Liskeard. However, if you are planning linear walks, the lack of a continual bus service along the south coast, both east and west of Looe, can be frustrating.

Ferries

Cawsand Ferry ① 01752 822784 ⓦ www.cawsandferry.com. A summer service that carries people, bikes, dogs and pushchairs from Cawsand Beach to Plymouth Barbican, with departures every 90 minutes from 09.30 until 16.30. The crossing takes 30 minutes.

Cremyll Ferry ① 01752 822105 ⓦ www.tamarcruising.com. A year-round passenger service between Cremyll and Admiral's Hard in Plymouth. The 15-minute crossing runs every half-hour at peak times. Check the website for seasonal and Sunday variations.

Tamar Passenger Ferry ① 01822 833331 Ⓦ www.calstockferry.co.uk. From Apr to late Sep a passenger ferry based in Calstock offers a regular service to Cotehele and Morwellham Quay on the Devon side of the Tamar.

Torpoint Ferry ① 01752 812233 Ⓦ www.tamarcrossings.org.uk. A 24-hour, daily chain-ferry service that transports vehicles and foot passengers between Plymouth and Torpoint, with ferries every 10 minutes at peak times.

Cycling and walking

So far, there are no specially designated cycle routes across this part of Cornwall, and you will need OS Explorer maps 107 and 108 to plot your own routes. Following the valleys of the **Tamar**, **Lynher**, or **East** and **West Looe** rivers is one of the best ways to plan a ride, but there's no escaping the steep hills and plunging valleys that characterise the region, and will test even the keenest adherents to the maxim that the views from the top of a long haul uphill reward the effort. The most useful websites to consult are offered by the endlessly resourceful Mannings at Rezare Farmhouse (*www.rezarefarmhouse. co.uk/tamar_valley_cycle_routes.php*) and the Chycor website (*www.chycor.co.uk/ holidays/cycling-in-cornwall*).

Rewarding areas for **circular coastal walks** include Rame Head and Mount Edgcumbe, where the peninsular character of the land means you can get waterside walking on both sides; and around Looe there's some impressive river scenery inland following the West Looe River. A 30-mile Discovery Trail follows the Tamar from Launceston to Plymouth; there's no continuous riverside route and planning circular walks isn't that easy, though the branch-line rail service from Plymouth to Gunnislake can be useful for return journeys. Kit Hill is excellent for a blustery stroll and the coast path east of Looe springs a curious meditational surprise for walkers.

Cycle hire

The greater part of the Tamar Valley AONB lies on the Devon side of the border, and if you are planning to explore this area by bike, cycle hire in Tavistock or Plymouth might be a better option. On the Cornish side of the Tamar there are just a small number of cycle hire outlets:

A Cornish walking festival

Mark Camp has been organising a walking festival since 2000, first in the Looe Valley, but now guided walks with local experts on local heritage or wildlife are offered all over southeast Cornwall in mid-September (*www.visit-southeastcornwall.co.uk*; follow links for Attractions and Activities, and Walking in Southeast Cornwall).

Cycle Action 1A Harvey St, Torpoint ① 01752 427265 ⑩ www.cycleaction-torpoint.com. Well placed for exploring the Rame peninsula, with daily or weekly hire and free delivery within a 15-mile radius of Torpoint.

Launceston Cycles 6 Southgate St ① 01566 776 102 ⑩ www.launcestoncycles.co.uk. They hire out bikes on a weekly basis only.

Accommodation

Berrio Mill Golberdon, Callington PL17 7NL ① 01579 363252 ⑩ www.berriomill.co.uk ⑥ enquiries@berriomill.co.uk. Two luxurious holiday cottages, sleeping two and four, look across the leat to a former mill, surrounded by unspoilt woods and fields, just yards from the River Lynher, where fishing for salmon and sea trout is all part of the deal. The Callanans, who live in the mill and are deeply committed to the Slow ethos, produce honey, fruit and vegetables for their growing jam, mustard and chutney business. Weekly tariffs at average rates for a very special place, particularly if you're into fly-fishing.

Botelet Herodsfoot, Liskeard PL14 4RD ① 01503 220225 ⑩ www.botelet.com ⑥ stay@botelet.com. A working farm of idyllic beauty in a green valley overlooked by an Iron Age hillfort, offering B&B in the farmhouse, self-catering in the adjoining cottage or another cottage just down the lane, two yurts, each in its own meadow – and camping for a very limited number of 'low-impact' tents in whichever of the fields closest to the farm is not being grazed by the cows. The Tamblyns have farmed here for generations, know the area inside out and their recipe for simple, unspoilt rural seclusion is perfect, and offered at average prices. Be sure to walk out to the vertiginous tree tunnel, made by Julie and Richard Tamblyn's father. Carl Honoré, author of *In Praise of Slow*, stayed here and loved what the Tamblyns have created.

Highertown Farm Campsite Lansallos, Looe PL13 2PX ① 01208 265211 ⑩ www.nationaltrust.org.uk ⑥ highertownfarmcampsite@nationaltrust.org.uk. When friends, camping for the first time with two very small children, asked me where they should pitch their tent, this was my first suggestion – and they loved it. Lansallos is a tiny unspoilt village, a short walk from a lovely beach and the campsite is in a field next to the church. It's owned and run by the National Trust, in a very relaxed kind of way, relying on the decency of those who camp there to make it work. A restored barn offers washing and drying facilities. Very cheap, but be sure to reserve a pitch in school holidays: it's a small site.

Little Wenfork Campsite Rezare, Launceston PL15 9NU ① 01579 370755 ⑩ www.littlewenfork.co.uk ⑥ info@littlewenfork.co.uk. Just outside Rezare, a very pretty village, close the Inny and well placed for exploring the Tamar Valley. A level paddock, with space for just a handful of tents and two ready-pitched bell-tents with logburners for 'glampers'. On the way to the small, spotless shower rooms you pass pens of smiley pigs and free-ranging chickens and ducks. Prices are a little above average.

The Old Luggage Van and the Travelling Post Office Railholiday Ltd, Haparanda Station, Nut Tree Hill, St Germans PL12 5LU ℗ 01503 230783 Ⓦ www.railholiday.co.uk Ⓔ DaveandLizzy@railholiday.co.uk. St Germans is a working station on the main line from Plymouth to Penzance, but quiet, flower-filled corners have been found for two railway carriages, converted into cosy, quirky self-catering accommodation. The Old Luggage Van sleeps two and has a woodburner; the TPO, which has a double bed, sofa bed and bunks, will sleep a family of up to six and has private access to 10 acres of woodland. Weekly rental close to average holiday cottage prices.

Pentillie Castle St Mellion, Saltash PL12 6QD ℗ 01579 350044 Ⓦ www.pentillie. co.uk Ⓔ enquiry@pentillie.co.uk. Fabulous, faultless B&B in a wonderfully restored late 17th-century manor house overlooking the Tamar. The Corytons are delightful, hard-working hosts who now have nine bedrooms available to guests and will cook a three-course dinner if numbers (minimum six) are feasible. Opera and theatre are performed in the garden during the summer and there are art study days, classic car and gardening events too. Upmarket prices, but worth every penny.

Rezare Farmhouse Launceston PL15 9NX ℗ 01579 371214 Ⓦ www.rezarefarmhouse.co.uk Ⓔ info@rezarefarmhouse.co.uk. No longer a farm, but a very comfortable village house offering four rooms (two doubles, one twin and one single), and breakfast with a menu using local organic products that takes some beating: homemade bread and granola, porridge cooked overnight in the Aga, pancakes with fruit from the garden alert you to the fact that the Mannings are not just brilliant cooks, but care deeply about the food they use. Dinners are also cooked on request. A great place to explore the Tamar Valley: fly-fishing can be arranged and bike and walking routes suggested. Prices are a little over the average; comfort, cooking and care, however, are way above the norm.

Treworgey Farm Duloe, Liskeard PL14 4PP ℗ 01503 262730 Ⓦ www.hideawayhuts.co.uk Ⓔ stay@hideawayhuts.co.uk. A shepherd's hut has been carefully transformed by Alec and Jo Craig into a lovely, simple double bedroom decorated in pale greys and blues, standing in a sheltered paddock beside woodland, where a very discreet and eco-friendly shower and loo complete the facilities. The farm has stables and riding is available for guests staying in the shepherd's hut or in the several upmarket holiday cottages that have been created from converted farm buildings. Prices similar to top-end B&B accommodation.

Westcroft Guest House Market St, Kingsand PL10 1NE ℗ 01752 823216 Ⓔ info@westcroftguesthouse.co.uk. A very special, distinctly upmarket B&B right on the seafront at Kingsand with three bedrooms done out in luxurious contemporary style. There's a star-gazing bathtub, four-posters, but it's not so posh that well-behaved dogs aren't welcome. Next door, the owners have created a superb gallery, aimed at bringing wider recognition to local artists.

Wringworthy Cottages Morval, Looe PL13 1PR ℗ 01503 240685 Ⓦ www.wringworthy.co.uk Ⓔ holidays@wringworthy.co.uk. Great set-up for children, with lots of friendly animals and both indoor and outdoor play spaces which include a heated swimming pool. The eight cottages, created from restored farm buildings, sleep two to eight and make it more like a little village: perfect for sociable families and a great base – if you can drag the children away – for exploring both coastal and inland areas around Looe. Good value and some very good deals for low season, last-minute breaks.

Tourist information centres

Liskeard Foresters Hall, Pike St ⓣ 01579 349148 ⓦ www.liskeard.gov.uk
ⓔ tourism@liskeard.gov.uk.
Looe The Guildhall, Fore St, East Looe ⓣ 01503 262072 ⓦ www.visit-southeast
cornwall.co.uk ⓔ looetic@btconnect.com.

Along the Tamar

Once filled with fields of daffodils, market gardens and orchards, the Cornish banks of the Tamar in springtime now see field margins and woodland understorey splashed with floral memories of those years in cream, yellow and white, the bare canopy above enlivened with occasional clouds of apple, cherry and plum blossom.

The river below **Launceston** descends to Plymouth Sound in no particular hurry: a lazy ribbon of meandering loops joined by the swifter currents of the Inny and the Lynher. Egrets perch in oaks undercut by the water, kingfishers skim above the surface and, during the winter months in the tidal reaches, avocets and spoonbills stalk the shoreline. Salmon and sea trout start running the clear waters in April heading upstream to their spawning ground, and the otter population is rising. With no small measure of justice, in 1995 both sides of the Tamar were together designated an Area of Outstanding Natural Beauty.

It's hard to fault the manmade additions to the landscape either. The soaring viaducts that span the river at **Calstock** and below **Saltash** seem only to enhance the beauty; and the same may be said of the great riverside houses at **Cotehele**, **Pentillie** and **Ince**. The relics of an industrial past – mines, engine houses, docks and warehouses – have crumbled with heroic grace beneath the meadow flowers and ferny woodland.

It would be strange if such an inspiring landscape did not attract artists, but on my last visit to the valley I became aware that Tamar artists are gaining in number and recognition; thanks to new galleries such as the tiny, but influential **Tayt Morden**, near Cotehele, a stronger voice and – though not a school – a distinct identity is emerging. Cornish art, which for so long has been focused around Newlyn and St Ives, now has a counterweight in the east of the county.

Exploring the Explorer 108

Nanette and Anthony Manning at Rezare Farmhouse (see above) put me onto an original and very well-structured website (*www.exploringexplorer108.co.uk*) which lists dozens of short walks (averaging 1.5 hours) around the Tamar, all within the OS map Explorer 108. Each walk describes not only the route and level of what the author, Kate Latham, describes as 'plodginess', but also the wild flowers and birds encountered on the way. A section titled 'small joys' adds enormously to the sense of place you get with each description. Comments here might include 'crisp winter meadows' or 'a complete walk without any cows!' (I found the 'Navigational Errors' section endearingly honest, too.) The **Ordnance Survey Explorer map 108** itself is obviously an indispensable accompaniment to these walks; helpfully, the site also offers a link to the OS online shop.

① The Inny valley

Having discovered the infant Inny while camping at Tregillis Farm and again at Trecarrel Manor (see pages 6 and 74), I was curious to see more of this pretty tributary of the Tamar, particularly around **Rezare**, where it drops through mixed woodland to Innyfoot. Look at the OS map, however, and you'll see a marked absence of public footpaths, for this is fly-fishing territory and the seatrout and salmon spawning grounds are carefully protected. Licences, day tickets and instruction are not difficult to organise, via Launceston Anglers Association (*www.gethooked.co.uk*) or Launceston Sports (*1 Market St, Launceston PL15 8EP; 01566 774127; www.launcestonsports.co.uk*).

Food and drink

Springer Spaniel Treburley PL15 9NS ① 01579 370424
ⓦ www.thespringerspaniel.org.uk. The watering hole of choice in these parts. Real ales come from Skinners, Sharpes and St Austell breweries, the food is very good and often locally sourced; much thought has been given to both the sensitively restored interior and the garden. Children and dogs welcome.

② Kit Hill

The close-up intimacy of river valleys is seductive, but there comes a point when you want to get up a hill and put the whole landscape into perspective. Kit Hill is the highest and most accessible peak between Bodmin and Dartmoor – and you can drive right to the top if you wish, which has the advantage of leaving you with lots of energy for exploring the 400 acres of granite heathland, quarries and ruins from a well-maintained network of tracks. The views from the summit are sublime and a happy half-hour can be spent doing nothing more than rambling about the summit, trying to identify places encountered at close quarters. Go early in the morning and you may see novice balloon pilots and their instructors slipping upwards and south, drawn by the airborne currents of the Tamar.

The summit is quite clearly defined by an earth embankment, now covered in grass, which turns out to be the remains of a folly, built in the late 18th century by Sir John Call of Stoke Climsland, whose estate, Whitefield Park, is now occupied by the Duchy College. The folly resembled a five-sided Saxon fort, built in commemoration of a 9th-century battle, fought on the lower slopes of the hill, which brought Saxon rule to Cornwall.

Bang on the summit stands a chimney, though from a distance it has a distinctly monumental appearance. This is the most significant relic of the 19th-century mine workings that riddle the hill, serving a steam-driven engine that pumped water and lifted ore from the innermost workings of the mine. For some reason, the chimney was built on the site of a prehistoric burial mound. In 1858, archaeological sensitivity and mineral exploitation, it seems, did not shake hands too often. There are, however, some 18 other barrows scattered around the hill.

Kit Hill belongs to the people of Cornwall. It used to be Duchy land, but in 1985 it was handed over to Cornwall County Council to celebrate the birth of Prince William.

Food and drink

Louis' Tea Room PL17 8AX ☏ 01579 389223. Right by the entrance to Kit Hill, and open all year, this is a friendly, steamy café in just the right place. Outside are llamas, rabbits and guinea pigs (not on the menu).

③ Callington

At first glance, Callington looks like a small market town that might have seen better days, but hop out of the car and you'll see that something quite extraordinary has been going on. The **Callington murals** started to appear in the late 1980s and now there are dozens adorning the walls of the town, some painted by professional artists, others by local schoolchildren, and hardly a year goes by without a new one appearing. You can follow them with a trail guide, available in many of the shops or the town hall. One of the best is a fanciful view of a secret pasty factory, as it might have been designed by Brunel, deep in the bowels of Kit Hill (it may be relevant that Callington's biggest employer is Ginsters of pasty fame), and I was very taken with the *trompe l'oeil* image of the interior of the old farriery, close to the building where Callington's horses were shod. Another striking image on the wall of the police station shows a beehive in an orchard; you don't have to spend very long here before realising that apistry plays an important part of local culture, culminating in the October **Honey Fair**, when bee-craft provides the focus for a popular jamboree.

Pevsner's *Buildings of England: Cornwall* describes the 15th-century church of

St Mary as 'ambitious' (certainly it is unusual in having a clerestory), but its size and grandeur are not only an indication of Callington's prosperity and strategic importance at the time, but also testimony to the private wealth of Nicolas de Assheton, a local justicier who died in 1465 and was largely responsible for funding the construction of the church; finely carved brass plates in the chancel carry images of him, his wife and their 11 children.

The **Callington Heritage Centre** (*Liskeard Rd, PL17 7HA; 01579 389506*) is housed in a former cemetery chapel, split in two for conformists and their non-conforming, Methodist brethren. The collection of local social and religious memorabilia is too large to be on permanent display in its entirety, so each year a theme is adopted to give exhibits an airing. Lynda Small, who helps curate the collection, told me that she thinks the collection of 'Chapel china' – tea services individually designed for each Methodist chapel and used for anniversary high teas (alcohol was forbidden of course) – might be the only collection of its kind.

Food and drink

Sleepy Hollow Farm Rising Sun PL17 8JB ① 01579 351010. Just off the A390 from Callington to Gunnislake, this used to be an egg farm with a café. Now it's a much-appreciated farm shop, café and restaurant, famous locally for its home baking.

④ Gunnislake

Gunnislake is soaked in history, from the narrow 16th-century bridge at its foot, where Parliamentarians fought their way into Cornwall, to the rich tin, copper, arsenic and wolfram mines that gave the town its considerable size and importance in the 19th century. The steep, wooded landscape around the town was painted by Turner, whose magisterial *Crossing the Brook* was first exhibited in 1815, and Betjeman waxed lyrical about this part of the Tamar.

The branch line from Plymouth terminates at the top of the hill above the town, and from here it's an easy walk to the **Tamar Valley Centre** (*Drakewalls, PL18 9FE; 01822 835030; www.tamarvalley.org.uk*), housed in a new, eco-friendly building, often used for art exhibitions and talks. It's a good place for picking up information about the latest heritage and leisure projects in the valley and maps of the valley trails. *Trails from the Track*, a series of self-guided walks accessible from stations on the Tamar Valley line, suggests a particularly good (though steep and muddy) five-mile walk from Gunnislake station that takes in a canalised section of the Tamar and passes through woodland, in which the relics of Clitters mine can still be seen.

⑤ Calstock

Spirits rise in Calstock, for the village is full of life both on and off the river and is decidedly photogenic: whitewashed houses and cottages spill down steep banks to the shore of the Tamar, where the wide, free-flowing river is spanned by the lofty arches of the **railway viaduct** built by John Lang, a Liskeard engineer, just over a century ago. A youthful pilot gig team were launching their distinctively Cornish six-oared rowing craft as I arrived, sponsored, they proudly told me, by Ginsters, the Callington pasty makers. There's a lively arts centre, based in the old **Methodist chapel**, tea rooms by the water, a really good quayside pub – and a rich history of mining, shipbuilding and river-based activity to explore. It's a pretty mile-and-a-half walk along the river to **Cotehele**, or you can take to the water in the **MV *Gloria*** (*www.calstockferry.co.uk*), a river launch which runs passengers up and down the river to the quay at Cotehele and across the water to **Morwellham Quay** on the Devon shore.

Food and drink

Tamar Inn PL18 9QA ① 01822 832487 ⑩ www.tamarinn.co.uk. Overlooking the quay, there are wooden benches both inside and outside, where at least half of this friendly village seems to gather in the evening with their dogs and kids. The drinking and eating is just as good as the setting: locally brewed ales from both sides of the river and reasonably priced pub food, with crayfish as well as Cornish burgers on the menu and homemade apple crumble or treacle tart.

⑥ Cotehele

St Dominick PL12 6TA ① 01579 351346 ⑩ www.nationaltrust.org; closed winter, but garden and estate open all year.

Cotehele is a proper working estate – only a handful of its 80 cottages are used as holiday lets – with a strong local identity that draws the neighbouring

Drawn to the Valley

Turner was not alone in finding the Tamar Valley a place of unique and inspiring beauty; there is now a large and diverse community of artists living, working and exhibiting here, rather in the way that St Ives drew artists half a century or so ago. Drawn to the Valley was formed in 2003, not only to promote the work of these artists, but also to promote the Tamar Valley AONB and contribute to the regeneration of the area through selling exhibitions and Open Studio events. Look out for their work at the Calstock Arts Centre, the Tamar Valley Centre, Tayt Morden (see page 87) and the Ashtorre Rock (see page 89).

population to its food markets, boat jumbles, wassailing and rural crafts workshops. The **Tudor house** at the heart of the estate is outstanding, virtually unaltered since its construction (on the site of an earlier family pile) for the Edgcumbe family which began during the last years of the 15th century. Magically, there's still no electric light, so on gloomy days a torch is a good idea for properly examining the tapestries and furniture commissioned by the original Edgcumbes. An alcove in the chapel contains a complicated set of cog wheels, weights and winding mechanism. These are the working parts of a turret clock, the oldest of its kind in the world to be still striking the hour (a turret clock has no face to show the passing minutes) and in its original position.

The **walled gardens** hidden in the wooded slopes below the house are lush and almost subtropical, thanks to the sheltering walls and frost-impeding presence of the river below. A short walk from the gardens along a woodland path high above the river brings you to the 'chapel in the woods', built by Sir Richard Edgcumbe in the late 1480s, shortly before work started on the new house. Richard had been an outspoken critic of Richard III and at Plymouth joined a failed rebellion against the king. As a result, the king sent the notoriously brutal Henry Bodruggan to Cotehele to sort matters out. The chapel marks the spot where Edgcumbe, hidden among the trees, escaped his pursuers by weighting his cap with stones and casting it into the river below. While Bodruggan believed him drowned, Edgcumbe made his way to Brittany, joined forces with Henry Tudor and re-emerged on the battlefield at Bosworth, which saw Henry victorious and his brave supporter able, at last, to return to Cotehele. But Richard Edgcumbe did not live long enough to see the new house built; it was his son Piers who oversaw the construction. Despite the decision by Piers's son (another Richard) to relocate the family seat to Mount Edgcumbe, (see page 91) ten miles downstream, in 1553, Cotehele remained part of the Edgcumbe estate until 1947, when it was handed over to the National Trust. Because it was only intermittently occupied for 400 years, no great reworkings of the building were undertaken (apart from a tower, added in 1627, which provided three extra bedrooms); take away the visitor signs, restaurant and gallery and there's very little that Piers or his father would not recognise. And they would probably appreciate it if the **Barn Restaurant** was not taken away, as it does an exceptionally good line in lunches, using produce derived from the estate and local farmers (*01579 351346 or 352711*).

A day is barely long enough to do justice to Cotehele. Down by the river, on the quayside you can wander into the boatshed, where repairs are undertaken to the old craft which still occasionally ply up and down the Tamar. The *Shamrock*, built for sea and river duties in 1899, is permanently moored here; her rudder was being given a new coat of paint by a chatty volunteer when I called in. There's a small free museum, devoted to the days when the Tamar was an industrial highway, full of ketch-rigged barges like *Shamrock*, huge ore-transporting vessels and passenger ferries too. Next to the arches of old

Canoeing on the Tamar

From Easter to September inclusive, **Canoe Tamar** offers three-hour guided trips in Canadian canoes, starting from Cotehele quay (*01822 833409; www. canoetamar.co.uk*). Paddling with the tide, the pace is relaxed and unhurried, the peace and stillness of the river as important as the informal exchange of information *en route*, and the bring-your-own-picnic break. Paul and Kate, who run Canoe Tamar also offer mountain biking, bushcraft courses and 'tree-surfing' (*01822 833409; www.treesurfers.co.uk*) at their base in Gulworthy, on the Devon side of the river.

limekilns, a handsome granite house is now The Edgcumbe Arms, a daytime-only pub and tearoom, perfect for riverside walkers with a thirst on. Cider made from apples grown in Cotehele's 'Mother Orchard' – home to dozens of rare local varieties of cider apple – and pressed in the ancient mill, is not to be missed.

Follow a gushing millstream, the Morden, for ten minutes through woodland and you find yourself at **Cotehele Mill**, which produces not only stone-milled flour, but also, since 2011, energy for the bakery and several workshops. It was here that I met Barry Mays, a greenwood furniture maker, who gave me an insight into what it's like to live in or around Cotehele, and we both agreed that 'Slow' just about summed up the year-round enjoyment of local food and drink, tradition and skills encouraged by the estate.

⑦ St Dominick

Follow the Morden upstream on a narrow lane to St Dominick, and between a bend and a bridge is a tiny art and craft gallery, **Tayt Morden** (*www.tayt-morden.co.uk*). The name is jokey, but the content of this small new gallery is seriously impressive. A collection of nine paintings by the late John Miller were on show when I visited. No wonder the local papers were excited, producing headlines such as 'Tiny Tayt pulls off Coup with collection of unseen Millers'. 'Artists enjoy saying they are exhibiting at Tayt Morden,' says owner, Ceri Taylor, who started the gallery in a disused toyshop in 2010. 'And it's important for our growing arts community to have somewhere we can be seen in the context of where we all live and work.' Another well-known Tamar Valley artist occasionally exhibiting here is Mary Martin. She and her partner, James Evans, who live just round the corner from the Tayt, have quietly been responsible for tracking down, grafting and planting dozens of lost apple varieties, once familiar in the valley. The mother orchard at Cotehele could not have been planted without their unsung, but hugely important contribution.

⑧ Saltash

Despite hosting the Cornish end of Brunel's triumphant railway bridge, 'Cornwall's 1st Place', as the town styles itself, couldn't look more unprepossessing if it tried. But it was sheer chance that I was passing **Elliott's Stores** in Lower Fore Street on one of the twice-weekly occasions when it opens to visitors (*Wed afternoons and Sat mornings, summer only*). Inside, I was instantly transported back to my childhood, and crikey, I thought – looking at the tins and packets – diets and packaging have changed a bit since then. The story is that Frank Elliott, who kept this grocer's shop and was vociferously anti-decimalisation, decided in 1973 to turn it into a museum, as a sort of protest (and also to avoid paying business rates on the property). Great fun for over-50s, even if you leave feeling slightly older and possibly queasier than when you went in. The views from Saltash over the estuary are pretty stunning, and one of the best places to enjoy them is from the windows or terrace of the **Ashtorre Rock**, a community-run café, right under Brunel's bridge (*www.ashtorrerock.co.uk*). This is the heart of the arts community in

The Royal Albert Bridge

Brunel's swansong, an engineering feat of heroic problem-solving, remains the crucial link in joining Cornwall to the rest of England by rail. Six years in the planning and six in construction, but the official opening by Prince Albert on 2 May 1859 was missed by Brunel due to ill health. Two days later, he was feeling fit enough to make the crossing in an open carriage; four months later, he was dead.

What made the project so complex was the Admiralty's stipulation that the river must remain navigable without interruption to its high-masted shipping. There was also a lack of available bedrock in the river bed for building piers on which high arches could be supported. Then, having come up with a clever solution, his contractor went bankrupt and Brunel was obliged to take on the contract for construction himself. Brunel was probably what today we'd call bipolar and his dark moods were not helped by these challenges.

But the single, mid-river pier was built and on 1 September 1857, watched by some 20,000 spectators, the first of the two oval-shaped, arched spans was floated out into the centre of the river between two barges. It took two hours, five navy vessels and 500 men to manoeuvre it through 45 degrees, working with the turning tide. The iron construction was gradually raised at a rate of six feet a week using hydraulic jacks until on 1 July 1858 it reached its final height, 100 feet above the water at high tide, as the Admiralty had prescribed.

On 10 July 1858 the second span for the Devon side was floated out into the river. Word had spread about the incredible spectacle and special trains were laid on to bring even more spectators from London. Less than a year later, Prince Albert walked across the bridge, while Brunel, bedridden and frustrated, could only imagine the applause.

Saltash, and there are always exhibitions, arts projects and classes going on in the studio upstairs.

⑨ Ince Castle

Elm Gate PL12 4QZ ⓦ www.incecastle.co.uk.

The handsome, four-square brick-built house (you can't really call it a castle) was built for Henry Killigrew, a Royalist and MP for West Looe in the early 1640s, just as Civil War was breaking out. Defeated and living in exile, Killigrew lost his house, but it was eventually reoccupied by his scandalous nephew who reputedly installed a wife in each of Ince's four towers, keeping each wife in ignorance of the others by claiming a plague of mice lay beyond the safety of their apartments.

Ince is privately owned, but the gardens are opened for one afternoon each month during the spring and early summer, and those lucky enough to be able to take advantage of these rare opportunities are well rewarded: the spring bulbs, woodland garden, formal sunken garden and walled 'summer garden' are the result of more than 50 years' careful and courageous planting by the late Lady Patricia Boyd and her daughter-in-law Lady Alice Boyd who lives there now. The views across the Lynher to the woodland gardens at **Antony** are superb.

Food and drink

The Rod and Line Tideford PL12 5HW ⓣ 01752 851323. On the A38 close to the turning to St Germans, this doesn't look much from the outside and you could easily drive past and miss it, but it's a gem (of the diamond in the rough variety), both for eating and drinking. Lots of people recommended it to me while researching this chapter, with Sunday lunch often getting a special mention.

⑩ St Germans

A handsome estate village with a grand church that was once known as Cornwall's cathedral frames the entrance to **Port Eliot** (*01503 230211; www. porteliot.co.uk*), a dreamy, castellated house, parts of which have stood here for over a thousand years. Sir John Soane was involved in much of the remodelling, creating a spectacular round room and generally reorganising the architecture to flood the new and elegant living quarters with light.

Only in England would you find such a gloriously shabby and eccentric stately home, and for a few months in spring and early summer it opens its doors to the public. Family portraits by Reynolds decorate the entrance hall, conventionally enough, but thereafter expect an eye-popping series of anachronistic, but much-loved possessions among the faded grandeur. A classic motorbike leans against an unfinished mural by Robert Lenkiewicz; a disco glitter-ball hangs from a gigantic French chandelier. Peregrine and Catherine, the present Earl and Countess of St Germans are unrepentant: 'Our collection

The Port Eliot Festival

It started in 2003 as a very low-key literary event, two decades after the 'Elephant Fayre' (a music festival with an 'if you can remember it you weren't there' kind of reputation). Now it's one of the biggest and most eclectic festivals in the southwest, styled as a 'celebration of words, music, imagination and laughter' (*www.porteliotfestival.com*). Food, fashion and flowers play a big part too, not to mention river swimming and camping larks. It's the new Cool Cornwall all over.

of vinyl records will stay propped up against the most prestigious piece of furniture in the house, a late 17th-century armoire in boule work [the art of inlaying brass designs in a veneer of tortoiseshell] in the Morning Room. The drinks table will stay in the Drawing Room – it has always been there and helps make the room feel lived in. We may replace the alcohol with coloured water, but not until we've seen how many visitors try to have a nip of brandy.

Food and drink

The Long Gallery St Germans, PL12 5LG ℡ 01503 230753 ℗ www.thelonggallery.co.uk. An art gallery also open for lunch, tea and cakes or Friday and Saturday evening tapas and drinks. Lovely courtyard lined with unusual plants and a small door takes you directly into Port Eliot.

The Rame peninsula

Across the River Lynher, a knobbly peninsula, dubbed 'Cornwall's forgotten corner' looks across the confluence of the Lynher and the Tamar, known as the Hamoaze, at the urban sprawl and dockyards of Plymouth. Two great gardens, **Mount Edgcumbe** and **Antony**, crown the eastern promontaries; all else is empty hilly farmland and long beaches sheltering beneath crumbling cliffs on the Channel shore. All the people seem to have been shaken down into the picturesque conjoined villages of **Kingsand** and **Cawsand** that once stood on either side of the county boundary with Devon. Some villages are distinctly Anglo-Saxon in name – Crafthole, St John, Millbrook – and have a remote air about them, though none is quite so lost as tiny **Rame**, an inspiring destination for Romantic souls, particularly on Christmas Eve when candles light the lonely chapel.

⑪ Antony House, Gardens and Woodland

Torpoint PL11 2QA ℡ 01752 812191 ℗ www.nationaltrust.org.uk; Apr–early Oct open three or four days a week.

The Carew Poles are a family of great gardeners to which the gardens and woodland at Antony, which has been their ancestral home for centuries, bear witness. The current owner, Sir Richard Carew Pole, was until recently President of the Royal Horticultural Society, his parents assembled important collections of camellias and day-lilies, and his forebears enjoyed the help and assistance of J C Williams of Caerhays, who gave his name to some of the greatest camellia hybrids. Earlier still, in 1792, Humphry Repton was called in to sweep away the lingering formality of the first gardens, created when a new house was built for the family between 1711 and 1721. Evidently the spirit of innovation and development remains strong: there is a thought-provoking collection of modern sculptures and surreal moments of recognition, for the topiary walk was used in Tim Burton's 2010 film of *Alice in Wonderland*.

Quintessentially Cornish, the **gardens** at Antony are perhaps best viewed in spring, when they are filled with the flowers of camellias, magnolias, rhododendrons and azaleas above the River Lynher with magnificent views of the estuary rich with wildlife.

The **house**, which opens to the public too, is rather splendid, though very much a lived-in home and not a museum. The **woodland garden** (which requires a separate admission), overlooking the Lynher is a dendrologist's dream, and even if you can't tell your *Taxodendrons* from your *Metasequoias*, the sheer loveliness of the woods, walks and water will take care of the rest of the day; **St John**, an attractive village, less than a mile from Antony, has a decent pub to head for when the gates close.

Food and drink

St John Inn PL11 3AW ℡ 01752 822280. Head for this 14th-century village pub, easy-going and full of character, serving local ales and home-cooked pub grub.

⑫ Mount Edgcumbe

Cremyll, Torpoint PL10 1HZ ℡ 01752 822236 Ⓦ www.mountedgcumbe.gov.uk.

So, I was wondering, what could possibly have induced the Edgcumbes to leave the loveliness of Cotehele? Here, ten miles south of Cotehele, they had a deer park and in 1547 work started on a new and very grand house. Perhaps by the late 17th century, when the move happened, Cotehele was looking rather dated and the new pile the more attractive residence of the two? A century earlier, it had certainly caught the eye of the captain of the Spanish Armada, who declared that he would live there when the war was over.

The mid 18th century saw grand landscaping works as the grounds were brought up to date in the new Arcadian style, by which time both the façade and the innards of the house would have looked quite different from the original Elizabethan design. A stray incendiary bomb hit the house in 1941, destroying almost all of the interior fabric of the building, though astonishingly the external walls remained intact. Today, it's clear that the rebuilding, which began in 1958, proved the silver-lining theory, as modifications to make the house lighter and more comfortable to live in could be incorporated into the restoration plan. Many of the older pieces of furniture and paintings did not survive the blast, but there are some superb tapestries from Cotehele and a joyous painting of a Cotehele tenants' dinner, dating from the 19th century.

The Cremyll foot passenger ferry to Plymouth deposits walkers at the eastern approach to the park, otherwise you are free to drive, cycle or walk through the thousand-acre park, to the house and formal gardens. Beyond here, unless you are following the coast path, which follows the wooded fringes of the park, a bike is the best way to get about and there are well-marked routes to follow. Paying to visit the house also gives admission to the Earl's **garden**, with its 400-year-old lime tree, cedar lawn and shell seat, decorated with shells reputedly provided by Captain Cook, whose voyages often began and ended in Plymouth harbour.

⑬ Kingsand and Cawsand

After the emptiness of the surrounding landscape, it can be a bit of a shock to find the peninsula's twin villages chock-a-block with visitors, enjoying the harbourfront views from the narrow streets and pavements, onto which, in Mediterranean style, tables and chairs spill. On my last visit the place was filled with the buzz of holiday chatter and the aromas of grilling fish and garlic. (This turned out to be a man barbecuing his mackerel on the harbour wall, but might just as well have come from any one of the harbourfront cafés and pubs.)

The two villages run into each other almost seamlessly, but the distinction was once important, as the stream running between the two marked the division between Devon and Cornwall, first established in the 10th century by Athelstan and not pushed back to the Tamar until 1844. A wall-mounted sign on the appropriately named Boundary Cottage close to the Halfway House Inn marks the old division.

During the summer, a **foot passenger ferry** leaves Cawsand Beach for Plymouth Barbican every 90 minutes or so. If arriving from Plymouth, be prepared to paddle the last few yards at low tide.

Food and drink

Cross Keys Inn The Square, Cawsand PL10 1PF Ⓣ 01752 822706 Ⓦ www.crosskeyscawsand.co.uk. The décor is definitely upmarket and the pub, overlooking the village square, is clearly popular with the boaty crowd. The well-kept real ales are popular with everybody though and the pub grub honest and unpretentious.

Halfway House Inn Fore St, Kingsand PL10 1NA ℗ 01752 822279
Ⓦ www.halfwayinn.biz. Cornish ales, such as Doom Bar and Betty Stoggs, local
fish and shellfish on the menu (best eaten in the bar; the dining room is not so
cosy) and the village male voice choir practises on Wednesday evenings. Child-
and dog-friendly.

Old Boat Store The Cleave, Kingsand PL10 1NF ℗ 01752 822568
Ⓦ wwwtheoldboatstore.co.uk. Arty café, with a relaxed ambience, overlooking the
sea. The menu is mainly vegetarian, plus fresh seafood when landed locally; take-
away picnics can be ordered with a bit of notice. A blue display cabinet is filled
with miniature bell-jars under which are displayed an odd collection of 'celebrity
leftovers', such as Pete Doherty's toast crust.

Rising Sun The Green, Kingsand PL10 1NH ℗ 01752 822840. Very jolly locals'
pub, friendly and welcoming. Spingo on tap (a much-admired ale rarely found
outside of its home town, Helston) and Skinner's Heligan Honey, too. An excellent
menu; live music Thu and Sat.

⑭ Rame and the Channel coast

Although only a mile up the hill from Cawsand, lonely Rame has a world's-
end feel to it. A scattering of small houses and a 13th-century church make
up the village, though the graveyard is filled to overflowing, there being no
cemetery in the twin villages below. Drowned boy sailors, smugglers brought
to justice, children, gig pilots and all their families, friends and enemies lie here:
a fascinating and poignant record of social history, inscribed in stone and slate.
Without electricity, the little church is lit by candles for services; the flickering
candlelight, brave against the winter night and black sea, creates a very special
atmosphere and ensures the Christmas Eve carol service is particularly well
attended.

Out on Rame Head, you can park by the volunteer coastguard building
and walk out on a spur from the coast path to a medieval stone chapel, close
to the site of an Iron Age cliff-fort, so utterly isolated that Rame feels almost
suburban by comparison. On a clear day, the headland just visible on the far
western horizon is the Lizard; to the south and east there are closer views of
shipping entering Plymouth Sound.

A clifftop road, overlooking the sandy beaches of **Whitsand Bay** wiggles
narrowly through scruffy chalet territory towards the MoD's Tregantle Fort
firing range, where it joins the steadier B3247 to Looe. If the red flags are not
flying, the beach below **Tregantle Cliff** is peaceful, wide and often empty;
easier access is to be found at **Sharrow Point** close by, which has National
Trust parking and steps down to the beach. The rip tides are ferocious.

∞∞∞

Food and drink

Blue Plate Main Rd, Downderry, PL11 3LD ℗ 01503 250308
Ⓦ www.blueplatecornwall.com. Accomplished gastro-bar, good at lunchtime for

a bowl of perfect soup, local cheeses or a plate of mussels and a glass of beer. The three-course dinners from the specials board are remarkable value considering the pedigree of the chefs at the helm.

Cliff Top Café Tregonhawke PL10 1JX ① 01752 822069. A gem of a greasy spoon, perched on the cliff side of the road between Rame and Freathy. Open all year, with a great friendly atmosphere that extends to children and dogs. The coffee is excellent, the cakes and scones homemade and the breakfasts just the job after an early beach walk.

The View Freathy PL10 1JY ① 01752 822345 ⓦ www.theview-restaurant.co.uk. Upmarket seafood eatery run by – though not necessarily for – surf dudes, with grand views over the sea. Fairly casual at lunchtime but distinctly smarter in the evening.

Around Looe

The hinterland east of Looe, hilly and wooded along the stream-fed valleys, is a world apart from the busy streets and harbour of the town. Narrow lanes and footpaths can be knitted together to make up some fairly challenging walks between Millendreath, the valley of the River Seaton and Bucklawren, for which you will need either the OS Explorer map 107 or the 'Bucklawren Countryside' walks leaflet, available in Looe TIC. It was a warm August day when I walked through Treveria and Keveral woods, following the Seaton path, and I didn't see another person all morning, just rabbits, roe deer and buzzards circling overhead.

⑮ The Sevenfold Labyrinth

In a field beside the coast path, midway between Looe and Seaton (grid reference SX282542), local resident Caroline Petherick has taken it upon herself to cut this meditational turf labyrinth, some 60 feet in diameter, giving walkers the opportunity to stop and reflect for a while. She identified the right spot by dowsing for the crossing of two ley lines and an appropriate blood sacrifice was made when her dog appeared with a freshly killed vole at the hole where the centre stone was about to be raised.

'You can go and sit there and realise the earth isn't such a bad place after all,' Caroline told me. 'It's just a gentle pleasure for people to enjoy. I live in a phenomenally beautiful place and I wanted to share it somehow.' Her next project is to create a refuge for coast-path walkers needing overnight shelter.

⑯ Murrayton Monkey Sanctuary

Murrayton House, St Martins, Looe PL13 1NZ ① 01503 262532
ⓦ www.monkeysanctuary.org.

It was swarming with children when I visited, but the affable keepers were doing a grand job, getting the message across that monkeys are not pets. While all eyes followed the monkeys as they pottered about in their huge, tree-filled, netted enclosures, the story of Leonard Williams unfolded. Williams, a teacher of Spanish guitar (and father of guitarist John Williams), was bequeathed a pet woolly monkey during the 1950s, and as time went on, acquired a few more. The leap from living in London with five pet monkeys to living in Cornwall came in 1964: here, in the large gardens, he could accommodate more and more rescued monkeys. By this time, Williams had come to understand the terrible effects of social deprivation on Amazonian woolly monkeys, and deplored the practice of slaughtering mothers in order to send their infants to pet shops and zoos. At Murrayton, the beasts were allowed to live as close as possible to their natural state in colonies, with minimal human contact, and with the first births, Williams saw his emerging colony regaining lost, instinctive skills and patterns of behaviour. However, attempts to rehabilitate young monkeys in their natural Brazilian environment foundered for all sorts of practical reasons, and now all the female monkeys are given contraceptive pills to stop the population growing beyond the means of the sanctuary, whose main responsibility these days lies in rescue and education.

The sloping site makes for good viewing, even when the monkeys are moving about high up in their enclosures or on rainy days, when they seek the shelter of the leafy canopy. There's a film room and a very good shop, or you can sit out the showers very happily in the Treetop Café, which serves child-friendly vegetarian food, cooked on the spot with local ingredients. The basket of apples on the counter came from the garden of the cook's mum.

Much of the monkeys' food comes from the sanctuary's gardens and orchards: local residents are invited to recycle vegetable waste in the sanctuary's giant compost stacks which all ends up in the garden.

⑰ Looe

Looe has everything you might expect of a Cornish seaside town: a sandy beach and fishing port, children crabbing off the harbour walls; quirky old buildings and steep narrow lanes oozing a history of smuggling and fishing; shops variously selling pasties or ice creams or fish and chips; beamy pubs and fishermen offering boat trips. I enjoyed the busy activity of Looe's fish market, the fun of being able to take a boat across the river to **West Looe** or down the coast to **Polperro**; I loved the unexpected music and the friendliness in a tiny crêperie, and it was great to be able to do it all by train.

But it all adds up to a bit of a mixed bag. I also watched, with embarrassment, a boat return ahead of schedule from a shark fishing trip, and disgorge its muscular, tattooed passengers, grinning all over at the skipper's refusal to accept their 'Ungentlemanly Behaviour on the High Seas'. I wonder what Nelson, the one-eyed grey seal, would have made of that. Nelson, who for 25 years made the sea around Looe his home and was much loved by local residents, became a kind of ambassador for all Cornish seals and his image and name were used in a successful campaign to increase awareness of Cornwall's

St George's (or Looe) Island

A mile out of Looe harbour, but only spitting distance from Hannafore Point to the north, the green, humpback form of St George's (or Looe) Island offers a tempting excursion for anyone looking for a quiet hour or two observing marine wildlife. The Cornwall Wildlife Trust runs a boat to the island from Easter to September (*01872 273939*), or check the information board by the Lifeboat Station in East Looe for sailing times. On arrival, there is a short briefing, given by one of the Trust's small team of volunteers who live and work on the island, about the kind of marine and island wildlife you might see and then you set off on your own to explore. The main house, built in the 19th century for customs officers to keep an eye on smugglers, was more recently home to the Atkins sisters, Babs and Evelyn, who bought the island in 1965, with a loan of £22,000. Their love of nature, at a time when the island might have been vulnerable to development, preserved the local biodiversity, and when Babs died in 2004, she bequeathed it to the Trust.

The woods and maritime heathland cover only 22.5 acres, but these are some of the least spoilt acres in Cornwall, rewarding close-up and respectful observation.

fragile seal colonies. When Nelson died in 2003, the town did not forget him. His statue, cast in bronze, was unveiled by Robin Knox-Johnston in 2008; it crowns the Pennyland Rocks, where the Looe River meets the sea.

If Looe is attempting to cast off its slightly tawdry reputation, it does so in style in early summer, when thanks to the RNLI, the town presents itself as a top Cornish foodiefest venue during the Looe Festival by the Sea (*www.looefestivals.org*). Local restaurateurs cook and serve up mainly seafood dishes all along the quay, and the Pengelly sisters, whose shop is supplied daily as the boats come in, set up a barbecue, filling the harbour with alluring whiffs of grilling fish.

The **Old Guildhall Museum and Gaol** in Higher Market Street (*01503 263826*) looks heavily restored from the outside, but this 15th-century building is still remarkably intact. The cells below and the magistrates' court above reveal an impressive stone and timber fabric, and the side rooms are stuffed with exhibits relating to Looe's boatbuilding, fishing and smuggling past. There is no room for storage, so everything's out on display – from a mastadon tooth to a grisly cat-o'-nine-tails.

Food and drink

Courtyard Café The Courtyard, Fore St, East Looe PL13 1AE ① 01503 264494. Just like walking into an old friend's home: there are sofas and papers to read, a guitar if you feel so inclined, a family-sized kitchen table to sit at and delicious sandwiches (the size of your head) on the menu.

Daisy's Café Castle St, East Looe PL13 1BA ① 07988 803315. A nice place to take children, and dogs are welcome too. Bright, cosy décor and luscious homemade cakes, daisy-shaped scones and spotty teapots.

Fisherman's Arms Higher Market St, East Looe PL13 1BW ① 01503 265800. Often packed with a jolly local crowd, one of Looe's more authentic pubs, with decent real ales, semi-spontaneous music nights and peat on the fire.

Larsson's 7 Buller St, East Looe PL13 1AS ① 01503 265368 Ⓦ www.larssonscoffeehouse.com. Something of an institution in Looe, thanks to Martin Noble (favourite artist: Carl Larsson), who has jammed more tables, music, good conversation, coffee and crêpes into a single space than you would think possible.

The Salutation Fore St, East Looe PL13 1AE ① 01503 262784. A locals' spit-and-sawdust pub, with low beams and a huge fire. Friendly staff, Doom Bar on tap and fish on the menu.

⑱ Talland Bay

Two pretty, sheltering coves with beaches, rockpools and summer-only cafés, and further towards Polperro, tiny Donkey Beach, are predictably popular in the summer. But I've been here in April sunshine and had the emerald and cobalt waters and soft sand almost all to myself. One improbably narrow, steep lane leads in and out of Talland; the village must heave a collective sigh at the seasonal influx of cars. On foot, following the clifftop coast path, the beaches are 45 minutes' walk from either Looe or Polperro; in summer there are, as one local resident put it, 'more skylarks than you can listen to with one pair of ears'. The church, wedged into a leafy shoulder of the cliff, stands almost alone (Talland is not so much a village as a cluster of scattered houses and farms) in a world of its own between the rising land and the open sea. The architecture is partly responsible for this feeling of self-containment: the tower, half buried in the grassy hillside, was built separately from the nave in the 13th century, but the gap was given a walk-through arch and roofed 200 years later, creating a narrow, cloistered approach between sheltering walls of granite.

⑲ Polperro

Seasonal boat trips venture from Looe to Polperro, a very enjoyable way to arrive in this picturesque fishing village, which has featured on more jigsaw puzzles and chocolate boxes than has been good for it. Alternatively, it makes sense to start in Talland Bay and walk a very pleasant mile or so along the coast path; otherwise you are more or less obliged to leave your car in the large Crumplehorn car park at the head of the valley and walk (or

take the electric 'omnibus'-style transport on offer) into the village, which takes less than ten minutes.

Although undeniably charming, the approach is crowded with touristy shops which may obscure its Slow appeal. Come very early on a summer morning, however, and the loudest noise is the River Pol, rushing beside the medieval lanes before disappearing under a 13th-century bridge and tumbling into the inner harbour. At this early hour, the hugger-mugger cottages and warehouses, threaded together by narrow paths around the stream and the harbour, where a small fish market still operates, or an unexpected encounter with a shell-encrusted façade of a fisherman's cottage, all make for enjoyable ambling. I couldn't help wondering how Polperro residents ever manage to get anything bigger than a medium-sized fish (let alone a fridge or sofa) into their houses. The **Polperro Heritage Museum of Smuggling and Fishing** in The Warren (*01503 2724230; www.polperro.org/museum.html*) is, as you might expect, dedicated to fishing and smuggling. The smuggling exhibits, which include tales of recent drug-smuggling activity, rather outdo the fishing ones in terms of excitement. Sadly, none of the exhibits address the vexing issue of furniture delivery over the ages.

Leaving Polperro by the westbound coast path, just a few yards on from the harbour and down a steep rocky path, you'll find a large semi-natural rock pool, big enough for half a dozen proper strokes, small enough for youngsters to get a taste of a wild, splashy swim.

Food and drink

Blue Peter Quay Rd PL13 2QZ ① 01503 272743 Ⓦ www.thebluepeter.co.uk. A welcoming, gossipy pub, full of laughter and locals and well known for its regular music nights. Blues Best, brewed specially for the pub by Sharp's, is always on tap, beside the usual suspects, Doom Bar and Tribute as well as cider from Cornish Orchards.

The Looe valleys

The branch line to Liskeard follows the leafy contours of the East Looe River, its single track occupying much of the footprint of the 19th-century canal that once ferried granite, copper and tin from the canal basin at Moorswater, just outside Liskeard, to the seaport at Looe. It's a peaceful journey, through broadleaf woods, shouldered by hilly farmland, serving a handful of small villages along the way. The West Looe River, muddily tidal and teeming with birdlife, is perfect for quiet woodland walks on either shore.

⑳ Along the West Looe River

For less than 50p, a little boat ferries passengers from the harbour at East Looe across the river to the town's westerly half, which is mostly residential. (You can walk across the bridge in half the time, but that's not the point.) The Looe library now houses the **South East Cornwall Discovery Centre**, where you can pick up the leaflet 'Explore Kilminorth Woods', or you can simply set off on the well-marked path to this oakwood nature reserve, which offers lovely views across the tidal shores of the West Looe River to broadleaf woodland on the far side.

On the north side, **Trenant Wood** belongs to the Woodland Trust, but is far less frequented by walkers and nature lovers, as it's quite difficult to find the way in. The trick is to head to the fiveways crossroads at Trenant Cross (grid reference SX246543) and head up the lane towards Polpever Farm. As the lane swings right, carry straight on up the track, to where it opens onto a wide grassy spot, where parking is permitted. Thereafter there are discreet signs indicating the footpaths through the woods and new plantations of native broadleaf trees, with glimpses of busy Looe far below across the river. It's a very special place to visit, which I would not have discovered had not Jo, from Treworgey Farm (see the *Accommodation* section on page 80) told me that it was her favourite walk.

㉑ Duloe

Jump off the train at **Causeland** and, after following the road south for about 400 yards, a footpath on the right leads through woods and fields to Duloe, passing the apple orchards at Westnorth Manor Farm on the way. This is the home of **Cornish Orchards** (*01503 269007;*  *www.cornishorchards.co.uk*), a cider farm run by Andy Atkinson, a true master of craft cider-making. April, when the orchards are in blossom, is the prettiest month to visit, and late October when the pressing is in full swing is the working end of the season. You won't get a guided tour, but if you catch Andy at a quiet moment he's willing to talk about the apples and the processes; juices and ciders can all be tried in the farm shop.

The footpath into Duloe spurs off beside the cricket pitch, and leads to a sheep-grazed paddock, where a Neolithic **stone circle** (oval to be more accurate), the smallest of its kind in Cornwall, sits unobtrusively beside a hedge. On the other side of the main road into the village, the **church of St Cuby** occupies an almost circular graveyard, which has given rise to speculation that this was once the site of an Iron Age hillfort. Inside the restored medieval church, there are several carved slate memorials to the wives and daughters of local landowners, dating from the 16th century.

The name of Maria Arundell is touchingly re-wrought as mixture of 'marigold' and 'laurel' and her short life likened to the brevity and beauty of those plants: 'Both feed the eye, both please the optic sense/Both soon decay, both suddenly fleet hence.'

Food and drink

The Plough at Duloe ① 01503 262556. This village pub, formerly Ye Olde Plough House Inn, had just been taken over and smartly relaunched under its new name by Barclay House (an upmarket Looe hotel) when I visited, but local reports were very positive, with the food receiving high marks. Real ales include the ever-popular Doom Bar, Tribute and Proper Job.

㉒ St Keyne

One of the joys of the branch line is that you can hop off at St Keyne, just round the corner from **Lametton Mill**, where the sound of music is likely to draw you towards a cavernous barn across the road from the old mill buildings. Paul Corin is the eccentric and charming *genius loci*, a man with endless bags of energy and enthusiam for restoring, displaying and enjoying his comprehensive collection of music machines, a collection started by his father, the last miller of St Keyne (*www.paulcorinmusic.co.uk*). Corin's own grandfather, Bransby Williams, who helped a young Charlie Chaplin start out on his career, can be heard in his role as Scrooge, on a Thomas Edison phonograph; a paper music roll fed into a 1927 reproducing piano emits a recording of Grieg playing one of his piano concertos in 1906; or if you ask, you can hear Rachmaninov or the great American jazz pianists of the 1920s and 1930s. The real star of the show, however, is a grand Wurlitzer organ, which was first played at the Regent Cinema in Brighton in 1929. This is what I could hear as I walked into the barn, played by Paul Corin with great affection and panache, to an audience of two spellbound teenagers and their mother: a marvellous moment.

A few minutes' walk along the road is a leafy spot where a **holy well** (grid reference SX248603) is supposed to confer marital authority on the first half of a newly wed couple to drink from it. You can almost hear the poet, Robert Southey, chuckling as he penned the last verse to his poem in which he tells of meeting a local Cornishman who believed in the well's magic properties:

I hastened as soon as the wedding was done,
And left my wife in the porch
But i'faith she had been wiser than me,
For she took a bottle to church.

㉓ Liskeard

'Fresh from the quaint old houses, the delightfully irregular streets, and the fragrant terrace-gardens of Looe, we found ourselves, on entering Liskeard, suddenly introduced to that "abomination of desolation", a large agricultural country town', wrote Wilkie Collins in *Rambles Beyond Railways,* when Cornish tourism was still in its infancy.

Today, good-looking towns that have resisted selling their souls to tourism are not thick on the ground in Cornwall, and handsome Liskeard is one of those I like best. Much of the town's good looks comes from the prosperity brought by the boom in mining during the 19th century, coupled with the Georgian vision of architect Henry Rice, who designed over a hundred houses in Liskeard for those who had grown rich on rising tin and copper prices. The **Liskeard Museum** (*Foresters Hall, Pike St; 01579 346087*) has a small display devoted to the architect, while the arts and heritage centre at **Stuart House** (*Barras St; 01579 347347*) has produced a Henry Rice Trail leaflet. This house is a real treasure; it was built 400 years before Rice first sat at a drawing board, and sheltered Charles I for a week during the Civil War. A couple of rooms are devoted to Civil War exhibits, but overall there's a wonderfully warm and intimate feeling about the granite and timber structure, which overlooks a courtyard garden, filled with clipped box and roses. This feeling stems, I'm sure, from the way the house is made available to the community. You can pop in for tea and homemade cake (for which a donation is asked) or sit in the garden; there are lunchtime concerts and evening lectures, craft fairs and demonstrations.

I couldn't help noticing, both in Stuart House and the museum as well as elsewhere in Liskeard's public buildings, some unusually beautiful doorknobs, made of blue glass. These are the work of local craftsman, Liam Carey of **Merlin Glass** (*Barn St; 01579 342399*), whose workshop can be visited by appointment. The shop is like a gallery in its showcases of these jewel-like glass knobs.

Part of Liskeard's charm is the high number of small, independent shops, like Liam's, which make it such an enjoyable place for pottering, but everyone I spoke to feared that many of these, like the famous weekly cattle market, held in the town centre, were at risk in such economically straitened times. Nevertheless, the agricultural show, held in July, remains one of the biggest events on the calendar and continues to uphold Liskeard's identity as an important centre for livestock sales.

Food and drink

60's Coffee Bar Windsor Pl, PL14 4BH ① 01579 340264. In an old butcher's shop, where the black-and-white floor tiles have been retained, Sandy Williams and Phil Hicks have created a joyfully atmospheric 1960s-style coffee bar, all the more authentic for being inexpensive and unpretentious. Period memorabilia adorns the walls, familiar songs play on the huge Wurlizer jukebox and Sandy and Phil are true aficionados of the era.

㉔ Carnglaze Slate Caverns

Near St Neot PL14 6HQ ⓣ 01579 320251 Ⓦ www.carnglaze.com.

Liskeard is fortunately placed for access both to the sea and Bodmin Moor. An evening at the tented, outdoor theatre at Upton Cross six miles to the north (see page 74), for example, is easily done from here. Even closer, on the Dobwalls to St Neot road, are the Carnglaze Slate Caverns, where evening concerts ranging from Tibetan chanting to glam-rock tribute bands are held in a cathedral-like, acoustically superb cavern. By day, you can wander round the former slate quarry (guided tours are obligatory at peak visiting times); the highest of the three vast chambers served as a rum store for the navy during World War II, the lowest is now filled by a spectacular, floodlit lake.Outside there are six acres of woods and gardens on a whimsical fairy theme to explore.

5. The Fowey Valley and Cornish Alps

Even by Cornwall's extraordinary standards of contrasts, you would be hard put to find a greater divergence in the landscape than in the few miles that separate the wooded, watery world of the Fowey, its towns and villages steeped in medieval history, from the almost lunar landscape of the clay pits above St Austell. Slow explorers will relish the individual characters of both – and gardeners (to whom the concept of Slow comes as readily as planting trees, I suspect), will discover here some of the most inventive and creative gardens in Cornwall, enjoying a brave, windswept garden on the cliffs of Polruan as much as a dazzling display of summer perennials in the Hidden Valley Gardens, or the ambitious Eden biomes and magnolia-filled slopes of Caerhays.

Industrial heritage is never far from view in Cornwall, but here the exploitation and export of China clay is current and active and still shaping the landscape. Rivers and streams run milky white around St Austell, cargo ships slip through the yachts and pleasure craft at Fowey to load up just out of sight at Carn Point; the conical white spoil heaps from the clay pits grow and change shape on the horizon. Cornish Alps, indeed!

Researching this chapter gave me some wonderful excuses to take to the water: paddling a canoe up Lerryn Creek, in the wake of Kenneth Grahame, riding the little passenger ferries from Polruan to Fowey and Fowey to Mevagissey and swimming in the turquoise sea at Lantic Bay. It also encouraged me to start rereading Daphne du Maurier, whose lyrical descriptions of the Cornish coast around Fowey had first enthralled me as a teenager. Walking in her footsteps above the beach at Polridmouth or gazing across the water to Bodinnick from the chain ferry animated my reading, and gave added allure to an already romantic landscape. The great thing about this stretch of the Cornish coast and estuary is that you don't need your own yacht to experience the thrill of seeing the land from the magically altered perspective of the sea. Returning to Fowey on the ferry from Mevagissey, I scanned the trees behind the red and white stripes of the Gribbin Daymark, hoping to glimpse the rooftops of Menabilly, the house that had been the inspiration for Manderlay in *Rebecca*. Then, like the novelist, cruising around the coast on *Ysdragil*, I saw 'the clay-hills hard and white on the western skyline. Then the slope of the Gribbin peninsula ... bracken-covered, green, and beyond it, hull-down between its coverage of trees, two chimney tops and the grey roof of Menabilly.'

Getting around

The A390 and A391 converge on St Austell, linking the town to Cornwall's principal arteries, the A38 and the A30, and Lostwithiel and Bodmin along

THE FOWEY VALLEY AND CORNISH ALPS

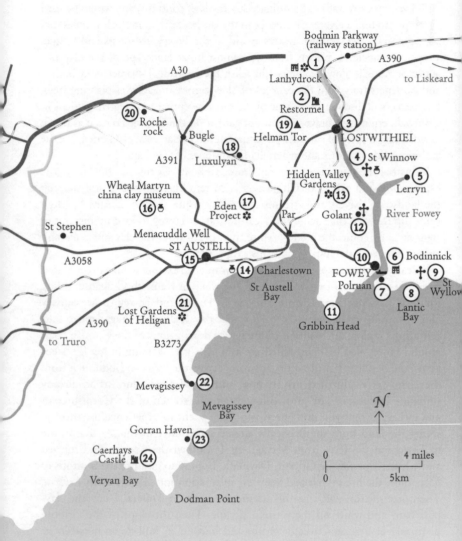

the way. Fowey, too is easily reached by road from Lostwithiel or St Austell (although it is unwise to even think of driving a car into its narrow, twisting streets). But east of the River Fowey, a tangle of tiny country lanes with desperately steep inclines make navigation a bit of an adventure; the six miles to Polruan from Lostwithiel could easily become 20 without a map. Similar adventures await those who venture into the cat's cradle of lanes south of Mevagissey, too.

Trains
Lostwithiel, Par and St Austell all lie on the main line from Paddington to Penzance and a branch line from Par runs northwest to Newquay, passing through the lovely Luxulyan Valley and, conveniently for walkers and cyclists, stopping at Luxulyan; Bugle and Roche are the next stops, more used by clay-industry commuters than visitors, but handy for cyclists accessing the clay trails or looking for the strangest of medieval hermitages.

Buses
The narrowness and steepness of the lanes around the Fowey estuary are impossible for buses to navigate, especially on the east bank, which keeps the local taxi cabs busy. On the west bank, even the simple journey north from Fowey to Lostwithiel means heading west first, and changing buses at Par. Around St Austell, buses run regularly to the major attractions: Eden Project, Wheal Martin, Mevagissey and Heligan, though beyond Gorran Haven the narrow, twisting lanes mean no buses, making Caerhays particularly inaccessible unless arriving by car or bike.

Ferries
There are no bridges across the Fowey below Lostwithiel, but a small eight-car ferry operates between Fowey and Bodinnick all year round. Queues for the ferry in the summer holidays are inevitable. The passenger ferry between Polruan and Fowey is a year-round service too; there are extra charges for dogs and bikes. Details of both services can be found at www.ctomsandson. co.uk. During the summer a passenger ferry crosses St Austell Bay between Mevagissey and Fowey, four or five times a day, depending on the weather (*www.mevagissey-ferries.co.uk*)

Cycling
A terrific section of the Sustrans NCN route 3 (the Cornish Way) passes through Caerhays, Mevagisssey, St Austell and Bugle and continues to Bodmin and Bude. Expect hills and clifftop views, plunging woods and white clay mountains. At St Austell, the route connects with the 'Clay Trails', offering off-road routes to Pentewan, Wheal Martin China Clay Museum and the Eden Project (*www.claytrails.co.uk*). The trails – particularly around Wheal Martyn – generally involve long inclines through spectacular wild country dramatically

altered by industry: clay pits, emerald pools and white spoil heaps, ruined chimneys and engine houses line the trails which were originally constructed for the transportation of clay.

Cycle hire

Pavé Velo Market House, St Austell PL25 3QL ① 01726 64950 ⓦ www.pavevelo. cc. An exciting new venture run by keen cyclists, father and son Nick andTom Finnemore (Pavé is a reference to the infamous cobbled Paris–Roubaix race in France), and very good news for cyclists on the Cornish Way, looking for a pitstop in the Feed Zone café and friendly chat. Bikes are hired by the day or for longer periods, advice and maps on local routes are always available too.

Pentewan Cycle Hire 1 West End, Pentewan PL26 6BX ① 01726 844242 ⓦ www.pentewanvalleycyclehire.co.uk. Right on the Sustrans route 3 and the gentle Pentewan section of the Clay Trails; bikes can be hired for upwards of half a day. Open Easter–end Sep.

Accommodation

Caerhays Estate Caerhays PL26 6LY ① 0800 032 6229 ⓦ www.nicheretreats. co.uk/caerhays. There are nine self-catering holiday cottages on the estate, all beautifully converted from estate buildings. The Fish Sheds (sleeps six) and Lime Kiln (sleeps two) are right on the beach, while the Lodge and Rabbit Warren are in the lovely gardens (see page 130). The Vean is a luxury country house (part- or fully catered accommodation), sleeping 16, furnished to suit the Georgian elegance of the building. Prices reflect the quality of the accommodation and the idyllic locations.

Court Farm Camping St Stephen PL26 7LE ① 01726 823684 ⓦ www. courtfarmcornwall.co.uk ⓔ info@courtfarmcornwall.co.uk. A campsite for stargazers: the low level of light pollution here has led to the creation of an observatory on the farm, which runs regular events for would-be astronomers. The land has been farmed by the Truscott family for 250 years and the quiet camping field is very much in tune with the family ethos of sensitive, sustainable land use. Expect average camping prices and don't forget torches - it really is very dark at night.

The Dwelling House at Fowey 6 Fore Street, Fowey PL23 1AQ ① 01726 833662 ⓦ www.thedwellinghouse.co.uk [email] enquiries@thedwellinghouse.co.uk. Highly recommended tea room with one double B&B in the centre of Fowey. Parts of the lovingly and sensitively restored house date from the 16th century. Very reasonable rates for such a special place.

Fowey Hall Hotel Hanson Drive, Fowey PL23 1ET ① 01726 833866 ⓦ www.foweyhallhotel.co.uk ⓔ info@foweyhallhotel.co.uk. Spacious and comfortable with a country house feel (there's a good-sized garden, too), families come here to unwind: the hotel is very child-friendly and there's nothing stuffy or pretentious about the elegance and luxury of the surrounds. And it's just a short walk from the beach at Readymoney Cove and the centre of Fowey. Prices are about double those of an average B&B.

Foye Old Exchange 12 Lostwithiel St, Fowey PL23 1BD ① 01726 833252 ⓦ www.foye-old-exchange.co.uk Ⓔ bandb@foye-old-exchange.co.uk. A B&B with a difference, close to the church in the middle of Fowey. Up until 1960, this was the Fowey telephone exchange and the owners, Celia and Michael Penprase, have acquired an extraordinary collection of telephones and telephonalia, all on display downstairs. Upstairs there are three double rooms (one has a four-poster); prices are average for Fowey. Note: there is no parking and it's a hilly walk to the nearest paying car park on the outskirts of Fowey.

Lombard Farm Mixtow PL23 1NA ① 01726 870844 ⓦ www.adventurecornwall. co.uk Ⓔ david@adventurecornwall.co.uk. There's a yurt, a tipi and two family-friendly cottages on this family-run idyll, all beautifully presented. Everything is geared towards making the most of the lovely outdoor location – canoeing and mountain-biking trips can be arranged.

Penquite Manor Youth Hostel Golant PL23 1LA ① 01736 833507 ⓦ www.yha. org.uk Ⓔ golant@yha.org.uk. A Georgian manor house in 3 acres of grounds overlooking the Fowey sounds like very upmarket holiday accommodation, but this is the Golant Youth Hostel, and a perfect spot for families on a budget. There's a kitchen for self-caterers, and a dining room where you can book an evening meal. Golant is a 20-minute walk: very pretty in daylight, but a torch is essential after sunset.

Tourist information centres

Fowey 5 South St, PL23 1AR ① 01726 833616.
Lostwithiel Pleyber Christ Way, PL22 0HA ① 01208 872207
ⓦ www.lostwithieltouristinformation.webs.com
Mevagissey St George's Sq, PL26 6UB ① 01726 844440 ⓦ www.mevagissey-cornwall.co.uk.
St Austell By Pass Service Station, Southbourne Rd, PL25 4RS ① 01726 879500 ⓦ www.visitthecornishriviera.co.uk. Hidden behind the Texaco garage on the Liskeard road out of town, it's convenient for drivers and cyclists on the Sustrans NCN route 3, but a fair hike from the train station if on foot.

The Fowey Valley

The River Fowey rises high on Bodmin Moor, in the shadow of Brown Willy, trickling through impenetrably marshy moorland before gathering pace in deep, wooded valleys on the southern fringes of the moor. Two or three miles short of Bodmin the green river valley takes a southerly turn, and overlooked by the grand old estates of Lanhydrock and the ruins of Restormel Castle, winds on to Lostwithiel, the medieval capital of Cornwall. Below Lostwithiel's ancient bridge the river becomes tidal, and the last six miles to the sea are sheltered by a glorious landscape of wooded hills and creeks, giving way to the purposeful movement of china clay by rail and ship above the yacht-strewn haven that lies between busy, popular Fowey and quieter, more self-contained Polruan. There's plenty of scope for Slow exploration here: the narrow streets of Lostwithiel, Fowey and Polruan make pottering a pleasure and the villages that lie in between, hidden among the woods and deep lanes, have a largely unselfconscious charm, unusual in Cornwall. The walking is superb, both above and below Lostwithiel, with a good network of well-marked footpaths on both sides of the river, while some of the most enjoyable canoeing in Cornwall is to be found in the tidal creeks below St Winnow.

This is the part of Cornwall that Daphne du Maurier loved with a passion and described so eloquently in her novels; and other writers such as Sir Arthur Quiller-Couch and Kenneth Grahame drew inspiration from the woods and water, too. On the beach at Readymoney Cove I saw a teenager, her iPod discarded, deeply immersed in *Rebecca;* and what better place than the riverbank in Lerryn to introduce the younger members of the family to Ratty, Mole and Toad?

① Lanhydrock

Bodmin PL30 5AD ① 01208 265950 Ⓦ www.nationaltrust.org.uk; National Trust.

Plenty of wow factor here, from the moment the pinnacled gatehouse comes into view, amidst a great sweeping roll of parkland, bisected by a long avenue of beeches. More wows as you look up through the formal gardens to the grand house, the church on the rising slopes behind and – if you visit in spring – the clouds of pink, red and creamy blossoms as hundreds of magnolias, camellias and rhododendrons erupt into bloom in the woodland garden. The formal gardens are an exercise in Victorian perfection: box-framed beds packed with a seasonal succession of bright bulbs and annuals, clipped yews and lawns so trim they might have been laid by a carpet-fitter. Inside the house, it's a bit like walking into the film-set for *Downton Abbey*: no fewer than 50 rooms inside the house are open to the public, furnished as they would have been in Lanhydrock's late Victorian heyday; the dining room is laid for dinner; the vast kitchens below reveal the colossal efforts of the 20 kitchen staff to keep the entire household fed and watered; and upstairs and well out of earshot, the nursery wing (designed to accommodate ten children and their nannies) and attics full of toys are as separate as the servants' quarters. The last time I visited, it was just before Christmas: a magic lantern show was in progress in the library and a wing-collared butler served me a tipple of mulled apple juice. All muddy from a wintry walk along the Fowey, I felt slightly under-dressed.

Lanhydrock is without doubt a jewel in the National Trust's Cornish crown, but it is a museum rather than a family home; great wealth does not guarantee heirs. The memorial plaques in the church tell the sad story of the last generation of the Agar-Robartes who made Lanhydrock great: the toll taken by World War I, and the last two sisters who died unmarried and childless. The estate came into the care and management of the National Trust in 1953. The church warden, who showed me how the altar had curiously migrated from the north to the east aisle, was also able to fill me in on the chequered history of the house and gardens. John Robartes, a wealthy merchant from Truro, built the original house in the mid 17th century on the site of a Benedictine priory. Four wings met at the gatehouse from which an avenue of sycamores unfurled towards the Fowey (a couple still survive). A century later, the east wing was demolished, leaving the gatehouse to stand alone, but opening up the views over the landscaped grounds. Fast-forward another century to 1857 and the high priest of the Gothic Revival, George Gilbert Scott, was busily employed, designing additions to the house which re-incorporated the gatehouse into the new garden walls. But scarcely was his work finished when, in 1881, fire destroyed everything bar the north wing, entrance porch and gatehouse, and the job of rebuilding fell to a pupil of Scott's, Richard Coad. Which is what you see today. After the fire, the layout was retained but the latest in gadgetry and creature comforts appeared, including an electric lift for taking trunks upstairs, a capacious bathroom, central heating and electric light.

During the winter months most of the house is closed, except on special opening days, but there's always a good log fire burning in the Servants' Hall café, a good pitstop if you've been exploring the woodland gardens (which remain open) and walks along the Fowey. The woods here take some beating: pass through the wooden gate (to your left as you approach the Servants' Hall) and the world suddenly changes. The Great Wood is criss-crossed with paths, each so inviting it's hard to know which way to turn, though the broad track that runs downhill to the river, known as the Lady's Walk, is perhaps the most popular – partly because it's the start of a lovely walk that takes in a stretch of the Fowey and brings you back to the house via the long beech avenue. In May, bluebells carpet the woodland floor beneath an emerging canopy of beech, oak and ash. And if you take one of the less-travelled paths, you'll discover an orchard of Britain's rarest tree, the Plymouth pear, established here, far from the danger of cross pollination, as part of a rare species recovery programme.

② Restormel Castle

Lostwithiel PL22 0EE ① 01208 872 687 ⓦ www.english-heritage.org.uk; open Apr–Oct; English Heritage.

His father, Richard Earl of Cornwall, had built castles at Launceston and Tintagel, but young Edmund had his eye on his father's latest acquisition: a motte and bailey hunting lodge overlooking a deer park and close to a little town, quaintly called 'The Place at the Tail End of the Woodland' (Lostwithiel in Cornish) that was rapidly prospering on tin, with its own port on the Fowey. Edmund's new castle, begun in 1271, was a circular edifice, built to impress. In fact it would have been dazzling: the high walls built of slate were rendered and limewashed white. Inside, there was even piped water. Edmund died in 1300, but Lostwithiel's glory years as a medieval Klondike City were already numbered; tinning activity upriver was causing the river to silt up, and by 1400 the port was available to only the flattest-bottomed craft. The castle was stripped and abandoned after the death of the Duchy's first duke, the Black Prince, and by the time of the Civil War it was already a ruin. Today, because there are so few vantage points from which the castle is visible, it's easy to visit Lostwithiel or even walk the path that skirts the hill on which it stands without a glimpse, but the walls still stand – and from their battlemented heights the views over the Fowey valley are sublime.

③ Lostwithiel

It's not difficult to be seduced by Lostwithiel. History oozes from its medieval stones and the river flows prettily beside Brunel's handsomely restored railway-carriage works (now flats and offices) and past invitingly grassy picnic places where you can dabble your toes in the shallows. Pottering comes easily here: antique and bric-a-brac shops, delis and cafés throng the main street; there's a free museum, dedicated to the town's far-from-dull history; and a cluster of characterful pubs serve locally produced food, ciders and ales.

But you'd miss an awful lot without some inkling of Lostwithiel's status and

Lanhydrock to Restormel Castle on foot

The train service between Lostwithiel and Bodmin Parkway is the key to making this a fine, car-free day's walking. (It's only seven miles, but hours can be spent exploring the house and gardens at Lanhydrock.) The footpath to Lanhydrock starts right by Bodmin Parkway and tracks the Fowey as far as the great beech avenue that leads to Lanhydrock House, a mile distant. Leave Lanhydrock by the Lady Walk through the Great Wood and the well-marked track to Restormel Castle picks up the Fowey again once it has skirted the waterworks. A quiet lane runs from Restormel to Lostwithiel, where there are lots of possibilities for refreshment before catching the train back to Bodmin Parkway; trains run roughly every hour.

importance in the 13th and 14th centuries, and its Civil War history. The best place to start is at the **medieval bridge**, which has spanned the Fowey for seven centuries. The Norman foundations of the first crossing are now buried under the road on the west side of the river, so what you see are 13th- and 14th-century arched additions, necessitated by a rapidly silting river altering its course.

The **Old Duchy Palace**, on the corner of Fore Street and Quay Street, is instantly recognisable by its solid buttresses and Gothic arched windows, suggestive of medieval ecclesiastical architecture. This however, was no church. The original building, constructed around 1292 – just as the paint was drying on the walls of Restormel Castle – was a vast administrative centre for the tin industry, for the Duchy and for Cornwall. Tin was brought here to be assayed, weighed and stamped; licences were granted for sale and export; stannary courts administered tin-related justice, the county court covered the rest; and wrongdoers were held in its prison. The oldest recorded strongroom for business activity was contained within its walls too, together with counting rooms – in effect, a prototype bank. In total, the complex covered two acres, overlooking the busy port. Like Restormel Castle, however, its glory was transient, ironically curtailed by the same industry that had created its wealth and prestige. Silt washed down by tinning activity blocked the port and Fowey, at the mouth of the river, prospered instead. By Elizabethan times, new wealth from tanneries rescued the sagging building, but it had lost much of its status. In 1644 some of the bloodiest and most destructive fighting during the Civil War took place in Lostwithiel, where a besieged Parliamentarian army fell to Royalist forces. The Duchy Palace was burned and in the slow reconstruction of the town, parts were dismantled to make way for new buildings in which much of the old stone was recycled. So although substantial, the building left standing today is just a fraction of the old palace, and though in the safe hands of the Duchy, has yet to find a new purpose.

The tower of **St Bartholomew's**, the parish church, was probably built in Edmund's time, and the Black Prince would have seen the nave under construction, during his periods of residence at Restormel in 1353 and 1365. (The Breton-style octagonal spire which neatly tops off the tower was added at the same time.) But like the palace, it suffered at the hands of the occupying army during the Civil War, when it was used as a garrison and stables. Records of 1644 tell of a horse christened at the font by Parliamentarian troops, who jeeringly called it 'Charlie' and of a barrel of gunpowder that was deliberately exploded beneath Royalist prisoners, cowering in the belfry.

The free **museum** on Fore Street (*www.museumsincornwall.org.uk; open Mon–Sat*) is housed in the Georgian corn exchange and run by local historians. Betjeman is reported to have said that there is history in every stone in Lostwithiel and his words are borne out here with a fascinating series of exhibits that runs into the old jail at the back of the building. One of the star exhibits though, pre-dates the town's glory days under Edmund. It's a small, gilded figure of Christ, dating from the late 12th century, found in a field near the town in 1894 and then lost again. It turned up exactly 100 years later, hidden in a desk.

The museum organises **guided walks** around the town every Thursday between April and September at 11.00, starting from the community centre, just off Liddicoat Road.

It seems appropriate that a town with so much ancient history should have become the 'antiques capital' of Cornwall, and there's a bit of a buzz on alternate Fridays when the popular **antiques market**, held in the community centre. comes to town. A good place to find information about Lostwithiel's antique shops and market is under the 'Go Shopping' section of www. lostwithiel.org.uk.

Food and drink

These days Lostwithiel has a name for promoting local food and drink producers and counts as one of the top **Slow Food** destinations in Cornwall. The food shops – butcher, baker, deli – are outstandingly good and on alternate Fridays the Cornish Guild of Smallholders run a terrific local produce market in the community centre (*www.cornishfood.org.uk*). October sees a 'grass roots' **cider festival** (*www. cornishciderfestival.co.uk*), growing in size and popularity each year.

Bellamama Deli 24 Fore St ① 01208 872524. A great spot to pick up picnic items or perch in the window seat for coffee and buns.

Duchy Café 10 Fore St ① 01208 873184. Cosy and traditional tea rooms doing breakfasts, lunches and afternoon teas.

Earl of Chatham Grenville St ① 01208 872269. A St Austell Brewery pub, popular with locals and serving good pub grub (the local sausages are excellent). Child friendly and well-behaved dogs welcomed too.

Globe 3 North St ① 01208 872501. Real ales at this pub include Skinner's Betty Stoggs and Doom Bar, as well as guest ales. Its established reputation for good food, sourced from local suppliers is well deserved.

Canoeing down the River Fowey

Lostwithiel is not a place to hurry through and that suited us, because we were planning to leave in a canoe, on the outgoing tide. By the time we had done exploring the medieval backstreets and alleyways, it was clear that the tide had been ebbing for some time, which was good, but not having canoed the river before, we had no degree of certainty about how long it would take to paddle ourselves clear of the muddy junction with Penpol Creek, three or four miles downstream and into the broader, deeper waters of the Fowey below Golant.

But it was a bright October morning and with the river flowing fast and shallow we put in on the slipway by the gateway to Coulson Park, with hopes that we would not find ourselves stranded on a mudbank, halfway to Fowey.

(Not least because in the early morning haste to seize the day, the sandwiches had been left behind.) The current took us gently out of the town and within minutes we were gliding past the rushy margins of Madderly Moor on our left and Shirehall Moor to the right: saltmarsh vegetation, stalked by herons and egrets. The water was very shallow now, and our paddles brushed the shingly river bed more often than was comforting. And, as the morning grew warmer and the tower of St Winnow appeared through the trees, the mid-river channel we were following dwindled to a winding trickle; on either side the receding tide had exposed huge mudbanks, making landfall impossible.

From time to time I would hop out and push the canoe along, the water barely covering my ankles. It was hardly the stuff of epic canoe journeys, and we were advancing at the pace of a slow shuffle, but it was  none the less magical. Waders and gulls poking about at the muddy shoreline barely glanced at us, the oak woods as we approached Lerryn Creek were the colour of tawny marmalade, and a slow locomotive pulling a seemingly endless string of trucks overtook us on the western bank. Our mid-river trickle forked between great mudbanks; we took a guess and paddled on, heartened by the deepening water and the rooftops of Golant, rising on the hillside ahead.

The tidal outflow had reached its lowest point as we finally emerged into deep water, rounded a bend and were suddenly dwarfed by a container ship; our train, which had been carrying china clay was unloading its freight. We passed, slightly awestruck by the sudden industrialisation of the landscape, and then it was behind us and we were passing between yachts at their moorings and Fowey was just ahead ... and so we landed, leaving the canoe in the car park by the chain ferry and, carrying the paddles, set off to explore the narrow streets of Fowey on foot.

We were thinking of returning to Lostwithiel by bus to collect the car, but spotted an empty table in Sam's and gave in to a late lunch. It turned out to be one of those lingering meals you don't want to end. Fish was on our plates and in the conversation with the cook, who came and sat with us for a while and talked about their new venture on the beach at Polkerris. By the time we had finished, it was clear the tide was rushing back upstream and all thoughts of catching a bus evaporated. This was a different river! Swept along by the tide, we only needed the paddles to steer, weaving our way back through the yachts and past the china clay dock; both ship and train had vanished. Lerryn Creek was rapidly approaching and after a minute's discussion we swung right, allowing ourselves to be propelled into the creek, between woods, muddily undercut by the water. For a mile we paddled and stalled and paddled, travelling as slowly as possible, to allow time for the swelling tide to carry us through the woods as far as Lerryn.

Boconnoc in bloom

The Cornwall Garden Society has over 1,000 members, and its annual show at the beginning of April in the grounds of Boconnoc (*Lostwithiel PL22 0RG; www. boconnoc.com*) attract many more visitors besides. The road out of Lostwithiel is nose to tail with cars heading towards this extravagant plant festival, timed to coincide with the flowering of Cornwall's finest camellias. The woodland gardens surrounding the house are open (for charity) every Sunday in May only, when the rhododendrons and bluebells are at their peak. It's a wonderful opportunity to see the recently restored Domesday manor (from the outside) too, bought in 1717 by Thomas Pitt (grandfather of the prime minister William Pitt) with proceeds from the sale of the whopping 'Pitt diamond'.

In the end, we just made it; the stepping stones that cross the creek were still dry, so we had wet feet for the last 50 yards as we hauled the canoe up to the landing beach, for collection the following day. The three-mile walk back to Lostwithiel through the oak woods of the Ethy estate and narrow hedged lanes was filled with dusky birdsong.

Experienced paddlers can hire a kayak from **Fowey Kayak Hire** (① *01726 833627* Ⓦ *www.foweykayakhire.co.uk*) for independent days or half-days out on the river. Accompanied trips for the less experienced are available at Fowey River Expeditions, run by the same outfit. **Encounter Cornwall** (① *07976 466123* Ⓦ *www.encountercornwall.co.uk*), based in Golant, offer guided canoe trips on the Fowey and canoe hire for those with recent experience of independent canoeing or kayaking.

④ St Winnow

A rural backwater hidden among the woods and cider orchards on the east bank of the Fowey, St Winnow is almost too lovely to be true. There's too little of it to be spoiled, just a tiny rough-and-ready farm campsite in an orchard you can sail or paddle to with your tent. There's a shed full of old tractors and agricultural memorabilia, calling itself a museum; tea and cakes are sold from a caravan; and an ancient church on the riverbank. The narrow lane that ends at the farm is not easy to negotiate by car; far better to arrive on foot or by bike, or by canoe, when the tide is high enough to land.

⑤ Lerryn

Straddling the uppermost reach of Lerryn Creek, where the diminishing water is crossed by a Tudor bridge – and stepping stones at low tide – Lerryn is one of those magical places that those who live there or discover while on holiday, hug quietly to themselves in the hope that it will always stay the same. Kenneth

Grahame loved Fowey and often visited Lerryn by water; it's nice to think that the creek is reflected in the leafy, watery world of *The Wind in the Willows*. (Ethy Manor, hidden in the woods above the village, some like to say, could have been Grahame's inspiration for Toad Hall.) This is a blissful place for children, with plenty of safe opportunities for messing about at the water's edge, or in boats or canoes, though the tidal ebb and flow is not to be messed with.

Although it swells with holidaymakers in the summer, the village is a real community, with a school, top-notch shop and pub. In December, between Christmas and New Year the village jollies itself up in fancy dress for the annual Seagull Race. Seagulls (lest your imagination be taking flight in the wrong direction) are a spluttery type of low-power outboard motor; lashed to pretty much anything that floats, the result is a water-borne type of pram race that would set Toad's heart racing.

Food and drink

Ship Inn ① 01208 872374. A perfect village pub: friendly, beamy and slate-floored, serving a good range of Cornish ales and above-average pub food. Children and dogs are made to feel very welcome.

⑥ Bodinnick

Daphne du Maurier's name will always be linked with Bodinnick, whose pretty cottages and ancient pub cling to an impossibly steep hill that terminates abruptly on the slipway of the small chain ferry that links the village to Fowey. Ferryside, the big white house with the blue paintwork, built against the cliff face to the right of the slipway, is where the 19 year old fell in love with this part of Cornwall. She persuaded her parents, who had bought the house for holiday visits, to let her use it as a writer's retreat. Soon after, she wrote in her diary: 'The lights of Polruan and Fowey. Ships anchored, looking up through blackness. The jetties, white with clay. Mysterious shrouded trees, owls hooting, the splash of muffled oars in lumpy water ... All I want is to be at Fowey. Nothing and no one else. This, now, is my life.'

Four years later, in 1932, Major 'Boy' Browning sailed into the Fowey estuary, looking for her. He had read her first novel, *The Loving Spirit,* and fired by her descriptions of the Cornish coast, was determined to meet the woman behind the prose. A few weeks later, they were married – at the lonely church of St Wyllow, high in the hills behind Polruan. Her husband's military career often took her away from Bodinnick, but Ferryside remained their base until 1943, when they moved into the grand house at Menabilly (Manderlay in *Rebecca*) on the other side of the Fowey.

Ferryside was restored by her son, Christian Browning, who lives there; the house is not open to the public.

The small chain ferry runs cars, bikes and foot passengers to and from

The Hall Walk

Despite being well known and well signposted, this four-mile riverside and creekside walk from Bodinnick to Polruan can be made to feel like an adventure, by using the all-year ferries to cross the river. You can start at Fowey, take the chain ferry to Bodinnick, then follow the Hall Walk, along the River Fowey and up the creek known as Pont Pill and back on the other side of Pont Pill to Polruan where the passenger boat takes you back to Fowey. The woods touch the water all along the shore and the path rises and falls, with the odd well-placed seat along the way. Allow yourself three hours, which will leave enough time to make the short detour to St Wyllow; allow longer if planning to explore Polruan and Fowey.

Fowey, all year round. (The alternative is to cross the river at Lostwithiel, six miles upstream.)

⑦ Polruan

Polruan looks across the estuary to fashionable Fowey with its packed streets and pubs, smart restaurants and celebrity residents and just seems to shrug, for it has the one thing that Fowey can't have: a picturesque view of Fowey across the water. Polruan's isolation from any main road (it's at least 45 minutes to Fowey on narrow lanes, via Lostwithiel) has given the village a quiet, self-contained character, much appreciated by its resident population of boatbuilders, artists, writers and retired folk and a community spirit that was described with great warmth by the volunteer coastguard I chatted to, while his gaze swept the sea and the estuary below his clifftop vantage point, beside the ruins of the 13th-century **St Saviour's Chapel,** built on 8th-century foundations. An hour or more passed easily in his company, as he told me of his concern that the volunteer coastguards, while offering an incredibly important service 'might put the professional chaps in coastguard stations threatened with closure out of a job'.

We talked too, of the brave and lovely **Headland garden,** perched on the exposed cliffside below us, and which opens on Thursday afternoons in the summer, and of the community's passionate regard for its heritage. This was something I had already noticed, down at the harbour, where a plaque proudly announces that the Old Coal Wharf had been acquired in 1963 'on the initiative of Polruan people supported by public subscription (and) administered by Polruan Town Trust since 1973'. The 14th-century **blockhouse** has been preserved by local initiative, too. Originally, there had been a similar building on the Fowey side of the estuary (which, with a sad shake of the head, they will tell you in Polruan, was allowed to crumble beyond hope of repair) and chains slung between the two buildings could be raised to prevent pirates or worse still, the French, from entering the harbour.

Food and drink

There are two cheerful pubs in Polruan, both owned by the St Austell Brewery: the **Lugger** (*01726 870007*) next to where the ferry lands is well placed for harbour-watching; the **Russell Inn**, up a side street, is smaller and full of character. (*01726 870292*). Both serve food and are child- and dog-friendly.

⑧ Lantic Bay

This is one of Cornwall's best south coast beaches, and the effort of getting to it from the National Trust car park (*PL23 1NP*) a mile away ensures it's never overcrowded. A wide horseshoe of pale sand, studded with outcrops of rock, and turquoise sea is the reward for those prepared to walk the sloping fields and plunging final descent. At low tide, a succession of smaller, sandy coves are revealed towards Polruan, often visited by boating families out of Fowey. The cove is known, however, for its occasional rip currents, and great care should be taken if you're contemplating a swim. From Polruan, the mile and a half of clifftop walking eastwards to here gets choice views all the way.

⑨ St Wyllow

Grid reference SX145515.

Restored, but not wrecked in the 19th century, the tall-towered church at Lanteglos-by-Fowey is buried quietly among the woods and fields, high above Polruan. Daphne du Maurier was married here and it's as romantic and lonely a spot as a novelist could wish for – but a long walk for the faithful of Polruan and the surrounding hamlets (though handy for the farm next door). Inside, the woodwork is particularly special and the Tudor bench ends, showing fish and faces, birds and animals, are among Cornwall's finest, which is saying something.

⑩ Fowey

The steep, narrow streets lined with jostling cottages, shops, cafés, pubs and restaurants are great fun to explore, though you may find yourself flattened against a wall each time a car attempts to squeeze past. Tantalising views of the glittering estuary are glimpsed through tiny passages, like windows onto the busy river. Enjoying Fowey from the water is an altogether different experience; in the early morning for instance, when mist still hangs over the river or at dusk, with lights glimmering, the town rises enchantingly from the shore.

Like Falmouth, at the mouth of the next river to the west, Fowey's waters are deep and wide, allowing heavy shipping passage for a mile or so upriver, where they lurk unseen from the town. But whereas on the Fal the container ships are merely heading to deep-water anchorage, on the Fowey they are heading to meet the china clay train at Carn Point dock. The incongruous mixture of huge freighters, pleasure boats and ferries is one of the special features of taking in the scenery from Fowey's waterfront: there's such a mixture of commercial and leisure activity to watch.

Fowey's architecture is equally fascinating: by turn Elizabethan, Edwardian, Georgian and Victorian, reflecting the non-stop development of the port from medieval times as it gradually took over from Lostwithiel, right up to the present day. The long and colourful history of Fowey is told in the town's **museum** in the town hall (*www.museumsincornwall.org.uk; Easter–mid Oct open Mon–Fri,*) full to bursting with model ships, nautical memorabilia, and other curiosities, such as the contents of a medieval 'garderobe' (or toilet), of particular fascination to social anthropologists investigating the diet of Fowey, c1400. Children obsessed with pirates will be impressed by the exhibits relating to the 'Fowey Gallants' a band of privateers licensed to attack French shipping in the Channel during the Hundred Years War, who got rather above themselves and saw any ship, friend or foe, as fair game. Privateers usually ended up as an embarrassment to those who had granted their licences in the first place and this lot of pirates was no exception. They were eventually tricked into a trap at Lostwithiel and several hangings took place to make the point. Nevertheless, you'll still see plenty of Fowey Gallants on the water today – it's the name of the local sailing club.

When you look across the water to Fowey, two buildings stand out, high on the hillside above the lesser rooftops: the church of **St Finbarrus** and behind it, the grey tower and castellated walls of **Place House**, home of the Treffry family since the 13th century. Sadly, it's not the original building: the house was rebuilt in the first half of the 19th century to suit the grandiose taste of mining tycoon, Joseph Treffry. The architectural historian Nikolaus Pevsner described it as 'elephantine'; a little harsh, perhaps. It's not open to the public as Treffrys still live in it.

Readymoney Cove begins where the town ends, so it's a predictably busy little beach, but nonethless perfect for paddling tired feet if walking the hilly peninsula. Sheltered by the encircling wooded hills that rise above it faces east – great for breakfast on the beach with the sun rising behind Polruan on the far shore of the estuary. **St Catherine's Castle**, on the rocky headland above the beach, was built around 1530 at an early stage of Henry VIII's plan to boost coastal defences against French invasion. (Pendennis and St Mawes, built a decade later, seem much more sophisticated by comparison.)

Food and drink

Fowey is packed with places to eat and drink; the ones with good views of the harbour get very busy in the summer.

The Lifebuoy Lostwithiel St ① 01726 834858. A tiny café with a nice, old-fashioned feel that does spectacularly good breakfasts. Everything on the menu comes from named, local suppliers, the fish fingers are homemade and best appreciated in the Lifebuoy's signature dish, the fish-finger butty.

Pinky Murphy's Café 19 North St ① 01726 832512. Inside, it's all colourful,

Joseph Treffry

The Treffrys have stamped their name indelibly on Fowey's history and the surrounding landscape. In 1457, when the French broke through the defences at the mouth of the harbour and ransacked Fowey, Place House was the prize they were denied thanks to the efforts of Elizabeth Treffry, who organised her household to repel the invaders by pouring molten lead, collected from the roof, onto the heads of the French. But it was Joseph Treffry, born three centuries later, who claims the greatest attention. Nicknamed the King of mid-Cornwall, he built a mining empire that encompassed the harbours he built at Newquay and Par, confronting engineering problems that even Brunel was reluctant to address. Copper, tin, granite and clay from his mines were funnelled through railways conceived and built by Treffry – and water, so necessary to the industry, was channelled through miles of leats, including one that ran over the ten-arch Treffry viaduct in the Luxulyan Valley.

mismatched furniture and quirky displays of seaside retrobilia; upstairs squashy sofas, newspapers and magazines – and a logburner. The menu is big on soups, smoothies and 'fatboy' hot chocolates: just the thing after a morning on the river.

Sam's Fore St ☏ 01726 832273. Specialises in local seafood, caught in the morning and dished up at lunchtime. There's a big choice of homemade burgers too. It's much loved by locals and with a no-bookings policy, the queues in the summer can be daunting.

Ship Inn Trafalgar Sq ☏ 01726 832230. Built in 1570 by John Rashleigh, the long history of the pub is displayed on the walls beside the open fire and oak panelling. It's now a St Austell Brewery pub, with a good seafood menu.

Literary Fowey

Fowey seems to exercise a particular hold over writers, in the same way that St Ives continues to draw its artists. Daphne du Maurier is the most famous of these, but the town also celebrates the work of Sir Arthur Quiller-Couch, poet, novelist, critic and likeable eccentric who lived on the opposite shore, just above Bodinnick. It was 'Q', as he styled himself, who penned the following memorable ditty:

Oh the harbour of Fowey
Is a beautiful spot
And it's there I enjowey
To sail in a yot;
Or to race in a yacht
Round a mark or a buoy -
Such a beautiful spacht
Is the harbour of Fuoy!

… leaving readers no chance of mispronouncing the name of his adopted home town.

A small bookshop-cum-exhibition space, the **Fowey Literary Centre** (*5 South St; 01726 833619*), shares the task with the museum of promoting these and other writers, both home-grown and from further afield, who owe their inspiration to the estuary.

The **du Maurier Festival** (*www.dumaurierfestival.co.uk*), held each May since its inception in 1997, has become a huge affair, spanning ten days and attracting big names as speakers; the events, which include music, exhibitions, guided walks, boat trips and open gardens, spill out into the neighbouring villages and countryside.

⑪ Around Gribbin Head

A demanding circular walk of six and a half miles starting and finishing in Readymoney Cove takes in the cove and beach house immortalised in Daphne du Maurier's *Rebecca*, the 84-foot-tall red- and white-striped Gribbin Daymark, a choice of delicious pitstops on Polkerris Beach and the last two miles of the Saints' Way.

The first mile and a bit to Polridmouth ('Pridmouth') Cove follows the clifftop coast path before descending steeply through woods to a sandy beach, separated from an ornamental lake by a raised walkway. The lake is the lowest of three created during World War II as a decoy to the gathering military activity in Fowey harbour during preparations for D-Day: the US 29th Division were loading ammunition for the Omaha Beach landing and lights were floated on the lake to distract approaching enemy aircraft. Out of sight, among the trees is Menabilly, the seat of the Rashleigh family since the 16th century. Daphne du Maurier lived in the house for the last 25 years of her life, enthralled by the secret spot which she had transformed, years before living there, into Manderley.

The coast path swings back up the cliff towards the Daymark, which is open on Sundays throughout the summer. The views from the foot of the stripy tower are impressive enough, but if you climb to the top, the views over inland Cornwall as far as Bodmin and the Tamar Valley to the east are outstanding. It was a Rashleigh of Menabilly who granted the land and materials for the building of a 'very handsome Greco-Gothic square tower', designed to ornament his view as well as contributing to 'the safety of commerce and … the preservation of mariners'. History does not record what the inhabitants of Lanlivery, up near Lostwithiel, thought about the Daymark. For centuries their church tower had been the landmark for ships entering Fowey, and in medieval times an annual coat of whitewash to the south face was paid for by the Crown.

Beyond the tower, the path follows the west-facing cliffs northwards to Polkerris with its views from the beach of the docks and sands of Par across St Austell Bay. The Rashleigh Arms is a much-loved pub almost on the beach

– the food and ales are excellent. Next door an upmarket café, Sam's on the Beach (an offshoot of Sam's in Fowey) attracts a youngish crowd, and there's also a third café, selling more conventional beach snacks. The trouble is you can get too comfortable in Polkerris, nicely placed for the afternoon and evening sun, and the walk back over the hills to Readymoney Cove starts with a bit of a climb out of the village to pick up the Saints' Way trail. But the walk back through Tregaminion Farm, crossing fields and streams is lovely and the last stretch along Love Lane, which follows an old packhorse route, is downhill and wooded.

⑫ Golant

An old pilgrim route (now a long-distance footpath) the Saints' Way passes the sequestered church of **St Sampson**, high above the picturesque village, which hugs the tidal shoreline of the river below (this is the only access point on foot to the west bank of the river between Lostwithiel and Fowey). Legend has it that King Mark married Isolde here; I was transfixed by the exhibition in the church in which the Tristan legend was retold in a series of creative floral arrangements, which thankfully, have been recorded for posterity in photographs. Despite some sympathetic renovation in 1842, the building has hardly been changed since it was consecrated in 1509, the date carved on the

The Tristan Stone

The tragedy of Tristan and Isolde unfolds between Ireland, Cornwall and Brittany, but much of the action centres around the court of King Mark, who was probably a genuine historical figure – a 6th-century Cornish chief and possible contemporary of Arthur.

If you are approaching Fowey by road, just after the turning to the Bodinnick Ferry, a large granite stone appears on the left, inscribed in Latin. The stone was moved here from Castle Dore, (a rather self-effacing Iron Age hillfort) just above

Golant, which has had a long history of association with King Mark. The stone marks the death of 'Drustanus', a Latinised form of Tristan, and names him as the son of Cunomorus, a Latinised form of Kynvawr, who was identified in the 9th century as Marcus Kynvauwr. There's no proving anything, but if the sad story of Tristan, Isolde and King Mark (so reminiscent of the Arthur–Lancelot–Guinevere love triangle) is the sort of thing you enjoy, then the roadside appeal of the Tristan Stone will be limited, but there are worse places than the mossy churchyard of St Sampson's to mull over the evidence.

arched roof timbers overhead. Three original box pews survive and both pulpit and stalls are clad in old recycled bench ends.

Golant is the closest village to the idyllically isolated **Sawmill Studios,** a residential hideaway (approached only by boat or footpath) that has attracted some heavyweight names from the music industry over the past four decades. The **Fisherman's Arms**, Golant's much-loved pub, is a proper local, unpretentious and welcoming to dogs and children. Given the proximity of the studios, there's no knowing who you might bump into.

⑬ Hidden Valley Gardens

Treesmill PL24 2TU ⓣ 01208 873225 ⓦ www.hiddenvalleygardens.co.uk; open late Mar–mid-Oct except Tue and Wed.

Tucked away in a fold of the landscape, below the railway line from Lostwithiel to Par, Peter and Tricia Howard have created a four-acre garden of intimate and intense beauty, filled with a rainbow palette of perennials, which lingers late into the season. It's unusual, in this part of Cornwall, to find a garden that isn't dedicated to spring flowering trees and shrubs; the Howards have done well to establish themselves at the forefront of a new breed of smaller Cornish gardens that really sing throughout the summer and autumn.

Around St Austell and the Cornish Alps

The white peaks and plateaus of the clay spoil heaps can be seen from 40 miles away, and suggest a lunar desert when seen in satellite images. It's a powerful, manmade landscape, crossed by roads and cycle trails where you feel a million miles from the leafy creeks and picturesque coves that decorate the Fowey, just a handful of miles away, or the rich seam of gardens that lie on either side of St Austell.

⑭ Charlestown

St Austell was served by several ports in its industrial heyday, but none prettier than Charlestown, named after Charles Rashleigh, who funded the entire project in order to provide the infrastructure to his and clay and copper exports. There was a foundry and tin-smelting house as well as dry-stores for clay; the level of activity during building (1790–1810) and after completion must have been phenomenal. It gets distinctly busy these days too: with its film-set looks, Charlestown has become a sort of open-air museum, thanks to the permanent presence of at least one or two splendid **square-riggers**, moored in the narrow harbour and the well-preserved terraces of Georgian houses and cottages. The *Earl of Pembroke, Kaskelot* and *Phoenix*, like all tall ships are breathtakingly handsome and earn their keep as training ships and film stars (*Kaskelot* starred in *Shackleton* and *The Three Musketeers,* the *Earl of Pembroke* in *Hornblower*, and years ago on TV's *The Onedin Line*), and there's the chance to go aboard when the ships are 'resting' between film and TV appearances. All three ships are replicas, built in the 20th century, but no less impressive. At various times in the summer, hands-on 'cruises' (don't expect cruise-style accommodation though) along the Cornish or Breton coast are available to novice sailors, looking for a taste of tall-ships adventure (*www.square-sail.com*).

The **Charlestown Shipwreck and Heritage Centre** (*01726 69897*), housed in a former dry store for china clay, concentrates on diving, salvage and rescue stories and exhibits, and you can explore the underground tunnels where clay was stored.

⑮ St Austell

St Austell is surrounded by so many good gardens, museums, walks and bike trails that it seems to have forgotten to look after its own identity, which has been slightly squashed by the large new shopping centre occupying the town centre. Followers of the architect Silvanus Trevail will have a field day though, peering up at sumptuous Victorian façades, and there's been a local sigh of relief that the lovely old **Market House** has been given a new lease of life, with cafés, shops and a local produce market on Saturdays. It's true too, that St Austell is gradually acquiring a new identity, as a centre for green technologies, that's partly due to its proximity to the Eden Project but also to the five 'eco-villages', heralded as models of sustainability which will soon be emerging from disused clay-mining sites around the town.

St Austell Brewery

Industry needs its ale (especially in an area where temperance was being vociferously preached) and Walter Hicks was the entrepreneur who saw the business opportunity. His family had been farmers for over 400 years, but he mortgaged the farm and set himself up as a maltster, then a wine-and-spirit merchant, before building his first brewery in 1869.

By 1893 the business had outgrown the building and the Walter Hicks Brewery moved to Trevarthian Road, where the family business has become something of a local institution, employing generations of the same families and, up until very recently, still using the 1890 belt-driven barley mill and heating mash in even older cast-iron tuns. The company is revered locally for other reasons too: as a supporter of local charities and because it makes a point of using Cornish barley and spring water. All this is good news, because the brewery owns a huge percentage of Cornwall's nicest and most historic village pubs. And I've never heard a bad word said about its best-selling ale, Tribute. In fact, it's thanks to the success of Tribute that the company has recently (if reluctantly) upgraded all its brewing equipment and has advanced well beyond the Tamar.

The brewery has a museum, shop and bar and runs entertaining guided tours throughout the year (*www.staustellbrewery.co.uk*).

Par's Gardens

Two of Cornwall's finest, yet least-known gardens, each with its own specialist appeal and character, lie within easy reach of the train station at Par, on the eastern side of St Austell. **Tregrehan** (*PL24 2SJ; www.tregrehan.org; open mid-Mar–end May and a day a week in summer*) has been home to the Carlyon family since 1565, and its 20 acres of woodland, Victorian kitchen gardens and greenhouses are evidence of the family's deep and knowledgeable affection for plants, particularly trees and shrubs from the southern hemisphere. Tom Hudson, the latest family member to take on the estate, is no exception: his collection of high-altitude Asian trees, brought back from recent expeditions, complement his cousin's camellia hybrids and Jovey Carlyon's superb pinetum. Tregrehan may be stuffed with glorious examples of unusual trees that will excite dendrologists, but the gardens (which are only open for a limited number of days in spring and summer) are quiet and unshowy; Tom Hudson likes to keep it that way.

The three acres of gardens at **Marsh Villa** (*PL24 2LU; 01726 815920 for opening times; www.marshvillagardens.com*), on the other hand, were created out of boggy dereliction less than 30 years ago, the work of one dedicated plantswoman, Judith Stephens. There's still 17 acres of impenetrable marsh, which has been left for wildlife, but also reveals the extraordinary transformation, by drainage and landfill, of the planted areas: a series of intimate, colourful, leafy, watery 'rooms', linked by a wandering grassy path.

Menacuddle Well

Grid reference SX011533. Pass under the viaduct on the Bodmin road out of St Austell, and after half a mile take the small turning on left, signed Brake Manor.

It's almost impossible to spot the entrance first time round, and the road past is fast and turning off it dangerous, but perseverance pays off: in a peaceful green dell, sheltered by old laurels, a clay-coloured stream bubbles and falls past a mossy granite shrine. The original building dates from the 15th century, but was heavily restored in 1922. Inside, the water runs crystal clear, unlike the milky stream outside, which is perhaps why so much faith has been attached to its curative powers for so many centuries. No matter whether you believe in this or not, it's a delightfully unexpected and secret place with a gentle atmosphere – on the grassy slope a granite Druid's seat is the spot from which to contemplate the well, and parking space has thoughtfully been provided for a couple of cars, too.

⑯ Wheal Martyn china clay museum

Carthew PL26 8XG ① 01726 850 362 ⑩ www.chinaclaycountry.co.uk.

The lady on the ticket desk sighed: 'People go to the Eden Project, because it's the big must-do and then they don't come here – despite being so close, it's too much to visit both in one day – and [although there's a reduction in ticket price if you've been to Eden] too expensive.' Which is a shame, because

Wheal Martyn is a wonderful surprise, both inside and out and helps to put Eden (which was created in an abandoned china clay pit) into its historical and environmental context.

Inside the museum, an animated portrait of William Cookworthy describes his discovery of china clay on Tregonning Hill (see page 157) and the revolutionary impact this had on porcelain production in England. There are examples of some of the earliest experimental pieces of English porcelain here and surprising examples of other uses to which the clay is put today, such as the manufacture of toothpaste, cosmetics and paints, while paper manufacturing scoops up around 70% of production.

Outside, looping paths through 26 acres of sloping woodland take you on a journey past waterwheels and trickling leats, drying yards and kilns, sheds full of engines and the odd art installation. What I liked was the freedom to explore without feeling overly directed or bombarded with information – discretion and fun appearing more important than overt pedagogy.

Unlike tin and copper mining in Cornwall, the china clay industry is very much alive and is still Cornwall's biggest industry; at the farthest end of the woods, the ground rises and opens onto a viewing platform, from which you gaze down over a vast pit, currently being worked by the Goonvean China Clay Company and Imerys Minerals Ltd, which between them produce 4,500 tons of clay a week. So huge is the scale of the operation that the diggers and bulldozers look like Dinky toys working the pit bottom. But having come up through the museum, all the activity going on below makes sense: the digging, the washing, the separation of the liquid sludge, the growing conical mountain of spoil ... it's an absorbing spectacle. I knew what Oscar Wilde meant: 'I love work,' he said. 'I can watch it all day.'

⑰ The Eden Project

Bodelva, St Austell PL24 2SG ① 01726 811911 ⑭ www.edenproject.com; reduced entry fees for those arriving on foot, by bike or by bus.

Eden seems to me to be like an onion, which gets more interesting as you strip away each layer. Beneath the dizzying ingenuity of the vast, honeycomb-inspired, dome-like greenhouses, constructed from steel-framed inflated plastic cells, the two plant-filled biomes (climatically defined ecosystems) that draw in visitors by the thousand each day, there are deeper issues at stake. Eden is all about supporting healthy plant communities – in the Rainforest biome, heated to tropical temperatures and humidified by a giant waterfall; in the warm, dry Mediterranean biome (as well as in the local Cornish biome outside the domes) – and pushes the message hard that we disrespect the plant world at our peril.

The less visible, but wider project here is a creative response to such perils: by encouraging healthy, sustainable human communities, too, where people are interested in where they live and find ways of sharing and celebrating local identity. People come to Eden for 'Neighbourhood Event Planning' workshops and 'Creative Community' ideas, Social and environmental projects, dreamt up at Eden, travel the globe – creating a garden in Kosovo or helping a village in Thailand reclaim local rainforest; young offenders are helped into work with outdoor training initiatives.

Eden gets predictably packed in the summer holidays, and the health warnings on entering the Rainforest biome are not to be taken lightly (carry drinking water; remove warm or heavy outer layers of clothing). But my last visit to Eden was on a freezing day in January, when the hot, humid atmosphere of that biome was a haven: blackbirds were singing their hearts out among the ripening papayas and their tropical cousins were scuttling about in the lush undergrowth; robins perched on the stumpy vines in the Mediterranean biome and the scent of wild thyme and lavender among the olive trees transported me back to a happy year spent on a Spanish island.

Between the Rainforest and Mediterranean biomes, you look down over a bakery and help-yourself kitchen – long wooden tables and benches, earthenware jugs, huge bunches of fresh herbs – and no queues.

I talked to Tim Smit when Eden was still on the drawing board, back in 1995; the Lost Gardens of Heligan was already an established success and his creative ambitions were leaping ahead: 'I can't begin to describe what the biomes will look like,' he said. 'It's tempting to think in terms of pyramids or Christmas puddings, but I don't want to influence or prejudice the architects working on the design. But this is fundamental: so often man is seen as an accretion in the environment, as somehow extraneous to it. My aim is to place the environment in the context of man.' And then, after a pause, he added, 'I must seem incredibly arrogant ...' He didn't. Determined, passionate, thoughtful and – two decades later – vindicated.

⑱ Luxulyan Valley

I have a soft spot for this wooded valley, with its tumbling river and soaring viaduct; hidden and self-contained, yet barely a mile from the Eden Project and the busy beach at Par Sands. Climbers come here to test themselves on the granite cliffs; industrial historians to potter among the relics of tin and clay and granite exploitation and seek out the 650-foot, ten-arch Treffry Viaduct (see page 119); walkers on the coast-to-coast Saints' Way find this the leafiest and most peaceful part of the long trail and children scramble for the odd rope swing to be found among the branches on the slopes of the river.

The train station at Luxulyan, at the head of the valley is handy for exploring the valley on foot; by picking up the Saints' Way markers, you can continue

Keynsham Library

Customer name: Harris, Charlotte (Miss)
Customer ID: ******0654

Items that you have borrowed

Title: Slow Cornwall and the Isles of Scilly
ID: 4100675240
Due: 05 August 2023

Total items: 1
Account balance: £0.00
15/07/2023 11:52
Borrowed: 14
Overdue: 0
Hold requests: 3
Ready for collection: 0

Did you know you can access thousands of
free eBooks and eAudiobooks with your library
card?
We've got eMagazines and eComics too! Visit
www.librarieswest.org.uk to start downloading
today.
Find out about all our events, activities and
latest news by searching for 'Bath and North
East Somerset Libraries' on social media or
visit our blog
bathneslibraries.wordpress.org.uk.

We'd love you to give us your feedback, or tell
us about an event or group you attended.
Scan the QR code to tell us how we're doing.

Silvanus Trevail

With such a wonderful name, and such a vast legacy of civic, commercial and domestic buildings all over Cornwall, you'd think everybody would have heard of the prodigious and talented architect and entrepreneur from Luxulyan. Not a bit of it: when he died in 1903 (he put a gun to his head in the ladies lavatory on a train leaving Bodmin) his name died with him.

Nine of the Cornish buildings funded by the philanthropist Passmore Edwards (see page 141) were designed by Trevail, and nearly 50 schools in the county as well as cottages and mansions, banks and churches. St Austell and Truro are stuffed with his buildings, but the coastal resorts are where he made a controversial name for himself. Trevail saw that tourism was about to boom in Cornwall and was determined to cash in on the top end of the market. In 1890, he formed the Cornish Hotels Company, with the idea of attracting wealthy visitors to Cornwall. He'd got it all cleverly worked out: the well-heeled would be able to travel the entire coastline, moving at their pleasure between the chain of upmarket hotels he had planned. The enormous and castellated Camelot Hotel at Tintagel is his work, as is the imposing Headland Hotel in Newquay, which sparked riots among locals when it was built on supposedly common land, overlooking Fistral Bay. He realised that infrastructure was important too, and fought local councils to improve (or in some cases, create) services to drinking water and sewage, attempted to push through rail connections between emerging resorts – and made a lot of enemies in the process. Despite his suicide at the age of 52, Trevail was buried in Luxulyan churchyard, a few yards from where he was born; his grave is marked by a granite cross he had designed the year before.

downhill to Tywardreath and Par (the next station on the branchline) and return to Luxulyan by train.

Food and drink

King's Arms Luxulyan PL30 5EF ℗ 01726 850202. A great pitstop: cosy and traditional inside, welcoming children and dogs, damp walkers and cyclists.

⑲ Helman Tor

Grid reference SX062615.

Northeast of Luxulyan and southwest of Lanhydrock, tucked away in a maze of tiny lanes, Helman Tor is one of the very special viewpoints of central Cornwall, with a path taking you up from its car park. From the top you look across to the Hensbarrow Downs, the Lanhydrock estate and the Gilbert Monument near Bodmin. A prized wildlife habitat and nature reserve (Cornwall Wildlife Trust) with wetland, heath, woodland and acid grassland, it includes Red Moor Memorial Nature Reserve.

⑳ The Roche rock

Some 270 million years ago, in the late Carboniferous period, when great shifts underground were occurring, fluid boro-silicates separated from the molten rock and bubbled up towards the surface, finally cooling and solidifying into a crumpled rock formation, which rises broodingly over Roche (pronounced 'Roach'), on the northern fringes of the Clay country.

A ruined hermitage, consecrated in 1409, crowns its craggy skyline, which can be reached by a wooden ladder. Some come here hoping for a glimpse of the rock's famous ghostly inhabitants. Chief among these is the 17th-century corrupt magistrate, Tregeagle, who after his death jumped a particularly nasty kind of demonic bail and was cornered here by a pack of hellhounds; there's also St Gundred, whose leprosy-stricken father removed himself to the rock to spare the other inhabitants of Roche from his affliction. Brave little Gundred stuck with her father to look after him, occasionally taking him down to rinse him in a local holy well, but ultimately perished with him on the rock. Parts of the horror film *Omen III* were filmed here, too. On a summer's day, however, with butterflies springing from the rough pasture at the foot of the rock, it's hard to see its presence as anything but benign and it's good to recall that in the Tristan and Isolde legend, this is where the lovers were hidden from the wrath of King Mark by the friar hermit, Ogrim.

㉑ The Lost Gardens of Heligan

I first visited Heligan in 1997, when the newly restored gardens were just starting to hit the headlines and TV screens. Everybody seemed to be talking about someone called Tim Smit who, with his friend, John Nelson, had stumbled across a forgotten Cornish garden and fallen in love with the mystery and melancholy. Hothouses and potagers lay in the tangled embrace of briars and a jungle of tree ferns and rhododendrons had swarmed over rockeries and terraces, hiding Victorian bee boles, borders and pineapple pits.

I remember admiring Smit's bold approach to the project: 'It's unhealthy to think that if something is old it must be good,' he said. 'And as Heligan was made at different times, over a number of centuries, it's impossible to be completely authentic.' What Smit envisaged was a living, lively restoration, with a team of eager, expert gardeners working to exacting Victorian standards of horticultural practice. I remember him saying too, that he wanted Heligan to make people say 'Wow!', not 'How nice'. He likened the experience to being at a rock concert: 'We're doing this garden for the people dancing and having a good time, rather than the sober theorists standing at the back.'

Nearly two decades later, the gardens are fulfilling that early ideal with conviction: it's a brilliant, dramatic place, immaculate where it should be immaculate, wild and jungly where wild and jungly are required; all is designed to wow the crowds that visit in great numbers. And I see no reason why Slow visitors should not be there at the front of the dancing crowd; 15 years after that first conversation, I was.

㉒ Mevagissey

The picturesque harbour and constant comings and goings of the colourful fishing boats are the stuff of Cornish dreams; no wonder Mevagissey is popular and its narrow maze of backstreets crowded with gifts shops and cafés. On the east wharf of the inner harbour, the free **museum** (*01726 843568; www. mevagisseymuseum.co.uk; open Easter–Oct*) is a gem. In the best tradition of local museums it contains a lovingly assembled mixed bag of exhibits relating to its residents: local boatbuilding exploits rub shoulders with a fondly remembered Mevagissey milkman with a penchant for motorbike racing; Andrew Pears, the man who invented the first bar of soap you would actually want to wash yourself with, is given a hero's corner; a Mevagissey pound note from the village's family-owned bank is sadly exhibited beside news of its bankruptcy in 1824; and there are quirky 20th-century ceramic models of surprised fishermen or a rapturous couple sharing a bath by Bernard Moss. The **aquarium**, housed in the old lifeboat shed, is a treat too, stocked and regularly added to by Mevagissey's fishermen.

I had my bike with me, and found Mevagissey made a great base for cycling trips along the off-road trail to St Austell, seven miles distant (following the Sustrans NCN route 3), where it linked with the Clay Trails which pass through Wheal Martyn and the Eden Project. The steepest section followed a branching track to Heligan, which (mercifully) is less than two miles from Mevagissey.

Model railways were the last thing on my mind as I cycled back towards the harbour, but I wasn't in a hurry and in the spirit of Slow research I parked the bike outside a small wooden building, advertising itself as the **World of Model Railways** (*Meadow St; 01726 842457*). What a treat: beyond the shop, which stocks everything a model railway enthusiast could hope to find, including owner and top enthusiast Paul Catchpole, a miniature Cornish landscape unfolded, complete with stone circle, china clay pits, tin mine, gardens (including a Glendurgan-ish maze), harbour with a film crew, bike race, wedding and engineering works. No fewer than 30 trains quietly threaded their way through the extraordinary landscape, which I followed, rapt, up one side of the room and down the other, until the landscape gave way with unexpected abruptness to an alpine village. 'Ah, well, you see,' said the knowledgeable Mr Catchpole, 'the man who built this liked to spend his winter holidays in Grindelwald.' There can't be many other places where you can travel from the Cornish Alps to the Swiss Alps in a dozen paces.

Food and drink

There's no shortage of places to refresh yourself in Mevagissey: the **Central Café** (*3 Market Sq; 01726 843109*) was recently voted one of the ten best fish and chip shops in England in a *Times* survey; **Cofro** (*14 Fore St; 01726 842249*) is an art and craft gallery (Cofro means 'keepsake' in Cornish) with a café, doing a nice line in locally made cakes and biscuits; and the **Fountain Inn** (*Cliff St; 01726 842320*) is a characterful pub, one of the first to be bought by Walter Hicks of the St Austell Brewery (see page 123), with a well-earned reputation for real ales and a terrific fish menu.

㉓ Gorran Haven

Like many Cornish fishing villages, Gorran is in two parts: a cluster of cottages and houses built around the harbour, and higher inland a 'churchtown', where the streets are broader, the houses bigger and the smell of fish (in the past) less invasive. Because of its relative inaccessibility by road, Gorran is one of the few picturesque places on the Cornish coast that seems to have escaped commercialisation – it's a community rather than a commodity, and while its two family-friendly beaches and cottages receive their fair share of families who return here year after year, it's not yet been overwhelmed.

Food and drink

Barley Sheaf ① 01726 843330. An upmarket, friendly pub, with a reputation for good eating, local ales and an excellent cider produced at Cotna Barton (who also supply the salads and vegetables), just outside the village.

㉔ Caerhays Castle

Nothing quite prepares you for the loveliness of that first view of the castle in spring, standing massive and at ease behind its lake and velvety green pastures grazed by Highland cattle, against a rising backcloth of a thousand trees enriched by clouds of cream and pink magnolia blooms and scarlet bursts of rhododendron. Visitors arriving by car or bike (the entrance is on the cross-Cornwall Sustrans route) are directed down a narrow country lane to park at **Porthluney Cove**, so arrestingly beautiful in itself that it is quite a shock to turn your back on the sea and find the castle and its grounds dragging your gaze towards an altogether different kind of beauty. The next shock is the discovery that this view (known as 'the cut') was only made possible by dozens

of unemployed miners hacking away with picks and shovels at the interposing hill during the mining doldrums of the late 19th century.

Completed in 1813, Caerhays was built by John Nash for the Trevanion family, but bankruptcy ensured their enjoyment of the palatial building was short-lived; since 1853 this has been home to the Williams family, who still live here and occasionally open the house to visits. Its 100 acres of gardens are open from mid-February until early June, giving

Democratising the camellia

Gardeners who love camellias have good reason to be grateful to the Williams of Caerhays, in particular to J C Williams (great-grandfather to the present owner) who produced the hardy, free-flowering and easy-to-grow camellias we enjoy in our gardens today. JC funded a number of expeditions to China by the great plant hunter George Forrest and turned the wooded slopes of Caerhays into a giant experimental nursery. But his real breakthrough came in 1923, when he crossed *Camellia saluenensis* and *Camellia japonica*, producing the first of the *williamsii* camellias. (The original parent plants can be seen growing either side of a green door on the entrance façade of the castle.) At last there was a camellia that was tough enough to withstand a British winter with the additional bonus of producing flowers that dropped off after flowering, instead of collapsing in an ugly mess while still attached to the plant. It seems the camellia gene has been passed on through the generations – the famous Burncoose nurseries at Gwennap were established by the Williams family and the passion for raising new hybrids remains as vigorous as ever.

visitors the opportunity to see the wonderful collections of magnolias and camellias at the height of their flowering season. The steeply pitched slopes make for a lot of legwork, but create their own rewards, offering unusually close-up views of the blooms from above as well as below. Although of historic and national importance, the collection of plants at Caerhays is far from being preserved in aspic. The current owner, Charles Williams, and his head gardener, Jamie Parsons, respond with astute commitment to the annual challenge of replanting slopes denuded by the ravages of phytophthora (all the old *ponticum* rhododendrons have had to go) or by old beeches and Monterey pines sent crashing by strong winds; ten newly planted acres of trees and shrubs have recently been opened up to visitors, too. On my last visit, in January 2012, the best moment was undoubtedly when Mr Parsons spotted one of his own hybrid magnolias planted on a south-facing slope, covered in downy black flower buds for the first time. His astonished and joyful reaction is unprintable.

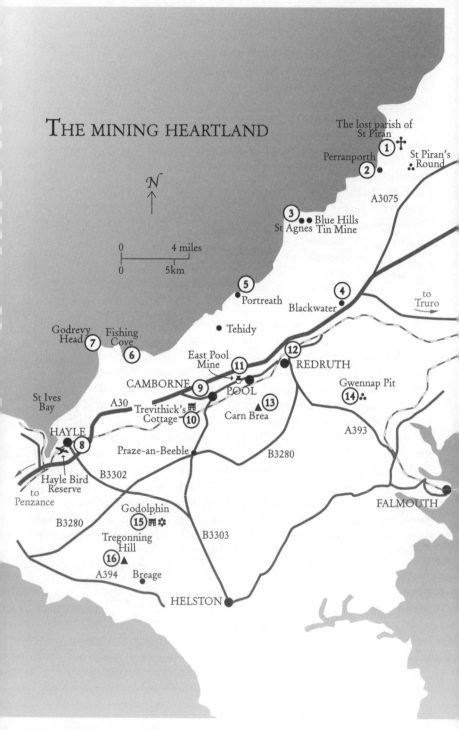

THE MINING HEARTLAND

The lost parish of St Piran
① ✝

Perranporth
②
St Piran's
Round

A3075

③ ● ● Blue Hills
St Agnes Tin Mine

N
↑

0   4 miles
0   5km

⑤
● Portreath
④
Blackwater
to Truro

Godrevy
Head ⑦   Fishing
Cove ⑥
● Tehidy

East Pool
Mine ⑪
⑫
REDRUTH

CAMBORNE ⑨   POOL   Gwennap Pit
⑭

St Ives
Bay
A30
Trevithick's
Cottage ⑩
Carn Brea ⑬

HAYLE
⑧
Praze-an-Beeble
A393

B3280

Hayle Bird
Reserve
to
Penzance

B3302

B3280

Godolphin
⑮

Tregonning
Hill
⑯ ▲   Breage

A394

B3303

HELSTON

FALMOUTH

6. THE MINING HEARTLAND

Cornwall's industrial heritage is stamped indelibly on the landscape, towns and coast over the whole county, but with no greater density – and pride – in the region of St Agnes, Redruth, Camborne and Hayle. I've extended the ground covered in this chapter southwards, to include the Godolphin estate and Tregonning Hill, as they form the largest of the ten separate areas which together create the World Heritage Site, established in 2006 in recognition of the importance of the Cornish mining landscape. There's enormous beauty here too, not just in the wild and natural beauty of the north coast dunes and cliffs or the wooded hills and farmland valleys of the interior, but in the decayed industrial architecture, softened by the steady encroachment of nature. You'll encounter a sense of place that grows on you and intensifies, especially after visiting one of the many museums dedicated to mining heritage, where the colossal human endeavour, which at its peak saw Cornwall meet two-thirds of the world's demand for tin and copper, is brought vividly to life. You really don't have to be an industrial archaeologist or have Cornish mining in your blood to appreciate the extraordinary inventiveness that went into extracting the shiny metals from lumpen ore, buried in wet ground, where efficient pumping was crucial to success and safety – nor the tales of courage, comradeship and survival that bound communities together.

The closure of the mines in the last century and the dispersal of the Cornish mining population to new, more profitable areas around the world was reflected grimly in the towns that had once prospered, but times are changing: affordable housing and studio space have brought an influx of artists to Redruth and Camborne, a multi-million-pound development of housing, offices and studios is rising from the wasteland of Pool – and Hayle, with its wave-energy Hub and historic waterfront is poised for a green, Docklands-style revival.

But it's not all about mining and its aftermath. The north coast is studded with safe, family-oriented beaches, and the giant dunes above Hayle and Perran Sands conceal all sorts of treasures, from glow-worms and butterflies, to buried explosives works, churches and sites of pilgrimage; among the dunes of Perran Sands you can lose yourself exploring the lost world of St Piran.

Getting around

The A30 provides a fast link from 'upcountry' to Redruth, Camborne and Hayle, from which its just a short hop on spur roads to Perranporth, St Agnes and Portreath. Heading south of Carn Brea into Godolphin country can lead into a muddle of tiny lanes, which all seem to tie up at the gloriously named Praze-an-Beeble, whence it's a straight, short run to Leedstown before plunging into small-lane territory again around Godolphin Cross.

Trains

Redruth, Camborne and Hayle are all served by the main-line service from London and Plymouth, making this one of Cornwall's most accessible regions by train.

Buses

Taking Redruth, Camborne or Hayle as your starting point, it's pretty easy to get around by bus and the north coast resorts are well served by spur routes, although some of the remoter places such as Godrevy have summer-only services. The 547 (Newquay–St Ives) offers a joined-up service, linking Perranporth, St Agnes, Portreath, Gwithian and Hayle, but sadly, this is a weekday service only. The Camborne to Helston bus (39) runs an hourly service, Monday to Saturday, stopping at Godolphin Cross, ideal for visiting the gardens and walking the Godolphin estate.

Cycling, riding and walking

This is great country for getting about by bike, horse or on foot, thanks to the well-signed routes forming the Mineral Tramways Mining Trails, which are centred around Camborne and Redruth, but also run from the north to south coast, from Portreath to Devoran on the Fal estuary. A map showing all the trails, heritage attractions, places for refreshment as well as bike and horseriding centres is available at visitor information centres, and there's an exhibition room dedicated to the trails at King Edward Mine. The map is also available for downloading at www.cornishmining.co.uk.

Cycle hire

The popularity of the mostly flat and well marked Mineral Tramways has encouraged a good network of cycle hire places and riding centres close to the routes.

Aldridge Cycles 38 Cross St, Camborne TR14 8EX ℗ 01209 714970 Ⓦ www.aldridgecycles.co.uk. Summer only; weekly or daily mountain-cycle hire.

The Bike Barn Elm Farm Cycle Centre, Cambrose TR16 5UF ℗ 01209 891498 www.cornwallcycletrails.com. Not just a cycle hire and repair place, but a farm with a shop selling local produce (real ale too, from Skinners) and a field for camping. Bed and breakfast is also offered in the farmhouse, four miles from Portreath on the coast-to-coast trail.

Bike Chain Bissoe Bike Hire Old Conns Works, Bissoe, Truro TR4 8QZ ℗ 01872 870341 Ⓦ www.cornwallcyclehire.com. Just outside the range of this chapter, but right on the north–south coast route and offering a large car park and café too. Bikes are hired on a daily basis, though longer hire periods can be arranged.

Hayle Cycles 36 Penpol Terrace ℗ 01736 753825 Ⓦ www.haylecycles.com. A friendly shop, offering daily or weekly cycle hire. Well placed for pottering around Hayle and the Towans or longer rides to Portreath and Tehidy Country Park.

Horseriding

Goonbell Riding Centre St Agnes TR5 0PN Ⓣ 01872 552063
Ⓦ www.goonbellridingcentre.com. Picnic and pub rides in the summer; horses and ponies for all ages (including the very, very young) and abilities.

Reen Manor Riding Stables Reen, Perranporth TR6 0AJ Ⓣ 01872 573064
Ⓦ www.reenmanorstables.com. Perfectly placed for exploring the sandy dunes above Perran Sands, or longer rides inland, with a stop for lunch at a local pub.

Wheal Buller Riding School Buller Hill, Redruth TR16 6SS Ⓣ 01209 211852
Ⓦ www.cornish-riding-holidays.co.uk On the slopes of Carn Brea; hacks along the mineral trails can be organised for all abilities; beach rides available for more experienced riders.

Accommodation

Beacon Cottage Camping Beacon Drive, St Agnes TR5 0NU Ⓣ 01872 552347
Ⓦ www.beaconcottagefarmholidays.co.uk Ⓔ beaconcottagefarm@lineone.net. The working farm is spread over the lower slopes of St Agnes Beacon, within easy reach of Chapel Porth; Trevaunce Cove is about 2 miles away on the coast path. It's a windy spot, but with glorious views out to sea; the seven paddocks and orchards, each with a limited number of pitches, offer shelter and are popular with families who return here year after year. Very reasonably priced and well placed for exploring on foot or by bike. There's a small shop selling milk and eggs from the farm.

Calize Country House Prosper Hill, Gwithian, Hayle TR27 5BW Ⓣ 01736 753268
Ⓔ jilly@calize.co.uk. Calize House is a substantial Victorian villa, with views over the rooftops of Gwithian to the Godrevy lighthouse and St Ives Bay. It's also a great B&B that works hard to support the local economy (breakfasts are sourced from farmers' markets) and is environmentally conscious too. Reasonably priced for above-average accommodation (there are four doubles as well as a two-bedroomed self-catering cottage).

Driftwood Beach Chalet Gwithian Towans, Hayle Ⓣ 01209 832042
Ⓦ www.tothelighthouse.co.uk. A wooden chalet, built in the 1930s, set among the dunes at Gwithian, lovingly renovated to provide a bright and airy living space. Not big or posh, but sleeps a family of six comfortably and is right there on the beach. Expect to pay upmarket prices for this slice of retro beach-holiday style.

Drym Farm Drym, Praze, Camborne TR14 0NU Ⓣ 01209 831039
Ⓦ www.drymfarm.co.uk Ⓔ drymfarm@hotmail.co.uk. A treat for gardeners and sybarites alike - comfortable farmhouse accommodation surrounded by 2 acres of richly planted Cornish gardens. A good spot for exploring local mining heritage sites and as well a both north and south coast beaches. The two double bedrooms (a small twin may also be available on request) provide upmarket luxury at affordable rates.

Godolphin House ① 0844 800 2070 ⓔ cottages@nationaltrust.org.uk ⓦ www.
nationaltrustcottages.co.uk. Recently restored and furnished with country house
furniture from local sales, the historic manor house is available for weekly rental
through the National Trust. There's a terrific atmosphere of the past (ghosts seem
to part of the deal) and enough space for 12 people to stay in style. Prices match
the sumptuous surroundings, but with a couple of large families sharing, prices
seem pretty reasonable.

Tourist information centres

Hayle Hayle Library, Commercial Rd ① 01736 75439.
Redruth Visitor Information Point, The Cornwall Centre, Alma Place
① 01209 216760 (Cornish Studies Library).
St Agnes 18 Vicarage Rd ① 01872 554150.

The north coast from Perranporth to the Hayle estuary

South of Holywell Bay, the windswept north coast is not short of variety:
craggy cliffs, towering sand dunes and vast beaches alternate with tiny coves,
accessible only to seal colonies and the most intrepid beach-lovers. Harbours
once dedicated to mining exports now cater to the surfing industry, while
in the hilly, wooded or heathy hinterland you are never far from the skeletal
remains of an engine house or chimney stack.

① The lost parish of St Piran

Behind the wide sweep of Perran Beach the largest sand dunes in Britain,
tufted with marram grass, rise to a height of 90 feet. The coast path
dips and rises along the safer margins of the shifting sands, giving a
seagull's-eye view of scudding sand-yachts and surfers far below. Turn the
clock back 1,500 years or so, and you might have glimpsed an Irish monk,
riding not a surfboard, but a slab of granite through the breakers and onto
the beach. This would be Cornwall's popular Celtic hero, St Piran, lashed
to a millstone and slung into the sea by a heathen Irish king, fearful of
Piran's reputation for performing miracles. Legend has it that the millstone-
cum-miraculous raft landed on the beach that still bears his name, and
on the level plateau above the beach Piran built a small oratory. The story
continues that Piran, having lit a fire on a black stone hearth, observed
a bubbling trickle of silvery metal rise to the surface and thus discovered
the existence of tin in Cornish granite. Which explains why Piran is the
patron saint of tinners, and why the Cornish flag is a white (tin) cross

(discovered by a Christian saint) on a black (granite) background.

How different the landscape must have looked in Piran's day, before the dunes took over. The 6th-century **oratory** – most probably a structure of wattle, daub and thatch, later replaced by stone as its importance grew – would have stood among fields and farms. However, blown in on north winds, the sands encroached and parishioners were forced to abandon it during the 10th century and build a new church, 300 yards further inland, across a stream. But, like the oratory, the church was eventually engulfed by sand and in 1804 it was removed, stone by stone and rebuilt at Perranzabuloe, three miles to the south. Today, it's a good walk – two miles from Perranporth – over the dunes to find the remains of both church and oratory, neither of which is particularly easy to locate. In fact, all that can be seen of the oratory is a small, humpy dune (among many, many other humpy dunes), marked only by a discreet information plaque and surmounted by a simple granite slab, inscribed with the name of the saint. Beneath the dune is an astoundingly ugly blockwork structure, built in 1910, to protect the oratory remains; it was deliberately buried in 1980 as a response to flooding and vandalism. The excavated foundations of the church are, however, still visible and the eight-foot Celtic cross (pictured on the cover of this book) speaks of the vast medieval graveyard that lies beneath the sand. From time to time, bones are revealed, including the skeleton of a mother holding an infant, found close to the entrance to the oratory.

Don't expect easy-to-follow waymarkers to guide you here; the best option is to follow the coast path north from Perranporth as far as the MoD fence and turn right, keeping the fence to your left and ignoring the huge concrete cross on a dune to the south. After half a mile, the oratory mound and plaque (grid reference SW768564) become visible. Continue in the same direction (skirting the deep stream bed) – looking out for St Piran's cross to guide you to the church, which, like the oratory, lies close to the MoD fence. Locals are well aware of the absurdity of such obscurity for a site of national importance: the oratory is believed to be the oldest building dedicated to Christian worship on mainland Britain and a charitable trust has been set up with the aim of uncovering and reopening the oratory (*www.st-piran.com*).

A circular walk from Perranporth to these holy sites joins a lane close to Gear

Farm (grid reference SW775554) from where a network of footpaths and lanes leads to **St Piran's Round**, a mile to the southeast, on the edge of Rose hamlet. This is a remarkably well-preserved circular earthwork, which may or may not have started out as a fortified Iron Age farm. What is sure however, is that the Round was used for centuries as a theatre for Cornish mystery plays as well as wrestling matches, fairs and preaching. A medieval pilgrims' road once bisected the circle and it's possible that Miracle plays were laid on here to reward and educate travellers approaching the oratory. The depression in the centre marks the place of a pit from which the devil would spring – to predictable gasps and jeers. These days, Cornwall's (secular) Miracle Theatre puts on plays here for one evening each summer and local and visiting Mummers will occasionally stage an event here too; it seems very little use for what is probably Britain's oldest 'Playing Place'.

② Perranporth

Once a mining village, Perranporth now appears to be dedicated to beach and surf, both in glorious abundance. At low tide, the level sands are a huge playground for sand-yachters too, skimming the beach as swiftly as the wheatears and stonechats skim the tufty heights and hollows of the dunes above. But Perranporth really comes alive and bares its soul for the weekend closest to 5 March when the village celebrates the arrival of its saint, and kicks off with a giant model of St Piran arriving on the beach (in a rigid inflatable), followed with pageants, plays and a procession across the dunes to the site of the ancient church and oratory. A thorough dash of Cornish nationalism is thrown in too, with lots of flag waving and lusty renditions of 'Trelawney' along the way.

The **Perranzabuloe Museum**, attached to the library in the Oddfellows building (*Ponsmere Rd, Perranporth TR6 0BW; 01872 573321; open Easter–Oct, weekdays and Sat mornings*) does a grand job of keeping Perranporth's identity from being submerged by holidaymaking traffic. Surfers should note the exhibit that reveals how the local coffin-maker, Tom Tremewan, spotting the new enthusiasm for riding the waves, sold coffin lids to tourists for this purpose in the 1920s. Perranporth was used as a training ground for the D-Day landings and wartime memorabilia includes the tiny uniform made for Jacqueline Fewins, the three-year-old mascot of an American battalion that was based here. And I liked the story of the shipwreck, that (for once) had a happy ending, when the skipper, who survived with his humour intact, commented 'I have been wrecked in different parts of the world, even the Fiji islands, but never among savages such as those of Perranporth.'

A short walk through the village to the southern end of the beach takes you up the cliff to **Droskyn Point**, where on a grassy ledge an enormous granite sundial was installed to celebrate the millennium. True to the spirit of Perranporth, the gnomon has been set to show *Cornish* time: 20 minutes ahead of GMT.

Food and drink

Bolingey Inn Penwartha Rd, Bolingey TR6 0DH ℗ 01872 571626.
Less than a mile from Perranporth, and accessible by a footpath that starts opposite the Co-op car park, Bolingey is a pretty hamlet with a superb old pub, both for eating and drinking. Local ales are well kept, vegetables come from the pub's allotment garden, lamb from a nearby farm, and ice cream from Callestick Farm, just up the road. Dog- and child-friendly.

③ St Agnes

The relics of an industrial past – chimney stacks and engine houses – crowd thickly around the the steep and narrow valley that shelters St Agnes on its plunging descent to Trevaunce Cove. But this is no grim mining village: St Agnes is a flowery, cottagey sort of place, with good shops selling local produce, galleries that reflect an established arty community and busy little beaches, popular with surfers. If you don't mind hills, there are some great walks, starting and finishing in the village, that take you up St Agnes Beacon, or along the wooded Jericho Valley or out onto the wild coast at Chapel Porth. Whichever route you take, the tin industry is never out of sight and if the lonely, lofty ruins intrigue you, it's best to go armed with the series of locally produced walking maps (*Ten Walks in and around St Agnes*) which tell the

John Opie RA

John Opie was just ten when he sold his first portrait, much to the disgust of his father, who was determined his son would follow him into the carpentry trade. But in 1776, aged 15, the St Agnes boy was released from his apprenticeship and delivered into the hands of Dr Wolcot, a Truro dilettante, who had spotted not only talent but the possibility of high earnings in the teenage prodigy. For six years, Wolcot touted Opie round Cornwall's big families, organising portrait commissions; then, encouraged by his protégé's rapidly developing artistic maturity, took his 'Cornish Wonder' to London. Opie was introduced to Sir Joshua Reynolds and from that moment his career, but decidedly not his sense of fulfilment, took off. Opie started to resent Wolcot's constant and exploitative presence and broke off their partnership; he then rushed into marriage with one of his prettiest and sadly, most immature sitters, and spent 13 years regretting everything and painting everyone. History subjects, especially the dramatic slashfest titled *The Murder of Rizzio*, painted in 1787, brought him wide acclaim and it can only be hoped that painting it brought him some kind of cathartic release from his marital troubles too. He died aged just 45, but not too unhappily: in his last decade he was made a Royal Academician (largely thanks to the Rizzio picture), divorced his wife who had mercifully eloped – and found blissful companionship in a second marriage. When he died, he was buried beside Reynolds, in St Paul's Cathedral.

stories behind the relics, on sale in the post office (they can also be downloaded at www.stagnesforum.com).

At the top of the village the **St Agnes Museum** (*Penwinnick Rd, TR5 0PA; 01872 553228*), housed in a former chapel of rest (divided neatly in half with one entrance for Methodists and another for Anglicans), likens itself to 'a Victorian Cabinet of Curiosities'. From the stuffed leatherback turtle at the entrance to the collection, to the hideously curling, six-inch (Edwardian) toenail, collected by William Whitworth, one of five generations of Whitworths to serve as doctor to the community, you can see what they mean. There are minerals and models (including one of the harbour which once occupied Trevaunce Cove), a painted ship's figurehead and dozens of photos of village scenes and characters. Upstairs, there's the paintbox of the Georgian society painter, John Opie, and pride of place is given to one of Opie's 20 self-portraits; Edward Opie, who like his role-model great-uncle, became a Royal Academician, is also represented by a portrait of the artist's father. Both portraits are arrestingly frank, but it is the intensity of John Opie's self-querying gaze that commands the attention longest.

Blue Hills Tin

Wheal Kitty, St Agnes TR5 0YW ① 01872 553341 ⓦ bluehillstin.com.

The last working tinners in Cornwall are father and son, Colin and Mark Wills. Theirs is a small operation, dwarfed by the towering remains of mine engineering in the surrounding hills which ceased operation decades ago. The Wills are not miners, but streamers and the real joy of visiting derives from the intimacy of the scale and the evident sustainability of what they do. Winter sees them hacking ore out of the exposed rock face on their narrow valley site and feeding it into the stream where it is crushed (one of the crushers is even driven by a working waterwheel), causing the heavier particles of tin to be separated out by the action of the water. Come the tourist season, Colin and Mark guide visitors through the various stages of purification, smelting and casting – and sell tin jewellery of their own design and making too. The tiny lane which swoops down into their valley from Wheal Kitty is breathtakingly steep and twisty; worth checking your brake blocks first if visiting by bike.

Food and drink

The Driftwood Spars Trevaunance Cove, St Agnes TR5 0RT ① 01872 552428 ⓦ www.drfitwoodspars.co.uk. A friendly pub, beamy and full of character, close to the beach, with its own microbrewery in the blue timber shed across the road. Local ales and real cider from St Buryan, and a terrific menu of locally sourced dishes. Popular with everyone: locals, surfers, families and hairy bikers.

The Secret Garden 1 Penwinnick Villas, Penwinnick Rd, St Agnes ① 01872 553168. Open in the summer only, and only when weather permits, for it really is a garden, where vegetarian teas are dished up among the flowers and foliage.

④ Blackwater

The A30 used to pass right through the main street, but now there's not much to tempt visitors to turn off the bypass and turn back into the village. However, Blackwater has the honour of being the birthplace of Cornwall's great philanthropist, John Passmore Edwards (his cottage is marked by a plaque), and a decent, unpretentious pub, the Red Lion Inn. From late July until the end of August, up to 1,000 visitors head to Blackwater each evening, heading for the Asylum – a sort of geodesic, tented structure at Tywarnhale Farm, on the outskirts of the village, to see the latest boundary-pushing and often magical offerings from Cornwall's Kneehigh Theatre.

Kneehigh Theatre

Kneehigh (*www.thekneehighasylum.co.uk*) has entertained families (and their now grown-up children) for over 30 years – in village halls and marquees, preaching pits and quarries, clifftops and woods all over the West Country. (It must be 20 years since my youngest and I were enthralled by *Fish Boy*,

---

John Passmore Edwards (1823–1911)

There's scarcely a town of any size in Cornwall that did not benefit from the generosity of the poor boy from Blackwater who hauled himself out of poverty through education and made language a weapon for liberating others from oppression and injustice. Libraries and institutes where the poor could advance their education without payment were his legacy to Cornwall – as well as other towns across the south of England – and he also built orphanages and art galleries, convalescent homes and hospitals, earning himself the title 'the Cornish Carnegie'.

As a young man, Edwards was a bit of a firebrand and abandoned work as a solicitor's clerk to write for a radical newspaper, where he earned peanuts, but fought for the abolition of hanging and flogging, spoke passionately against war, rallied to the cause of the trade unions and opposed all forms of social injustice. By the age of 28 he was owner of his own paper, *The Public Good*, but his enthusiasm outdistanced his means and he was bankrupted. For ten years Edwards slaved to repay every penny owed to his creditors, and was rewarded by better fortune in the form of a happy marriage and the clever purchase of London's first evening paper. Notwithstanding libel actions (as when, for example, his paper lashed out at a parliamentary candidate for being more suited to representing Sodom and Gomorrah than Rochester) Edwards made a mint, and that was when the busy philanthropy started. His first project was to build an institute with a library that included a section for children in his home village, Blackwater. Few lives are lived better than this: there was never any trace of Victorian smugness, and even towards the end of his life, something of the young radical in Edwards led him to refuse a knighthood.

performed in a hut somewhere near Bridport.) Kneehigh's gift is for creating an anarchic fairy-tale world: subversive, colourful, darkly funny, music-filled performances that have now found fame around the world, enabling the company to set itself up with a huge, tented performing space in Blackwater, known as the Asylum. Consider yourself lucky if you can get hold of a ticket, though. Ticket prices have shot up to the point where they are out of reach for most local families (it's actually cheaper to see Kneehigh at Sadler's Wells in London than at the Asylum), but even so they sell out fast and you never read a bad review.

⑤ Portreath and Tehidy Country Park

Between Camborne and the sea, the Bassetts of Tehidy, a wealthy and influential mining family, built a succession of increasingly lavish houses, surrounded by gardens, lakes and a deer park. They built a harbour, too, at Portreath, from which copper and tin could be exported, while coal to drive the mine engines arrived on incoming vessels. But thanks to the profligacy of the last Bassett to reside at Tehidy, in 1916 the house and park were divided and sold. The house reopened as a TB sanatorium, but was destroyed by fire, just two weeks after receiving its first patients. A new hospital and houses were built around the core of the ruin and although the hospital has closed, this part remains a private residential area. Since 1983, however, the wooded grounds have been a public space, much appreciated by residents of Redruth and Camborne. It's not a place where you're likely to find solitude, but is good for a morning or afternoon's sheltered ramble, when the wind is blowing hard on the North Cliffs. A bike route runs through the park and if you follow it from east to west, the route follows a gentle downhill slope, emerging by an inexpensive little café, run by a friendly family in a wooden hut at the coombe entrance.

Food and drink

Beach Café Portreath. Built into the wall of the car park, right on the shingly beach. Roger is open every morning, serving up bacon butties to surfers even on Christmas Day.

Polcrowjy Tea Room. Beside the coombe entrance to Tehidy; open all year, Fri–Sun in winter. Prices are about half what you'd expect to pay in a NT tearoom; the cakes are out of this world.

⑥ Fishing Cove

The clifftop path from Portreath to Godrevy Head offers tantalising glimpses of secret beaches, occupied only by seals, thanks to the general inaccessibility of the shore from the cliffs. Fishing Cove, protected from the westerlies by Navax Head, is the exception; it's a far from easy scramble down the cliff, but at low tide the beach becomes a perfect horseshoe of soft sand, lapped by a peacock-blue sea, shallow and safe for swimming. Its unspoiled seclusion makes it a favourite both with naturists and nature-lovers. If approaching from Portreath, look out for the Hell's Mouth Café on your left; just after and on the right is a free-parking area, giving onto the coast path. Follow the path west in the Godrevy direction for about 300 yards until the vertigo-inducing track down to the cove appears on your right.

⑦ Godrevy Head and the Towans

In summer, the two National Trust car parks are packed to overflowing and the three miles of west-facing sandy beach between Godrevy Head and Hayle freckled with bucket-and-spading families and surfers. The Towans (Cornish for sand dunes) are dotted with chalets and caravan parks, but alive with butterflies and skylarks among the duney vegetation.

It's hard to believe that a large part of the Upton Towans was the site of a dynamite factory in the early 1900s, but a scattering of ruined buildings and parts of the old tramway can still be seen. The dunes hide other secrets too: further north, close to Gwithian, a pre-Norman oratory, dedicated to the Celtic saint Gothian, was rediscovered when a local farmer decided to dig out a pond in 1827. It's since been reclaimed by the sand but Gwithian's 13th-century church, built on safer ground, has survived despite being almost entirely rebuilt in Victorian times. The Methodist chapel in Gwithian, built in 1810, is one of the prettiest thatched buildings in the county.

Tread softly in the dunes at dusk and you may see glow-worms, too. Between Godrevy Head and Navax Point you can look down the sheer cliff to seal colonies, who come here to breed and raise their young. It's a long way down and access (even if it were possible) is prohibited, so a pair of binoculars is a good idea. Out of season, it's a lonely wilderness, visited by migrant birds and the walk to Godrevy Head,  with its island lighthouse and views across the bay to the bright lights of St Ives, is a good way to work up a feeling of Romantic melancholy, or at least, following in the footsteps of Virginia Woolf, whose novel *To the Lighthouse* was drawn from memories of childhood holidays spent here, a Mrs Ramsayish type of introspection.

Food and drink

The Jam Pot Gwithian Towans TR27 5BT. A much-loved beach café (the homemade cakes are legend in these parts) in a historic building, shaped something like a jam pot, but in fact a coastguard lookout built in the early 19th century.

Red River Inn Gwithian TR27 5BW ☎ 01736 753223. Named after the stream close by that used to run red with the run-off from iron ore in the mining areas upriver, this is a Free House, with a jolly atmosphere and fine menu of local ales and dishes. Family- and dog-friendly.

The copper and tin towns: Hayle, Redruth and Camborne

The real joy of going Slow is the way that the unlikeliest of places reveal themselves, heart and soul, and often in a most unexpected fashion. In fact, it was harder to find the beating heart of some of Cornwall's more fashionable resorts than it was in this trio of post-industrial towns that are working with passion and integrity towards a distinctive and sustainable future.

⑧ Hayle

These are interesting times for Hayle, home to the latest developments in wave-energy technology: a multi-million-pound redevelopment plan has been put forward for the harbour area, which is intended to give it a mini-Docklands kind of facelift. You can see the thinking – Hayle is built around water: pools, creeks, wharves and the River Hayle itself; then there is the town's wealth of Victorian industrial architecture, just right for offices and loft apartments. But for the time being, the slightly scruffy harbour and Penpol Creek with its faded boats tied up along the narrow wharf, faced by a row of characterful shops (Bigglestone's Hardware is particularly nice) and the odd café, will suit those who enjoy pottering and nattering and watching the dabchicks scuttle about the banks or the gig team, scooting across the harbour at high water. Hayle is big on watersports as well as lifeguard training, and one of the gig rowers grimaced pointedly as we discussed the new proposals: 'Whatever they end up building, it would be nice if all the watersports could have a clubhouse.'

In the 19th century, Hayle developed rapidly, thanks to its booming copper industry, into a town of two tribes and two halves, which is why it's not very obvious today where the town's centre lies. One tribe consisted of the Harvey's Foundry workforce who had their own commercial and residential centre known as **Foundry,** in the region of the White Hart Hotel on the west side of town, while the other tribe was the Cornish Copper Company, which occupied the town to the east, known as **Copperhouse**. The Passmore Edwards Institute sits diplomatically between the two on the waterfront, but there are still granite posts dotted about the town, marked with H or CCC, which were erected to settle territorial disputes by formalising the tribal boundaries. 'Copperhouse' territory is also identifiable by the use of shiny black blocks in the construction of many of the older buildings. The material is scoria, the slag waste produced from smelting copper ore; it was a brilliant piece of recycling, but unless it has acquired a patina of lichen, not terribly attractive.

On the other side of Copperhouse Pool lies **Phillack**, a rural outpost of Hayle, with its back to the grassy dunes that give it some protection from

The Wave Hub

Ten miles offshore, a £42 million project is Cornwall's great hope for generating green energy from waves. In reality, it's a giant electrical socket, connected by an undersea cable to the national grid, operating as a test site for wave-energy devices designed around the world. The website for the hub wasn't working when I looked, but I found all the local knowledge about who was in testing and who had pulled out in Bigglestone's Hardware shop.

northerly gales. Heads swivel as they pass Phillack's St Austell Brewery-owned pub, on account of its name, the Bucket of Blood. It's dark and beamy inside, playing up to its reputation of being haunted (long ago, the landlord let his bucket down into the well and drew up the blood of a murdered customs man). Phillack's Victorian church, St Felicitas, built on the remains of a Norman church and even older Christian Celtic site, is granite, but the churchyard's retaining wall is built of scoria. St Felicitas, in Copperhouse territory, was Hayle's only Anglican church, so the Foundry tribe tended to go to the church in St Erth, until the decision was taken to build a new church in Hayle to cater for them. This was the imposing St Elwyn's, completed in 1888, which stands on a rise overlooking the junction of harbour and Copperhouse Pool. Needless to say, there were two Methodist chapels; the Copperhouse one has been demolished, but the Foundry chapel is now a galleried indoor shopping and gallery space, Pratt's Market, specialising in crafts and antiques. Just around the corner, in a nicely converted range of old foundry buildings, Foundry Yard is a mixture of studios and craft workshops. Opening times are not guaranteed, but there is a general policy of opening to visitors on Thursdays.

A good way to explore Hayle and its watery environs on foot is to cross over the iron bridge by the harbour and follow the **George V Memorial Walk**, fragrantly lined with subtropical planting, from the open-air swimming pool all along the back of Copperhouse Pool, from which Hayle's grander buildings stand out with clarity. Returning to the town over the Black Bridge, it's a straight run down through shops and terraced houses to St Elwyn's Church where the harbour joins Penpol Creek. I've already mentioned the row of interesting shops and cafés along Penpol Terrace, but there's a good reason to cross the road to the grassy wharfside: here is the memorial to Hayle-born Rick Rescorla, who died while helping over 2,700 people to safety from New York's World Trade Center on 11 September 2001.

Hayle's birds

Hayle's watery environment and tidal exposure of marshy mudflats is an important overwintering ground for all sorts of wildfowl and visiting migrants; the whole estuary, much of which is owned by the RSPB, is hugely popular with birdwatchers, from those who enjoy the avian spectacle from the comfort of the car by **Copperhouse Pool** (there's free parking space by the outdoor swimming pool on the Phillack side of the water), to seriously tooled-up photographers, crouched silently behind zoom lenses in the hide at Ryan's Field, close to the A30. Copperhouse Pool is famous for its rarities, often spotted flitting between the pool and the main estuary. For most people though, just observing the resident population of shelducks, redshanks, curlews, herons, egrets and gulls going about their business, or enjoying the seasonal influx of pattering dunlins, sandpipers and turnstones, and the flocks of plover and lapwing, is quite enough.

With all this free and natural bird entertainment on hand, a trip to the bird sanctuary at **Paradise Park** (*16 Trelissick Rd, Hayle TR27 4HB; 01736 751020; www.paradisepark.org.uk*) might seem an unnecessary expense, but behind the gaudy advertisements are seven gorgeously planted acres of serious conservation at work and children seem to love it especially on dry afternoons, when some of the birds are allowed out of their huge and imaginatively designed aviaries and fly freely. Like the Monkey Sanctuary near Looe, Paradise Park was created by a single individual, whose hobby developed into a passionate cause. It began with a pair of parrots, kept as pets. Mike Reynolds (who, in his professional life, led the Milky Bar Kid advertising campaign in the 1960s and 1970s) soon saw his love for the birds advance into a concern for the threat to wild populations; in 1989 he set up the World Parrot Trust, a charity which supports conservation and education projects around the world.

One of the trust's greatest successes was a project to save the rare echo parakeet of Mauritius, whose numbers in the wild had dwindled to around 15 known individuals by 1990 but can now be measured in hundreds. Reynolds, who died in 2007, also set up the world's first ever Parrot Action Plan, which has become a blueprint for conservation programmes around the world. His family still runs the conservation centre at Hayle and one of the latest projects is to re-introduce the red squirrel to Cornwall.

I went, because I wanted to find out more about their chough breeding programme. David Woolcock, the head keeper, explained that the relatively recent wild population of choughs in Cornwall (see page 195) has been traced genetically to a very small number of breeding pairs, who arrived on the Lizard, blown off course from their native Ireland. 'Imagine if the human population of Hayle were descended from just one couple,' he said, keeping a perfectly straight face. 'You'd hope for some new blood to strengthen the gene pool, wouldn't you?' Indeed you would. Which is why at Paradise Park they have been breeding Welsh choughs, with the future aim of introducing them to the wild, but purely Irish, population. However would you do that? 'A straight egg swap,' replied David. 'We simply swap our Welsh chough eggs with eggs from the nests of the wild birds. The parent birds should not notice a thing.'

Food and drink

Bird in Hand Trelissick Rd ⓣ 01736 753974. At the entrance to Paradise Park, and run by the same family, this pub is big on music nights with local bands often performing. The pub brews its own speciality ale, Paradise Bitter.

Johnny's Café 50–51 Penpol Terrace ⓣ 01736 755928. A vegetarian café, named after the owner's father, with monthly (extremely popular) evening openings for dinner, when booking is essential. Very informal and friendly, plenty of art on the walls and local and recycled gifts to buy as well. Breakfasts are top dollar here: porridge or pancakes with maple syrup, toast made from organic bread, and superb coffee. The mixed salad is highly recommended at lunchtime.

Richards of Cornwall Carwin Farm, Hayle (just off the A30, close to the West Cornwall Retail Park roundabout at Loggans Moor) ⓣ 01736 757888 ⓦ www.richardsofcornwall.co.uk. This is a fantastic farm shop, selling fruit, vegetables and salads direct from the farm and daffodil bulbs too in the autumn. Lots of organic Cornish dairy and meat and a superb frozen counter, where you can buy fruit and vegetables by the scoop.

Salt Kitchen Bar Foundry Sq ⓣ 01736 755862. At the Foundry end of town, Salt looks like the shape of things to come in Hayle: industrial architecture close to the water and a contemporary Mediterranean-style menu based on local ingredients.

Scarlet Wines The Old Forge, Griggs Quay, Lelant ⓣ 01736 753696. Scarlet is a wine shop, delicatessen and café. It smells blissful when you go in and the small menu of tapas includes local mussels and mackerel as well as more Spanish dishes such as marinated Manchego cheese and herby aranchini.

Trevaskis Farm Gwinear TR27 5JQ ⓣ 01209 713931; shop 01209 714009 ⓦ www.trevaskisfarm.co.uk. An awful lot of good stuff happens at Trevaskis: it's an organic farm and kitchen garden with an educational as well as a productive mission; there's a comprehensive farm shop every bit as tempting as a Waitrose with a huge deli counter, and a café/restaurant, that opens for breakfast, lunch and dinner, six days a week and lunch on Sundays.

⑨ Camborne

Outsiders to the region tend to lump neighbouring Camborne and Redruth (and Pool which lies between) together, often with a shudder of horror at the thought of visiting the urban centre of Cornwall's post-industrial heartland. It's a rather outdated attitude, though, typified by S P B Mais in his 1950 book *We Wander in the West*, where talking of Camborne-and-Redruth he writes: 'neither of which ... has much to offer the stranger in search of beauty except some very virile Rugger'. He was right about the rugby though; Camborne and Redruth have distinct identities and a history of rivalry, played out with concentrated ferocity on the rugby pitch. And Pool in the middle is in the process of receiving a multi-million-pound development scheme, just as South Crofty mine at its centre is starting to produce tin again after its closure in 1998.

It's true that Camborne doesn't go out of its way to entice visitors; most of the signposted attractions are to mining heritage centres in the vicinity, but I like it all the more for its self-contained reticence. A visit to the public loo, just off Commercial Square for example, brought me face to face with a pair of beautifully carved, clearly contemporary, wooden gates. 'The Outlaws Hide in the Forest' ran the lettering, above a man in a tree looking at a fox and holding his finger to his lips. There was no plaque, no explanation, just the carved words 'Beunans Meriasek'. I found part of the answer in Camborne's church, the other in the Driftwood Spars, a St Agnes pub (see page 140). Standing in a large and leafy churchyard, **Camborne's parish church** is a lovely amalgamation of Norman, Tudor, Georgian and Victorian building. It's dedicated to St Martin and St Meriadoc, Meriasek in Cornish. The 16th-century mystery play *Beunans Meriasek* tells the story of the saint coming to Camborne and founding the church. (And in the Driftwood Spars the new brewer, Peter Martin, turned out to be a versatile chap as it was he who had carved the gates.) The church revealed some other surprises, too: in the main sanctuary, the panelling and seat along the walls are made from 15th-century bench ends showing a mermaid, a unicorn and other mythical creatures, but the best treasure lay under the altar cloth in the Lady Chapel. There, with the help of the church warden, I looked at the 10th-century altar slab, inscribed in Latin with its sponsor's dedication and five Norman reconsecration crosses, originating from the chapel of St Ia, near Troon, a couple of miles away.

Camborne is stuffed with grand **Victorian architecture** that speaks of prosperous times and Victorian benevolence. As you might expect, there's a Passmore Edwards Library, designed – as so many of Edwards's donations were – by Silvanus Trevail. A statue of Richard Trevithick, with a model of the Camborne locomotive tucked under his arm, stands outside looking up the hill on which he tested the full-size version of the machine to destruction in 1801. By the time the library was built, Camborne already had a literary institute, complete with classical portico and lecture room, on the edge of Commercial Square, and two enormous Wesleyan chapels. All these are still standing, but no such respect was shown for the internationally renowned **Camborne School of Mines,** which was demolished in 1974 and replaced with a supermarket. It's no exaggeration to say that Camborne was the Oxbridge of the mining world; from 1888 anyone associated with minerology, mines and mine engineering anywhere in the world would have heard of Camborne. (The school still exists, as part of Exeter University, located at the new Tremough campus in Penryn.)

Shopping

On the second Saturday of the month, a general market spills around the fountain at the centre of Commercial Square. This now incorporates a farmers' market, a positive indication of Camborne's growing demand for locally produced meat, fish, cheese and vegetables.

Richard Trevithick (1771–1833)

Camborne salutes its favourite son each year on Trevithick Day, on the last Saturday in April, with steam engine displays, street parades and dancing along the route of the inventor's most famous steam-driven experiment 'up Camborne Hill and down again' (as the song goes).

Trevithick was every bit as brilliant as (and probably more versatile than) his contemporary, Sir Humphry Davy, but his genius did not extend to capitalising on what his fecund mind produced and his adult life was spent lurching from one financial pit to another. In the highly profitable and hugely competitive world of Cornish mining in the late 18th and early 19th centuries there was endless demand for new technology to solve the problems of deep shaft flooding and transportation, and steam was seen as the way forward.

But whereas everyone has heard about James Watt and George Stephenson, outside Cornwall, Richard Trevithick's name has got lost along the way. He may have been unworldly and open to exploitation, but his vast and eclectic record of achievement is none the less impressive: pumping engines, steam locomotion, lifts, turbines and floating docks – there was clearly something of the Leonardo in him. His one real stroke of good luck and judgement came in his marriage to Jane Harvey, a daughter of the Hayle Foundry empire. Throughout his frequent and financially disastrous trips away from home, which included 11 unprofitable, danger-filled years in South America, and a last, desperate year in London, where he died a pauper, she never faltered in her fondness or support.

⑩ Trevithick's Cottage

TR14 0QG ☏ 01209 612154 to make an appointment to visit the cottage during its open afternoons.

Lois Humphrey invited me to enjoy the small, but colourful garden while she took a couple who had arrived just ahead of me inside the whitewashed, thatched cottage in Penponds.

It's been extended since the Trevithicks lived here and quite how Richard, a local mine captain, and Anne Trevithick raised Richard junior and his five sisters in such a confined space is hard to imagine.

Only the parlour on the ground floor can be visited and this only on Wednesday afternoons between April and October (just as well for the Humphreys, who live here, by arrangement with the National Trust). What you see is a tiny, but perfectly unspoiled Georgian living room, panelled and carefully decorated with portraits, memorabilia and photographs that give flesh to the Trevithicks and the way they lived.

Richard left home in 1797 when he married Jane Harvey, but the couple returned to live here with their own children in 1810, for a brief period, when ill health and bankruptcy forced them out of London. Lois and I looked at the portrait of the steadfastly loyal Jane, who waited 11 years for her husband to return (empty-handed) from South America. And we looked at the portrait of Trevithick, a big man with gentle, unworldly eyes, gazing back at the small room that can barely have contained his restless energy or her enduring patience.

⑪ East Pool Mine

Trevithick Rd, Pool TR15 3ED ℗ 01209 315027 Ⓦ www.nationaltrust.org.uk.

You'll know when you're getting close: the northern site of the museum is easily identified from a distance by its towering chimney stack, with EPAL (East Pool and Agar Ltd) picked out in white bricks.

I can't imagine the great steeplejack Fred Dibnah being happier than here (and I'm sure he must have visited because I saw his signature in the Trevithick Cottage visitors' book), watching the great, oiled shafts of the two enormous beam engines in action. The museum is split between two sites, one on each side of the main road that links Redruth and Camborne. The engine at Taylor's Shaft, on the north side, was manufactured by Harvey's of Hayle, and designed to pump water from the deep mine; the engine on the south site, at Mitchell shaft, was engineered by Camborne's dynastic family engineering firm, Holman's, and designed to work a winding mechanism, or 'whim'. Although no longer powered by high-pressure steam (electricity does the job now) the two great beasts, pumping away to their own steady rhythm, are none the less impressive

The Heartlands Project, Pool

The road uniting Camborne and Redruth used to offer a disheartening prospect of abandoned, scrappy mining buildings and retail trading estates. There's still some of that on offer, but a huge new development, powered by photovoltaic energy and fuelled by a biomass boiler, is rising from the industrial ashes, which is determined to give Pool a fresh start and a wildly different image. Centring on the beautifully restored Robinson Mine, where a new mining heritage centre has just opened, an eco-friendly cluster of houses, artists'

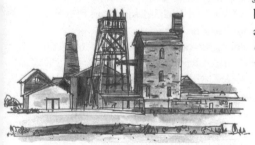

studios, offices and community buildings have sprung up, grouped around a market place while the rest of the 19-acre site is well on the way to becoming a lush green landscape, filled with trees, pools and places for play. I was particularly taken with the Diaspora Gardens, filled with plants native to the Americas, South Africa, Australia and New Zealand, and representing the spread of Cornish miners and Cornish mining technology across the globe. There's endless, exciting scope for botanical exchange of plants and people across the globe, which would establish Heartlands on not just the Cornish, but the wider horticultural map. The whole project is ambitious, certainly – one of its stated aims is to make Heartlands a centre for Cornish arts – but there's much local pride in the project, which augurs well for the future.

⑫ Redruth

Once the financial capital of the mining world, Redruth is chock-full of history, written all over its handsome Victorian architecture. The town leans out in three hilly directions from its centre in Fore Street, where since 2008 a bronze sculpture of a miner, arms flung out wide, feet firmly on the ground, appears to be on the point of launching into flight. It's a striking image for a town which saw both boom and bust, when two-thirds of its mining population were forced into emigration as their industry collapsed. I like the ambiguity of the miner's gesture: the artist, David Annand, seems to have caught both the heroism and the suffering, the rootedness and the eventual flight of the Cornish miner.

Every one of the old buildings in Redruth has a story to tell, but none more poignantly encapsulates the rise, fall and emerging restoration of Redruth than the preserved ruins of **Druid's Hall** in Penryn Street. This was built in 1859 as a cultural centre of commensurate grandeur for such an important town, containing a library, vast assembly room and theatre. In 1910, as Redruth's fortunes were on a downward roll, and the cultural centre closed, it was given a new lease of life as a cinema. In post-war years the building, which had once

Old rivalries

Not to be outdone by Camborne's Richard Trevithick, Redruth has its own hero of steam invention: the Scot, William Murdoch, whose life and works are celebrated in mid-June on Murdoch Day, with a similar blast of noise and colour to that of Camborne's Trevithick Day. Murdoch was James Watt's most ambitious and creative employee, but Murdoch's interest in 'strong steam' engineering (where the steam rather than the vacuum created produces energy) cut no ice with Watt, who saw it as risky and experimental. So when Trevithick showed up on Murdoch's Redruth doorstep, the frustrated Scot was delighted by the young man's curiosity and enthusiasm and gave him a demonstration, using a little model engine that ran round his drawing-room floor.

When Trevithick married, he and Jane moved into Redruth, taking accommodation next door to Murdoch. Redruth partisans are in no doubt that Murdoch was the victim of industrial espionage, perpetrated by Trevithick, who went on to claim 'strong steam' as his own invention. Secure in this knowledge, visitors can move about the streets of Redruth safely (unless that is, you're wearing the cherry-and-white colours of Camborne rugby club on the day of the derby match).

represented the civic pride of Redruth, was transformed into the Zodiac Bingo Club, destroyed by fire in 1984. Only the intriguing shell of the structure remains and this now encloses a small garden, planted in 2000, symbolic of the new Redruth, rising not so much from, as within, the ashes of its past.

Walk through the garden and you emerge in a small street, next to a 14th-century stone cross, which marked the entrance to **St Rumon's Chapel**. The medieval chapel was demolished in the 17th century and replaced with a modest house, where **William Murdoch** lived, with (for a brief period) the Trevithicks as neighbours for the last two decades of the 1700s (*open Mon, Wed and Fri mornings*).

The best place to start exploring Redruth's past is the **Cornwall Centre**, just up the hill from the sculpture in Alma Place. This is where anyone interested in tracing their Cornish roots or anything to do with Cornwall's past will find themselves eventually, and the entire history of Cornwall is displayed in a sequence of stitched and sewn pictures displayed on the walls. The visitor centre (in the same room as the Cornish Studies library) offers three different heritage trail maps that explain the significance of all Redruth's important buildings and make for enjoyable ambling.

Redruth's mining history is important, but it hasn't consumed the town's identity entirely. Artists and creative businesses are increasing in numbers to the point where the **Krowji studios**, just off Blowinghouse Hill (*West Park, TR15 3AJ; 01209 313200*) can describe themselves as 'Cornwall's largest creative hub'. Krowji is housed in an old grammar school that has been converted into dozens of artists' studios and offices. The studios open for a Christmas weekend in December and again in May/June for the **Cornwall Open Studios** fortnight, and in between there's usually at least one exhibition or event to visit, and music on Wednesday evenings in the Melting Pot Café (see below). Krowji is also headquarters of the **Miracle Theatre** (*www.miracletheatre. co.uk*), Cornish to the core, and much loved for their wildly popular outdoor performances all over the county in the summer.

Moseley Museum

Tumblydown Farm, Tolgus Mount, Redruth TR15 3TA ① 01209 211191.

This private collection of vintage boys' toys, housed in a barn on a working farm just north of the A30, is not so much a toy museum as a tribute to Frank Hornby. Model trains and Meccano made Hornby's name a legend, and by the 1950s his Liverpool-based business was running at peak capacity to meet demand. But competition eventually undid the company, which was bankrupted in 1979. Phone first to make an appointment to see the collection; owner Colin Saxton will take you round. He's also created a display of coal-mining exhibits and is building a collection of narrow-gauge locomotives, rescued from local mines and which run on a short length of track between the horse paddocks.

Food and drink

The Melting Pot The Old Grammar School, West Park, Redruth TR15 3AJ
① 07915 252757 ⓦ www.themeltingpotcafe.co.uk. The whole room is an
unbridled, sumptuous collage made from pieces of everyday junk donated by
café regulars. Open weekdays only, for breakfasts and lunches, and dinner on
Wednesday evenings when there's live music, often salsa or jazz. The lunchtime
curries on Fridays are very, very good.

⑬ Carn Brea and the Great Flat Lode

Just to the south of Camborne and Redruth, the humpback ridge of Carn Brea
is one of the great landmarks of west Cornwall, crowned as it is with what looks
from a distance like a giant chess piece, and a little lower down embellished
with a fortress-like building. You can drive up to the village of Carnkie, just
short of the summit, but it's infinitely more interesting to walk, bike or ride the
eight-mile track that loops around the hill, through gorse and stunted thorn
taking in the many vestigial remains of engine houses, smelting works, mine
shafts and chimneys along the way: basilica-like wrecks of a lost civilisation.
It's funny sometimes how nature and the ruins of industrial architecture work
so well together – the landscape would not be half so interesting without the
ruins and the ruins would not look half so appealing without the soft, green
wrappings of nature.

The monument on top of the hill was erected in 1836, to honour Sir
Francis Bassett of Tehidy. It's known as the Dunstanville rather than the
Bassett monument, in recognition of the title bestowed on the bravest and
most popular of the Bassetts, who marched 65
miles with his miners to reinforce Plymouth's
woefully inadequate defences from the threat of
a combined Spanish and French invasion in
1779. A little way down the hill, the restored
castle, one room of which perches on top of
a colossal outcrop of granite boulders, was
originally built by a medieval Bassett, more as
a hunting lodge than as a defensive fortress. It
now contains what has to be one of Cornwall's
least expected delights: a Jordanian family-run
restaurant (see below).

The well-marked trail around Carn Brea is known as the Great Flat
Lode, a reference to the rich vein of tin-bearing ore (lode) underground, which
while not exactly horizontal, was far from vertical, as most tin lodes tend to
be. This accounts for the proliferation of shafts along the trail: how much
easier it was to hit the lode with a sequence of short shafts than the single deep
shaft that most lodes required, with galleries off, from which the ore could be
hacked. The mine owners had other reasons to be grateful to the GFL; the
copper-bearing ore above had been exhausted by 1870, and the discovery of

tin below kept the mines open for several decades longer than expected, finally closing in 1917.

To make a full day of the walk, there are a couple of worthwhile places to stop at on the way: King Edward Mine and the Shire Horse Farm and Carriage Museum, both on the southern section of the trail.

Food and drink

Carn Brea Castle Carnkie, Redruth TR16 6SL ① 01209 218358. Very hard to find and get to (it's down a pot-holed track, somewhere near the summit of Carn Brea) especially on a dark evening, but the reward for intrepid and determined diners is pure magic: candle-lit granite walls that are 700 years old, a Jordanian welcome, (you will meet Mr Sarwalha, who had the imagination and courage to set up a family restaurant here in 1989) and superb food on a Middle Eastern theme. See if you can persuade Mr Sarwalha to let you climb up to the roof; the views across Cornwall are sublime.

The King Edward Mine Museum

Troon, Camborne TR14 9DP ① 01209 614681 ⓦ www.kingedwardmine.co.uk.

'What we have here is either priceless treasure – or a pile of junk, depending on your point of view,' grinned the man on the admissions desk, 'but none of it can ever be replaced.' I am no industrial archaeologist, but one of the real pleasures of researching this chapter has been the opportunity to engage with some of the characters who keep Cornish mining history alive and accessible. The engineering principles may be roughly the same, whichever mine you visit, but each mine has a different story to tell, and the voices that tell the story are worth listening to. In this case, it was Ben, a young graduate of the School of Mines, who explained the history and machinery of the mine and set the enormous waterwheel into action. Since 1901, when the mine was refurnished with the latest in mining equipment for training purposes, all students of the Camborne School of Mines have done their practical training here, both above and below ground. There's some lovely footage on display of students here in the 1930s, all tweed-suited and Brylcreemed, learning surveying techniques and playing a game of impromptu football among the old buildings.

Shire Horse Farm and Carriage Museum

Lower Gryllis, Treskillard TR16 6LA ① 01209 713606; open Easter to end Sep Sun–Fri 10.00–16.00.

There's a serious conservation issue at this bucolic farm southwest of Carn Brea, where octogenarian Harry Gotts has been breeding Suffolk Punches – a breed of heavy horse on the verge of extinction – all his adult life. As a boy, Harry was evacuated during the war to a farm where horses were being used as draught animals, and he's never looked back, though it saddens him to have witnessed the rapid decline of the breed in post-war years. 'We hope to see a

Cornish Methodism

There's nothing like an industrialised, working-class community for generating a feeling of 'Us and Them', and by the middle of the 18th century mining communities across Cornwall were feeling about as far removed from the mine-owning 'Thems' as was possible. Even on Sundays, there was no getting away from the feeling of alienation, shuffling into a church which seemed to represent a similarly distant, incomprehensible authority, accessible only to the toffs in the front pew.

So when the Wesley brothers, Charles and John, arrived in Cornwall in 1743 (it was the first of 32 whirlwind tours of preaching by John), preaching personal rather than institutionalised faith and salvation, it was taken up by the working classes with gusto. What's more, it meant not being restricted to worshipping in church with the local toffery; services could be held in cottage parlours, farm buildings or even woods and quarries. Chapels began to spring up, but that didn't change the basic fact that Methodism was comforting, comfortable and spoken in everyday language.

But as the numbers of chapels increased, many of the old Anglican churches in Cornwall were falling to pieces and watching their congregations dwindle. This in turn generated its own dynamic response: by the mid-1800s, a huge rebuilding initiative to preserve the old parish churches was launched and dozens of Victorian architects rolled up their sleeves.

foal born here every year,' he says, 'but that doesn't alter the fact that more Suffolk Punches die than are born in the UK each year.' He keeps Clydesdales and shire horses here too, and there's a working forge where you can see the horses being shod. Harry also gives ploughing demonstrations and is happy to talk about his collection of over 40 horse-drawn vehicles, which includes the largest collection of horse-drawn buses in the country.

⑭ Gwennap Pit

3 miles south of Redruth, on the edge of a small village; TR16 5HH; grid reference SW741400 ℗ 01209 822770; visitor centre open Spring bank holiday to end Sep.

This one of the most important places on the Methodist map. In 1762, John Wesley wrote, 'The wind was so high that I could not stand at the usual place at Gwennap; but at a small distance was a green hollow capable of containing many thousands of people. I stood on one side of this amphitheatre towards the top and with people beneath on all sides, I preached.' He returned on no fewer than 18 occasions, once (reportedly) attracting a crowd of 32,000, which seems a slight exaggeration: the pit is impressive enough, but surely not that big. The grassy tiers were cut out by local miners in the early 19th century, to make seating easier for the crowds which continued to flock to the site; today the annual Whitsun service (as well as regular summer services) continues to draw large audiences. There's an indoor chapel next to the entrance and a small visitor centre.

Godolphin country

South and west of Camborne, a maze of roads winds through undulating farming country, dotted with small villages and hamlets, littered not only with remains of the mining industry, but relics of older activity too, in the form of isolated barrows and standing stones, earthworks and abandoned settlements. Bassett mines give way to Godolphin estates and less than five (crow-flown) miles from Camborne, the trickling beginnings of the River Hayle have been crossed and the wooded entrance to the headquarters of the once-powerful Godolphins lies ahead.

⑮ Godolphin

Godolphin Cross, TR13 9RE ℗ 01736 763194; National Trust.

An entry in the visitors' book compares the gardens at Godolphin most unfavourably with Lanhydrock's manicured acres, which gives everybody who loves the place a good giggle.

Parts of Godolphin's gardens are over 700 years old and much of the special atmosphere derives from the feeling that time and horticultural fashion have slipped past, leaving a sort of leafy, self-contained lushness, just on the right side of unkempt, that the 17th-century poet, Andrew Marvell, would have recognised and loved: 'Society is all but rude,/ To this delicious solitude.' The head gardener was moving on to another position when I visited, but she assured me that the National Trust, which acquired the property in 2007, has no intention of 'improving' the gardens, despite massive recent renovations to the buildings that have seen the creation of a discreet visitor centre/tearoom in the old piggery and conversion of the main house into an upmarket holiday let. (The house can still be visited during the first week of each month when lettings are suspended to allow visitors access.)

Originally the gardens were laid out as eight squares, enclosing in the ninth square a small castle, erected in or around 1300. The castle was pulled down in the late 1400s, and a new house built, set around two courtyards, embellished by generations of Godolphins, until by the mid-1600s, it was ranked as one of the biggest houses in Cornwall. Just one courtyard survives today, with its chief glory intact: the double-height, colonnaded north façade, an idiosyncratic blend of Tuscan classicism and English battlements. The Civil War halted the building programme and although the Royalist Godolphins recovered their wealth and influence the house was left increasingly unoccupied and ultimately more or less abandoned until 1937, when Sydney and Mary Schofield bought it from a local mining man and initiated a loving and sensitive restoration of what remained of the house.

Beyond the gardens, there are 550 acres of National Trust-owned estate woods to explore, beneath which lie the source of Godolphin wealth: tin- and copper-mine workings, some dating back to the 16th century. The old engine houses, engulfed now by trees, reminded me of those ruined jungle temples you find in Cambodia or Peru; those of a more prosaic temperament might find the allusion a little far-fetched and suggest a head-clearing stroll up Godolphin Hill, which pushes its bare crown above the treeline and offers bracing views of both north and south coasts and everything in between.

Food and drink

You're not far from Helston or Porthleven (see *Chapter 8*) by the time you get to Godolphin or Tregonning, but there's a decent pitstop at Breage on the way.

The Queen's Arms ① 01326 573485. A big, friendly pub, serving home-cooked, locally sourced food and local ales, this is dog- and child-friendly, too. At the back there's parking and hook-ups for camping cars, and when I asked about putting up a tent, I was shown across the road to a delightful grassy spot, in a walled enclosure adjoining the churchyard.

⑯ Tregonning Hill

Several footpaths lead to the summit, but the shortest and most accessible route starts in Balwest, where there's free parking in a field during the summer months (park on the grassy triangle at the start of the track at other times) and an information board and map by the gate. The views from the top are stupendous, a huge reward for an easy climb of well under a mile, along a track that is well used by mountain bikers too. From the war memorial that stands close to the trig point, you can see both the north coast and the great, glinting arc of Mount's Bay, St Michael's Mount dwarfed by distance and height. Godolphin Hill, a mile away to the north, though just lower by 30 feet, is similarly reduced to molehill proportions. A short walk southeast along the summit ridge leads to a Wesleyan preaching pit in a disused quarry and a plaque commemorating William Cookworthy's discovery of china (kaolin) clay here in 1746. Cookworthy, a young chemist from Plymouth, had spotted local miners were using Tregonning clay to repair their furnaces, and guessed that if it could withstand such high temperatures without cracking, it must have similar properties to kaolin-type clay, from which porcelain was made. He was right: Tregonning Hill was full of it and British porcelain-makers' dependency on imported kaolin from China was about to end. The reason why Tregonning Hill bears no resemblance to the 'Cornish Alps', is that the clay here turned out to have a high mica content, and the pits were abandoned as 'kaolin fever' spread east and purer kaolin was found around St Austell. Cornwall's most profitable industry ever had been launched.

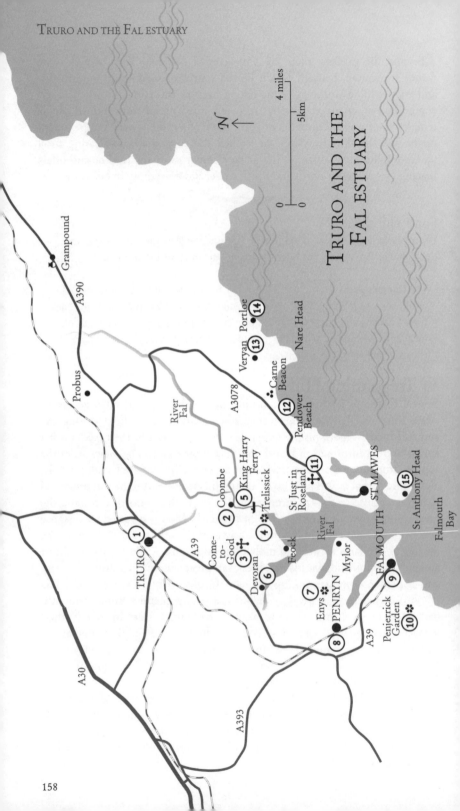

TRURO AND THE
FAL ESTUARY

7. TRURO AND THE FAL ESTUARY

From Truro to Falmouth by river, there is not one inch of unloveliness, the estuary shores designated in their entirety an Area of Outstanding Natural Beauty. Herons, silent and still observe the water, egrets gather in oak trees and oystercatchers sweep down to the muddy banks at low tide. And the sorrowful cry of the curlew echoes around the tidal creeks, epitomising the soft, green loneliness of these very special hidden places.

Although it's common to refer to the whole estuary as the Fal, the Fal is just one of several rivers that flow into the deep, wooded ria (meaning a flooded estuarine valley) below Truro, where the Allen and Kenwyn flow into the Truro River. The Truro is joined by the Tresillian at Malpas, and it's not until further downriver that the Fal cuts in from the east. On the west bank, the Carnon and Kennal join in at Restronguet Creek and the Penryn River merges with the generous embrace of Falmouth harbour. Here, with the sea in sight, the estuary widens hugely and becomes known as the Carrick Roads, narrowing only marginally where Falmouth and St Mawes face each other across a yacht-filled mile of sea. It's a busy estuary, populated not only by sailing boats and passenger ferries, but also towering container ships, heading to the deep moorings above the King Harry Ferry, where they sit out the lean times, surrounded by dense oak woods, absurdly out of place beside the red-sailed oyster boats, dredging the river bed the traditional way, through the autumn and winter months.

The western banks of the estuary are the busiest, with a student population at Falmouth and Penryn contributing to the youthful, arty buzz that distinguishes both these towns from other Cornish harbours. There's a heady mix of culture here, encompassing music and the visual arts, gardens and regional cuisine that erupts into a summer-long series of festivals against the backdrop of the river. While not so much goes on across the water, the Roseland peninsula has an idyllic waterfront, both riverine and coastal, fringed with sandy, secluded beaches, busy harbours, bright with yachts and dinghies – and some of the smartest hotels in the county. Inland, it's quietly pastoral and dotted with well-heeled little villages, farms and harbours all the way down to its remote, southernmost tip at St Anthony Head.

Getting around

It's no fun driving through Truro or Falmouth during the morning and evening rush hours, and as the university campus at Tremough expands Penryn gets busier and busier in term-time, too. If arriving by car in Falmouth during the summer months, take advantage of the 'Park and Float' scheme, which is more expensive than Park and Ride (both operate out of the Ponsharden car park), but gives you the joy of arriving in the middle of Falmouth by boat.

Summer brings a concentration of cars to narrow lanes of the Roseland peninsula, and long queues for the King Harry Ferry. This is a lovely way to cross the river at its narrowest point – and it cuts miles off the road trip around the head of the estuary, but at peak times can end up being the slower option. However, getting around on public transport is easy, and there's every reason to dump the car and arm yourself with an integrated ferry, bus and train pass.

The **Fal Mussel Card** (it should have been called the Fal Oyster Card, but London Transport argued against) comes in two forms. The Local card is valid on ferries only (particularly useful for car drivers commuting on the King Harry Ferry); the Visitor card covers travel on the Maritime Branch Line, local buses (including the 550 which covers the Roseland peninsula) and all the classic ferry routes, up, down and across the river (*www.falriver.co.uk/mussel*).

Trains

A two-carriage train shuttles up and down the west bank of the estuary every half-hour between Truro and Falmouth Docks, stopping at Penryn and Falmouth Town (The Dell) on the way. The Maritime Branch Line has proved a phenomenally successful service: packed with students and commuters on weekdays and only marginally quieter at weekends.

Buses

Walkers on both sides of the river are well served, with buses from Truro covering the main villages on the Roseland peninsula and linking with the passenger ferry from Falmouth to St Mawes. Falmouth, which is anathema to cars in the summer, has a great round-the-town service departing every 20 minutes from the Quarry car park. The free *Fal River Cornwall Area Guide Book* shows how it all fits together and suggests bus- and ferry-linked walks.

Ferries

The King Harry Ferry from Feock to Philleigh is the only means of getting a car across the river below Truro, but is much used by walkers (it's free for foot passengers) and cyclists (50p per bike). The service runs all year and is staffed by a very friendly crew. In summer, there's often a chap selling bags of Fal mussels on board.

The other year-round service is the foot passenger ferry between Falmouth and St Mawes. Details for both are on www.kingharryscornwall.co.uk/ferries.

From the beginning of April to early November a small, open boat (fuelled ecologically by old chip fat) ferries walkers from St Mawes across the Percuil to Place Creek, on the southernmost tip of the Roseland peninsula.

Other summer services link Falmouth to Truro and points in between, such as Flushing, Mylor and Trelissick – go to the Town Quay in Truro or Prince of Wales Pier in Falmouth or you can find all the details online at www.enterprise-boats.co.uk

Cycling

There's good cycling to be had on both sides of the estuary and you can take bikes cheaply on all the passenger ferries. The Sustrans Cornish Way crosses the Fal on the King Harry Ferry and winds pleasantly down to the beach at Pendower (where you'll have to carry your bike over a footbridge) and rejoins the coast again at Portloe. Steep hills and twisty, single-track lanes are the price to be paid for detours to the remoter shores of the Fal around Lamorran woods.

A free booklet *7 Bike Rides from Truro on Tarmac: Tarmac, Sweat and Teas* is an inspiration. The author has already produced a similar booklet for mountain bikers, *8 Mountain Bike Rides from Truro. Mud, Sweat and Beers.* Both guides give detailed information of circular routes, illustrated with photos, but you will need an OS Landranger map (204) to plot the route first, or else you'll be stopping at every junction to see where to turn. You can pick up a copy at Devoran Creek Cycle Hire or at the Old Quay Inn in Devoran, which is next door.

Cycle hire

Bike Chain Bissoe Bike Hire Old Conns Works, Bissoe, Truro TR48QZ ☎ 01872 870341 Ⓦ www.cornwallcyclehire.com. Well placed for exploring the network of Mineral Trails which fan out west of Truro; bikes can be hired by the day or week and there's a café too, beside a large car park.
Devoran Creek Cycle Hire Behind the Old Quay Inn, Devoran ☎ 01872 863142 Ⓦ www.devorancreekcyclehire.com. From Devoran a surprisingly level cycle route leads 11 miles to Portreath on the north coast; it's also a perfect spot to tackle a complete round-the-estuary ride, using the passenger ferry from Falmouth to St Mawes.

Accommodation

Upmarket hotels and self-catering cottages are thick on the ground here: the Duchy, the Falmouth, the Greenbank and St Michael's Spa are all to be found in Falmouth; the Tresanton in St Mawes and the Nare on the coast cater to the well-heeled on the Roseland side of the estuary. A selection of B&Bs and campsites are listed on www.falriver.co.uk.

Carnebo Barn Trenoweth, Mabe, Falmouth TR10 9JJ ① 01326 377454. The approach is up a rough track west of Falmouth: the car-free, inexpensive campsite is intended for walkers and cyclists looking for a spot of back-to-nature camping and an evening round the fire-pit. There's a solar-powered shower, compost loo and a cold tap, but just down the hill is a pristine, icy cold pool in a small disused quarry. A pre-erected bell-tent, sleeping four, is a handy option.

Come-to-Good Farm Feock TR3 6QS ① 01872 863828 Ⓦ www.cometogoodfarm. co.uk Ⓔ info@cometogoodfarm.co.uk. A very reasonably priced B&B in a glorious rural spot, close to the thatched Quaker meeting house of the same name (see page 170). A double room and family suite (sleeping four) each have their own bathroom. The farm has chickens and sheep, and children are encouraged to collect the hen eggs for breakfast. There are hands-on courses for those interested in learning lambing skills or looking after their own poultry.

Little White Alice Carnmenellis TR16 6PL ① 01209 861000 Ⓦ www. littlewhitealice.co.uk Ⓔ enquiries@littlewhitealice.co.uk. In a wild and remote corner of the granite landscape close to Stithians Lake, about 6 miles west of Penryn, are these six beautifully designed, eco-friendly cottages, sleeping two to eight, and a studio where the owner teaches weaving from home-grown willow. Hand-crafted kitchens and the last word in eco-luxury bedrooms and bathrooms at average holiday cottage prices. There's a natural swimming pool, looking just like an emerald pond, a fire-pit and Cusgarne Organics deliver boxes of farm produce on request. The name is a version of the local tin mine – wheal white allis.

The Observatory Tower Trelawney Rd, Falmouth ① 0844 800 2813 Ⓦ www. cornishgems.com. The white tower, looking rather like a lighthouse, is one of Falmouth's landmarks. Built in 1867 on the highest point in Falmouth as a weather observation tower, this is now a quirky but very upmarket self-catering let, sleeping four in some style. The top floor has blackout blinds and a camera obscura, handy if there's an eclipse.

St Anthony Head Cottages National Trust Holiday Cottages ① 0844 8002070 Ⓦ www.nationaltrustcottages.co.uk Ⓔ cottages@nationaltrust.org.uk. Out on the wild, remote St Anthony headland, the former office buildings of the World War II observation post have been converted by the National Trust into four small holiday cottages. Tiffy's, the Lieutenant's and Captain's quarters each sleeps two, the Major's Quarters sleeps four and is suitable for wheelchair users.

Tourist information centres

Falmouth Fal River Visitor Information Centre, 11 Market Strand, Prince of Wales Pier ① 0905 325 4534 Ⓦ www.falmouth.co.uk.

St Mawes The Roseland Visitor Centre, The Millennium Rooms, The Square ① 01326 270440 Ⓦ www.stmawesandtheroseland.co.uk.

Truro Town Hall, Boscawen St ① 01872 274555 Ⓦ http://tourism.truro.gov.uk.

Truro and around

Cornwall's only city may not have the tourist-pulling power of Falmouth or the Roseland, but it is a rewarding destination for Slow explorers, especially if time is spent discovering its gentle riverine setting.

① Truro

A city with lots of Slow attributes, that looks prosperous and well cared for, Truro is a place to be enjoyed on foot and at a leisurely pace. Truro's small by any city standards, with a population of around 19,000, but that serves to make it all the more approachable. It looks good from a distance too, settled snugly in its shallow valley, the three pale towers and spires of the neo-Gothic cathedral soaring high above the surrounding rooftops; it's hard to believe that such a defining landmark has stood there for only a little more than 100 years.

You don't get much of a sense of Truro's strategic position as a riverhead port, however, unless you take to the water (Enterprise Ferries run a boat from Town Quay to Falmouth) and get a view of the docks and warehouses that line the approach to the quay and a glimpse of the two small rivers, the Kenwyn and the Allen, that flow through the town to meet at this point. The Kenwyn disappears almost immediately beneath the piazza-like expanse of Lemon Quay, but the Allen can be followed on foot, through the Memorial Gardens and car park beyond to the leafy lanes behind the cathedral.

Truro's Celtic and Norman origins were modestly built on fishing, farming and tin; it was Penryn, a few miles downstream, with its internationally important Glasney College, that became the happening place in medieval times. But Truro had stannary-town status, a safe port and its prosperity as a commercial and industrial centre grew to heady heights in the 18th and 19th centuries, under the stewardship of one family in particular, the intriguingly named Lemons. William Lemon (1697–1760) was a self-made mining tycoon, who married well, invested shrewdly and was twice mayor of Truro. Known locally as 'the great Mr Lemon', he had great visions for building and improving the town, but it was his grandson, also named William, who put the plans for the creation of a grandly terraced avenue in place and thoroughly revamped the layout of Truro. By the time he died in 1824, the town was being frequently compared to Bath in terms of architectural and social scenery. Important Cornish families came to Truro to 'do the season' – it was in the fashionable Assembly Rooms that dynastic unions were forged by anxious Georgian mamas and papas, intent on securing family wealth. The name of Lemon is everywhere you look in Truro: Lemon Street is still grandly Georgian, Lemon Quay is the city's new festival and market place, Lemon Villas is just as it sounds; a local barbershop calls itself Lemon Heads. But the man on top of the tall Doric column at the head of Lemon Street is not who you might imagine; this is Truro's hero, Richard Lander – equal and contemporary (had he lived longer) of David Livingstone, in charting the dark heart of Africa.

Orientation in Truro is fairly straightforward, with the compact historic centre lying around and immediately south of the cathedral, now gleamingly unwrapped from a long period of restoration. **High Cross**, by the cathedral entrance, is dignified by the 1780 façade of the **Assembly Rooms**, decorated with handsome Wedgwood plaques representing Thalia (the Muse of actors), Shakespeare and David Garrick. But the façade is all that's left: the splendid theatre-cum-ballroom that lay behind has long gone, and the arched Georgian windows now display pasties. A few steps away, **Millpool** is a quiet, leafy spot beside the River Allen and overlooked by the cathedral café; there's a 1930s police box by the bridge over the river, which occasionally lends itself to an extremely small art exhibition or installation.

A wander down St Mary's Street takes you past the **Old Grammar School** (now a pleasant wine and tapas bar of the same name), founded in 1597; Humphry Davy, the inventor of the miners' safety lamp, went to school here, shortly after the retirement of its legendary headmaster, George Conon, who described the establishment as 'the Eton of Cornwall'. William Lemon (the elder) enrolled himself here as an adult; having missed out on education in his early years, the mining tycoon humbly decided to make a start on his Latin and Greek. Whether or not he was allowed to bring his pet chough into the classroom (until it was accidentally shot by one of his junior classmates) is a matter for conjecture.

Just around the corner, the many gabled and chimneyed building, known as **Coinage Hall** (built as a bank in 1848) contains a marvellously old-fashioned tea room on the first floor with grand views of the Italianate **town hall** and the shops along **Boscawen Street**. Between Coinage Hall and the town hall, **Princes Street** (how can you resist entering via Squeezeguts Alley?) was clearly the place to build your house if you were anyone in the mid 18th century. **Princes House**, designed by Thomas Edwards, was built in 1739 for the chough-loving Lemon, and the **Mansion House** was the town residence of Lemon's chief assistant, Thomas Daniell. Edwards was once again the architect, but his brief was different in one important respect: the house was to be built of Bath stone. Thomas Daniell had married Elizabeth Elliot in 1754; as a wedding gift, Elizabeth's uncle, Ralph Allen, a Cornishman living in Bath, gave them the stone extracted from quarries he owned for the house. The gift had a secondary purpose: Allen had spotted a market in Truro and wanted to showcase Bath stone as cheaper, paler and altogether more desirable than the local Newham stone. The Mansion House took seven years to build – from 1755 to 1762 – at a cost estimated to be in the region of £8,500. And as an advertisement it worked; even the cathedral, when it came to be built just over a century later, was built partly of Bath stone. The problem though, is that Bath stone is not as resistant to the Cornish weather as the local stuff, resulting in the recent restoration work to the cathedral.

The completion of the Daniells' house meant the Enys residence, started in 1706 in neighbouring Quay Street, quickly became known as the **Old Mansion**

House, another fine example of early Georgian town house architecture. On a more domestic scale, **Walsingham Place**, a perfectly preserved crescent of Georgian cottages, set Betjeman's heart racing with relief that it had not been lost to the post-war building boom. And you can almost hear the Poet Laureate muttering 'Proportion, proportion, proportion' to himself, wandering the length of **Lemon Street** with a smile on his face.

Among all this Georgian splendour, the concreted-over harbour known as **Lemon Quay** is something of an anomaly and when the large bronze statue of a naked drummer balancing on a ball, costing £95,000, was unveiled in 2011 as part of the annual arts festival, eyebrows were raised, giving protesting twitterati a field day. The **Hall for Cornwall**, with its entrance on the quay, gives the place a lively buzz on theatre or music nights, but the quay really comes to life during the city's jamborees, which include not only the Arts Festival in late April but also the Music and the Cornish Food and Drink festivals in September, and an impressive **City of Lights Festival** in November, when enormous paper lanterns, wittily representing everything from dragons to (clothed) musicians are paraded through the streets to the quay.

Truro Cathedral

Truro's Victorian masterpiece is the first Anglican cathedral to be built on a new site since Salisbury Cathedral began to rise from the ground in 1220. It needed to be impressive: for 800 years Cornwall had been denied its own bishop, and decades of intense lobbying finally paid off when, in 1877, the diocese of Cornwall (which had last been held at St Germans, in the 10th century) was finally re-established on Cornish soil, at Truro. There were other contenders for the honour – St Germans, naturally, put up a good case; Bodmin too. Even St Columb threw its hat into the ring.

Richard Lander

Truro's hero is the boy who grew up in the Fighting Cocks Inn, listening to seafarers' tales and walked alone to London aged nine, looking for adventure. By the age of 14 he had spent three years in the West Indies and within five years he had seen something of Europe too, earning his keep as odd-job boy and servant to a succession of wealthy employers. Aged 21 he joined the Scottish explorer Hugh Clapperton's expedition to chart the course of the Niger from source to sea; all the expedition members died of fever, apart from Lander, who received a hero's welcome when he eventually returned home to write a hair-raising account of his adventures.

Two further expeditions to Nigeria followed, partly fuelled by the dangerous mission of attempting to eliminate human slavery; the first, on which he was accompanied by his younger brother, John, was counted a success. The second ended with his death, after a gunshot wound turned gangrenous.

Truro had a parish church in the town centre, but it was in a shabby state by the 1860s and it was assumed that it would have to be pulled down to make way for the new building. But the architect, **John Loughborough Pearson**, made a convincing case for incorporating the south aisle of the old church into the new building and won further approval by putting an unobtrusive bend in the main axis, thus avoiding the cost of purchasing an 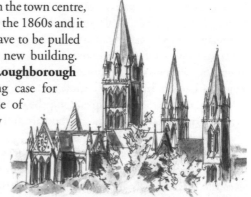 extra block of land to the south. It's cleverly done: you have to stand in the centre of the nave and look up and down to register the six-foot difference in alignment between the nave and chancel. Pearson's extravagantly Gothic vision, topped off by three spires, was completed in 1910, 30 years after the first stone was laid.

Inside there's lots to admire. Pearson worked closely with the sculptor **Nathaniel Hitch**, a man with the ability to make stone seem like butter in his hands. The vast stone **reredos** behind the high altar is by Hitch, and as you look around, other intricately detailed relief carvings by the same hand stand out with clarity. While I was admiring the reredos, an elderly Truronian nudged me and pointed up at a tiny bit of blue glass, evidently a repair, in the stained-glass windows, high above the altar. 'That's the only bit of wartime damage,' he chuckled, 'but it's not what you think. A bored boy chorister with an air rifle did that, and the emergency repair hasn't been replaced.' He was gone before I thought to ask him how he knew.

I was in for another surprise. A large painting, titled *Land of the Saints*, caught my attention. It's a heaven's-eye view of the entire county, painted with astonishing topographical virtuosity, with every one of its parish churches lit by a tiny beacon of light, painted in 1980 to help celebrate the cathedral's centenary. The surprise for me was the artist: my first-ever visit to Cornwall had been to meet **John Miller** in his garden studio at Sancreed in 1993. I knew him then for his almost abstract – now iconic – images of Cornish sea and sky; I had not guessed at the sacred in his work, but in front of the immense and lighted panorama it now made sense.

If you can make it to the cathedral for Friday lunchtimes there's a free world-class recital on the magnificent **Father Willis organ**, which is raved about by visiting organists. Recitals start at 13.10 and are deservedly well attended. The choir too, has an international reputation and can be heard at evening prayer daily at 17.30 or at 10.00 and 16.00 during Sunday services. The cathedral shop sells CDs of their music and there's a terrific coffee shop and restaurant in the **Chapter House**, which stays open for pre-concert suppers.

The Royal Cornwall Museum

The Royal Institution of Cornwall – the organisation that still owns and manages the Royal Cornwall Museum and Courtney Library in River Street – was founded in 1818 for 'the promotion of knowledge in natural history, ethnology and the fine and industrial arts, especially in relation to Cornwall'. It's currently undergoing quite an extensive refurbishment, designed to shake off its slightly dusty image, but the exhibits, spread over two floors, are some of Cornwall's finest: the Rashleigh collection of minerals (collected by Philip Rashleigh of Menabilly between 1760 and 1811) is of international importance; the most valuable finds from Cornish Bronze Age settlements are on display and the gallery contains the best collection of paintings by the Newlyn School outside Penzance's Penlee Gallery as well as some superb portraits by Opie (see page 139). Perhaps the least Cornish of the exhibits is an Egyptian mummy (still in its wrappings).

Entry is free, there are daily activities for children in the school holidays and the monthly lunchtime lectures are rated highly by those with a finger on the pulse of Truro's cultural agenda.

Food and drink

The **farmers' market** on Lemon Quay is held every Wednesday and Saturday and is one of the best around – it's the sort of market you'd be proud to show to a visitor from France or Italy. There's game according to season, locally caught fish and smoked cheeses from Penryn. **Nancarrow Farm** have added a terrific homemade burger stall to their stand selling home-reared organic beef, lamb and mutton; pork comes locally from the Lugg's **Primrose Herd** and the much-feted **Cornish Duck Company** is there on Saturdays, too. Fresh river mussels from the Fal are cooked on the spot by the **Cornish Mussel Company**, soup from the excellent **Cornish Soup Company**, best mopped up with bread from the **Cornish Mill**.

Indoors, **Lemon St Market** (just off Lemon St) has an extremely good collection of food shops, including **Baker Tom**, **Halzephron Herb Farm**, which does a nice line in sprouted seeds as well as jams and chutneys, and a super deli, **The Larder**, which also does healthily yummy take-away lunches and picnics. Upstairs, the **Lander Gallery** café is nicely informal among a mouth-watering collection of Cornish art for sale.

Skinner's Brewery, close to the docks (*Riverside View, Newham; 01872 245689*) produces Truro's much-loved ale, Betty Stoggs, among other favourites, such as Cornish Knocker and Heligan Honey, found all across the county. There are daily tours (and tastings) of the brewery which has won more awards than any other brewery in the West Country – not bad going with St Austell Ales and Sharp's just down the road. For a taste of Skinner's outside the brewery, go to the **Old Ale House**, one of Truro's oldest pubs, with an atmosphere to match; it's on the corner of Quay St (*01872 271122*). Lunch for the hungry is a feast, cooked and presented in cast-iron skillets, with half a loaf on the side.

There's no problem finding a place for a bite around the cathedral and city centre, though if you're after an old-fashioned (indeed, Victorian) tea room, with uniformed waitresses and leaf tea served in proper china, you should head up the stairs of Coinage Hall, and squeeze past an enticing secondhand bookshop to **Charlotte's Tea House** (*01872 263706*).

Around Truro

To appreciate the estuarine setting of the Truro, it's worth exploring the river scenery that's close by. One of the best ways to approach the city is by river from Falmouth; Enterprise Ferries run daily trips according to the tide in the summer months, with a stop at Malpas on the way (*www.enterprise-boats.co.uk*).

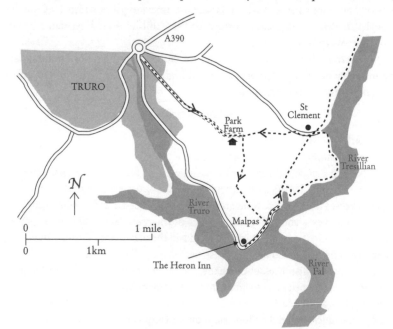

If you find yourself thinking you'd like to see more of the river and have a couple of hours to spare, there's a fine circular walk that takes in a good pub and two idyllic riverside villages linked by a wooded footpath, just a mile or so south of Truro.

A wander up the lane signposted Malpas leading off the big roundabout by the river leads past Truro School and onto high ground where you get your first proper look at the river.

The lane turns into a footpath leading to Park Farm, beyond which the drive offers a right-hand turning over the hill and down into Malpas and the waterfront. The Heron Inn (*01872 272773*) is family-friendly and very good for food – lots of people come by boat to eat here in the summer. The road from Truro ends in Malpas, but if you continue through the houses and cross the bridge over a stream in the woods you have the option to reach St Clement by either a hillside footpath (which culminates in a superb view of St Clement's Church) or continue along the river on a permissive path through the woods. You can extend the walk from St Clement, where a riverside public footpath extends along the Tresillian River northeast for a further mile. On the lane out of the village a footpath on your left leads back to Park Farm and the track back to Truro School and the roundabout.

Idless woods

Another decent walk a mile or so north of Truro takes you on a circular route through the Forestry Commission-owned Idless woods, (confusingly marked on the OS map as St Clement Woods). A circular route takes you past an Iron Age hillfort and a pretty branch of the infant River Allen in less than an hour. Unfortunately phythophthora has left its mark here in recent months and scores of larch have been felled in an attempt to halt the tree disease (also known as rapid oak death, despite oaks being thankfully immune), much to local chagrin.

Along the river to Falmouth

The journey by road and river between Truro and Falmouth paints two entirely different pictures: the road is a rather bleak artery which gives no hint of the beauty of the riverside harbours, gardens and wild, marshy creeks busy with wildfowl that lie within a mile or two of its austere path.

② Coombe

The cottages clustered around the shore of the creek were once home to oystermen and dredgers, their incomes and larders supplemented by the orchards of cider apples and local speciality plums that rose behind their houses. Generations of children grew up around the creek, learned to sail or row out into the deep waters of the Fal and returned with the tide to the lighted windows along the shoreline. It's all very different now. At least seven of the 19 cottages in the estate-owned hamlet have recently been transformed into smart holiday lettings; more are planned as the ageing tenants disperse – the community is on the verge of extinction. This was the story I heard from one elderly resident of Coombe, who felt keenly the loss of the community he had raised his children in. He had just returned from committing the ashes of a neighbour to the creek, early one morning at high tide, observed by a circle of old friends in their rowing boats. Later he sent me the following lines:

No tears, no outward signs of grief;
Perhaps a long, soft sigh as the ashes spill into the creek.
A moment of love and profound memory.

The glassy calm of the mistbound morning tide.
The melting sun just warming through.
Oars paused dripping and then slowly dipped as all the boats
Disperse and make for home.

I have a feeling it was not just his neighbour that he was mourning, and his words stayed with me as I walked the footpath through the woods above the creek and found unexpected solace in a deliciously planted teagarden overlooking the river. **Halwyn's** (*01872 272152; www.halwynsteagarden.com*) is the sort of place where you get loose-leaf tea served in bone china teacups and homemade scones and jam. Approached from Coombe by the footpath, or by a very narrow lane (beyond the turning to Old Kea), it's not the best place for cars, which soon clog up the narrow lay-by parking. But there's a tiny beach at the bottom of the garden, which is served by the Pandora Rover, a foot ferry run on a voluntary donation basis (see page 172). From here, you look across to the **Smugglers Cottage** on the quayside at Tolverne; it's now a café, run by the Tregothnan estate (whose much-vaunted tea plantations nestle among the woods on the far shore), but imagine the scene here in 1944, when General Eisenhower addressed 27,000 American troops before they embarked for the D-Day landings. His chair is preserved in an upstairs room of the cottage.

③ Come-to-Good

There's a footpath over the fields from Coombe to Come-to-Good, which is a lovely name for this cluster of houses and beautifully restored Quaker meeting house, built of whitewashed cob and thatch, dating from 1710, making it one of the earliest to be built in Cornwall after George Fox's travels (and travails) in Cornwall in 1656. The village's name is still the subject of some debate. One theory is that it derives from Cwm-ty-coit meaning 'the coombe by the dwelling in the wood'. Others think that because the name does not appear before the late 17th century, by which time the community's Quakers were

The Kea plum

Take the footpath from Kea to Cowlands and Coombe during late July and August and you'll see orchards laden with small red or black fruit, more like damsons than plums. The salt and wind resistant Kea plum is native to this valley, and the fruit highly prized for its high pectin content, which makes it eminently suitable for jam or chutney. People say the plums are too sharp to be enjoyed as dessert fruit, but the ones I tasted, at the end of August, were sweeter than I'd been led to believe – the red ones were especially good. You'll find produce made from Kea plums on sale in local farm shops, and the jam and chutney labels could soon be wearing a new badge for an application has been made to the European Union to give the Kea plum PGI (Protected Geographical Indication) status.

gathering for meetings in a local disused building, it may well be an ironic reference to the meeting house.

Inside, the interior has hardly changed since it was built: light streams through the lattice windows onto the wooden benches and plain, limewashed walls. It's a place of absolute peace and serenity; the grassy garden around the building is awash with snowdrops in February.

④ Trelissick

Feock TR3 6QL ⓣ 01872 862090 ⓦ www.nationaltrust.org.uk; National Trust.

From Easter to September, ferries from Truro, Falmouth and St Mawes drop off and pick up passengers from the pontoon at the bottom of the garden – which would get any garden off to a flying start, and in this case invests the whole experience with a kind of poetic quality. It's a steep climb through the densely planted slopes, but the stupendous views on all sides and the rich diversity of exotic trees and shrubs make it all the more worthwhile. And all along the main path are inviting diversions: grassy glades, shaded by the pick of the world's most beautiful trees, now grown to maturity; little summerhouses and a footbridge over the sunken lane which leads to the King Harry Ferry invite you to discover yet more acres of handsome specimen trees and shrubs. You encounter vivid herbaceous borders too, designed to extend the colour in the garden through to autumn, national collections of photinias and azaleas, and closer to the main buildings, walls swarming with roses and wisteria. One of the best-known images of Trelissick – especially visible on the road approach – is a round tower, capped with a steeply pitched conical slate roof, as though it had been lifted from a French chateau or fairy tale. It was a cleverly disguised water tank, built in 1865, and used for irrigation and fire control; now it's an unusual National Trust holiday cottage.

By contrast to the Rapunzelesque tower and romantic gardens, the house, when it finally comes into view, is a model of classical restraint: Nikolaus Pevsner described it as 'the severest neo-Greek mansion in Cornwall'. It was built in 1824 for Thomas Daniell (whose mining-magnate father was known as 'guinea-a-minute' Daniell). Daniell junior, however, had a gift for losing the money his father had earned and 30 years later, he was forced to sell the family pile. Trelissick's next owner, Carew Davies Gilbert, added to the house and planted many of the fine collection of trees, but the gardens really came to life in the last century, when the new owners, Ronald and Ida Copeland, began to fill the grounds with the rich menu of plants seen today. Ronald Copeland was a director of Spode and the gardens provided many of the floral models for the famous porcelain designs. Sadly, the collection was sold and dispersed in 2013 and can no longer be visited.

⑤ The King Harry Ferry

The clank of heavy chains is part of the soundscape on this stretch of the Fal, and the latest ferry, launched in 2006, has glass panels allowing you to see the impressive chains in action. The 300-yard crossing is all too brief – there's just time to take in the mussel beds and birdlife, get a glimpse of an incongruous container ship or two, mothballed while their skeleton crews wait for commercial activity to resume – and then the cars are rolling off again, cyclists prepare for a steep uphill exit and walkers shuffle their maps and look hopefully up at the sky. There's been a crossing here for more than a thousand years, as it's on an old pilgrim route to St Michael's Mount and the name refers to pious Henry VI, to whom a chapel in the woods on the east bank was once dedicated. The first chain ferry rumbled across in 1888, saving travellers' (and their horses') legs 26 miles of road via Truro and Tresillian. As green statistics go, the ferry's are pretty impressive: each year five million car miles are saved, which equates to 1,870 tons of CO_2 emissions.

⑥ Devoran

At the head of Restronguet Creek, Devoran's cottages sprang up as a result of an initiative to recover tin from the mud at the end of the 18th century, and as its quay facilities and tramway into the mining areas west of Truro expanded, so the population increased to the point where a church was called for. Devoran's church is pure Victorian, but its claim to fame lies in its architect, J L Pearson, who went on to design Truro Cathedral some years later. The churchyard turns out to be a treat for garden-minded people: wild meadow flowers and Cornish

The Pandora Rover

① 07772 302232; Jul and Aug, Wed–Sun.

When fire destroyed the 13th-century thatched Pandora Inn on the waterfront of Restronguet Creek in March 2011, the sense of shock and loss all around the Fal was enormous. But after painstaking restoration, the pub reopened its doors just under a year later. The pontoon by the pub has given its name to an on-demand passenger ferry, perfect for walkers hopping from one creekside walk to the next, which chugs around the upper reaches of the estuary – Pandora, Restronguet, Point Quay, Loe Beach, Mylor harbour, Turnaware, Trelissick, Smugglers Cottage, Halwyn and Roundwood Quay. Running costs are covered by Cornwall Ferries Ltd and passengers are asked to donate what they feel is a fair price for the passage and these donations are passed on in full to whatever charities are being supported that year. Bikes and dogs go free, although bad dogs are threatened with a charge of £10 per toothmark (and that's just on the woodwork).

hedgerow plants are clearly encouraged, but there's also evidence of careful planting too – there are camellias, palms, roses and escallonia, berberis and even a crinodendron. This is no accident, for Devoran is where the great plant hunter, Thomas Lobb, was buried in 1894, and Carclew Manor (just across the creek) is where he and his brother William (who also became a renowned plant hunter) worked as boys before being taken on by the great Veitch nurseries in Exeter. (Carclew Manor was destroyed by fire in 1934, but the gardens where the Lobbs worked have been restored and open occasionally for charity.)

Food and drink

The Old Quay Inn ① 01872 863142. Devoran's pub is a gem: inside are log fires, old wooden tables and papers and magazines to read. The food is exceptionally good, the local ales are well kept and there's a friendly feel to it all. At the back, a steeply terraced garden has pockets for seating while benches at the front overlook the creek.

⑦ Enys

St Gluvias, Penryn TR10 9LB ① 01326 259885 Ⓦ www.enys.co.uk.

Cornwall is not short of places where each May bluebells steal the show, giving the rhododendrons a run for their money, but Enys must come near the top of the list. Although the gardens are open from April to September, the majority of visitors come to witness the extraordinary blue phenomenon in the tree-fringed part of the grounds known as Parc Lye, believed to have been undisturbed since medieval times. The house and gardens, which have been home to the Enys family since 1272, however, have undergone great transformations: the Elizabethan manor was destroyed by fire in the early 1820s and the old walled garden was pulled apart to make way for a less formal design. In 1833 John Samuel Enys engaged Henry Harrison, a London architect, to produce designs for the garden as well as the house. He created the Ladies Garden (now called the Flower Garden), which leads through a stone arch into the Colonel's Garden, named after Colonel Enys (1757–1818). Colonel Enys had an unusually large nose, and I was delighted to discover that the small enclosure has just been replanted as a scented garden, a befitting tribute to the Colonel's great conk. But it was J D Enys (1837–1912) who made the biggest contribution to the planting; he was a great traveller and regularly sent seeds and plants home from New Zealand and Patagonia, which have now grown to maturity.

⑧ Penryn

I've completely fallen for Penryn; its history and its future seem to have found a nice balance and while the huge influx of students at the new **Tremough campus** have ruffled a few feathers of the indigenous population ('you can't get a seat on the bus these days') shops are busier, cafés are flourishing and a new line of creative businesses are starting to line up beneath the wind turbines on the zero-carbon buildings of **Jubilee Wharf**.

Penryn's history is not dissimilar to that of Lostwithiel – it was a town of enormous significance in medieval times, which dwindled with the loss of its port as silt made it increasingly difficult to navigate. And just as Lostwithiel found itself superseded by Fowey, so Penryn lost out to Falmouth, with its deep, accessible harbour. But Penryn's chief glory, before the Reformation saw its decline and ultimate destruction, was **Glasney College**, known throughout Europe as a centre of learning. It was built in the late 13th century, on the instructions of the Bishop of Exeter (whose diocese included the whole of Cornwall) and the collegiate church was nothing less than a slightly scaled-down replica of Exeter Cathedral. Virtually nothing left of it remains today – just a grassy playing field and a few bits of architectural masonry – but there are several houses in Penryn, notably in **Easom's Yard**, that clearly benefitted from pieces of the ecclesiastical pile. The free **museum**, housed in the early 19th-century market house, bang in the middle of Penryn's main street, tells the story – with a model, maps and drawings – and the complex of cloisters, chapter house, refectory, infirmary, mills, houses, deer park and fish pond, as well as the cathedral-like church, makes a powerful impression. As the local ditty goes: 'Penryn was a flourishing town/When Falmouth was a furzy down.' Despite the loss of Glasney, Penryn continued to grow rich, exporting granite, tin and copper from its port and its streets filled with the handsome houses of its prosperous merchants. Falmouth may have snatched the lucrative customs house away from the port in 1650, but the town continued to hold its own, until the general decline in mining and quarrying took a grip and decay set in during the last century. But Penryn was lucky – incredibly lucky – to have its many handsome Tudor, Jacobean and Georgian buildings saved in the 1970s by a mammoth listing and restoration project, in which 200 buildings were rescued from near dereliction. No other Cornish town has as many listed buildings and it all makes for very pleasant ambling around the streets, opes (alleyways) and squares. The museum has put together a heritage trail (no mere leaflet – it's the size of a small book) that takes you through the town's architectural and social history.

What saves Penryn from being just a heritage town is the new lease of life it's been given by the groundbreaking eco-architecture on Jubilee Wharf, the Innovation Centre at the Tremough campus and resident or working population of artists and designers – many of whom are graduates of Falmouth Art School, just down the road. Just opposite the museum, for example, in Lower Market Street, **Open Space Galleries** (*01326 373415*) exhibits contemporary local art; a wander up the hill to West Street brings you to the **Malcolm Sutcliffe Glass Gallery** (*01326 377020*), a light and airy exhibition space and workshops where you can sign up for a lesson in glass-blowing. There's more superb glass down on Jubilee Wharf at **glassbydesign** (*01326 218812*) and, a step away, you can look through the windows at printmaking in action – it could be a class of novice woodcut students or experienced copperplate engravers – at **John Howard Print Studios** (*www.johnhowardprintstudios.com*).

But it was only while chatting to the volunteers in the museum that it dawned on me how much contemporary Penryn, full of new ideas and buildings and students from far beyond the Fal, in a curious way, is reliving its medieval past.

Jubilee Wharf

What an intelligent and brave piece of town planning this is. Completed in 2007 to the designs of Bill Dunster, a pioneering hero of zero-carbon urban housing, the two linked buildings (which bear more than a passing resemblance to an old riverboat, with an upturned hull for a roof) sit comfortably in their slightly scruffy harbour surrounds, surrounded by tall ships' masts, beside which the four, almost silent wind turbines look quite at home. Local labour built the project and wherever possible, local and reclaimed materials found their way into the construction and it's all been given a cladding of Cornish cedar and larch.

There are flats, workshops, offices and a nursery, all nicely mixed so that the wharfside community feels properly integrated, helped along by the Zedshed (a community space, so called because Zed stands for zero energy development) and a café which has been raved about the length and breadth of Cornwall.

$$\infty\!\!\infty$$

Food and drink

Cornish Cuisine The Smokehouse, Islington Wharf, TR10 8AT ℡ 01326 376244. You'll see their stall at the farmers' markets in Truro and Falmouth, but this where to find them, in the deli, when they're at home. It's a small family business and they smoke not only salmon, but duck, game, chicken and cheese using wood from Cornish fruit trees in the smokehouses.

The Famous Barrel St Thomas St, TR10 8JP ℡ 01326 373505. In the one of the most picturesque backwaters of Penryn, the pub is named by the huge barrel you walk through once inside. Sharp's Doom Bar is the local ale and there's usually a guest ale too. There's no food, but you're welcome to bring your own and sit by the logburner or outside in the leafy walled garden. Family- and dog-friendly

Miss Peapod's Kitchen Café Jubilee Wharf ℡ 01326 374424 ⓦ www. misspeapod.co.uk. It's in a great spot, overlooking the boats tied up on the quay and the marshy shores across the water. Families are made especially welcome – there's a wooden play kitchen and an unobtrusively healthy children's menu. Sunday breakfasts go on until lunchtime, with local smoked mackerel and poached eggs from the happiest flock of Plymouth Black Wing hens in the neighbourhood on the menu which has lots to offer vegetarians and an intelligently ethical flavour. The occasional music evenings are highly rated by locals of all ages.

Mylor and Flushing

The novelist Katherine Mansfield and her husband John Murry fled Zennor for Mylor in 1916, after a short-lived attempt at braving the wild, north coast of Penwith in the company of D H Lawrence and his wife, Frieda. Lawrence wrote 'it is too bleak and rocky for them. They want the south side, with trees and gardens and softness'. The world (at least the world that comes to Cornwall) is still divided into those that come for the wildness, the remoteness and austerity that characterises so much of the north coast and those that come for the gentle, leafy rivers and creeks, sheltered harbours and lush gardens of the Fal estuary (as well as the easy access to the cosmopolitan civilisation of Truro and Falmouth). And it doesn't get cosier than Mylor, with its snug, whitewashed cottages, green riverbanks and tree-fringed churchyard. If you want to get on the water, little motor launches, sailing dinghies and punts can be hired at the harbour.

Its close neighbour, Flushing, has terraces of pretty Queen Anne houses and cottages built by Dutch immigrants from Vlissengen in the 17th century. The small harbour is busy with local fishing and sailing boats, and has retained a lot of character; other parts of the village have been so smartly renovated that you could be in a Kensington mews.

⑨ Falmouth

Falmouth must rate as one of the most appealing places to live in England; it's the sheer diversity of what it has to offer that makes it so fortunate. There's the sparkling beauty and almost Mediterranean glamour of the wide estuary and harbour, the grit and guts of a large, working dockyard, a Victorian-style seafront with beaches, hotels and exotic gardens, a ribbon of old streets, packed with good shops and art galleries – and a rich history of maritime adventure written all over its engaging quays and alleyways. The population of art students adds another dimension too: there's a youthful liveliness about the town, that brings guitars and campfires to the beaches on summer evenings, art to the foreground at summer show time and a buzz to the cafés and bars. Rainy-day families wanting an alternative to beach and boats are well looked after in Falmouth, too. The maritime museum and Pendennis Castle make a special effort to woo children and the free Falmouth Art Gallery has been a winner of the Guardian Family Friendly Museum competition.

You can circumnavigate Falmouth in a couple of hours on foot and get a good feeling for all the different faces of the town. Pendennis Castle, high on the headland beyond the docks calls for a bit of extra time and effort; the bus from the town centre runs from July to October only.

The Killigrews' Falmouth

Falmouth wouldn't be the place it is today without the Killigrews, who took up residence on the muddy shores of the estuary towards the end of the 13th century. A wander down Grove Place towards Discovery Quay and the

Maritime Museum takes you past their handsomely restored manor, **Arwenack House**. It was converted during the 1980s into private accommodation, but in its medieval and Elizabethan incarnations, was home to 16 or so generations of this enterprising and occasionally scandalous family. (Everyone in Falmouth has heard of Lady Mary Killigrew, a throat-slitting pirate, whose death sentence was commuted by a frankly admiring Elizabeth I to a spell in prison.)

In 1598, when Sir Walter Raleigh visited Arwenack, the house stood alone on the shores of the river; the nearest church was at Budock, a good mile away over the hills and all the boats went to Penryn or Truro. Raleigh couldn't help pointing out what a great spot for a harbour lay before the house; the point was taken, but by the time of the Civil War, the Killigrew fortune – built largely on piracy and abuse of government posts – was starting to evaporate. John Killigrew bankrupted himself trying to found the new town and build a lighthouse on the Lizard (see page 206); and while his divorced wife stayed on at Arwenack, Parliamentary troops seized the house and set fire to it. His brother, Henry Killigrew (whom Elizabeth I described as 'dull'), was forced to abandon his new home at Ince Castle (see page 89) and rally to the Royalist cause: Henry was one of the heroes of the terrible siege of Pendennis Castle. Loyalty to the Crown did the family – and Falmouth – no end of good; Charles II granted the town its charter (despite furious opposition from Penryn) in 1661 and within a decade a church had risen in the new town centre, ingratiatingly dedicated to 'King Charles the Martyr'.

With royal favour riding high, and Killigrews pushing hard for the geographical superiority of their port to be recognised, the packet ships were transferred from London to Falmouth in 1669. This was a prize worth having – packet ships carried mail and gold bullion to all corners of the empire and the rewards for controlling the service were immeasurable. The Killigrews should have prospered enormously, but through accident and heirlessness they managed the exact opposite.

The **Killigrew Monument** opposite Arwenack House is a strange sort of memorial to such a colourful clan; the tall granite pyramid was erected in 1737 on the instructions of Martin, the last Killigrew of Arwenack, and was deliberately left without any kind of inscription. Oddly, when the pyramid was taken apart and moved to its present position, two empty glass bottles were found inside, creating even more of a mystery. A stroll through the pretty terraces of Regency, Georgian and Victorian houses on the slopes above Arwennack reveals the decline in the family fortune, as the land behind the manor was sold off piecemeal.

Curious Cornwall (*www.facebook.com/curiouscornwall*) offer guided walks describing the dodgiest moments in Falmouth's history as well as creative workshops for adults and families.

Rainy-day Falmouth

Falmouth's art galleries are a joy. The **Falmouth Art Gallery** (*The Moor; 01326*

313863), with its wonderful collections of Cornish impressionists, prints, portraits and very funny automata, knows how to put on a good exhibition. It's the attention to detail that counts: placing exhibits that children will enjoy at the right height for them; using humour in interpretation that even grumpy teenagers can't resist – I've never been in and not seen children enjoying themselves. And it's free.

Beside the Wave (*Arwenack St; 01326 211132*) exhibits and sells big-name contemporary Cornish art – landscapes by Richard Tuff, Andrew Tozer and Paul Lewin all feature there regularly. And it's always worth a look to see who else is up-and-coming; exhibitions change every month.

The Royal Cornwall Polytechnic Society, known simply as **The Poly** (*24 Church St; 01326 319461*) is Falmouth's much-loved arts centre, which has recently regenerated itself, fuelled by local support and enthusiasm.

Close to the harbour, in an elegant house built for the Fox family in 1740, the **Great Atlantic Gallery** (*48 Arwenack St; 01326 318452 or 788911*) exhibits work by Cornish artists with an established or emerging reputation. It was here I discovered the work of Gill Watkiss, whose windswept figures, seen setting out for blustery walks on the beach or through moorland puddles, epitomise the reality of living with Cornish weather.

The **National Maritime Museum** on Discovery Quay (*01326 313388*) opened in 2003 to great acclaim and you can see why: every inch of its imaginatively designed space engages you instantly, from the moment you enter the main hall where a flotilla of iconic boats are suspended overhead, to the underwater viewing chamber where you can see what's really going on in the harbour – a cormorant diving for a fish, perhaps. Year-long exhibitions focus on the epic and sensational treasures in the collection. Falmouth's maritime history has been given tremendously lucid exposure recently by the publication of *The Levelling Sea*. The author, Philip Marsden, who lives close to Falmouth, is much in demand at the museum and his talks sell out rapidly, but do get a ticket if you can.

There's a lot to be said for visiting a subtropical garden in summer rain: the air smells fresh and damp, the dripping foliage acquires a lush intensity and often it's just you and the blackbirds, sheltering under the same palm. The **Fox-Rosehill gardens** are very discreetly hidden on the beach-facing slopes of the town, beside the buildings of the **Falmouth School of Art**. The Quaker shipping magnate, Robert Were Fox (who retired to Penjerrick; see page 181), lived in the house that the school now occupies, and started to fill the gardens with exotic plants in the mid 19th century. His family continued to fill the gardens, introducing Australian gums and New Zealand cordylines (this mild, south-facing pocket of Falmouth is often referred to as 'Little Australia'), until handing it over to the town in 1974. The open day, held over the first weekend in June, is a lovely event, with plant sales, talks and picnics, well supported by locals, whatever the weather.

The seafront

The three connected beaches, **Gyllyngvase**, **Tunnel** and **Castle**, on Falmouth's south-facing shores, get very busy with students 'revising' at the first hint of sunshine; it takes a few more minutes, walking west, to find the quieter shores of **Swanpool Beach** and its brackish pool, just across the road, a scruffy but essential haven for wildlife and waterfowl.

Several of the grand Victorian hotels that once lined the seafront have been converted into luxury flats, saving the prom from losing its dignified charm; Gyllingdune House, set back from the prom on the clifftop was sold after just two generations of occupancy by the Coope family to Frederick Horniman, (who was later to found the Horniman Museum in south London). The gardens had a tunnel entrance to their own private beach, both of which became open to the public when the house was bought by the town in 1907.

Gyllingdune Gardens are approached by steps opposite Tunnel Beach; one surprise leads to another. First there's an extraordinary quarry garden with shell grottoes and a fernery – then around a corner, a beautifully restored Edwardian bandstand sits in the grassy centre of an elegant, glass-roofed cloister, beyond which lies the old mansion, converted to a concert hall in 1911. It was opened by Princess Alexandra, since when it has been known as Princess Pavilion.

Shopping

There's a very attractive cluster of independent shops in the **Old High Street**, where you'll find some of the oldest buildings in Falmouth, on the hill leading up to the old town hall. Among the food shops listed below, you'll find retro clothing at the **Black Cat Boutique**, secondhand books at **Colin Benford Books**, as well as guitar shops, quirky gift shops and antiques.

Food and drink

Falmouth celebrates its centuries-old oyster harvest in mid-October with the **Fal Oyster Festival** held on Events Square (in front of the maritime museum). The Fal is the only place in the country where oysters are dredged by traditional methods – by the last oyster fleet working under sail or oar – and deserves its celebration. If Falmouth were in France, they wouldn't be hand-dredged, but there would be oyster bars up and down the town, crowded with locals; here, they're a luxury and served in style at **Rick Stein's Fish and Chips & Oyster Bar** on Discovery Quay (*www. rickstein.com*).

Falmouth farmers' market is held every Tuesday on The Moor, a lovely, traffic-free square, bringing together a particularly rich seam of farm shop producers around the Fal, many of whom you'll find at the Truro farmers' market on Wednesday or Saturday. The **Natural Store** (*01326 379426*) is towards the top end of High St sells everything organic and **Stones Bakery** (*07791 003183*) on the other side of the street, make their own muesli and crackers as well as superb breads. The flapjacks and focaccia are in a league of their own.

The Chain Locker Quay St ℡ 01326 311085; open all day. A great spot with lots of window seats for harbour watching, bare boards and masses of nautical memorabilia on the walls. Ales are from Sharp's and Skinner's and food comes in generous helpings.

Dolly's Tea Room 21 Church St (above the Falmouth Bookseller) ℡ 01326 218400. Retro-themed tea room that turns into a slightly louche (Dolly's description, not mine) wine bar in the evening. New to the Falmouth scene and popular with the arty crowd.

Espressini 39 Killigrew St ℡ 07890 453705. This friendly café, very close to the farmers' market, does terrific lunchtime food inspired by what's local and seasonal at very reasonable prices. Rupert, the owner, takes great interest in all his suppliers and can give you chapter and verse on the origins of the coffees and hot chocolates he serves. The special leaf teas are excellent, too.

The Front Custom House Quay ℡ 01326 212168. The barrels are lined up on the wall as you walk in, giving the impression that a real ale festival is taking place. But this is everyday: Matt the landlord keeps a terrific range of local and guest ales and ciders and regularly scoops up awards from CAMRA. It's not all about real ale – there's also Breton folk singing and dancing on Monday nights. The sign outside says 'we're a pub, so bring your own grub!' and lots of people do. It's handily next door to the highly rated **Harbour Lights** fish and chip shop and opposite the **King's Pipe Pasties**. (The King's Pipe is a witty nickname for the brick chimney beside the pasty shop, where contraband tobacco was burned.)

Greenbank Hotel Harbourside ℡ 01326 312440. The restaurant deserves a special mention as a beacon of Slow cuisine. Sanjay Kumar, who contributed to the introduction of this book, and is one of the chief movers and shakers in the Cornish Slow Food movement, was head chef here until recently; Fiona Were runs the kitchen now and is equally committed to small, local producers and seasonal menus. You don't have to spend a fortune either: some of the best harbour views can be enjoyed over a tea or coffee.

Pea Souk 19 Church St ℡ 01326 317583. The miniscule, bohemian vegetarian café, serving Middle Eastern food has a devoted following. Salads come from the owner-cook's own garden and other dishes might include rose-scented *basbousa*, aubergine rolls stuffed with coriander and walnut paste, beetroot and dill dip or a tagine with homemade *labneh* and lemony coriander salsa.

Provedore 43 Trelawney Rd ℡ 01326 314888 ⓦ www.provedore.co.uk. Off the beaten track and much cherished by locals – a tiny but brilliant café-cum-tapas bar, with an olive tree in the courtyard garden to sit under and drink coffee made by Tim, a proper *barista* in true Mediterranean style. In fact, it gets my vote for the best cup of coffee in Cornwall. Thursday and Friday evenings, when Tim produces his favourite Spanish dishes, are worth getting to early as there's no booking. Cash only.

The Seven Stars 1 The Moor ℡ 01326 312111. A legendary pub, run by five generations of the same family. Legendary for its perfect pints of Bass, Sharp's and Skinner's, legendary for refusing to serve food other than crisps and legendary for its unchanging décor. Its loyal, burping, dry-witted regulars would rather die than be seen with a mobile phone at the bar and there would be a riot if anything was ever altered.

⑩ Penjerrick Garden

Budock, Falmouth TR11 5ED ℗ 01872 870105 ⓦ www.penjerrickgarden.co.uk.

If you're the sort of person who is put off visiting a garden by the sight of huge car parks and visitor centres at the entrance, or find you have little enthusiasm for crisply edged lawns and immaculate borders, Penjerrick will be your kind of place. There's no car park – you just park carefully on the grass-edged drive – and the entrance fee goes into an honesty box. The owner, Rachel Morin, is unrepentent: 'Penjerrick Garden has got everything a garden enthusiast needs: plants, plants and more plants, secret corners, winding paths, thriving shrubs, towering trees, lush green. Do not visit Penjerrick, however, if you prefer neatly laid out flower beds or if you are looking for a cup of tea – you will not find either of them here. It is 'just' a garden – and that's all we could wish for.' A pair of gumboots, she adds, is highly advisable.

The gardens were planted by Mrs Morin's Victorian forebears, a branch of the Fox family, who were also responsible for creating great gardens at Trebah and Glendurgan (see page 200). Robert Were Fox, whose enthusiasm for exotic plants led to the creation of the Rosehill gardens (see page 178) in Falmouth, retired to Penjerrick in 1872 and spent the next five years filling the gaps in the gardens that his son, Barclay Fox, had laid out 20 years earlier. Barclay's sister carried on planting after her father's death, working with Samuel Smith, Penjerrick's head gardener, who was thoroughly caught up in the contemporary craze for rhododendron hybridisation. Today, the garden is a lush jungle: wildly overgrown, but not unloved, and best visited in a spirit of romantic adventure.

The Roseland peninsula

South of the Fal, the Roseland peninsula licks the gateway to the estuary with a long tongue of land, cleft by the Percuil River, unbridged for the length of its two-and-a-half-mile journey inland. The two neighbouring headlands thus created could not be more different: north of the Percuil is fashionable, upmarket St Mawes, much favoured by the yachty crowd and linked all year to Falmouth by the to-ing and fro-ing of the passenger ferry and to Truro and St Austell by the much-improved A3078. For walkers, St Mawes is the gateway to St Just in Roseland, with its picturesque church in a garden at the water's edge. To the south, the St Anthony headland is remote and wild, accessed only by a single-track lane or, in summer months, by the open boat that crosses the Percuil from St Mawes. The coastal shoreline of the peninsula conceals a string of harbours, coves and beaches of quite immoderate loveliness all the way to Nare Head.

Inland are deep, quiet woods, threaded by spindly lanes, the fingertips of marshy creeks and a scattering of hamlets and farms. Provided you're not in a hurry, it's a lovely place in which to get lost.

One of the things that gives the Roseland its rather grown-up air is the absence of commercial entertainment on offer; visitors come here for boats, beaches, walks and good eating. And for the last two weeks of October, the Roseland Festival delivers an elegant programme of literary, artistic and musical events, held in pubs, hotels and churches around the peninsula.

⑪ St Just in Roseland

I count myself lucky to have made my first visit to the creekside village by sailing dinghy, zigzagging across the glittering blue expanse of the Carrick Roads from Mylor. Nothing quite prepared me, as we dodged through the thicket of masted craft moored in St Just Creek, for that first glimpse of the 13th-century church at the water's edge, and the lush canopy of exotic tree ferns, fan palms, monkey puzzle and Western red cedars, vast rhododendrons and magnolias that rises behind. Maybe if you live there you get used to its beauty, though it's hard to believe you would. Arriving on foot from St Mawes, some months later in winter, the approach from the slopes above the church was no less magical: the lychgate framed the short, grey tower below, camellias bloomed, fuzzy magnolia buds looked ready to burst and even the periwinkle was in flower, sheltered by the mild microclimate of the creek and protective shoulders of the hill behind.

It was John Garland Treseder, a Victorian nurseryman, recently returned from Australia, who spotted the potential of the site for exotic, subtropical plants,

Divine graffiti

An elderly lady I know described a visit she had made years ago with her husband to the little church at St Anthony. 'We were enchanted by the antiquity and deep sense of peaceful seclusion,' she said, 'and then the verger appeared, anxious to show us a pillar, on which he claimed a young Jesus had scratched his name.' Local legend has it that Joseph of Arimethea, accompanied by his young nephew, landed on the Roseland peninsula and stories abound of the traces left on their journey from Cornwall to Glastonbury. 'Well, we peered at the pillar,' she continued, 'but it was hard to make out anything in the gloom. I think the verger must have been disappointed by our reaction.'

A family of plantsmen

John Garland Treseder's father was a Truro nurseryman, but young John Garland and two of his brothers had fancied their chances as gold prospectors and took off for Australia in 1853. Plants, however, proved more lucrative than gold for JG, who over the next 40 years founded a small empire of plant shops and nurseries as well as designing gardens in Victoria and New South Wales. He returned to Cornwall in 1895 to take over the family nursery, laden with seedlings and seeds of subtropical plants, as well as the first Dicksonias (tree ferns) that were to find their way into all the great Fox gardens around Falmouth and Trewidden, near Penzance. The garden would just be starting to look established in the 1920s when H V Morton wrote 'I have blundered into a Garden of Eden that cannot be described in pen or paint ... I would like to know if there is in the whole of England, a churchyard more beautiful than this ...You stand at the lychgate and look down into a green cup filled with flowers and arched by great trees. In the dip is the little church, its tower level with you as you stand above. The white gravestones rise up from ferns and flowers.' Inevitably, by the late 1970s, the garden reached a point where it needed restoring and replanting; Neil Treseder, JG's grandson, who was running the family nursery, took on the task. More recently, a new memorial garden was added to the higher slopes above the lane to the church; the cost of garden maintenance is £25,000 a year (which makes you gasp a little), but Morton would not be dismayed.

and he was lucky to find the rector of St Just an enthusiastic plantsman, willing to co-operate. The Reverend Humfrey Davis had ideas too, for embellishing the churchyard. The path from the lychgate to the church is lined with 55 small granite tablets, each bearing a pious quotation. Most of the ankle-height words of wisdom are taken from the Bible or hymns, but one or two are of his own composition.

⑫ Pendower Beach and Carne Beacon

A mile of south-facing, firm golden sand, sheltered from east winds by the bulky presence of Nare Head: **Pendower Beach** (which runs seamlessly into Carne Beach to the east) is long and deep enough to absorb everyone. Families come here because it's safe and easily accessible; the proximity of the Nare, one of Cornwall's most upmarket hotels, idyllically positioned just above the beach, is a bonus for those who like their beach life to be tempered with a bit of luxury. Even in summer there's a feeling of wide open space, and in winter it's a huge playground for dogs and their owners.

Keen walkers will want to carry on along the coast path to the heights of Nare Head and on to Portloe, a stiff three miles further on. A very useful bus service from Truro connects Portloe with Veryan, Portscatho, St Just and St Mawes.

While you're down on the beach a tumulus is visible on the skyline to the east. Having heard that **Carne Beacon** was one of the largest Bronze Age burial barrows in England, possibly containing the relics of the 5th-century King Geraint, I set off to find it. Surrounded by sheep and sugar beet and approached by a short wooden ladder, the tumulus gave nothing to indicate its significance; in fact, it looked like nothing more than a turfed-over reservoir. Despite local objections that it was a historic site, the mound was used during World War II as an enemy aircraft lookout post, and kitted out with observation equipment – but all that remains now is a concrete plinth.

Food and drink

For a spot of sybaritic refreshment, the **Nare Hotel's restaurant** (*01872 501111*) does an afternoon tea that includes a glass of champagne, smoked salmon sandwiches, local strawberries and homemade scones.

⑬ Veryan

Veryan is a village of two halves: Veryan Churchtown and Veryan Green, the road at each end flanked by a pair of small round cottages, topped with thatched conical roofs; entering the village is rather like passing through the stubby towers of a solid medieval fortress. The five **roundhouses** (the fifth is in the village behind the school) were the idea of the Reverend Jeremiah Trist, who had them built in 1817. Quite why he chose to build them this way is a matter for speculation: many guidebooks like to say they were built to house each of his five daughters or that no corners leave the devil no place to hide, but the likelihood is that the Revd just had a leaning towards the picturesque and liked round buildings. There's no evidence either that any of his daughters lived in them. In fact, documentation reveals that he was captivated by a round cottage built for £42 at St Winnow, near Lostwithiel, by his friend Charles Vinicombe Penrose. In 1811 Penrose published its floor plan as suitable for a workman's home. History does not record what the first tenants thought of their circular accommodation as they struggled to find a place for granny's dresser.

The village is as picturesque as the roundhouses guarding the road in. Immaculate whitewash and thatch, a trickling stream and flowery gardens decorate the area around the church green, which was heavily restored in the mid 19th century, but sits no less attractively for that in its leafy surrounds. With a pub, a shop and an art gallery, Veryan poses no problems for potterers and it's a perfect base for exploring the safe beaches on Gerrans Bay, the summer gardens at

Poppy Cottage in Ruan High Lanes or **Ruan Lanihorne**, tucked away in the backwoods of the Fal, and watching oystercatchers stalk the tidal creek.

~~~~~~~~

Food and drink

King's Head Ruan Lanihorne TR2 5NX ⓘ 01872 501263. In a tiny, tucked-away village, beside a tributary of the Fal, the pub is a treat for those who are serious about enjoying their food and drink. Skinners of Truro supply the ales, some of the wines come from a friend's vineyard in France and the food is a constantly changing menu based on fresh, local ingredients. There's no children's menu.

⑭ Portloe

Two upmarket, foodie pubs, a cluster of freshly painted cottages and an art gallery scattered around the prettiest of harbours tell you that – although catches of lobster and crab are hauled up its narrow beach almost daily – Portloe no longer relies on fishing for its main income. It's so picturesque it could easily be a film-set, so there's no surprise to discover it is often used for just this purpose. Mary Wesley's *The Camomile Lawn* was filmed on the cliffs just above the village.

⑮ St Anthony Head

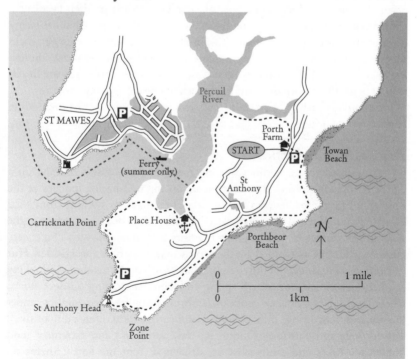

Freakishly you can undertake a supremely rewarding circular walk that is almost entirely coastal around a peninsula-within-a-peninsula, taking about three hours at an ambling pace and starting from Porth Farm, near the head of the Porthcuel River, then going either way – clockwise or anticlockwise – southwest to St Anthony Head and its lighthouse and back on the other side of the peninsula. In summer, the passenger ferry from St Mawes lands at Place, close to St Anthony, and there are National Trust car parks at Porth Farm and St Anthony Head, both just yards from the coast path. Three hours, however, will not be enough for Slow explorers or secret beach addicts: there is the **ancient church** in St Anthony to explore, tucked away behind the imposing **Place House**, built in 1840 for the Spry family and the three gloriously sheltered coves, known collectively as **Molunan Beach**, below the west-facing cliffs that look across to Falmouth docks.

A short, uphill detour, through gorse and craggy Monterey pines, brings you to the top of the headland, just above the **St Anthony lighthouse**. The views of Falmouth and the mouth of the estuary are sublime from this lonely, windswept vantage point, which served as a World War II observation post, where traces of 1904 gun emplacements can still be seen. It's now owned by the National Trust, who have restored the observation offices and let them as unconventional holiday cottages. From here too, **St Mawes** and **Pendennis** castles, built each side of the estuary mouth as part of Henry VIII's coastal defences against the French and Spanish, stand out clearly on their headlands.

There's another superb beach on the cliff path that tracks the Channel-facing coast of the peninsula. **Porthbeor** cove is all soft gold sand and craggy rocks that seem to slither down to the shoreline, while a mile further north, though less than 200 yards from the muddy car park at Porth Farm, **Towan Beach** feels as perfectly remote as any of the less accessible coves along the way.

The footpath back to St Anthony crosses a stream and fields before finding Porth Creek and the shores of Percuil and the ferry landing at Place.

Beaches and barbecues

It's not unusual to see families braving the winter chills and cooking up a Christmas lunch or New Year's day picnic on the well-heeled beaches of the Roseland; I met someone who had spent a Christmas Day walking from Nare Head to Portscatho and been invited to share more than one glass of champagne and venison sausage (as well as a heap of mince pies) along the way. This cheery outdoor gathering is typified by the crowd that gathers at the **Hidden Hut** (*www.hiddenhut.co.uk*), on the coast path just north of Portscatho, overlooking Porthcurnick Beach, for superb spring and summer evening outdoor feasts, where local lobster, mussels, pork or lamb might be featured, sizzling under the sky. Everyone brings their own plate and cutlery (and often a dog or two): it's very jolly and convivial. During the day, hot drinks and extremely good homemade cakes and sandwiches are dispensed from the hatch; there's no indoor seating, just a grassy bank with a great view over the beach.

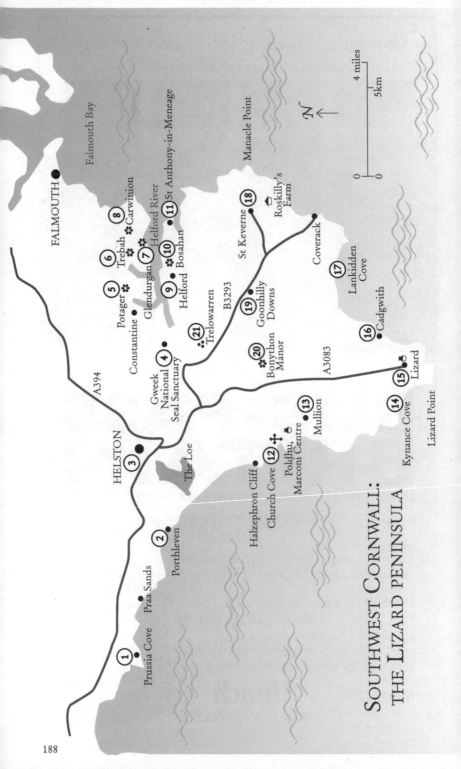

SOUTHWEST CORNWALL:
THE LIZARD PENINSULA

8. SOUTHWEST CORNWALL: THE LIZARD PENINSULA

The Slow lane starts here: away from main roads, crowded beaches, jammed harbours and busy towns, this part of Cornwall is perfect for quiet exploration and unhurried hours spent just looking, listening and absorbing the very diverse character of the peninsula. More of an island, in fact, than a peninsula, the Lizard has a coastline that faces not only west and east, but south for a few miles as well, while the Helford River carves a broad path through the hilly, wooded landscape to the north.

Lush and lovely gardens face each other across this wood-fringed river and footpaths ramble past muddy boatyards, secluded beaches and leafy creeks that can only be glimpsed or guessed at from tarmac roads. Tiny, unspoiled coves lie far below the southern cliffs where, if you search, pebbles of red or green serpentine that sit smooth and heavy in the hand can be found. Gaze skywards and you may be lucky enough to see a pair of choughs – Cornwall's emblematic bird – tumbling overhead.

In stormy weather, the furious sea breaking over the harbour wall at Porthleven from the safety of a pub window is compelling viewing; but beneath the lichen, coastal village churchyard tombstones remember the victims of the many shipwrecks on the Lizard's unkind reefs and bars. Inland, miles of heathland teeming with butterflies are criss-crossed by tracks passing ancient tumuli, half-hidden beneath the gorse and heather. Westwards, the empty heath gives way to an aquamarine sea, embraced by rocky coves, where pale sandy beaches are revealed as the tide recedes. When a couple of friends from New Zealand who had been working in London, asked me where they could find the kind of barefoot, natural maritime world they were pining for, I knew they would be happy here, staying at Henry's Campsite, a haven for lovers of a wild and simple way of living under canvas by the sea.

The remote exposure to the Atlantic has proved irresistible to the pioneers of communications technology too. Marconi built his famous transmitters on the promontory at Poldhu, from where the first transatlantic radio messages were sent in 1901. Six decades later, the biggest satellite station in the world rose from the abandoned radar station at Goonhilly Downs, and now plans are advancing to turn the redundant station into a space-science centre, fulfilling the prophecy (for some) that Arthur will rise again.

Enjoying local food and drink forms a vital part of Lizard life. Organic ice cream, made by the Roskilly family, is hard to miss and pasties from Gear Farm or Anne Muller in Lizard village are, like Vicky's Bread, legendary in these parts; freshly caught crab is a harbourside treat, and Helford Creek cider and apple juice will go down well with fans of real cider. Micro-breweries include Lizard Ales and the much-loved Spingo, brewed at the Blue Anchor in Helston. Trelowarren and Porthleven are rapidly establishing themselves as places where Slow food is championed and on the eastern side of the Helford, the vegetarian menu is supplied from the veg patch at the Potager Garden.

Getting around

Helston sits midway between Falmouth and Penzance on the A394, which is not the fastest of roads, particularly in the summer holidays, but the A3083, which branches off at RNAS Culdrose on the outskirts of Helston, offers a swift route south to Lizard village.

The B3293 swoops off this to St Keverne in the east and Coverack, a little further to the south. Beyond these roads, however, you'll need a map and a good sense of direction to get around the tangle of narrow lanes that link the remote villages and hamlets around the Helford River or inland from the coast.

Trains

Getting about by rail is not an option in this part of Cornwall; the branch line from a junction near Camborne that once served Helston closed in the early 1960s.

Penzance and Redruth are the nearest main-line stations; the busy line from Truro to Falmouth links up with bus routes that take in the big gardens on the north side of Helford River.

Buses

Your options for getting about by bus are pretty good. Helston is the hub: the T34 connects with trains at Redruth and goes all the way to Lizard village and there are regular services from Helston to Penzance, Falmouth, Truro and Camborne.

At Helford you can catch a seasonal foot ferry to the north bank of the river where both Glendurgan and Trebah gardens are easily reached on foot and pick up the service to Falmouth. In the summer months, the 401 runs from Helston to St Ives, calling in at Trevarno and Godolphin House on the way.

Truronian, the main bus operator, offers decent-value Day Rover tickets for unlimited travel on one day.

Cycling

There are no official bike routes through the peninsula, so the OS Explorer map 103 is the best tool for planning a ride. The biggest question left unanswered by the map, however, is the problem of crossing Loe Bar with a bike.

It can be done, though pushing a bike over 400 yards of shingle is not much fun, and crossing in wild weather, when waves smash across the bar, is extremely dangerous. The picturesque solution is the five-mile, largely level detour around the Loe, through the National Trust's Penrose estate and Helston (there is a bike path on the short stretch of main road past RNAS Culdrose).

On the east side of the peninsula, the little boats that offer a seasonal foot passenger service between Helford and Helford Passage will do their best to accommodate a bike or two; and as there are hardly any riverside lanes or tracks upstream from here, it's great for cyclists and walkers wanting to see a bit more of the Helford River.

Cycle hire

Porthleven Cycle Hire 1 Chapel Terrace, Porthleven TR13 9HS ① 01326 562976 ⓦ www.porthlevencyclehire.co.uk. Daily and weekly cycle hire, suggested routes and even guided rides are available. Free collection and delivery; helmets, locks and toolkits all part of the deal.

Accommodation

The Hen House Tregarne, Manaccan TR12 6EW ① 01326 280236 ⓦ www.thehenhouse-cornwall.co.uk ⓔ henhouseuk@aol.com. Grown-up eco-luxury B&B plus self-catering barn surrounded by organic meadows, where visitors are encouraged to relax among the wild flowers or indulge in a spot of stargazing. Breakfast eggs come from hens in the garden, everything else from local suppliers and Sandy makes her own bread. Dog-friendly, but no under 12s. Good value in the upmarket Helford area.

Henry's Campsite The Lizard TR12 7NX ① 01326 290596 ⓦ www. henryscampsite.co.uk. What's so good and unusual about the location of this camping spot is that it is right in Lizard village, with its shops and pubs and bus service as well as being just a field away from the beach and coast path. But what makes it so special is the laid-back, camp-fire ambience; there's banked seating round the firepit for a small crowd, so when the guitars come out, it's more like being at a mini-festival of a very green persuasion. Cheap and extremely cheerful camping.

Kynance Cottage Next to Kynance Cove Café ① 01326 290436 ⓦ www.kynancecovecafe.co.uk ⓔ cottage@kynancecovecottage.co.uk. Just big enough for a couple with two small children wanting to ditch the car for a week (you'd have to: the car park is nearly a mile away along a rough track). The café-cum-shop and beach crowds mean you'd be far from isolated during the day, but just imagine having one of Cornwall's most perfect coves to yourself as dawn broke. Not cheap, but until the other two cottages are renovated, the only place to stay is right here, in the cove.

Love Lane Caravans and Campsite Roskilly's Organic Farm, Tregellast Barton TR12 6NX ① 01326 340406 ⓦ www.lovelanecaravans.com ⓔ holiday@ lovelanecaravans.com. A gypsy caravan and pretty shepherd's hut are among the eclectic mix of classic caravans dotted around the edge of a field, close to Roskilly's ice-cream farm. There's also a pink two-berther, a sleek Airstreamer, a 'hippy-bus' and a huge safari-style tent, all beautifully kitted out with retro furnishings. The communal areas include a firepit and volleyball net, shack-style kitchen, compost loo and bathroom. A nice and not too expensive alternative to camping, especially if holidaying with other families.

Penmarth Farm Coverack ① 01326 280389. Henry's campsite is wildly popular and often full, but Ben Roskilly on the hill above Coverack offers simple, cheap camping on the farm.

Trelowarren Mawgan TR12 6AF ① 01326 221224 ⑩ www.trelowarren.com Ⓔ info@trelowarren.com. Eco-luxury doesn't come any greener or more comfortable than this, and the lovely, leafy Trelowarren estate is a byword in Cornwall for successful sustainability. There are 18 self-catering houses and cottages, sleeping between four and ten, all heated from a single biomass boiler, fuelled by coppiced wood from the estate. Bring bikes for cycling through the estate to the craft centre, restaurant or the pebble-bottomed swimming pool in the old walled fruit garden. It's a serious treat to stay in one of these fabulous cottages – reflected in the prices.

Tourist information centre

Helston and Lizard Peninsula 79 Menage St, Helston ① 01326 565431.

From Prussia Cove to the Helford River

A journey across the north of the peninsula takes you from some of Cornwall's most glorious – and treacherous – coastal scenery to the secret, leafy creeks and beaches of the Helford River, taking in handsome old Helston and busy RNAS Culdrose on the way. Unlike the rivers Fal and Fowey to the east, the Helford has no large towns or harbours facing each other across the yacht-filled estuary: instead, there are tiny creekside hamlets, subtropical gardens, broadleaf woodland and marshy banks strewn with dinghies and canoes pulled up above the muddy tideline.

① Prussia Cove

A small but free private car park is a generous gift to visitors anywhere on the Cornish coast; add to that a superb, though quite unheralded, little bakery that also sells locally produced cheeses, meats and drinks and you have a brilliant spot for starting a walk and picking up a picnic on the way. The track to the coast path reveals a cluster of totally unspoiled houses and cottages, all part of the Porth-en-Alls estate. The Tunstall-Behrens family who own the estate host a twice-yearly international gathering of musicians, giving the

Spring blooms on coast path

Walkers following the track from the car park to the coast path at Prussia Cove will notice the stone-built 'Cornish hedges' have been planted with tamarisks: the new feathery foliage and sprays of pink flowers in May look delicate, but are particularly suited to the salty, maritime climate. The clifftops are carpeted in pink thrift, yellow bird's-foot trefoil, purplish-blue kidney vetch and white sea-campion at this time of year, but one of the oddest sights is dodder, which forms a tangled mat of pinky-red stems and attaches itself parasitically to gorse and heather, looking as though a careless passer-by has been chucking out pocketfuls of string.

opportunity for both the young and the experienced to learn and perform together. It's an inspiring place – the sea is cobalt and turquoise, the coves sheltered and the rocky shoreline as ruggedly picturesque as anything you might find on a remote Aegean island. No wonder the music is inspired. Concerts held in local churches are listed on www.i-m-s.org.uk.

Prussia Cove is a generic name for this small stretch of coast, rather than belonging to an individual inlet. The name derives from Cornwall's most famous 'free trader' (smuggler if you must), John Carter, who since boyhood had taken Frederick the Great of Prussia as his hero and role model. During the last decade or two of the 18th century, the self-styled King of Prussia and his brother, Harry Carter, lived here and used the shelter of Bessy's Cove to land contraband, in days when dodging the excise man was considered an honourable trade. The cliffs are riddled with underground passages and tunnels leading from coves to cottages; it's all pure Daphne du Maurier.

To the west, a lovely two-mile stride along the cliffs leads to Perranuthnoe (you can return by an inland route across the fields); to the east, the coast path takes you past Kenneggy Sands, a quieter, less-visited beach than the hugely popular Praa Sands, a little further on. If you decide to make it a circular walk and follow the footpaths from Praa Sands back to Prussia Cove, you pass through the yard of Lower Kenneggy Farm. Look out for Oxo and Marmite, two gentle, hefty oxen who have replaced the tractor here.

② Porthleven

Porthleven has become something of a foodie destination in recent years, and hosts an annual Festival of Food and Music in April. Not that it's another Padstow in the making – the working harbour and often violent seas give the town a rather gutsy identity, and keep the small fishing community visible among the art galleries, delis and cafés. Not many harbours face – open-mouthed as it were – the prevailing wind, but this one, built in the early years of the 19th century, was designed specifically as a safe haven for boats driven by southwesterlies into this corner of Mount's Bay. The decision to build the harbour came after the loss of the frigate, HMS *Anson*, wrecked on Loe Bar, a mile to the south, with catastrophic loss of life. It was just a few days after Christmas 1807, and the ship had been on her way to Brest to support the blockade of the Napoleonic fleet. It was with a grim sense of justice perhaps, that French prisoners of war were used for the dangerous work of clearing the shingle bar that held the sea back from the marshy valley that lay behind. Two of the *Anson*'s canons, dragged up from sea bed, now face each other across the harbour. Another can be seen outside the folk museum in Helston.

Storm-watching is Porthleven's answer to theatre. On the south side of the harbour mouth the road narrows and twists around a granite-built clock tower on the corner of the town hall and the beach, punctured with jagged rocks, is revealed below. In really bad weather, this road is closed as waves crash right over it and dash against the clock-tower. But it's a marvellous show when seen from a position of safety, when the massive incoming waves offer an awe-inspiring spectacle of unstoppable energy.

Food and drink

Whether it's humble fish and chips or locally caught lobster, standards are high in Porthleven when it comes to eating, and never more so than in April, when the Festival of Food and Music (*www.porthlevenfoodfestival.co.uk*) draws in producers and chefs from all over Cornwall.

Amélies at the Smokehouse Harbourside ① 01326 554000 Ⓦ www.amelie sporthleven.co.uk. Fresh, local food (fish from the Porthleven fleet), served in a clean, contemporary setting: the wide doors open right onto the harbour. Open all year.

Corner Deli 12 Fore St ① 01326 565554 Ⓦ www.thecornerdeli.co.uk. If the lovely shop windows don't draw you in, the delicious aromas will. A couple of window seats allow you to enjoy terrific coffee (served with a homemade biscuit), and there are wood-fired oven pizzas to take away in the evenings as well as an incredible array of comestible Cornish and Italian goodies on the shelves.

Kota Harbour Head ① 01326 562407 Ⓦ www.kotarestaurant.co.uk. A New Zealand couple with a passion for fresh seafood (Kota is Maori for shellfish) and organic, local produce, have done much to put Porthleven on Cornwall's gastronomic map. Their latest venture, **Kota Kai** (*01326 574411*), on the top floor of Celtic House (almost next door, but on the north side of the harbour) is a more relaxed affair, and much enjoyed by local families; there are lots of sofas, a children's room, film nights and menu of delicious nibbly things and dishes on an Asian theme as well as live jazz every Sunday lunchtime.

Ship Inn Mount Pleasant Rd ① 01326 564204 Ⓦ www.theshipinncornwall.co.uk. Built into the rocks on the north side of the harbour, it's the ideal spot to sit out a storm and watch the waves breaking – over a pint of Doom Bar, so to speak. The pub is child-friendly, and the menu proudly excludes chips and pasties.

The Cornish chough

Cornwall's emblematic bird – a crow with a long, curved red beak and red legs, given to aerobatic displays – disappeared from the county in 1949, as post-war agriculture became increasingly intensive and reliant upon pesticides. Choughs, which feed off the kind of insects found on grazed pasture close to their cliff nests, such as woodlice, spiders, ants and beetles, didn't have much of a chance. But a general change in land management on the Lizard tempted the first breeding pair to return to the cliffs at Lizard Point in 2001 and a small colony, closely watched and guarded by local volunteers, has re-established itself. Choughs are also gaining in numbers on the south Penwith coast and the chough breeding programme at Paradise Park in Hayle envisages chicks hatched in the wild in the near future (see page 146). For up-to-date news of sightings and hatchings, www.cbwps.org.uk has all the latest chough gossip.

The Loe

Between Porthleven and Helston, one of the best spots locally for walking and cycling follows the contours of the freshwater lake, known as the Loe. Fed by the River Cober, but blocked from running into the sea by a huge (and growing) dam of sand and shingle, the Loe is one of those geography-textbook examples of lagoon formation. Not everybody can agree, however, when Loe Bar was formed. The idea was made popular in Victorian times that the Cober was navigable as far as Helston at the time of the Norman invasion and that the site of the current boating lake was once a busy port; it's a likeable theory, but sadly lacking in evidence. A more probable explanation is that the Bar was formed at least 6,000 years ago, deposited by rising sea levels as ice melted across the globe.

No matter: the lake is stunningly, silently beautiful and lies within the Penrose estate, now owned and managed by the National Trust. The route through the estate passes a mock-Roman bathhouse, at the foot of a great sweep of immaculate, landscaped pasture that falls away below the Georgian façade of the house, hidden on either side by woods and water. It's a good idea to bring binoculars: there's a birdwatchers' hide by the lake which is a haven for wildfowl – widgeon, teal, mallard, shoveler, pochard, tufted duck and coots are common – and there were a pair of crested grebes the last time I visited.

You can follow the Cober through the woods (carpeted with bluebells in May) to Helston and catch a bus back to Porthleven or cross the marshy junction of river and lake on wooden boardwalks, emerging by the derelict remains of Lower Nansloe Mine, and do the complete **six-mile circuit** of the lake, crossing the shingle of Loe Bar to return to the starting point. There's a car park and map board at the entrance to the Penrose estate or limited parking where the road from Porthleven comes to an end on the cliff above Loe Bar. On the eastern side of the Bar, a memorial to the lives lost when HMS *Anson* ran aground here in 1807 serves as a stark reminder of the maritime dangers of this part of the coast.

③ Helston

Helston's identity is a complex one these days; on the one hand, the town leans heavily on its old buildings and traditions, whilst on the other, it's home to RNAS Culdrose, where 3,000 military and civilian personnel are employed in training, defence and air-sea rescue.

Helston's prosperous past is written all over the splendid houses that line the streets between St Michael's Church and the old shops, pubs and civic buildings on Coinagehall Street. This was one of Cornwall's five stannary towns, where ingots of copper and tin from the surrounding stannary had to be brought to be assayed, weighed and stamped in the Coinage Hall before they could be sold. Each ingot had a small corner – a 'coin' – cut off for assaying its purity, a task which brought phenomenal commercial activity to the town. It wasn't just the  loss of 1,200 miners' jobs when Wheal Vor, was threatened with closure in the early 19th century, it was the knock-on effect to other trades in the town that filled Helston with fear. Small wonder that the Helston banker and lawyer, Humphrey Millett Grylls, who used his personal wealth to keep the mine open, was revered: the **Grylls Arch,** an imposing castellated gateway to the ancient bowling green at the bottom of Coinagehall Street, was erected in his honour when he died in 1834.

The town had faced a different kind of shock and salvation a century earlier, when **St Michael's Church** was struck by lightning and had to be demolished after the ensuing fire. Lord Godolphin, whose family had grown rich on local tin since Tudor times, sprang into action and personally funded the building of the new church, completed in 1763. Though built of local granite it's hardly Cornish in character; the architect employed by Godolphin was Thomas Edwards of Greenwich, a keen admirer of Nicholas Hawksmoor – which is why some elements of St Michael's are reminiscent of St Alfege's, a Greenwich church, designed by Hawksmoor in 1718.

It's not just the buildings in Helston that speak of stannary wealth: deep granite channels, or '**kennels**', bubbling with running water play an important part in defining the town's character (as well as punishing careless roadside parking). These kerbside rills are channelled into the town by a sophisticated system of leats and sluices, some of which date from medieval times, from the infant River Cober, across the Wendron Valley and a couple of miles north of Helston. Their purpose is not known for certain, but the usefulness of a continual supply of running water for maintaining street hygiene, particularly around the tanneries, can be imagined. From the top of the town the kennels branch out (invisibly in some streets, where they have been covered over) sending a constant trickle of water through the town, which eventually ends up back in the Cober.

Helston is perennially associated with its ever-popular and ancient **Flora Day** celebrations held in May to celebrate the feast day of St Michael. From early morning until late afternoon, the streets are thick with dancers, flowers, foliage and spectators, chasing out the winter and singing in the spring. It's an exhausting business, which involves the whole community, lots of Cornish flag waving, joyful renditions of 'Trelawney' and 'Hal-an-Tow' as well as ritual dragon slaying, but the key event is the midday Furry Dance. Led by the Helston silver band, couples dressed as though they are going to Royal Ascot, parade and twirl through the streets to the well-known tune, which – be warned – stays in your ears for hours, if not days, afterwards.

For over 60 years, Helston has also been synonymous with helicopters, thanks to the busy presence of **RNAS Culdrose,** one of the biggest naval air stations in Europe, which has swelled the population and brought new energy to the town. The station is the search and rescue base for the whole of the South West and you can watch the Sea King helicopters swing into action and other airborne activity from a small viewing car park, outside the perimeter fence. The café here is open in the summer only. The Air Day, held in July, is a hugely popular local event and, as on Flora Day, the roads around Helston are best avoided unless you're coming to take part.

Helston Folk Museum

Market Pl, TR13 8TH ℗ 01326 564027 ⓦ www.cornwall.gov.uk; open Mon–Sat 10.00– 13.00 plus afternoons in school holidays; free, but donations gratefully accepted.

Housed in the old butter and meat market, the exhibits are arranged where the stalls once stood, like mini-museums, on either side of the sloping, granite thoroughfare. It's all very engaging and the volunteers and staff are happy to chat knowledgeably as they polish the brass. As you enter, an enormous granite runnelstone and 18th-century cider press, both from the Trelowarren estate, take centre stage. Thereafter, an eclectic mix unfolds of Edwardian uniforms, Chapel china, pre-war groceries, Marconi memorabilia and Victorian domestic equipment, until level ground indicates you have arrived in the old drill hall, into which the museum expanded in 1999. Here, some of the highlights include a costume gallery, a horse-drawn hearse and a Victorian schoolroom. Upstairs, in the loft are displays of toys, garden equipment, bicycles and an exhibit that tells the story of champion boxer, local lad Bob Fitzsimmons.

Henry Trengrouse

While virtually everybody has heard of Sir Humphry Davy and his invention of the safety lamp that saved so many miners' lives, few people outside Helston remember Henry Trengrouse, inventor of the ship-to-shore rocket-fired safety-line, forerunner of the 'breeches-buoy', that has helped to save thousands of mariners' lives across the globe.

Born and bred in Helston, where his father was a builder, Trengrouse was among the number of appalled bystanders that watched, helpless, as HMS *Anson* foundered and broke on Loe Bar and more than a hundred men drowned just yards from the shore on the morning of 29 December 1807. The catastrophe made a profound impact upon him, and over the next ten years he poured £3,000 (which, as a cabinetmaker, was money he could ill afford) into developing his rocket-propelled lifeline.

The prevailing design, submitted to the government by George Manby in 1808, was for a mortar that fired a line from shore to ship – which was proving neither accurate nor practical. (Who, in the confusion and distress of a shipwreck, is going to catch a snaking line and attach it to the right part of a breaking ship?) But whereas Manby received £2,000 from the government for his troubles, Trengrouse was given merely a royalty of £50 as he relinquished manufacture to the Admiralty. (The Tsar of Russia, rather embarrassingly for the Admiralty, sent Trengrouse a personal letter of thanks and a diamond ring.) For the rest of his life, Trengrouse continued to design safety equipment for ships, including the 'Bosun's Chair' and a prototype life jacket.

There's an exhibition dedicated to his life's work in Helston Folk Museum and the Trengrouse memorial stone in St Michael's churchyard honours a man who died, unjustly, in poverty.

Drink

The Blue Anchor 50 Coinagehall St ⓣ 01326 562821. A thatched pub at the lower end of Coinagehall St – there's even a thatched anchor on the roof – that appears hardly changed since monks lived here in the 15th century. Fireplaces, cosy snugs, wooden settles and flagged floors, and four strengths of Spingo beer, brewed at the back, make this a place of pilgrimage for aficionados of real ale and lovers of proper old-fashioned pubs.

④ Gweek and the National Seal Sanctuary

The oddly named village of Gweek slopes down to its bridge at the tidal limit of the Helford River, where there's a busy boatyard and a very decent pub, the Gweek Inn (*01326 221502*), that does good food. There are lovely wooded lanes leading to Mawgan and Trelowarren; anyone planning a bike ride or walk through the Lizard should make sure they make this route part of the itinerary.

Gweek is best known for the **National Seal Sanctuary** (*0871 423 2110;*

www.sealsanctuary.co.uk; open all year round), which does valuable work rescuing and rehabilitating injured or orphaned seals found on the Cornish coast, before releasing them back into the wild. It's not a zoo or theme park, and visitors sometimes baulk at the cost of admission, but the centre relies on entrance money and donations alone for its survival. There's a permanent community of old-timers, deemed unsuitable for release and a constantly changing population of pups and older seals in various stages of recovery. Tender-hearted adults and children will want to dig deep into their pockets once they spot the sanctuary's adoption programme.

⑤ Potager garden

High Cross, Constantine TR11 5RE ℗ 01326 341258 Ⓦ www.potagergarden.org.

This is one of my favourite places in Cornwall: not only is the garden inspiringly well planted, staggeringly productive and managed on organic principles, the whole place – including the café, workshops and everybody who works here – seems to exude happiness and creativity. The result is a virtuous circle; it came as no real surprise that while chatting to the garden's new owner, Mark, and one of Potager's founders, Dan, that a young lad, who was on a cycling and camping holiday, was welcomed when he asked if he could pitch his tent in the wood-fringed field at the bottom of the garden for a few days and earn his keep by helping the gardeners.

The influence of Falmouth University is clearly felt here. Peter Skerrett, co-founder of Potager, taught at the Falmouth School of Art and I recognised his name from the contemporary altar of yew and glass in a side chapel of Truro Cathedral. The architectural and sculptural elements of the garden are handled with true artistic vision; Dan Thomas is a plantsman with a terrific eye for colour. A superb **vegetarian café**, run by a young Breton and his Swiss girlfriend (who met at Falmouth University of course), uses produce straight out of the garden which is served at rustic tables in an eco-efficient greenhouse the team have designed and built themselves. On Friday evenings in the summer they also serve dinner; as night falls, diners have the wonderful garden to themselves.

Just down the road is **Constantine**, one of those well-heeled, but equally dynamic rural communities where the arts are placed high on the agenda. The **Tolmen Centre** (*Fore St; 01326 341353; www.tolmencentre.co.uk*) is where it all goes on, from classical guitar festivals to film, contemporary dance and drama, occasionally fresh from the Edinburgh Festival.

The shores of the Helford River

It's wood-fringed riverside beaches and lush gardens all the way between **Helford Passage** and **Mawnan Smith**. Swimming is safe, the south-facing shoreline sunny, and an undulating coast path joins it all together. The further east you walk, the more secluded the beaches become: **Porth Saxon** and **Porthallack** are particularly seductive and perfectly placed for shelter and late afternoon sunshine. Both **Trebah** and **Glendurgan** gardens can be approached from their beach entrances; getting to **Carwinion** gardens means a short hike up the road from Mawnan Smith.

South of the river, the lush dairy pastures, woods and coves give discreet shelter to some of Cornwall's most desirable real estate. And, where the river meets the sea and tidal Gillan Creek, the ultimate backdrop is offered to those who are happiest messing about on a boat.

Food and drink

There are good pubs at either end of the walk – the **Ferryboat Inn** (*01326 250625*) at Helford Passage and the dark and cosy **Red Lion** (*01326 250026*) in Mawnan Smith, with locally caught fish and game on the menu.

⑥ Trebah

Mawnan Smith TR11 5JZ ① 01326 250448 ⓦ www.trebah-garden.co.uk.

The Falmouth branch of the Fox family were hugely into their gardens. Quaker businessmen and women of enormous wealth, with ships at their disposal, the Foxes were able to fund plant-hunting trips around the world and in the sheltered narrow valleys south of Falmouth found ideal conditions for creating gardens of colourful exoticism that have since become identified as a particularly Cornish style of garden.

Dazzling collections of camellias, rhododendrons, magnolias, palms, pines and tree-ferns, a stream-fed valley and, beyond a clump of craggy Monterey pines, a glimpse of a blue cove: this is the stereotype, and no garden pulls it off quite so magnificently as Trebah. Charles Fox, whose elder siblings were busy making gardens at Glendurgan (next door) and Penjerrick (closer to Falmouth), moved here in 1838 and spent the next 40 years planting and developing the garden. Successive owners (who included car designer, racing driver and orchid breeder Donald Healey) continued to enhance the planting, but perhaps none more so than the Hibberts, who bought a rather run-down Trebah in 1981, intending to make it their retirement home. Within days of arrival, they found themselves drawn into an exciting programme of restoration and replanting, which continues today. Tony Hibbert, his children, grandchildren and great-grandchildren, remain very much at the living heart of the garden; 'we must always', says Tony, 'plan and plant for 200 years ahead'.

⑦ Glendurgan

Mawnan Smith TR11 5JZ ① 01872 862090 ⓦ www.nationaltrust.org.uk; National Trust.

While Charles Fox was busy at Trebah, his elder brother Alfred and sister-in-law Sarah had been hard at work making a garden (and producing 12 little gardeners to help them with the weeding) in the next-door valley, above the miniature fishing village of Durgan. The brothers' shared passion for plants must have proved of mutual benefit to both gardens, but despite this and very similar geographical features, the two gardens are quite distinct in character today. Glendurgan's squishy-contoured laurel maze and wilder, looser planting on the valley slopes is more romantic in its appeal; Trebah is busier, both in plants and visitors, drama and energy. Talking to Trebah's head gardener, Darren, I was surprised at how little was the flow of ideas and plants between the two gardens today. Glendurgan is a National Trust garden, and perhaps more involved with other Trust gardens than with its immediate neighbour.

⑧ Carwinion

Mawnan Smith TR11 5JA ① 01326 250258 ⓦ www.carwinion.co.uk.

Another long, narrow valley garden with a distinguished pedigree; the Rogers family of the Penrose estate were cousins of the Foxes of Glendurgan and Reginald Rogers laid out the garden here towards the end of the 19th century. There must be something in the genes, for the garden is managed today by Reginald's grandson, Anthony Rogers. Carwinion has all the elements of its grander, bigger neighbours, but is more intimate and, I think, more creative in its planting. An impressive collection of bamboo is showcased here: glorious glossy canes in green and yellow, black and pink, all carefully labelled. Art exhibitions, family-oriented events, cream teas and theatre play a big part in the garden too. Carwinion is highly rated by chief gardener, Dan, at Potager garden, where there's a similar kind of energy and creativeness.

⑨ Helford and around

'Just stand on the quay and wave – the ferry will soon come,' said the village postwoman as I quizzed her about crossing the river from Helford to the north shore. Sadly, my lonely waving was to no avail; it was a day or two before Easter and the ferry service had not yet resumed. The silver lining turned out to be the **Down by the Riverside Café** (*01326 231893*), in the old chapel by the (compulsory) car park on the edge of **Helford**. The village – just a clutch of whitewash and thatch, surrounding a tiny harbour – is inaccessible to cars, ridiculously pretty and quite clearly holidayed in rather than lived in.

Kestle Barton (*01326 231811; www.kestlebarton.co.uk*) is a 20-minute stroll from Helford, on a wooded circular walk that takes in the slightly creepy Frenchman's Creek, immortalised by Daphne du Maurier. An exciting conversion of farm buildings has resulted in a new arts venue that reflects the affluence of the Helford, with gallery, designer garden café and stunning, eco-sensitive accommodation.

Food and drink

Shipwright Arms (*01326 231235*) in Helford is popular with the boaty crowd and the location, close to the river in the middle of the village, is idyllic.

⑩ Bosahan

Manaccan TR12 6JL ① 01326 231351; open by appointment, Mar–Sep, Mon–Fri.

With a trio of great gardens on the opposite side of the river, unsung Bosahan is the kind of place you need to know about, rather than stumble upon, as although visitors are welcome, a little bit of advance notice is required. There's a kind of lost valley feeling here, among the giant tree-ferns and podocarpus, metasequoias and cork oaks; in fact, most of the very distinguished tree planting, carried out in the 19th century by the owner of Bosahan, Arthur Pendarves Vivian, has now reached monumental proportions in the benign, riverside climate. Under the stewardship of a new generation of Graham-Vivians, the two valleys are being gently, though extensively restored.

The nearest village is **Manaccan** where the church has acquired status locally, because a 200-year-old fig tree grows from the wall of the tower.

Food and drink

In Manaccan, **South Café** (*01326 231331*) offers upmarket, locally sourced food and other refreshment in a contemporary setting.

⑪ St Anthony-in-Meneage

There can be few nicer ways to spend a Slow morning or afternoon than pottering or paddling around Gillan Creek. Sailaway, a small family-run shop on the beach at St Anthony (*01326 231357; www.stanthony.co.uk*), hires out kayaks, toppers, dinghies and motor launches: the rest is up to you, though tuition is available for the inexperienced. Whichever way you point your craft, the views are sublime. Turn seawards and thread through the moorings to Dennis Head, braving the swell to enter the wide mouth of the Helford; turn inland and find yourself gliding through a green world, where kingfishers flash through the leafy shadows and swans patrol the margins of their watery world. The tide is everything: at low tide the creek becomes a muddy expanse of beached boats, crossed by stepping stones at its narrowest point. Turn your back for an hour and the sea has slid in, doubling the depth of the view in the upside-down reflections of boats, woods and cottages.

Food and drink

It's gloriously uncommercialised here; the only offering is **Sid's Fish and Chip Van**, which comes to Manaccan on Tuesday evenings throughout the year.

The peninsula

The 20 miles or so of Lizard coast are rich in gorgeous beaches, often tucked away far beneath the high cliff path; great fun for Slow explorers, hunting for serpentine, shells or seclusion. Inland, among the heathery downs to the west and gentle woods and farmland to the east, there are equally sequestered discoveries to be treasured: a standing stone or fogou, an ice-cream farm, the saddest of churchyards and a garden filled with South African exoticism.

⑫ Church Cove

A golf course, a sandy beach and a church with a separate tower, half-buried in the cliff, make incongruous neighbours, but these are the ingredients of Church Cove. There's been a chapel here since the 5th century, but what you see today is a Victorian restoration of a storm-damaged 15th-century church; the bell tower dates from the 13th century.

There have been terrible shipwrecks here and it's easy to imagine a desperate

seafaring population building their church at a little distance from the village of Gunwalloe, right on the beach, where everybody would cluster for news or hope when a fishing boat or (fingers crossed) treasure-laden galleon went down on the rocks. Inside the church two surviving parts of a rood screen made from wreckage of the Portuguese ship, the *San Antonio*, can be seen. She was wrecked at Gunwalloe in 1527, *en route* from Lisbon to Antwerp, on a wild January night. Dollar Cove, just below the church, is still visited by treasure-seekers, and the odd gold or silver coin might yet be found.

Food and drink

There is an excellent pitstop if you are exploring the coast between Gunwalloe and Church Cove.

The **Halzephron Inn** is a 500-year-old free house overlooking the sea, on the lane south out of Gunwalloe (*01326 240406*). Local ales, Skreach cider and top-notch, locally sourced food.

⑬ Mullion

Busy Mullion is one of the few places on the peninsula with shops and banks and the picturesque cove and harbour, preserved by the National Trust, is an absolute magnet for artists. It's not for those wanting to escape the crowds, but the church of **St Mellanus** right in the centre of Mullion itself is too interesting to miss. The hugely studded south door is 13th century and contains a dog-door, which operated much like a cat-flap. It's nice to imagine the shepherds sitting quietly in the congregation, while their conscientious dogs popped in and out, keeping an eye on the flocks in the fields outside. The carved bench ends are a real delight: you can see caricatures of clergymen and drinkers as well as more sober Christian imagery and an intriguing rendition of Jonah in the belly of the whale. They were preserved from destruction during the Reformation by local carpenters, who covered them neatly in plain pine boards. Not so fortunate was the carved rood screen; although one of the most eye-catching things in the church and a brilliant piece of 20th-century craftsmanship, only the tiniest bit of the 15th-century original remains. The barrel-vaulted roof is even more recent, completed in 1987, but faithful to the Cornish style and built of pegged oak and lime-and-horsehair plaster.

The Marconi Centre, Poldhu

For details of opening times see ⓦ www.marconi-centre-poldhu.org.uk; free, though donations are very welcome.

The year 1901 was a significant one for Guglielmo Marconi: in January, when he received a wireless communication from the Isle of Wight at his experimental station close to Lizard village, he proved that radio signals could travel well over the horizon. By December he was on the other side of the Atlantic in Newfoundland, celebrating the arrival of a Morse signal from the transmitter he had erected on Poldhu Point. To mark the centenary of this event in 2001, the Poldhu Amateur Radio Club opened the Marconi Centre, close to the spot where Marconi's four transmitters had stood. It's run by volunteers, who use it as a base for the amateur radio club, and because of this it's open all year round on Tuesday and Friday evenings, and some afternoons too. Their enthusiasm is infectious; even teenagers wedded to their mobile phones find it hard to remain aloof here, among the headsets, dials, frequency static and radio chatter, where the everyday marvel of long-distance communication seems somehow more real than a digital tweet.

Marconi's experimental station close to Lizard village is also open to visitors (*www.lizardwireless.org*); it may look just like a wooden hut in a field, but it is the oldest Marconi radio transmitting station to survive in its original state, its interior virtually unchanged since 1901. The story of wireless transmission is picked up with a slightly different slant at the Telegraph Museum in Porthcurno

Beach gallops

If the sight of horseriders cantering across the beach at low tide fills you with longing, the place to go is Newton Farm (*01326 240388*), between Poldhu and Mullion. Rides can be arranged for both novice and experienced riders, ranging from one to five hours. Hats can be borrowed and boots hired.

(see page 233). By 1929, Marconi's profitable network, which had been sold to the Post Office, was causing concern to those who had invested heavily in the overland and undersea cable-laying projects. Competitive wireless communication was deeply unwelcome and, with something approaching skullduggery, Marconi's invention was appropriated by the new Cable & Wireless Company.

⑭ Kynance Cove

Beaches don't come any lovelier than this, and the long walk and steps down to the cove from the huge National Trust car park on the cliffs, is busy with families for whom the trudge is amply rewarded. What makes it so special are the pinnacles and islets of serpentine rock that create loose divisions and sandy niches around the cove, which as the tide recedes, add a naturally sculpted architecture to the crescent beach – and create pockets of shade, a thousand rock pools and vantage points for children playing pirates.

Just above the beach, a wide grassy slope offers a broad view of the whole cove, the emerald and turquoise water and the entertainment of beach activity.

Food and drink

Kynance Cove Café ① 01326 290436 ⑩ www.kynancecovecafe.co.uk. Roofed with photovoltaic tiles, this eco-friendly place on the grassy shelf above the beach seems almost too good to be true; the loos are fed by spring water and waste treated by a 'bio-bubble'. And that's not all: the toilet-block roof is a mixture of turf and meadow flowers, helping the structure blend into the hillside.

⑮ Lizard

The most southerly village in mainland Britain has a degree more charm than the most westerly point at Land's End. Both are busy and attract lots of tourists especially in the summer, but Lizard is no theme park and the village has a lived-in feel.

Food and drink

Lizard has a proper butcher's and nice deli (and **Ann's Pasty Shop**, which is probably the most famous pasty shop in Cornwall); the pubs and cafés make the most of locally produced food and drink and the gift shop windows display polished local serpentine rock.

Hidden Lizard Victorian Tea Room, Gweal Crease Barn, TR12 7NX ① 01963 291033. Quite apart from the teas, there's a lot going on here: a working forge, with horseshoeing demonstrations, a small museum of Victorian domestic life and a garden. Inside the first-floor tea room there are old photos of the village and a viewing gallery that looks down into the forge.

Lizard Lighthouse

① 01326 290202 ⓦ www.trinityhouse.co.uk; tower and visitor centre open throughout the summer and school holidays.

The story goes that protests from local villagers, actively caught up in wrecking and looting ships, prevented a lighthouse from being built on this dangerous part of the coast until 1619, when Sir John Killigrew poured his own funds into building a beacon tower on Lizard Point. The poor man seems to have been hated both on land and at sea; resentful local builders dragged their heels and Killigrew's attempts to recoup his investment by collecting voluntary tolls from passing ships was met with derision, to the point where King James I imposed a levy of a halfpenny per ton of ship safely passing the light. The response from shipping agents was so aggressively negative that the idea was dropped and only four years after its beacon was lit, the first Lizard lighthouse was demolished and Killigrew was declared bankrupt.

For over a century, the idea was debated and rejected until finally winning the support of Trinity House, and a twin-towered building, linked by the keeper's cottage, was built in 1751. With a coal-fired lantern burning in each tower, the bellows men had their work cut out. The keeper, positioned between them in his cottage, would give a blast on a cow-horn if he saw them relaxing their efforts.

It's all a bit different today, where just one of the towers is used and an automated white electric light flashes every three seconds.

The Witchball Lighthouse Rd, TR12 7NJ ① 01963 290662. Organic ales from the Chough Brewery, just down the road, scrupulous sourcing from named local suppliers and lobster, landed at Cadgwith in the morning, is often on the menu at lunchtime; utterly lacking in pretentiousness and offering extremely good value.

⑯ Cadgwith

There's something deeply attractive about Cadgwith: everybody wants to be a part of this tiny, world's-end community, wedged into a cleft in the serpentine rock, where tractors haul fishing boats, laden with crab and lobster, up the beach and sea shanties are sung in the beamy pub in the evening. Cadgwith's cosy, salty loveliness was burnished even brighter in *Ladies in Lavender*, the 2004 film about two spinster sisters (played by Judy Dench and Maggie Smith) who rescue a shipwrecked young musician and bring him into the community.

There's no room for visitors' cars in Cadgwith, which have to be left in the car park on the hillside behind the village. The walk down takes you past thatched cottages, with miniscule gardens brimming with colourful exotics and a very small church, made out of corrugated tin and painted bright blue.

Nigel Legge, who makes traditional lobster pots out of withies, and helps to keep the pub supplied with fresh crab and lobster, runs boat trips out of the harbour and knows how to tell a story or two (*www. lobsterpots.co.uk*). But the tallest fishy story from Cadgwith is true: when pilchard fishing was at its peak, the Cadgwith fleet held the record catch for Cornwall, with 1.3 million pilchards landed in a single day.

On the south side of the harbour, the cliff path rises steeply, and what looks like a huge, sea-filled crater is revealed, far below. Known as the **Devil's Frying Pan**, this is a collapsed cavern, and in wild weather, the sea swirls menacingly through an arch into this cauldron-like hole. However, it's only fair to point out that on a calm day, at low tide, with a seagull or two bobbing about, it's clear that the heat under the frying pan is not always turned up high.

Food and drink

The **Cadgwith Cove Inn** (*01326 290513*) adjoins an old pilchard cellar, where the fish would have been salted and pressed; pilchards are no longer on the menu, but the crab sandwiches are rather good and there's singing in the bar on Tuesday and Friday evenings.

⑰ Lankidden Cove

Grid reference SW756166.

On my OS map, I see my daughter has written 'not for the faint-hearted'. It was indeed, a bit of a scramble to get down, though ropes had been thoughtfully provided to help with the last section. Getting back up to the coast path took ages. This is probably one of the loveliest and most secluded beaches on the Lizard coast, which disappears completely at high tide, so unless you have studied your tide timetable, you may have to wait to gain access – and then work extremely hard for the pleasure such beauty and remoteness offers. Which is as it should be.

The narrow promontory that forms the western cliff behind the beach is the site of an Iron Age cliff-fort, known as **Carrick Luz**, Cornish for Grey Rock. But unlike other parts of the Lizard where serpentine is predominant, the grey rock in question here is crystalline gabbro. Going back about 380 million years, as continents advanced and collided, the earth's mantle and crust were shoved up to the surface, appearing as serpentine and gabbro respectively. Carrick Luz appeared where a fissure in the serpentine forced the gabbro to rear through. If this sort of thing interests you, go to Coverack Beach at low tide, where the exposed rocks offer a textbook geology lesson in igneous rock formation. In fact, Coverack is one of just a handful of places in the world where you can actually see the junction of mantle and crust exposed on the surface of the planet. As the information board by the car park in Coverack explains, 'as you walk south across the beach, you're travelling to the centre of the earth'.

⑱ St Keverne

It's hard to believe now that the thatch-and-whitewash village, surrounded by fields and woods, has had a such a sad history of burying the victims of shipwrecks. No fewer than 500 men, women and children who perished on the notorious Manacles, a submerged reef about a mile offshore, lie in the churchyard. Even today, there are some in the village who can remember their grandparents talking about the day the *Mohegan* went down in 1897 and 106 people drowned. Everybody in the village was involved in some way, giving shelter to those who survived, acting as pall-bearers, creating wreaths or digging the mass grave that eventually received more than 50 victims.

The village hero, however, is Michael Joseph, the blacksmith ('An Gof' in Cornish) who, with the Bodmin lawyer, Thomas Flamank, led a peaceful uprising against an unpopular new tax, levied by Henry VII in 1497. Why should Cornwall, argued Joseph, be obliged to pay the King for the cost of sending an army to squash the Scots? But Joseph was no rabble-rouser; people followed him because of his brave and clear opposition to injustice. The rebellion swiftly dissolved at the Battle of Blackheath, where Flamank and Joseph were taken prisoner. Their execution at Tyburn ten days later was an unpleasant exercise in Tudor butchery. Their frightened followers were sent home (no point executing all those taxpayers) and the county subjected to a humiliating and costly fine.

Food and drink

There are two pubs in the village square, the **White Hart** and the **Three Tuns Hotel**. The latter, under popular management, has been refurbished. Both offer local ales and top-notch pub grub.

Roskilly's Farm

The Roskillys – a talented and likeable family of farmers and artists – have been farming at Tregellast Barton just outside St Keverne for generations, and added artisanal ice-cream making to their activities in the 1980s. The farm (*01326 280479*) is open and you can watch the beautiful herd of Jerseys being milked, see the ice cream being made and drive yourself mad trying to choose from the long list of flavours available in the shop and farmyard café, **The Croust**. Gooseberry and elderflower sorbet topped my personal and, I am proud to say, extensively researched list of favourites. Toby Roskilly's furniture is on show in the gallery-shop and his sister, Bryanna Roskilly, is the stained-glass artist, whose work decorates the Croust. She now has her own ice-cream café, **Archie's Loft** (*01326 281440*), overlooking the beach at Coverack, a couple of miles away.

⑲ Goonhilly Downs

Head inland from the coastal villages and coves and you're soon confronted with an empty expanse of level moorland, dotted with grazing ponies as part of a heathland management scheme. Of course, it's far from empty, particularly from a naturalist's point of view – much of the heather is a type found only on the Lizard (and parts of Ireland) and there is a rich population of other heathland plants: tormentil and devil's-bit scabious, black bog-rush and purple moor-grass, as well as orchids and the extremely rare hairy buttercup.

Merlins and barn owls hunt here, and on still summer evenings, the eerie cry of the nightjar can be heard. And there are butterflies in abundance – skippers, graylings, meadow browns and silver-studded blues. There are tracks through the nature reserve (car parking is available close to the satellite station, on the B3292) and a couple of hours can easily be lost, rambling around, with a pair of binoculars at the ready.

RAF Dry Tree

A scattering of brick and concrete ruins, slowly disappearing beneath brambles and grass on Goonhilly Downs, is all that remains of a **World War II radar station**, staffed by women from the WAAF, whose job it was to give early warning to the RAF bases at Predannack and Portreath of approaching enemy aircraft. Tracks fan out from the car park and a looping circular walk takes an hour or so to complete. There's a stillness and silence here, made all the more poignant by the looming presence of the giant satellite dish, Antenna One ('Arthur'), which soars above the northern perimeter fence. The base was named Dry Tree, rather grimly, after the gallows tree that stood at the junction of five parishes. The Dry Tree standing stone, which was set upright again in 1928 (after losing its head to careless road-makers), has a singular presence, which I admit I found rather unsettling.

What makes walking here really interesting is that Goonhilly's history, both ancient and relatively modern, is never far from the surface – from the redundant satellite dishes of the Goonhilly Satellite Earth Station (see box) to the Bronze Age burial mounds and medieval turf stacks that litter the heath. Without some kind of guide, however, it's easy to be mistaken; the little hillocks dotted across the downs at regular intervals are neither Neolithic nor medieval in origin, but simply the remains of a grid of obstructions erected during World War II to prevent German gliders landing on the level, treeless plateau.

Merlin and Arthur: the Goonhilly Satellite Earth Station

The Goonhilly Satellite Earth Station must have been one of the most exciting places to work in Britain when it was at the cutting edge of communications technology in the early 1960s. The first aerial, nicknamed **Arthur**, tracked the Telstar satellite and its 79-foot-diameter dish is now a listed monument. It was followed by Uther and Guinivere, Lancelot, Tristan and Isolde to track the the increasing number of satellites being launched into space. **Merlin**, the biggest dish at 98 feet in diameter, was constructed in 1985; in total there were 25 operational aerials of all shapes and sizes, transmitting international phone calls and TV programmes, as well as connecting shipping communications around the globe.

But in 2008, British Telecom announced it was transferring its satellite operations to Madley in Herefordshire, keeping Goonhilly open as a museum only. When the museum closed in 2010, there were fears that the whole station would go into decline, but the latest news is that the Earth Station is to be given a new lease of life as a space-science centre, scheduled to open to the public in 2013. The plan is to connect Goonhilly to a global radio-astronomy network, exploring what Brian Cox would call 'the origin and fate of galaxies', and the big dishes will be upgraded to provide a communications link with deep-space missions in the future. As the old Cornish legend predicted, Arthur and Merlin will rise again.

⑳ Bonython Manor

Cury Cross Lanes TR12 7BA ⓣ 01326 240550 ⓦ www.bonythonmanor.co.uk; gardens open mid Apr–mid Sep Tue–Fri.

Iconic Cornish gardens such as Trebah, Glendurgan and Trelissick are thick on the ground in the sheltered valleys of the Helford and Fal, but you really don't expect to find a great garden just a mile or two short of Goonhilly in the middle of the peninsula. What's more, Bonython has a style of its own, and is one of a handful of newish gardens which are redefining the Cornish garden scene.

Sue and Richard Nathan arrived at Bonython from South Africa in 1999, bringing with them a love of South African plants, buckets of horticultural curiosity and a sense of adventure. The walled gardens that you enter on arrival pay colourful though respectful homage to English mixed border planting, but once in the valley beyond, where a series of orchards, lakes and ornamental parkland merges with the tree-fringed landscape, the adventure starts. The planting is relatively recent but mould-breaking, and the lakeside slopes, using bold grasses and plants native to the Cape, are inspired. A garden hut offers do-it-yourself teas and coffees, and Sue, who is a great plantswoman, is usually in the garden; she's a mine of friendly information.

㉑ Trelowarren and Halliggye Fogou

A long drive sweeps up and downhill through the wooded estate of **Trelowarren**, home to the Vyvyan family for 600 years. The 13th baronet, Sir Ferrers Vyvyan, now runs the estate with impeccable green intelligence and the carbon-neutral holiday cottages, craft centre and restaurant are among the best of their kind in Cornwall.

But way before the drive straightens out in the final approach to the manor, there's a strange adventure to be enjoyed. A notice by a lay-by points the way to the **Halliggye Fogou**, a hundred yards or so up the hill that was once an Iron Age hillfort. During daylight hours between April and September, the iron gates are open at the entrance to this prehistoric underground chamber, which is thought to have been constructed at the same time as the fort. It's dark once you're down the steps, the roof is low and the passage twists away from the entrance, so a torch is essential. No-one knows the purpose of these fogous, about a dozen of which have been found in the far west of Cornwall, and this one is the longest and best preserved of them all. There is unlikely to be anyone else around; there is something surreal about returning to the world after a few minutes in the confines of this ancient, atmospheric place.

Food and drink

Gear Farm Shop Just outside the estate, on the road to St Martin; TR12 6DE Ⓣ 01326 221150. A wonderful place to pick up a picnic. There's a quiet camping field too on this child-friendly farm.

New Yard Restaurant Trelowarren TR12 6AF Ⓣ 01326 221595 Ⓦ www.newyardrestaurant.co.uk. Just a few minutes' walk away from Halliggye Fogou; the menu reflects the Vyvyan ethos of enjoying and making the best imaginative use of the estate and other local farms' abundant seasonal resources.

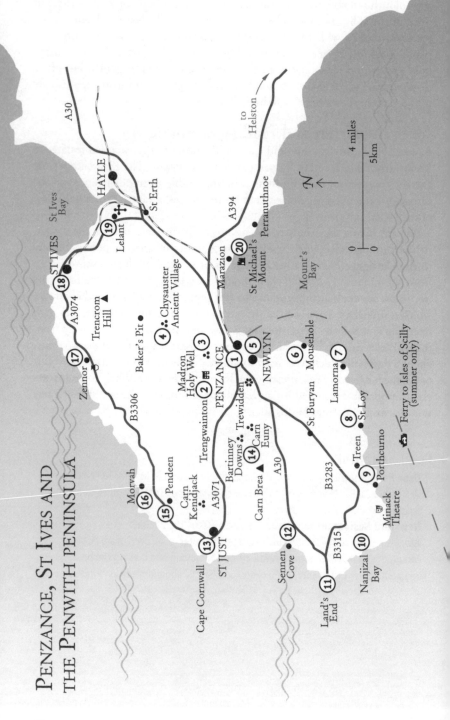

PENZANCE, ST IVES AND
THE PENWITH PENINSULA

to
Helston

A30

HAYLE

St Erth

St Ives
Bay

ST IVES

Lelant

19

A394

Marazion

20

St Michael's
Mount

Perranuthnoe

Mount's
Bay

4 miles

5km

18

A3074

Trencrom
Hill

Chysauster
Ancient Village

Baker's Pit

4

3

Madron
Holy Well

1

5

NEWLYN

6

Mousehole

7

17

Zennor

B3306

2

Trengwainton

PENZANCE

Trewidden

St Buryan

Lamorna

St Loy

8

Bartinney
Downs

14

Carn
Euny

A30

B3283

Treen

9

Porthcurno

16

Morvah

15

Pendeen

Carn
Kendjack

A3071

Carn Brea

12

Sennen
Cove

Minack
Theatre

10

Nanjizal
Bay

Ferry to Isles of Scilly
(summer only)

13

ST JUST

Cape Cornwall

11

Land's
End

B3315

212

9. Penzance, St Ives and the Penwith Peninsula

A peninsula at the end of a peninsula: small wonder that Penwith feels remote from the rest of Cornwall, let alone the rest of the country. Driving down the long A30 can be a grim affair, but that first, almost unreal glimpse of St Michael's Mount and the wide blue sweep of Mount's Bay never fails to lift the spirits, creating the feeling that some kind of threshold is about to be crossed to a wilder, older, more mysterious part of Cornwall. Penzance, which dominates the bay and makes a kind of gateway to the peninsula, has a special character entirely in keeping with its position. It's no surprise that so many artists, writers, archaeologists and historians – as well as a healthy smattering of good old-fashioned eccentrics – have found their way down here over the years. As my Cornish neighbour likes to say, with enigmatic knowingness: 'shake the stocking and all the nuts will gather in the toe'.

From the summit of Chapel Carn Brea you get a feel for a good chunk of Penwith and its history, as well as its siren appeal to artists. Approached from the narrow, twisting road between Crows-an-Wra and the Land's End airport, this hill is a far from strenuous climb, but the visual reward suggests you've scaled something much bigger. You can perch at the summit on a ruined Bronze Age burial chamber and think you're on an island, for on a clear day, sea and sky dominate for as far as you can swivel your head. The Isles of Scilly are a smudge on a horizon punctuated by ponderous tankers; smaller fishing vessels plough briskly through the white-capped swell; and waves which have travelled the Atlantic dash against the Longships lighthouse, enveloping it in dramatic clouds of foaming spray. Away to the east, St Michael's Mount is palely visible through a gap in the hills, and northwest beyond the offshore twin peaks of the Brisons, there's a glimpse of Cape Cornwall, believed for centuries to be the real Land's End.

At your feet, to the south and west, lies a green patchwork of fields and farms, bounded by hedges of wind-sculpted gorse and hawthorn; there are very few trees. Villages linked by ancient roads and tracks and the landmark church towers of St Buryan and Sennen are just discernible in the folded landscape where Davies Gilbert's rhymes, composed of nothing more than names of hamlets and farms, still echo down the lanes:

Vellandrucha, Cracka, Cudna,
Truzemenhall, Chun, Crowzenwra;
Bans, Burnnhal, Brane, Bosfranken,
Treeve, Trewidden, Try, Trembah.

Turn northwards, however, and Penwith Moor looms on the horizon, littered with prehistoric sites and abandoned tin mines, its craggy hilltop carns rising abruptly above the jagged north coast. There's a wild beauty here in the rough, windswept moors and cliffs, which is easy enough to appreciate when the sun is shining, but when the drenching clouds roll in, it can all feel rather raw and bleak. It's fortunate for many that St Ives, with its cosy and picturesque streets and alleyways, cosmopolitan galleries and lively, art-filled culture, is part of the north coast scenery too.

The eating is good in Penwith. Fish and crab from Newlyn and St Ives rarely come fresher to the fishmonger's slab; local dairies produce fabulous ice creams and farmers' markets start the season with astonishingly early potatoes and Cornish asparagus. After years of decline, craft cider is making a strong comeback (under the promising name of Skreach) in Penwith and many real ale enthusiasts claim that their favourite pint, brewed on the premises, is to be found at the Star in Crowlas.

Getting around

Penwith is well served by public transport, although you'd never guess, given the choked roads and bulging car parks at peak moments during the summer months. Double-decker buses (some open-topped in summer) trundle around the spectacular coast road, from Penzance to Land's End and on, through St Just and Zennor to St Ives, but I've rarely seen them more than half full. And St Ives, where it is particularly difficult to find a parking space outside the big field car parks on the outskirts, is reached by one of the prettiest branch-line train rides in England.

Yet you'll see lots of cyclists – and need to watch out for them – pedalling hard down the A30, particularly as you get close to Land's End – the end of the road, quite literally, for thousands of charity cyclists and walkers.

Trains

It's not quite the Orient Express, but the **Night Riviera** – the sleeper service which has rocked passengers to sleep between Paddington and Penzance since 1877 – is hard to beat for sheer civilisation and romance. I can't imagine anything sweeter than leaving grimy London at shortly before midnight and waking up to find the Cornish coast outside your window. It's not often that arrival by train presents a visitor with the best introduction to a town, but **Penzance** offers a glorious exception to this dismal rule. As you roll into the terminus decorated with huge panels of the Penwith landscape by local artist, Kurt Jackson, it's hard not to be thrilled by the wide blue sweep of Mount's Bay, crowned at one end with the battlements of St Michael's Mount and at the other with the crowded slate rooftops of Newlyn. One stop before Penzance is **St Erth**, where the branch line to **St Ives** connects with the main-line service.

Spared from Beeching's axe in the 1960s because of its popularity, the line skims the Lelant Saltings, a marshy sanctuary for migrating and native waders and sea birds. Climbing steadily, it turns to meet the surf and sandy beaches of St Ives Bay, where it runs along the rise above Porth Kidney Sands, Carbis Bay and, 15 minutes after leaving St Erth, enters St Ives. Train rides rarely come more appealing than this.

Buses

Two bus operators, First and Western Greyhound cover the Penwith peninsula pretty comprehensively. Route maps and timetables can be downloaded at www.firstgroup.com and www.westerngreyhound.com.

From mid-April until the end of September, the round-the-coast double-decker bus (First 300), linking **Penzance** to nearly every village on the 36-mile journey round the tip of the peninsula to **St Ives**, is an invaluable resource for Slow explorers and walkers doing the coast path in sections, wanting to get back to base, with **Land's End** a particularly useful bus stop.

Cycling

The wind blows hard in Penwith, and the hills are not for the faint-hearted. However, the visual rewards are staggering and for me the 18-mile, twisting clifftop road from St Just to St Ives (with a pitstop in Zennor) provides some of the best (and sweatiest) hours to be had on a bike in Cornwall. The **First and Last Trail** is part of the Sustrans cycle route 3 (the **Cornish Way**), linking Land's End to Bude, and this section takes you as far as Hayle, via a quiet and mainly inland route, with some decent stopping places for refreshment *en route*.

Cycle hire and tours

You can pick up a bike from **Land's End Cycle Hire** (*www.landsendcyclehire.co.uk*) in Trewellard, a couple of miles east of St Just. Given a day's notice, they will deliver and collect your bike to a drop-off point around the coast and, if you're interested, suggest the least hilly routes. In the middle of Penzance there's the **Penzance Cycle Centre** (*1 New St; 01736 351671; www.cyclecentre.co.uk*) offering bikes for daily or weekly hire. Alternatively, **Cornish Cycle Tours** (*www.cornishcycletours.co.uk*) organise 3- or 4-day (depending on your cycling fitness) tours of the Penwith peninsula, using the coastal road, starting in St Just.

Walking

Penwith has some of the most dramatic of all Cornish **coastal walking**. The entire stretch is worth savouring, but particularly around Zennor Head, Gurnard's Head, Morvah and Cape Cornwall, and the superb walk from Land's End past Nanjizal and Treryn Dinas to Treen. Tim Locke, the Slow series editor, has a happy memory of taking the bus from Penzance to Land's

End and following his favourite stretch of the coast path to Treen, before catching the same bus back to Penzance.

Inland, northern Penwith has the edge over the area further south: the moors, prehistoric sites and ruins of mine buildings punctuate the landscape perfectly with points of interest to head for, and an exceptionally fine route taking in all these aspects is described on page 240.

Further inland, the mini summits of Chapel Carn Brea and Trencrom Hill give sweeping views quite out of scale with the minimal effort involved in getting to the top.

Accommodation

The useful website www.cornwallfarwest.co.uk, not affiliated to the tourist office, is used by owners of all types of accommodation in Penwith to advertise their stuff.

The site has an excellent interactive map, particularly good for finding out-of-the-way campsites and B&Bs.

Abbey Hotel Abbey St, Penzance TR18 4AR ① 01736 366906 ⓦ www.theabbey online.co.uk ⓔ hotel@theabbeyonline.co.uk. Jean Shrimpton, fashion icon of the Swinging Sixties, bought this hotel in 1979, bringing country house elegance and colour to the 17th-century town house overlooking the harbour. Today, her son Thaddeus runs the hotel with the same dash and friendly eccentricity. Expect log fires, tea in the pretty garden, French armoires, crisp linens and wool blankets rather than duvets – and upmarket prices for all this. Visiting dogs please note: there is the promise of an extra sausage at breakfast if you have been well behaved.

Boscarne Farm Crows en Wra, St Buryan TR19 6HR ① 01736 810366 (no website or email). A cosy B&B, very reasonably priced, with an understandably loyal following. All four rooms have sea views and the two doubles have half-tester beds. There's also a twin and bunk room, making it ideal for families. Evening meals are optional, and breakfasts are cooked on the Aga. A real gem.

Boscrowan Farm Heamoor, near Penzance TR20 8UJ ① 01736 332396 ⓦ www.boscrowan.co.uk ⓔ elizabeth@boscrowan.co.uk. A mile north of Penzance, David and Elizabeth Harris's 25-acre smallholding is a model of small-scale sustainability. The two competitively priced cottages, Peace and Plenty (sleeps four) and Ring and Thimble (sleeps two), have their own garden spaces, where old wheelbarrows are planted with salads for guests to help themselves to, and Elizabeth encourages visitors to pick cosmos and sweet peas too, as an alternative to buying imported cut flowers for the cottages. Children should bring wellies if they would like to help feed the ducks and chickens.

Boswednack Manor B&B Zennor, near St Ives TR26 3DD ① 01736 794183 ⓦ www.boswednackmanor.co.uk ⓔ boswednack@ravenfield.co.uk. Set in three acres of organic meadows, vegetable, fruit and flower gardens, overlooking the wild north coast, the rambling Victorian farmhouse offers good-value, traditionally furnished rooms and vegetarian breakfasts. A 20-minute walk across the fields brings you to Zennor; the coast path at Gurnard's Head is even closer, making it a popular B&B with walkers.

Cove Cottage St Loy, St Buryan TR19 6DH ① 01736 810010 ⑩ www.cornwall-online.co.uk/covecottage-stloy Ⓔ thewhites@covecottagestloy.co.uk. An idyllic, secluded spot, overlooking a superb subtropical garden and the sheltered cove of St Loy: a first-floor hideaway for two people – four-poster bed included. A very special B&B (dinner served in rooms by arrangement), priced accordingly.

Grove Cottage B&B Trescowe, Germoe TR20 9RW ① 01736 763624 ⑩ www.cornishcottagewithrooms.co.uk Ⓔ roomenquiry@cornishcottage withrooms.co.uk. A lovely garden surrounds this old cartwright's house, brimming with exotics. Well placed for exploring the Lizard peninsula and Godolphin estate as well as Penwith, and close to the glorious coast around Prussia Cove. The two attractively furnished double rooms and one single, are very reasonably priced and breakfasts are a celebration of local produce.

Gurnard's Head Near Zennor, St Ives TR26 3DE ① 01736 796928 ⑩ www.gurnardshead.co.uk Ⓔ enquiries@gurnardshead.co.uk. A lot of thought has gone into the very comfortable bedrooms; not cheap, but just right for a bit of indulgence. Friends of mine who run a market garden on the Roseland peninsula spent their Slow honeymoon here, arriving on the round-the-coast bus, which passes the doorstep. Some of the best walking on the north coast can be enjoyed from here. The pub downstairs is a highly rated eating spot, serving contemporary dishes of lovely local grub.

Gypsy Caravan Primrose Cottage, Levant Lane, Trewellard, Pendeen TR19 7SU ① 01736 787585 ⑩ www.gypsycaravanbandb.co.uk Ⓔ holiday@ gypsycaravanbabdb.co.uk. Just 300 yards from the dramatic clifftops and National Trust-run Levant Mine, this authentic gypsy caravan is a godsend for budget-conscious walkers looking for a bit of cosy, quirky luxury at the end of a day's hike. The painted wagon sleeps two comfortably (there's space for one dog in the cubby underneath the bed) and there's even a TV next to the little logburner. Breakfast is served in the conservatory, next to the shower room.

Land's End Hostel Trevescan, Land's End TR19 7AQ ① 07519 309908 ⑩ www.landsendhostelaccommodation.co.ukⒺ Susie@landsendhostel accommodation.co.uk. Spotless bargain-priced hostel accommodation, plus an en-suite twin B&B; near the coast path.

Primrose Valley Hotel Porthminster Beach, St Ives TR26 2ED ① 01736 794939 ⑩ www.primroseonline.co.uk Ⓔ info@primroseonline.co.uk. Just yards from the beach and close to the Tate, the presentation of this small (ten-bedroom) eco-friendly, family-run hotel is as good as its location. Local producers are well supported (the bar stocks only Cornish beers, for example) and much emphasis is placed on employing a friendly, local team all year round. Prices are very reasonable for this kind of eco-luxury in the centre of St Ives.

Secret Garden Caravan & Camping Park Bosavern House, St Just, Penzance TR19 7RD ⓣ 01736 788301 ⓦ www.secretbosavern.com ⓔ mail@bosavern. com. There are just 12 pitches (for tents or caravans) in this old walled garden and orchard, close to St Just. A community farm next door has eggs and veggies for sale and a lovely walk from the doorstep takes you down the Cot Valley to the coast at Porth Nanven. If the site is full, try the rugby club on the outskirts of St Just, which offers basic camping (for tents) in a pretty spot.

Tourist information centres

Penzance Near the bus station ⓣ 01736 335530 ⓦ www.visit-westcornwall. com. Welcome to West Cornwall centre run by the NT and staffed by enthusiastic volunteers.
St Ives The Guildhall, Street-an-Pol ⓣ 01736 796297 ⓦ www.stivestic.co.uk. Reprieved after a brief closure in 2011, St Ives fought back and set up an excellent website.
St Just The Library, Market St ⓣ 01736 788165.

① Penzance

As I was approaching Penzance while researching this book, a pirate, complete with cutlass, hat and boots (but alas, no parrot) was attempting to hitch a lift out of town. (In 2011 Penzance stole the world record from Hastings for the greatest number of 'pirates' assembled in one place.) How different Penzance's identity might be today if Gilbert and Sullivan had stuck to the original title – *The Robbers of Redruth* – for their 1877 operetta *The Pirates of Penzance*. Pirate-spotting aside, Penzance is a rewarding place for curious pottering, which is the best way to get a grip on the town's multi-faceted identity. 'It's a bit flaky,' says Jean Shrimpton, who lives here and owns the Abbey Hotel. 'Penzance is not a prim-and-proper town.'

Like many other coastal settlements in Cornwall, Penzance grew up in two parts – a cluster of houses around a natural safe haven and, on higher ground, the church and market place. There's been a long history of accusation that high-ground Penzance has always turned its back – socially, aesthetically and financially – on its seafront and harbour, but the whole town is united from top to bottom for the lively, week-long festivals of **Golowan** and **Montol**, which have revived the old Celtic summer and winter solstice celebrations respectively.

The quirky heart of Penzance lies on the slope between the harbour and the former **Corn Exchange** (now Lloyds Bank). **Chapel Street**, uniting the port with its town, is a happy mix of Georgian and Recency town houses, as well as older buildings, many of which have been turned without loss of character into art galleries and antique shops, bars, restaurants and the odd specialist boutique. Sir John Betjeman may have grumbled that Penzance was 'turning into Slough', but you'd have look beyond Chapel Street and be feeling fairly dyspeptic to agree. To the west a labyrinth of squares and terraces of Regency houses, secret gardens and lamp-lit alleyways leading off **Morrab Road** contains two of Penzance's finest treasures: **Penlee House**, set among exotic public gardens, contains the largest collection of work by the **Newlyn School**, and the **Morrab Library,** planted within the subtropical **Morrab Gardens**, is one of the last and most beautifully positioned independent libraries in the country.

If you arrive by train, you step straight out onto what used to be the northern dock of the **harbour**, partially filled in 1968 to create a large car park. The granite walls are still visible though, if you peer behind the cars. Nevertheless, the view across the bay is so entrancingly dominated by St Michael's Mount and the hope of seeing dolphins that you are distracted from some of the uglier planning decisions of the 20th century along the front. This is the leisure end of the harbour – and where on Monday and Thursday evenings you'll see the dinghy club setting out to race around Mount's Bay and pilot gig crews in training. The older, working harbour and dry dock is now much diminished as a commercial port and plans to redevelop it as a marina and bigger ferry terminal for the Isles of Scilly come and go with the tide. But this is where Penzance's story began: when merchant shipping travelling between the west of England or Ireland and the continent, fearful of the confused and treacherous seas beyond Land's End, would land and haul their cargo across the moors to and from boats moored at St Ives. A 6th-century chapel dedicated to St Anthony was built on the spur of granite that provided the earliest safe haven, and the harbour was called Pen Sans, the Holy Headland.

The chapel went centuries ago, but the granite spur remains visible. Known as the **Battery Rocks** (a small defensive position was built there during the Napoleonic Wars), it projects a little way into the sea beyond the high white walls of the splendid Art Deco **Lido** that has won the battle to stay open during the summer months. **St Mary's** Church, built in 1834, put an end to the long trudge up to the old parish church at Madron. You'll often hear choir and orchestra rehearsals as you pass and concerts in the church are frequent.

There are spring and autumn days when at high tide the waves dash against the Promenade, sending cliffs of spray over pedestrians, cars and guesthouses – and summer days when, beyond the flapping, colourful banners that line the seafront, tall ships lie peacefully at anchor in the quiet waters known as Gwavas Lake between the Battery Rocks and Newlyn. Occasionally, you'll see the square brown sails of a Cornish lugger, but best of all is when a pod of dolphins are sighted, arcing through the bay or riding the bow wave of a motor launch.

Sir Humphry Davy

His statue, a favourite perch for seagulls, stands at the head of Market Jew Street, a stone's throw from the house where he was born. Davy, who was something of a Renaissance Man, admired by the likes of Napoleon and Samuel Coleridge, is best known for his invention of the miners' safety lamp in 1815 and his name must have been blessed a thousand times in tinners' cottages up and down the peninsula. Remarkably, Davy refused payment or patent – he knew he could help prevent the appalling methane explosions in the mines, caused by the naked flames of candles attached to the miners' helmets, and so he did. The principle was simple; by enclosing the oil-burning wick in a fine-gauge wire mesh cage, oxygen could enter and keep the flame alive, but the flame could not escape and ignite the methane. There's an example of a Davy lamp, made around 1817, in the Penlee House Museum (see below).

It's unfortunate that Davy is also remembered for his discovery of nitrous oxide (laughing gas) which he considered an excellent cure for hangovers. It became a bit of an embarrassing obsession; his first lecture in 1801 at the Royal Institution in London on this very subject was a roaring success, and launched his career as a popular scientist.

An accident forced him to take on an assistant and his experiments with young Michael Faraday went far down the road in the development of electrical energy. (Davy reportedly said that Faraday was his greatest discovery.) Somehow, the brilliant polymath also found time to write *Salmonia*, a book on fly-fishing published in 1828, a year before his death.

Up on the hill, in town, the main shopping streets, **Causeway Head** and **Market Jew Street** (jow being the old Cornish word for Thursday) hang on to a largely local identity; and though shops, galleries and restaurants come and go with alarming rapidity, Penzance retains a gritty vibrancy and a sense of purpose that has not submitted either to tourism or cloning.

The Morrab Library and Morrab Gardens

① 01738 364474 ⓦ www.morrablibrary.org.uk; free guided tours every Fri 14.00.

If you have a library and a garden, you have everything you need.
Cicero

Samuel Pidwell, brewer, mountain climber, mayor of Penzance and secretary of the Royal Geological Society, built this handsome, four-square house in 1841 with money made importing wine from Lisbon. The library, formed in 1801, has been in occupation since 1889, when the building was acquired by the Penzance Town Council.

Of just 30 independent libraries in the UK, this is the only one in Cornwall; the nicest thing about the Morrab ('by the sea' in Cornish) is the unstuffy atmosphere in the elegant, book-lined rooms and the colourful characters who work there and use it.

'You never know who's going to come through the door, says Annabelle Read, who has been chief librarian here for over 25 years. Her predecessor was a fan of the detective novel and besides Cornish history and periodicals, Celtic studies, art, biographies and travel, the largely open-access shelves are filled with crime fiction. The tradition has continued: 'Lots of people come here to meet other people or borrow the latest Donna Leon.' The Morrab has it all: winter lectures, coffee and good conversation – and enough rooms for peaceful browsing too. Non-members can buy a very reasonably priced visitor's ticket for a single day.

It stands in over three acres of subtropical gardens, laid out in 1888 and much loved by the local community. Joe Palmese, the gardener, has acquired a reputation as a top propagator and locals will often bring back seeds from far-flung holidays for him to raise. When a letter appeared in the local newspaper criticising the gardens for their lack of colourful bedding and apparently unkempt appearance there was an outcry as dozens of locals wrote back protesting the beauty of the gardens and the great work done by Joe and the volunteers.

Penlee House Gallery and Museum
Morrab Rd, TR18 4HE ☏ 01736 363625 ⓦ www.penleehouse.org.uk; closed Sun.

A Victorian mansion in the lovely Penlee Memorial Gardens houses the country's largest collection of work by the Newlyn school, which included Stanhope and Elizabeth Forbes, Walter Langley and Norman Garstin – and their later successors, Alfred Munnings, Laura Knight and 'Lamorna' Birch. It's a friendly, busy gallery and the café that spills out into the gardens makes it a popular spot, especially on warm days. There are two floors of exhibition space where you can gaze happily at vanished Cornwall, its fishermen and their wives and children – one of my many favourites is a summery view of the Abbey Slip and inner harbour by Stanhope Forbes. What makes this painting particularly special is the plaque beside it which tells of the passion aroused locally by the threat of its sale and the successful campaign to keep it at the Penlee.

There's no permanent collection on display, but frequently changing exhibitions, so check before coming if you've set your heart on seeing a particular painting (if it's not on display, and you give her a bit of notice, director Alison Bevan will open the storeroom for you). Upstairs, a couple of rooms are dedicated to local history – there are some wonderful examples of Roman gold necklaces and wristlets found on a Penwith farm as well as costumes, mining equipment and examples of Newlyn copperware.

The Newlyn school

Alison Bevan, Director, Penlee Museum and Gallery

In the 1880s, numerous British painters began to arrive in Newlyn, many of whom had trained in Paris or Antwerp. Most had also spent time painting in Brittany; in Newlyn they found a similar source of inspiration, but closer to home and with a direct rail link to London.

Like Brittany, Newlyn offered scenes and lives scarcely touched by the Industrial Revolution, with plentiful, cheap accommodation and willing models. Soon, a host of artists settled, forming the colony known as the 'Newlyn school'.

The first resident artist was Walter Langley, who moved to Newlyn in 1882. In 1884, Stanhope Forbes arrived, writing to his mother that 'Newlyn is a sort of English Concarneau and is the haunt of many artists.'

By September 1884, there were at least 27 resident artists, including Frank Wright Bourdillon, Frank Bramley, Percy Craft, Elizabeth Forbes, Norman Garstin, Thomas Cooper Gotch, Frederick Hall, Edwin Harris, Harold Harvey, Albert Chevallier Tayler, Ralph Todd and Henry Scott Tuke. Many more artists visited the village during this period, for both long and short periods, while others who were recognised as part of the 'Newlyn School' based themselves in St Ives, Lelant or Falmouth.

Initially, the artists were united by a desire to paint '*en plein air*', depicting the lives of the villagers in a rural naturalist style. As the colony declined and the common ethos evaporated, Stanhope and Elizabeth Forbes founded their school of painting, bringing a new generation of artists to Newlyn, including Dod and Ernest Procter and Frank Gascoigne Heath.

This re-energising of the colony attracted further artists, such as Samuel John 'Lamorna' Birch, Alfred Munnings, 'Seal' Weatherby and Harold and Laura Knight, many of whom later settled in Lamorna, forming the Lamorna group, often referred to as the later Newlyn school.

Chapel Street

www.chapelstreet.co.uk

A wander up Chapel Street from the harbour offers some rich pickings for Slow explorers. A plaque on number 25, the **Brontë House**, reveals that Maria Branwell, mother of the Brontë sisters, lived here. And so she did, until a visit to an uncle in Yorkshire in 1812 at the age of 29 changed her life forever. She died when her children, Charlotte, Anne, Emily and Branwell, were very young, and it became the turn of her sister Elizabeth to leave the Penzance family home for the parsonage at Haworth where she raised the infant writers, doubtless feeding them on Penwith legends and ghost stories, every bit as wild as stories bred on the Yorkshire moors. At least, that's how Daphne du Maurier liked to imagine things, endowing Elizabeth with the gift of having awakened in the authors of *Wuthering Heights* and *Jane Eyre* 'that narrative power, that sense of the dramatic which is such a part of the Cornish character, moulding them, unconsciously, to the shape of their maternal forebears ... rugged as the granite on the moors of West Penwith.'

Futher up the hill on the same side of the street, the **Egyptian House** is an architectural curiosity – an eye-popping mixture of Georgian town house and painted sarcophagus with a virtuoso display of geometry in the multi-paned windows. It's strange that the architect is something of a mystery, although the likeliest candidate is P F Robinson who had built the similarly styled Egyptian Hall in Piccadilly in 1815, when the vogue for all things Egyptian was at a peak. The coade-stone façade (which was simply grafted onto a pair of much older shops) was created around 1835, for John Lavin, and created a suitably impressive entrance to a collection of minerals he displayed on the ground floor. The Landmark Trust acquired the building in 1968 and restored the façade to its former glory. Three apartments for holiday letting were also created, one on each floor above the shop which now occupies the ground floor.

On the other side of the road, the **Union Hotel** is worth a peep, although its finest treasure, an unrestored Georgian theatre, languishes out at the back, where it is used as a garage. Howie, the landlord, is saddened that an attempt to rescue the derelict building failed to gather enough support, but if you ask nicely, he'll show you the old theatre playbills, Georgian dining room and the Assembly Rooms on the first floor (where news of Trafalgar and the death of Nelson was first announced on English soil, which explains all the Nelsonabilia in the bar below). In the bar there are blackened stones on the wall by the entrance – apparently dating from when Penzance was torched by a Spanish marauding party in 1595. (The Turk's Head, also on Chapel Street, is one of the few buildings to have survived.) The hotel bar is a good venue for jazz – look out for the Bennett Brothers, who appear regularly and belt out some of the best trad jazz you'll hear this side of New Orleans.

A step away, the telephone exchange building has been transformed into an important exhibition space for contemporary art. **The Exchange** (*Princes St; 01736 363715; www.newlynartgallery.co.uk*) is particularly striking after dark when its colourful glass exterior (designed by Penwith artist Peter Freeman) is lit up by green and blue ripples of LED lighting that responds to the movements of people on the pavement outside or the weather.

Food and drink

Penzance farmers' market is held in and outside St John's Hall every Friday and you'll find several good places to pick up picnic ingredients in the surrounding streets – **Lavenders** in Alverton St, **The Granary** in Causeway Head, and **Archie**

Brown's in Bread St has a lunchtime restaurant upstairs, reminiscent of that icon of vegetarian cuisine, Cranks. **Ian Lentern**, the butcher's shop on Chapel St, sells locally sourced meat, and the best wet fish is down the hill on the wharf (next to Willy Waller's) where **Stevensons**, the biggest fishing fleet operating out of Newlyn, sell their catch.

The Bakehouse Old Bakehouse Lane, Chapel St ① 01736 331331 ⑩ www. bakehouserestaurant.co.uk. Tucked away down an alley off Chapel St, this is a long-established favourite with locals and justly so: food is fresh, local and beautifully presented by friendly staff.

Crown Victoria Sq ① 01736 351070 ⑩ www.thecrownpenzance.co.uk. Always a good buzz in this small, friendly pub on the corner of a small square behind Market Jew St. Real ales include Otter, Landlord and Heligan Honey and there's a simple menu of homemade pizza or local steak at very reasonable prices. Landlord Josh has started up his own microbrewery, so look out for Cornish Crown on the pumps.

Mackerel Sky Café Bar 45 New St, Penzance TR18 2LZ ① 01736 448982. Cornish produce is given priority here – fish come from Newlyn and beef from the local butcher – and the menu changes with the seasons. Exceptionally friendly service, very reasonable prices and a bright, bistro-ish feel attract families at lunchtime; in the evenings, it attracts a lively, youngish crowd.

Navy Inn Queen St ① 01736 333232 ⑩ www.navyinn.co.uk. Just behind the promenade, near the Battery Rocks, the Navy's reputation for good local ales and food has been growing rapidly. Owner and chef Keir Meikle is passionate about local food and his cookery demonstrations are an important part of the Newlyn Fish Festival (see page 228).

Ricardo's 1 Taroveor ① 01736 366353 ⑩ www.ricardospizzas.com. Penzance mourned when Ricardo and his pizza van departed for Australia, but eventually he returned, bringing with him a cast-iron, wood-fired oven from Brisbane, which he had reclad and riveted by the last coppersmith in Newlyn. Now installed in a small (and unfortunately loo-less) restaurant at the top of Causewayhead, the aimiable Ricardo has reinvented the humble pizza and united the town's foodies in admiration. There's pasta and fresh, imaginatively composed salads too – and real Italian ice creams. Not licensed, but you are welcome to bring your own bottle; £1 corkage.

Willy Waller's Ice Cream Parlour Unit 14B, The Wharf ⑩ www.willywallers. co.uk. Behind the vividly coloured shopfront, the homemade ice creams are as good as ice cream gets, which is saying a lot in these parts.

Shopping

The bright, contemporary **Lighthouse Gallery** (*www.lighthouse-gallery.com*) is in Causeway Head, a pedestrian street with a cinema and a good collection of independent shops that includes a specialist soap-maker, ironmonger, organic grocer, florist and clothing shops. In Chapel St, the **Stoneman Gallery** (*www.*

stonemanpublications.co.uk) exhibits and sells many of the big names in contemporary Cornish art and fine art auctioneers, Barnes Thomas, often have a Newlyn school painting in the window. There's no shortage of antique and bric-a-brac shops in Chapel St, where at number 62, vintage clothing addicts will make a beeline for **Boudoir** (*www.facebook.com/boudoirpenzance*). Further down, the **West Cornwall Cigar Company** (*www.cornwall-cigar.co.uk*) is a truly old-fashioned tobacco shop: sweet-smelling, unpretentious and well informed.

Once a month there's a jolly auction of old and not-so-old household furniture and 'effects' at **Lay's Auction Rooms** opposite the Pirate Inn in Alverton; there are regular sales of fine art, jewellery and antiques, too (*www.davidlay.co.uk*).

Penzance's hinterland

As Penzance grew wealthy in the 17th and 18th centuries on the back of tin and copper, fish and farming, the grandees at the top of the economic pile built substantial houses for themselves on the hillside north of the town. They were not the first to appreciate the grand views over the bay: the Chysauster settlement of Iron Age roundhouses on the heights above Penzance commands a spectacular view of Mount's Bay and the surrounding moors. Down the deep lanes and ancient bridleways between Penzance and St Ives lie some of Cornwall's most secret and special places: Boswarthen Chapel, the Bodrifty roundhouse and Baker's Pit.

② Trewidden, Trengwainton and Trereife

Slow travel does not usually involve much excitement on the ring road, but the A30, as it bypasses Penzance to the north, is an exception.

Trewidden (*TR20 8TT; 01736 351979; www.trewiddengarden.co.uk*) was built in the 1830s for the Bolitho family, who still live there. (Bolitho is a name synonymous in Penwith with tin mining and banking.) The house is not open, but there are 13 extravagantly leafy acres of gardens, planted in the 1880s on the site of an ancient tin mine – granite ingot moulds and smelting basins lie dotted about. Successive generations have added to the planting and the tree-fern pit, giant rhododendrons and camellias, secret pools and twisting paths create the impression of a lush, jungly maze.

Almost next door to Trewidden is the delightful **Trereife** (*TR20 8TJ; 01736 362750; www.trereifepark.co.uk*), pronounced *Treeve*: a Queen Anne house and pretty gardens run by the endearingly eccentric Le Grice family. House and garden are currently only open on Wednesdays, and the younger generation of Le Grices are giving it a Ruth Watson-inspired rebirth as a B&B; it's looking very promising

In contrast to Trewidden, **Trengwainton Gardens** (*01736 363148; www. nationaltrust.org.uk; National Trust*), created around a long drive and lawn-with-a-view, seem open and airy, but are no less densely packed with sublime examples of magnolia, rhododendron, camellia, eucryphia, podocarpus and hundreds of other species of trees and shrubs. On the main lawn an eight-sided toposcope, carved in slate by a much-admired local artist, Joe Hemming, depicts all the real and symbolic ingredients of Penwith life, legend and industry: tinned sardines, a scythe, a tinner's shovel, a fishing boat, a mermaid, a woodcock, a lizard and the Bolitho emblem of lamb and flag.

The gardens are owned by the National Trust, but the grand house at the end of the drive is still owned and lived in by a branch of the Bolitho family. Under the stewardship of acting head gardener Phil Griffiths, Trengwainton is on a mission to involve local primary schools and families from the less privileged parts of Penzance in learning how to grow vegetables in the vast walled gardens, originally constructed by Sir Rose Price in the 19th century, to the supposed dimensions of Noah's Ark.

Polgoon Vineyard and Orchards

Rosehill, Penzance TR20 8TE ① 01736 333946 ⑩ www.polgoon.co.uk; guided tours Apr–Nov, Wed, Thu and Fri afternoons, followed by wine tasting in the shop; visitors' room open all year.

You see the elegant pink or green labels of Polgoon's wines, ciders and juices in all the best Cornish delis and restaurants these days, and further afield too, as the good news spreads. The leafy crown of Penzance and Mount's Bay make a spectacular backdrop to the young vineyards and orchards, planted on the south-facing slopes of an old flower farm, although fine views often come with a weathery sting. Kim and John Coulson planted the first vines in 2003 and their success was instant: with the fruits of their first harvest in 2006, they won the Waitrose Trophy for the best still rosé in 2009. But thanks to the weather, the harvests in 2007 and 2008 were awful, so the enterprising Coulsons decided to plant apples, which are more weather-resistant than vines, and add sparkling cider, made the French way, to their stable of delicious drinks.

③ Madron Holy Well and Boswarthen Chapel

Leaving Madron on the narrow lane to Morvah, you'll see a sign on your right indicating the well and chapel. A woodland track takes you from the parking area for several hundred yards until the trees open out and a pool appears, overhung by a goat willow to which coloured strips of cloth and little personal items have been attached. 'Clootie Trees' are often seen by sacred Celtic wells and the hopeful-minded leave these fragments with their wishes or prayers in the tree. A little way beyond, in a walled enclosure are the remains of a simple chapel dating from the 6th century or possibly earlier; water from the same spring that feeds the well is channelled into a stone basin, which is why it's often described as a baptistry. There's no denying the atmosphere of peaceful sanctity here, and wilted flowers and candle stubs on the granite slab altar leave you in no doubt that this place still sees active worship.

④ Chysauster Ancient Village

Badger's Cross TR20 8XA ① 07831 757934 ⓦ www.english-heritage.org.uk; English
Heritage; open Apr–Oct.

A couple of miles northeast of Penzance, the Iron Age village of Chysauster is
a hugely evocative archaeological site, set high on a south-facing slope looking
over Mount's Bay. The remains of eight, granite-walled Iron Age dwellings
and a larger community building lead off what is thought to be the earliest
identified village street in England and, although roofless, the mossy walls give
a distinct impression of what family and community living would have been
like before and during the Roman occupation. Each dwelling is composed of
small, semicircular chambers leading off a central, circular atrium that would
have been open to the sky, a design peculiar to this part of Cornwall. It's a great
place for children too: there are acres of cropped turf to run around (and a nice
selection of wooden swords and bows at the entrance kiosk).

For more of the same, on a smaller scale, that you can wander into at any
time of year, the remains of the Iron Age village at **Bodrifty** (grid reference
SW445354) lie in a remote and rugged valley, below Mulfra Quoit, just three
miles north of Penzance. A roundhouse has been constructed with the utmost
authenticity at Bodrifty Farm, which can be visited by arrangement with the
owners – and you can even stay in it (for details, visit www.bodriftyfarm.
co.uk). **Carn Euny** (see page 238) is equally remote, evocative and accessible
all through the year.

Baker's Pit

With time on my hands after visiting Chysauster, I went looking for Baker's Pit
(grid reference SW481359) a wildlife reserve and wood-fringed lake, buried in
an unfrequented, though truly idyllic Penwith valley.

Having returned to the road and turned left, the footpath I was looking for
appeared after three or four hundred yards on my left. The path ran uphill,
eventually passing the Castle an Dinas quarry on top, continuing on to
Nancledra in the valley ahead. A purple sign on my left indicated Baker's Pit,
which ran down a flower-filled hillside, emerging eventually at a tree-fringed
lake of quite staggering beauty. The path skirted the lake, arriving eventually
at a preserved clay pit works and a concrete landing stage beside the water.
The lake is the flooded clay pit, the water clear and very inviting on a hot
August afternoon; two swimmers were quietly enjoying the cool green solitude
far out in the middle of the water. I felt I was in the middle of nowhere, but
just a short walk further down the same footpath by which I had arrived,
took me to a tarmac road, a hamlet called Georgia and a tangle of footpaths
offering alternative routes back to the Chysauster car park. Cornwall Wildlife
Trust manages the nature reserve; the website www.cornwallwildlifetrust.org.
uk, offers an alternative walking route around the nature reserve from Georgia,
where there is parking space for two or three cars.

Food and drink

Coldstreamer Gulval Churchtown TR18 3BB ① 01736 362072 ⑩ www.
coldstreamer-penzance.co.uk. Run by three local lads – Tom, Dick and Harry –
the pub has a jolly, welcoming atmosphere and a terrific reputation for food
these days – delicious bread is baked each day in the kitchen, which makes the
lunchtime sandwiches rather special; local ales and cider are also on the menu.
Engine Inn Cripplesease, Nancledra TR20 8NF ① 01736 740204 ⑩ www.
theengineinn.co.uk. On the B3311, high on the moors between Penzance to St
Ives, this is a favourite locals' spot for Sunday lunch. Beers come from Sharp's and
Skinner's and there's usually a guest Cornish ale too. Child-friendly and dog-
friendly.
Gallery Latitude 50 Cripplesease, Nancledra TR20 8NF (opposite the Engine
Inn) ① 01736 741052 ⑩ www.gallerylatitude50.co.uk. Corinne Carr is French and
her beautifully presented craft gallery and café reflect her innate sense of style.
Corinne produces her own brand of unfussy knitwear at the back of the gallery in
gorgeous Italian wool, dyed to the blues, green and russets of Penwith moors and
coast. The coffee, as you might expect, is superb – as are the homemade cakes.

The south coast

To the west of Penzance, the south coast, with its cosy, wooded valleys running
down to the sea and picturesque fishing villages tucked into narrow coves,
contrasts vividly with the bleakly craggy north coast and its ruined remnants
of the mining industry. Mousehole, Lamorna and Porthcurno may have
delivered themselves up gratefully to tourism, but a short walk inland and you
are among old farming communities. The village scenes in the 1970s cult film
Straw Dogs were filmed in St Buryan, where on a Friday evening the tractors
parked outside the pub may outnumber the cars. Older communities too lie
hidden beneath the fields of 'broccly' (cauliflower to outsiders), daffodils and
potatoes, emerging in desolate pastures as standing stones and circles and by
roadsides as stumpy, weatherworn Celtic crosses.

⑤ Newlyn

I have a soft spot for Newlyn: it's got the integrity of a hard-working community
that is not overly concerned with how it looks to tourists and wears its cultural
history without any great fuss. You hear French as well as Cornish trawlermen's
voices in the post office queue and around the harbour the air is thick with
the screams of seagulls, the smell of diesel and fish. It's a working port, the
largest and busiest in the southwest, dominated by one name which you see
everywhere: W Stevenson. Stevenson's hold a wonderful collection of old
photos of Newlyn, which are put on public display during the Fish Festival,
held each year on the August Bank Holiday. Net-makers and rope-makers,
fish-packers and engineering trades all work from the sheds and warehouses

around the harbour. The **Seaman's Mission**, open to all, is where to go for a fry-up and cup of tea – or a (peculiarly Cornish) card game of euchre while the weather sorts itself out. It's been under threat of closure for some time, but the gutsy local community is working hard to keep it open.

Newlyn has always been famous for its coppersmiths, and on top of the roof of the Seaman's Mission perches a galleon-shaped weathervane, made by coppersmith Tom Batten in 1911. On the road out of Newlyn to Penzance there are more wonderful examples of the work of Arts and Crafts coppersmith John Mackenzie on the wall of the old Passmore Edwards gallery, now the **Newlyn Art Gallery** (a sister gallery to the Exchange Gallery in Penzance), which puts on regularly changing exhibitions of contemporary and 20th-century art. The large square panels on the façade representing earth, air, fire and water are all green and sadly corroded from exposure to the elements, but worth a respectful look. Today, Mike Johnson and his small team keep the Newlyn tradition of coppersmithing alive.

One of the best times to visit Newlyn (and dinky, touristy Mousehole, just around the headland) is at Christmas, when both harbours are filled with an incredible display of lights, representing lobsters and mermaids as well as more traditional robins and sleighs, and many of the fishing boats are lit up too. Christmas light-watching is so popular that the narrow road from Newlyn into Mousehole gets choked with cars as dusk falls; it's essential to arrive early or prepare for a long walk.

Food and drink

The independent butcher, baker, greengrocer, cheese shop and three excellent (all slightly different) fishmongers make shopping locally for local food easy and enjoyable in Newlyn.

The pubs along the harbour are about as far removed from gastro-chic as you like, but brilliant for a pint of Betty Stoggs or Doom Bar and fishy gossip, the best of which is completely unrepeatable. The more respectable stuff can be found on the harbour's entertaining blog (*http://blog.through-the-gaps.co.uk*).

Sadly, the pilchard factory with its small museum was converted into flats in 2006, but Newlyn pilchards have hit the upmarket deli shelves with their pretty tins showing pictures by Newlyn school artist, Walter Langley. Read the small print carefully, however, and you'll see that the Cornish pilchards are now cooked and tinned in Brittany before returning to grace the shelves of **Trelawneys**, one of several fish shops fronting the harbour.

⑥ Mousehole and Paul

Dylan Thomas spent his honeymoon in **Mousehole** (pronounced 'Mouzal') in 1937 and found it 'the loveliest village in England'. He would still approve, for despite the inevitable conflict between narrow, twisting streets and motor vehicles, second homes and tourist trade, the cosy, cottagey good looks and picturesque harbour have remained intact. But the village only starts to reveal its character when you start pottering about the maze of tiny alleys behind the harbour. Here, you might find a retired fisherman's cottage, decorated all over with bits of painted boat and shell – or a hand-carved tablet that reads: 'These net Lofts were gutted and rebuilt during 1998 to the specifications laid out by National Heritage and the Chief Building Officer of Penwith. The workforce was led by the beer-drinking cricketer Treve Laity with assistance from beer-drinking gig racers David Roberts and Tim "Budgie" Burgess. When sober the wood butchery was carried out by Julian Barned and Ben Marshall. The plumbing was installed by Geoff Pappin whose dislike for water, unless laced with alcohol, was well known. This gallant sober, hic, upright band of men started in January and completed the whole job in September. Butts 1998.'

Another plaque, beside the oldest house in the village, its porch jutting over a courtyard on granite pillars, records that 'Squire Jenkyn Keigwin was killed here 23rd July 1595 defending this house against the Spaniards.' (The offending cannonball sits on the windowsill of the house, now privately owned.) The rest of Mousehole's inhabitants, it appears, were paralysed by an attack of fatalism. The Spanish raid was the subject of a prophecy, inscribed in Cornish on the Merlin rock on the south side of the harbour. It read : 'They shall land on the

The Penlee lifeboat disaster

If you are making a special journey to see the Mousehole Christmas lights, you need to know why they are turned off for an hour each year on 19 December.

On 19 December 1981, the *Union Star*, a coaster with eight on board, suffered engine failure and was blown towards the coast by hurricane-force winds. As the urgency of the situation became clear to the Falmouth coastguard, the Penlee lifeboat, stationed in Mousehole, was requested to launch. Before the *Solomon Browne* slid down its ramp into towering waves, Coxswain Trevelyan Richards refused to allow the son of one crew member to board, saying 'No more than one from any family on a night like this.'

In an astonishing feat of bravery and seamanship, Richards managed to bring the lifeboat alongside the stricken ship and the message was received that four on board had been transferred to the lifeboat. However, when an attempt was made to go back for the remaining crew, radio contact with Falmouth abruptly ceased. In the terrible hours that followed, the truth dawned over Mousehole that all eight lifeboatmen had been lost to the storm, as well as all eight from the *Union Star*.

Today, the lifeboat operates out of Newlyn. The Penlee lifeboat station is closed and shuttered; no lifeboat has since been launched from its ramp. The eight unpaid, volunteer lifeboatmen of the *Solomon Browne* were posthumously honoured with RNLI medals and outside the lifeboat station a memorial plaque headed SERVICE NOT SELF lists their names.

Rock of Merlin, Those who shall burn Paul, Penzance and Newlyn.'

On the hill going out of Mousehole towards Raginnis, the **Wild Bird Hospital and Sanctuary** (*01736 731386*) is open all year, receiving injured, orphaned and – occasionally – oiled birds. Founded in 1928 by sisters Dorothy and Phyllis Iglesias, the hospital hit the headlines in 1967 when the *Torrey Canyon*, carrying 120,000 tons of crude oil, foundered on the Seven Stones reef between Land's End and the Isles of Scilly. Images of horribly oiled birds were relieved by the news that in many cases they could be cleaned and saved. Over 8,000 oiled birds passed successfully through the hospital after the disaster. Admission is free, though donations are always welcome.

Paul, on top of the hill behind Mousehole, is the village's 'Churchtown'. During the Spanish raid, the church was badly burned; it was rebuilt in 1600 and again as storms took their toll on the building. The churchyard wall contains a memorial to Dolly Pentreath, who died in 1777 at the age of 102, the last person in Cornwall to speak only Cornish.

∞∞∞

Food and drink

A few days before Christmas the traditional **stargazy pie** is made and served in pubs throughout Mousehole and Newlyn. It's a pie with no fixed ingredient, apart from whole, small fish, such as sardines, their heads poking through the pastry lid. The pie is made to celebrate Tom Bowcock's marvellous, life-saving haul, supposedly sometime during the 16th century, when terrible December weather had grounded the fishing fleet and the village faced starvation

The Old Coastguard Hotel The Parade, TR19 6PR ① 01736 731222 ⑩ www. oldcoastguardhotel.co.uk. Given a new breath of life by the Inkin brothers (who run the Gurnard's Head on the north coast); beneath the hotel, the bar has splendid views and a garden looking out over the sea, a roaring fire in winter and a nice selection of books and paintings, country furniture and a relaxed atmosphere. Good, local food, well-kept Cornish ales and excellent wines.

⑦ Lamorna

Lamorna and Lamorna Cove are like chalk and cheese: the village is a ribbon of pretty houses in the deep and wooded Lamorna Valley: a mossy, ferny place, with orchards on the sunny slopes and an artist lurking behind nearly every window. The cove it opens onto is an oddly oppressive place. The eastern slopes where granite used to build the Bishop Rock lighthouse was once quarried appear threatened by an arrested granite rockslide and around the expensive harbour car park are notices beginning with a daunting list of Nos and Don'ts. If you can stomach these, then the coast path to Mousehole, returning by an inland route, is a very enjoyable three-mile circular walk. Similarly, by following the coast path west out of the harbour, you can walk to Tater-Du lighthouse (the first part is a bit of a rocky scramble) and return on an inland footpath via Tregiffian, Rosemodress and Tregurnow farms; OS Explorer map 102 is handy for the field-crossing on the return route.

If you find yourself in Lamorna during the summer months, look out for signs announcing that the garden at **Chygurno** is open. The garden clings to the side of a south facing cliff overlooking the cove and is a tour de force of creative, subtropical gardening in a seemingly impossible location.

Food and drink

Lamorna Pottery Lamorna TR19 6NY ℗ 01736 810330 ⓦ www.lamornapottery. co.uk. By the bus stop, in a wooded dell a mile short of Lamorna village. Homemade cakes and scones, and a good lunch menu are served in a lovely garden when it's fine. Indoors, pottery by resident potter John Swan (and others) is for sale. Superb for short walks in the bluebell woods across the road.

⑧ St Loy and Penberth

The bus from Penzance to Land's End passes through St Buryan and Treen, making a superb four-mile walk, taking in the woodland cove of St Loy and the miniature fishing haven of Penberth, quite achievable in a morning or afternoon. A footpath from the pub in St Buryan runs in an almost straight line down to the coast at St Loy, crossing level farmland and ancient parish boundary stones. The downhill section through woods to St Loy cove is carpeted in bluebells in May. A rugged mile of coastpath drops into Penberth, where you can pick up the footpath to Treen. You may however, wish to wander up the lanes to Treen instead: the cottages and gardens are a treat and many have cut or potted flowers at the gate beside an honesty box. The short stretch of the B3283 encountered between Penberth and the turning to Treen has several salad and veg items on the roadside stalls and the hand-drawn sign indicating local wine should not be ignored. And there's a great café-cum-village shop as well as a pub in Treen while you wait for the bus.

Food and drink

Treen Local Produce Café and Shop TR19 6LG ℗ 01736 811285; open May–Sep daily. Free-range pork from Lamorna and 'Ewephoric' rare breed Ryeland lamb from Sancreed available in the shop and seasonal, unsprayed veg from local growers, bread made in the village as well as Cornish cheeses and ice creams. Café menu includes homemade hummus, pies and cakes.

⑨ Porthcurno and St Levan

The steep-sided valley ends in a perfect beach of soft white sand – and a second, smaller beach at low tide, when Pedne Beach (much loved by naturists) is accessible too. Here are a large car park, beach café, pub and village shop well stocked with local produce; 200,000 visitors a year venture down the narrow lane on their way to the world-famous Minack Theatre, perched high on the cliff overlooking the beach. A vertigo-inducing steep flight of steps leads from the beach to the theatre, the road up is similarly tortuous, but the 504 Western Greyhound bus (from Penzance to St Just) manages it; the 1 and 1A double deckers from Penzance turn round at the beach.

The lane continues past the entrance to the Minack as far as **St Levan**, an easy stroll away. The church has delightful bench ends showing a jester, pilgrim, shepherd, fisherman (possibly St Levan himself) and some curious portraits. Outside in the churchyard is a smooth mound of granite, neatly split in two. Records of the rock go back to pre-Christian times when it was associated with fertility rites. The large granite cross was strategically interposed to prevent such goings-on. The coast path route back to the Minack takes you past the old holy well and the steep steps down to **Porth Chapel Beach** pass the barely identifiable cliffside ruins of St Levan's Chapel, thought to date from the 6th century. The beach has a dreamt-of beauty; I remember it on a sunny March morning at low tide. Two surfers and their little dog were making the first prints across the damp sand while a seal rolled around in the surf.

Food and drink

Just a short walk further along the coast path brings you to the tiny cluster of cottages at **Porthgwarra**. One of the smallest buildings turns out to be a shop, selling tea, coffee, ice creams, cakes and pasties (*01736 871998; www.porthgwarrashop. co.uk*). Perfectly placed for coast path walkers, but closed in the winter months.

Porthcurno Telegraph Museum

Eastern House, TR19 6JX ☎ 01736 810966 ⊛ www.porthcurno.org.uk; open Mar–Nov daily and Dec–Feb Sun and Mon.

New funding is bringing important changes to this historic hub of global communications. The museum has always drawn in those fascinated by old communications technology – from needle telegraph to ticker tape telegrams – but there are still too many 'WWWICs' (Women Who Wait in the Car') for the museum's liking and at the time of writing it was revamping some of its exhibits and layout and adding a café to make it more visitor-friendly. But nothing much will change in the Tunnels: a series of deeply evocative, bomb-proof chambers that were built into the cliff behind the telegraph station during World War II. The atmosphere is still authentically 1940s and the wonderful volunteer staff are mostly retired employees of the station, delighted to demonstrate how the old machines work.

The cable station (the whole village, in fact) goes back to 1870, when the first cable to Bombay was laid, disappearing under the sea from Porthcurno Beach. It's quite a thought that by the turn of the century, the tiny valley, where young men from all over the world (for which, read 'Empire') came to be trained, was a multi-cultural community and hot spot of cutting-edge technology. The smart white houses and cottages all date from the centre's Edwardian heyday, though there are still plenty of people about who can remember when you needed to show your ID before you could enter Porthcurno.

Minack Theatre
TR19 6JU ① 01736 810181 Ⓦ www.minack.com.
Rowena Cade moved to Porthcurno from Derbyshire with her mother in the 1920s and soon after conceived a plan to construct an outdoor stage on a craggy bit of rock in the garden for a production of *The Tempest* by the local am-dram society. That was just the start; the production proved so successful – with the backdrop of the sea and sky, the acoustics of the cliffside gully so perfect – that she roped in her gardener and his apprentice to help her build a proper amphitheatre, with tiered banks, an access road and steps down to the beach.

The magic of the place is unfailing, even when the weather is unkind. Friends of mine saw *Under Milk Wood* at the Minack; a group of dolphins came out to play in the sea below, completely upstaging the actors for a moment or two, until with genius improvisation their antics were drawn into the play.

The visitor centre, café and extraordinary exotic garden are open all through the year. The programme of performances starts in May and finishes in September.

⑩ Nanjizal Bay
I consider myself indescribably fortunate to live within easy striking distance of this supremely beautiful Penwith beach. There's no easy access by road (at Polgigga take the Porthgwarra turning and park by the side of the road after 400 yards), just a muddy farm track to Higher Bosistow Farm and then fields and heathery clifftops to the coast path. The beach – pale sand and a scattering of boulders – is finally reached by wooden steps. You're more likely to see seals than other people, especially out of season. Look left for the Song of the Sea, a slender natural arch in the rock through which the sea glints, or rushes at high tide. Low tide is a good moment to find the beach, when caves and rock pools are revealed.

Nanjizal faces west, so is not much good for sun in the mornings, but wonderful for late summer evenings, when the water is almost warm enough for swimming in comfort. There's a pleasant, looping walk back, following the stream that gushes down onto the beach, through Bosistow Farm (watch out for the dogs) or you can branch left and follow the footpath to Trevilley Farm to Trevescan, for the bus stop and refreshments.

Food and drink

Apple Tree Café Trevescan, Sennen TR19 7AQ ① 01736 872753 ⑩ www.
theappletreecafe.co.uk. Nick bakes the bread, Helen makes the cakes and delicious,
simple breakfasts and lunches using local produce. There's a warm, friendly, family
atmosphere here, much appreciated by the local community, which close to
Land's End finds itself surrounded by so many tourist facilities. Paintings by local
artists hang on the walls and there are knitting and sewing workshops as well as
special food events in the evenings.

⑪ Land's End

Coachloads of people arrive every day in the summer to wander up to the
Land's End signpost, which points variously to the likes of the Falkland Isles
(6,658 miles) and Moscow (1,586 miles), and then wander back through the
sticky trap of shops, cafés and 'experiences' to the coach, no doubt relieved to
have ticked that particular box. The relief must be enormous too, for those
completing an 'End-to-Ender', having walked, jogged, cycled or wheelchaired
from John o'Groats, 874 miles to the north, to glimpse the huddle of white
buildings at mainland Britain's most southwesterly point. But consider the
sadness of one charity fund-raiser, setting out for John o'Groats from Land's
End, who tripped over the sign announcing his departure, broke his ankle, and
got no further.

The best way to approach the headland is on foot, following the coastpath
from Sennen, just over a mile to the north. There's more of a sense of occasion
as you approach over the cliffs, with the spray dashing over the Longships
lighthouse and sea churning below, than arriving at a massive car park. This
way too, you get to see the impressive remains of Maen Castle, a huge Iron Age
hillfort, recently cleared of undergrowth by the National Trust. Approaching
from the south, the nearest parking to the coastpath is at Porthgwarra or as
described for Nanjizal Bay, above.

⑫ Sennen Cove

The beach is busy with families and surfers all through the summer – it's a
beautiful sweep of sand, washed by some of the best surf in Cornwall, patrolled
by lifeguards (including Sennen's remarkable life-saving dog, Bilbo) and fringed
with rock pools. It's easily accessible and parents of children taking part in the
daily surf schools can sit on the raised terrace of the smart café-bar-restaurant
(*The Beach; 01736 871191; www.thebeachrestaurant.com*) right by the beach
and watch it all going on below. There's a small handful of beach-related shops
at the harbour end of the cove and an art and craft gallery (*www.round-house.
co.uk*) in a black-timbered, circular building that houses the old capstan,
formerly used for winching boats out of the water. More experienced surfers
often head further north to the next (un-lifeguarded) beach at **Gwynver** which
is emptier and wilder as it involves a much longer walk. In the evening camp
fires are lit as the long trudge up the cliffs is delayed until darkness falls.

The north coast and Penwith moors

The landscape takes on an entirely different character beyond Sennen. Remote, windswept and treeless, the granite mining villages that line the coast road have been repopulated in recent years by artists and writers, responding to the wild energy of the dramatic coast and wuthering moors.

⑬ St Just

For a brief period during the mining boom in the 18th century, the population of St Just and Pendeen was greater than that of Liverpool and Manchester. Migrant families lived in disease-ridden, makeshift camps and shanty towns, which vanished as quickly as they sprang up, though the legacy of the industry is to be seen everywhere in the skeletal engine houses and chimneys on moorland and clifftops – and the rows of terraced granite cottages that housed the mining families once the population had shaken down to a sustainable level.

St Just, England's most westerly village, is a busy, likeable place, with a surprising amount of things to see and do and good places to eat and drink. There are numerous art galleries in and around the village, representing the work of local artists: it's worth looking at www.just-arts.co.uk if you want to spend a day pottering round St Just's studios, as several of them are tucked away or only open by appointment. In the town, the Great Atlantic (*5 Bank Sq*) exhibits and displays work by some of the bigger names in Penwith; the Turn of the Tide Studio (*35 Fore St*) is a more intimate affair, run by husband and wife team, Gabrielle Hawkes and Tom Henderson Smith, exhibiting their richly coloured and highly evocative responses to the local landscape.

The week-long community arts festival, **Lafrowda** (*www.lafrowdafestival. co.uk*), is held in July, with outdoor events centring on the medieval Plain-an-Gwarry, a splendidly preserved, grassy medieval playing place. The highlight is Lafrowda Day, when the streets are decorated and there's live music, folk dancing and lots of people in strange costumes.

Food and drink

Vivian Olds, the tiny butcher's, tucked away in Chapel Rd (*01736 788520*), has almost a cult following in Penwith. Pub menus and restaurants name him as their supplier with pride. **Bollowal Farm** (on the lane out to Cape Cornwall) has a stall of home-grown veg, always well stocked.

Cook Book 4 Cape Cornwall St ℹ 01736 787266 ⓦ www.thecookbookstjust. co.uk. Playing a big part in St Just's family-friendly, arty, bookish identity, the café-cum-bookshop is a St Just institution. Upstairs, three creaky-floored rooms are lined with a fabulous collection of secondhand books for sale; downstairs homemade breakfasts, teas and lunches are served in the friendly café. Children and dogs welcome.

Kegen Teg 12 Market Sq ℡ 01736 788562. A friendly café where everything is homemade, including bread, soups and burgers. Good vegetarian selection too.

King's Arms Market Sq ℡ 01736 788545. A welcoming, beamy sort of pub with a log fire that positively beckons you in on chilly days and a deservedly good reputation for food and St Austell ales.

McFadden's Market Sq ℡ 01736 788136. The steak pasties come in three sizes, but even a small one will set you up for a day's walking. Also good for local meats and cheeses.

Star 1 Fore St ℡ 01736 788767. A St Austell Brewery pub which has retained its character as a locals' haunt. Monday evening is folk music night, when ten or more local musicians will gather round the table in the front window and play whatever takes their fancy.

Cape Cornwall

A cape is where two seas meet and for centuries the rocky promontory was thought to be the real Land's End. It's a good five miles north of the true southwestern tip of mainland Britain, but what it lacks in commercial razzamatazz, it gains in lonely grandeur. There is a small car park and a rough footpath out to the topmost crag, where a chimney-like tower bears a plaque recording the gift of the promontory to the National Trust by Heinz in 1987. Almost invisible, perched on a ledge beneath the tower, is the volunteer coastguards hut: you can pop in and ask if there have been any sightings of dolphins or basking sharks – and beyond that, nothing but sea until the coast of Labrador.

By the side of the Carn Gloose road just southwest of Cape Cornwall, near a trig point and marked by an information sign, is **Ballowall Barrow**, an extraordinarily elaborate Bronze Age burial chamber. It was completely unknown until 1878 when Cornish antiquarian W C Borlase discovered it under mining rubble. The barrow includes an entrance grave, a cairn, several individual burial cists and a number of ritual pits. What you see is very striking, if not entirely authentic: a central oval structure, 35 feet across with walls up to 10 feet high and all around this a passage with outside walls forming a 'collar' of the same height, built by Borlase to protect the interior. Close by, non-members are welcome at the café of the **Cape Cornwall Golf Club**, England's most westerly and most wind-blown course. The egg and bacon baps are highly recommended.

⑭ Chapel Carn Brea and Carn Euny

The dome-shaped hill between Crows-en-Wra and the little Land's End airport is known as **Chapel Carn Brea** (not to be confused with Carn Brea, which overlooks Camborne and Redruth). An easy walk from the small car park (grid reference SW389284) to the summit reveals stunning views over the peninsula, described in the introduction to this chapter. An equally rewarding mile of footpath leads from the same car park, northeast over Tredinney

Prehistoric Penwith

There is a greater concentration of prehistoric sites in Penwith than in any other part of England; the moors are littered with standing stones, circles and quoits (a capstone supported by three or more uprights), 3,000-year-old village settlements and mysterious fogous – subterranean passages of uncertain usage – hide their secrets beneath the turf, gorse and bracken.

Some are easily seen from the road, such as **Lanyon Quoit** beside the road from Madron to Morvah or the **Merry Maidens**, a stone circle in a field adjoining the B3315 Lamorna–Land's End road. Iron Age cliff-forts at Treen (**Treryn Dinas**) on the south coast (confusingly there's another Treryn Dinas at Treen near Pendeen on the north coast) and Land's End (**Maen Castle**) can all be seen from the coast path. Others need to be tracked down on foot, with a map. The perfectly preserved **Boscawen-Un stone circle** is, local farmers tell me, occasionally still used for pagan celebrations and rites. This is no surprise – the local post office in St Buryan has a card in the window advertising the benign services of the village's resident witch. However, Boscawen-Un is so well hidden that it's more than likely (in daylight hours) you'll have the spot to yourself. There's limited space for parking beside the A30, a mile west of Drift, where a small sign indicates Boscawenoon Farm and the footpath to the circle.

Many, but not all Penwith's ancient sites come under the care and protection of CASPN (Cornwall Ancient Sites Protection Network) formed in 2000 after a number of sites were vandalised. The network involves organisations as diverse as English Heritage, the Cornwall Wildlife Trust and the Pagan Federation.

Common, in the shadow of Bartinney Down and past a very natural, gurgling holy well that marks the site of St Euny's Chapel, to the ancient hut settlement at **Carn Euny**. The site is managed by English Heritage, but there's no kiosk or fee for entering, and the sense of private discovery is overwhelming. The low stone walls of the roundhouses are clearly visible, beneath a soft blanket of turf and wild flowers and the entrance to a mysterious fogou is also apparent. This remote and beautiful acre lies on a south-facing slope, overlooking the south coast; it's a place to linger, maybe with a picnic rug and a jug of local cider.

⑮ Pendeen

The village is typical of this part of the north coast – a huddle of granite miners' cottages, a village shop and pub, Methodist chapel and Anglican church – but Pendeen is a gateway to a section of the coast path that takes in an astonishing heritage of **World Heritage mining sites** from the desolate and much-photographed cliff-side ruins of **Botallack**, past a working beam engine at **Levant Mine** and **Geevor Mine**, kept alive as a museum by the heroic efforts of former miners. The path continues past the windy headland and the lonely Pendeen lighthouse, before dropping down to the pristine, empty sands of Portheras Beach. Turn inland from Pendeen and you're straight onto the moors, dominated here by the craggy top of Carn Kenidjack overshadowing the **Tregeseal stone circle** to the south.

Levant Mine and Beam Engine

Trewellard TR19 7SX ⓣ 01736 786156 Ⓦ www.nationaltrust.org.uk; National Trust.
Inside, the oldest working mine-serving steam engine in the country (1840) can be seen in the engine house of Levant Mine, which was close enough to be incorporated into the Geevor Mine in the 1960s. Both mines had shafts running half a mile out to sea, and steam engines worked both the pumps and the winding mechanisms. Both mines too, are now flooded to sea level. Outside, the gritty post-industrial landscape is matched by remorseless cliffs and a turbulent sea; as you wander in the direction of Geevor, an information board shows photos of anguished women waiting for news of the 31 miners who lost their lives in 1919, when the crude mineshaft lift, known as a 'man-engine' collapsed. There are still plenty of old folk around Pendeen today who grew up never knowing their grandfathers.

Geevor Tin Mine

Trewellard TR19 7EW ⓣ 01736 788662 Ⓦ www.geevor.com.
Throughout the 1980s, Cornish tin mines that had survived the general decline of the previous century were forced, like their coal-producing counterparts elsewhere in the UK, to cease operations. The miners at Geevor, however, firmly believed that their profitable, productive mine would stay open. It was not to be. Nevertheless, after closure many from the community threw their indomitable spirit into keeping the pit alive as a museum. Alive is the right word: you can walk, stooping, down the narrow, damp passages once trodden by the tinners and meet former miners who will talk with pride and good humour about the lives they led before 1990. 'First day down there, it was the noise that got me. Three great drills going flat out and no escape from the noise. I got home that evening and told father it wasn't for me. I won't repeat his reply.' Above ground, everything has been preserved just as it was on the day the mine stopped working and a superb museum tells the whole story, including film footage of that last working day.

It's an exceptional and profoundly moving experience (greatly enhanced by wearing sensible shoes), which fully justifies the slightly above average admission fee: the mine is kept open by this and public donation alone.

Food and drink

Lunches, including homemade soups and pasties in the **Counthouse Café** (01736 788662) at Geevor, are excellent, and locals book early in the week for the superb roast dinners cooked for Sunday lunchtimes only. There's a good crowd of pubs around Pendeen, too: the **Queen's Arms** at Botallack and **Trewellard Arms** at Trewellard are both good for local ales and traditional pub grub; in Pendeen itself, the **North Inn** is a picturesque, CAMRA award-winning pub with a decent garden and the **Radjel Inn** is a St Austell Brewery pub; both do good food and are family-friendly.

⑯ A circular walk from Morvah

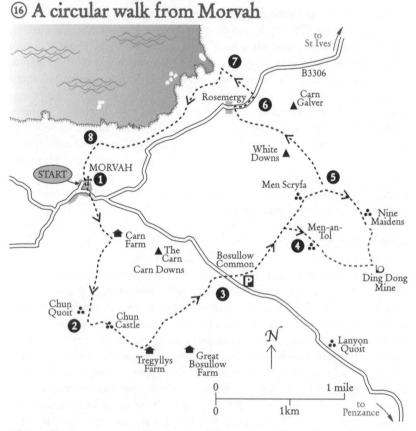

This walk encompasses 4,000 years of history as well as offering grand views over moorland and sea and a wild stretch of coast path. Most – but not all – paths on the route are well signposted. There's limited roadside parking at Morvah; or use the lay-by at Bosullow Common at point ③.

Morvah, where the walk begins and ends, is on the 300 bus route from St Ives. Morvah has a **coffee shop** and gallery in the Schoolhouse Arts and Community Centre (*01736 787808; www.morvah.com*).

① Leave Morvah on the B3306 St Ives road and at the first bend follow the marked footpath southeast over granite stiles and pasture towards Carne Farm. Film buffs will recognise the house where *Straw Dogs* was filmed in 1973 silhouetted on the skyline. Skirt the farm to the right and follow the signs uphill to **Chun Quoit**.

2 Chun Quoit, with its convex capstone, resembles a giant granite mushroom and you can just make out the remains of the cairn of boulders that once encircled it. This Neolithic burial chamber, along with Lanyon Quoit, just over the hill to the southeast, is one of the best preserved in Penwith. Turn left (due east, uphill) to **Chun Castle**.

Chun is a contraction of Chy-Woon, meaning 'House on the Hill'. First raised as a defensive stronghold in the 2nd or 3rd century BC, the circular remains of granite roundhouses can just about be discerned beneath the bracken and brambles. Leave the hillfort by the entrance and turn left, following a well-beaten track down the hill to the buildings of **Trehyllys Farm**. Here you find yourself at the start of the mile-long lane which joins the Madron–Morvah road almost opposite the lay-by.

3 Reach the road at **Bosullow Common** (note that the telephone box marked on the OS map at grid reference SW418344 has been removed) opposite a large lay-by. Cross over to the lay-by and follow the signed footpath.

4 After half a mile to you reach a point where you can turn right into a field to see the Bronze Age monument **Men-an-Tol**; this is a striking stone alignment of pillar – upright stone ring (known as a Crick stone) – pillar. This arrangement of stones is unique and theories and superstitions have surrounded them for centuries. Return to the main track and continue up the hill. Soon on the left, in a field there is a huge standing stone, **Men Scryfa** (said to be inscribed in Latin in the 5th century commemorating one Riolobran, son of Cunoval).

5 200 yards further on, at a grassy crossroads (grid reference SW430354), branch off to the right and make your way up to the **Nine Maidens stone circle**. The name is misleading: there are 11 stones and it's thought there were at least another seven. With the ruins of **Ding Dong Mine** now looming on the horizon, this is a rather brooding place, distinctly sinister in fog. Especially as there are old mine shafts lost in the scrub off the main footpath.

Return to the grassy crossroads and go straight ahead. The path heads northwest over the hill and then drops, with breathtaking loveliness towards the sea. Carn Galver looms craggily to the right.

6 Turn right onto the road at Rosemergy, then turn left on the signed footpath to the coast after 100 yards.

7 Turn left on the coast path; be prepared for some unavoidable and deeply boggy patches, particularly as you get close to Morvah. It's unwise to stray off the path, to keep your feet dry, as there several unmarked mineshafts in this area. But the views of the sea and fearsomely jagged Wolf Rocks are ample compensation for damp socks.

8 Turn left for the footpath inland to Morvah, emerging by the church.

⑰ Zennor

At Zennor one sees infinite Atlantic, all peacock-mingled colours, and the gorse is sunshine itself. Zennor is a most beautiful place: a tiny granite village nestling under high shaggy moor-hills and a big sweep of lovely sea beyond, such a lovely sea, lovelier even than the Mediterranean... It is the best place I have been in, I think.
D H Lawrence, from a letter to Katherine Mansfield and John Murry (1916)

Lawrence is not alone; lots of people fall for Zennor's charm and the list of the village's notable residents, if only temporary, is quite astounding. In no particular order it includes: the artist Patrick Heron, Emperor Haile Selasse (who sat out the war years here), Virginia Woolf, Arnold Foster (the first Secretary General of the League of Nations), Vera Atkins (who directed an all-female British spy ring) – and one local resident told me they had encountered the Dalai Lama, roaming the hills above Zennor Quoit. Sadly for Lawrence, however, the couple he hoped would help him and his German wife, Frieda, found a writers' colony in Zennor, refused to be seduced. Katherine Mansfield and her husband John Murry fled to Mylor (see page 176) quite unable to appreciate Lawrence's passion for living 'like foxes under the hill' at their isolated farmhouse among the wild gorse and bleak granite.

An entire room at the immediately engaging **Wayside Museum** (*TR26 3DA; 01736 796945*) in the middle of the village is devoted to Zennor's ability to attract VIPs of every stripe. The museum is laid out in a series of outbuildings surrounding the garden of a 16th-century miller's cottage and contains a lovingly assembled collection of local farming, mining and domestic artefacts from the Bronze Age onwards. The corn mill has been painstakingly restored and the waterwheel still turns on days when flour is being produced, a mesmerising process to watch. At the time of writing, however, the museum is up for sale and the owners fear that if a buyer cannot be found who wants to take it on, the collection will be dispersed.

Most visitors to Zennor make a beeline for the church and Tinners Arms, handily side by side. (The first version of the pub in fact, was built in 1271, to house the masons building the church.) The **church**'s great treasure is a 600-year-old seat with a carving on its side panel of a mermaid, holding a comb and mirror. Zennor has a particular fascination with mermaids, stemming from the local legend of Matthew Trewella. Trewella, the curate's son, had a fine singing voice, which proved irresistible to the mermaid Morveran, who flipped and flopped her way into the church to hear him sing. The moment he laid eyes on her, he was enchanted and following her back to the beach, disappeared under the waves of Pendour Cove.

Food and drink
Tinners Arms TR26 3BY ☎ 01736 796927. Flagstone floors, open fires, local

ales and tasty food – as well as folk music on Thursday nights – the Tinners is a deservedly popular pub, with a jolly atmosphere on both sides of the bar.

⑱ St Ives

Crowning the north coast of the Penwith peninsula, where wide, white beaches meet the gorgeously blue waters west of the Hayle estuary, St Ives has a luminous beauty quite unlike anywhere else in Cornwall. The town rises behind its working harbour and five sandy beaches – a maze of narrow streets and whitewashed fishing cottages (known as 'Downalong'), giving way to Victorian terraces and villas tucked away behind leafy gardens ('Upalong'), sheltered from westerlies by the high Penwith Moors.

Drawn by the light and abundance of cheap studio space in old net lofts and pilchard cellars, artists have flocked here for well over a century. I have a particular fondness though, for Breon O'Casey, who had a slightly different take on St Ives's appeal. The artist moved to St Ives in the late 1950s, at a time when the town was attracting kindred rebel spirits from all over the international art world. 'They talked about the artists being attracted to St Ives because of the light,' O'Casey later wrote. 'That's all balls: it was the sense of camaraderie against an, at best, indifferent, and at worst, hostile, world that drew them.' Whatever the reason, as Patrick Heron observed, St Ives is unique in being the only small town in Britain to have acquired an international reputation in the art world. That spontaneous assembling of artists such as Ben Nicholson, Barbara Hepworth, Naum Gabo, Peter Lanyon, Roger Hilton, Patrick Heron, Terry Frost and Bryan Wynter produced a dynamism and energy that lasted well into the 1970s; the town is still an important centre for art, but the original mood cannot be manufactured. There are times when St Ives reeks as much of nostalgia for its lost bohemia as of harbourside chips and pasties.

Today, the town is still rich in artist's studios and galleries, among which **Tate St Ives** (*01736 796226; www.tate.org.uk/stives*) is pre-eminent. Built in 1993 on the site of an old gasworks, the gleaming white façade overlooks Porthmeor Beach and the curved entrance porch, where there are stands for surfboards, produces a subtle echo of the waves breaking on the shore below. Inside, the bright, white galleries host a broad programme of exhibitions (there is no permanent collection on display) of international modern and contemporary art as well as special commissions and works from the Tate collection. The views over sea and sky, framed by windows in the top floor café, are as riveting as any of the displays; for a moment, as you

approach, you are beguiled into thinking you are looking at a blue abstract by Mark Rothko, who also visited St Ives and almost set up studio in Lelant. During the summer holidays the gallery organises beach workshops, popular with families, at all other times indoor 'art safaris' offer children a route round the gallery, providing buckets of crayons and paper.

The Tate also manages the **Barbara Hepworth Museum and Sculpture Garden** (*01736 796226; www.tate.org.uk/stives/hepworth*) a short, but steep, step away on the corner of Barnoon Hill and Ayr Lane. This is a truly delightful spot – far removed in spirit from the commercial tourist crush in the streets closer to the harbour and beaches. The museum occupies both floors of her studio: downstairs an informative introduction to Hepworth's life and creative journey into abstract sculpture – and what binds it to human experience and the landscape – is a vital prelude to understanding the work on display in the room above and the small, leafily chambered garden with its summer house, untouched since her death in 1975.

A wander up the hill known as The Stennack (the B3306) takes you to the hugely famous and influential **Leach Pottery** (*01736 799703; www. leachpottery.com*), founded in 1920 by Bernard Leach and Japanese potter, Shoji Hamada. Scores of potters were trained here, some from abroad, others from just down the road: while the museum celebrates the life, work and influence of its founders, the studios continue to produce 'Leachware' and provide training, apprenticeship and internships for international and local pottery students. There are family-friendly 'Clay days' during the school holidays, perfect for budding potters. A superb collection of Leach/Hamada-inspired pottery can also be found down by the harbour, in Fish St, in the spacious **St Ives Ceramics** gallery (*01736 794930*), set up by John Bedding, a former assistant to Leach.

It helps, but it's not essential to be a fan of modern art in St Ives. The **beaches** are what bring the crowds flocking in. Porthminster Beach, just below the branch-line station, is a long, safe, clean sweep of sand with beach huts and a fine café-restaurant. Porthmeor Beach, in front of the Tate, is great for surfing and the Harbour Beach is in the town centre, fronted by shops and cafés and backed by the solid granite harbour wall. Out of season, on a sunny morning, you may find you have it all to yourself; during the summer holidays it's chock-a-block with families and everyone with a take-away gravitates here for munching with a view.

At the end of the harbour, the **St Ives Museum** (*Wheal Dream; 01736 796005*) makes a pleasant alternative to the crowded shops and streets just a short step away. The large building occupies the spot where stone was taken for filling in the granite walls of the harbour pier, designed by John Smeaton (of Eddystone lighthouse fame) in 1767 and has had a remarkable history – first constructed in the 18th century as a pilchard-curing cellar, then extended to become a chapel; in the 20th century it saw use as a laundry, cinema and

The Knill legacy

It's hard to miss the odd, pyramidal monument on top of Worvas Hill, just south of St Ives. It was built in 1782 on the instructions of the mayor and customs inspector of St Ives, John Knill, who intended it to be his mausoleum. Even by Cornish standards, Knill was eccentric. In his will, he stipulated that he was to be remembered with a ceremony performed once every five years at the monument on the feast day of St James in July. In detail he described how the procession was to include ten little girls (daughters of sailors, fishermen or miners only, please) dressed in white, as well as two widows (in black) and a fiddler (colour of costume optional). They were to dance around the monument three times, then sing the Old 100th psalm, accompanied by the incumbent mayor, customs officer and vicar. Knill, who died in 1811, was able to attend the first of these ceremonies. The tradition continues to this day; the next Knill ceremony is due to take place on 25 July 2016.

hostel for shipwrecked sailors awaiting repatriation, with a dairy and pottery on the ground floor. The museum, which started in a small way when the Sailors' Mission closed in 1969, now fills both floors of the large building with an eclectic assortment of shipping, fishing, mining and farming memorabilia. Downstairs there are short films about local characters and life in St Ives; upstairs the volunteers are a cheerful bunch of gents who are happy to chat knowledgeably about the exhibits.

Food and drink

Allotment Deli 30 Fore St ℗ 01736 791666 ⓦ theallotmentproduce.co.uk. A good spot for picking up picnic ingredients from Cornish producers, with friendly, helpful staff dedicated to promoting local food.

Blas Burger Works The Warren ℗ 01736 797272. Rapidly acquiring a reputation for fantastic food, including ethically sourced local meat and fish and veg from nearby allotments. (Locals are invited to contact them if they have a glut of 'yummy food'.) Small and cosy inside, but when full, take-aways are available – the beach is a short step away.

Digey Food Room 6 The Digey ℗ 01736 799600. A deli specialising in Cornish, Spanish and Italian delicacies; the café is open for breakfasts, lunches and 'all-day' treats, which must mean Cornish Buccaneer real ale from the Wooden Hand Brewery near Truro and cider from Cornish Orchards.

Porthminster Beach Café ℗ 01736 795352 ⓦ www.porthminstercafe.co.uk. Much praise has been heaped upon this beachside café that grows its own salads on the slopes above the footpath from the branch-line station. Fresh, local and friendly – plus great views of sea, sky and beach.

Crossing the peninsula: from St Ives to Marazion

St Ives on the north coast and Marazion on the south coast are just six miles apart as the chough flies. The St Michael's Way – a fine cross-country walking route which traces an old pilgrim route to St Michael's Mount – manages to double the distance, starting in Lelant and following the glorious beaches on the western shores of the Hayle estuary to St Ives, before turning south towards Trencrom Hill, from the summit of which the craggy form of St Michael's Mount can be seen, raising its glorious profile against the sparkling sea.

⑲ Lelant

Overlooking the salt marshes and mudflats of the Hayle estuary, Lelant is a favourite spot for birdwatchers, especially in the winter months when migrant wildfowl home in on the wide and tidal shoreline. There's no footpath between the railway and the water south of the village, so most serious twitchers head for the large car park at the Lelant Saltings station or go down to the hide at Ryan's Field, close to the A30. Walkers will find the start of the St Michael's Way at St Uny's Church and within five minutes the soft sandy path gives way to the fast-flowing River Hayle and the wide open expanse of Porthkidney Sands. The novelist Rosamund Pilcher was born in the village, which makes it a place of pilgrimage for her enormous German following. (Several of her novels, set in Penwith, have been televised in Germany, which explains the obsession.)

⑳ Marazion

The pretty fishing village gets choked with visitors during the summer months, and the grassy seafront on the approach from Penzance is littered with expensive car parks. The bus (513 or 515 Western Greyhound from Penzance) is a better option, or if the tide's not too far in, it's a pleasant walk along the sandy beach from the car park at Long Rock (on the beach side of the railway line) a mile away. If you can coincide your visit to within an hour or so of low tide, the causeway to the Mount is exposed, but there are plenty of cafés, gift shops and galleries in Marazion to while away the time.

Marazion Marsh

A very attractive section of the St Michael's Way passes through this RSPB reserve which occupies Cornwall's largest reedbed, noisy in spring with the songs of several different species of warbler. In autumn, two unusual migrants – the spotted crake and aquatic warbler – are regular visitors to the reedy marshes and in recent years, bitterns have become regular winter visitors (although patience is required to see them).

A particularly interesting collection at the Summerhouse gallery exhibits the work of local artists. There is always something on display by Michael Praed, who paints not only the surrounding seascape, but the mines of the north Penwith coast. An extraordinary book he hand-wrote and illustrated in his twenties has recently been donated to the Penlee museum in Penzance: it documents his journey through the mining landscape, with pencil annotations by the miners he met on his fascinating journey.

St Michael's Mount

Marazion TR17 0EF ℗ 01736 710507 Ⓦ www.stmichaelsmount.co.uk.

The entire essence of Cornwall appears to have been distilled into this immoderately picturesque icon of Cornish myth and history, a quarter of a mile from the mainland. Saints and tinners, soldiers and fishermen, Royalists and Parliamentarians, artists, gardeners and architects have all left their mark on the island, but it's far from pickled in its past. A community of about 50 live in the houses and cottages clustered around the harbour and the castle is home to James and Mary St Aubyn, who have been in full-time residence since James's uncle, Lord St Levan, retired to the mainland in 2003. When the cobbled granite causeway is exposed at low tide, it's just a five-minute walk to the island from Marazion and a chalked notice informs you of the time by which you must leave in order to avoid being cut off by the tide. There are boats too, and the island's amphibious bus-boat, although getting lost and missing the tide is not very likely, for unless the castle and its gardens are open, there's only the small harbour to explore and the Sail Loft restaurant, run by the National Trust, who share the responsibility for the island with the St Aubyns.

Visitor numbers to the castle and gardens have risen hugely in recent years, which makes it distinctly busy in the high season. Nevertheless, there are grassy slopes for picnicking and the views from the castle battlements over the terraced gardens – cleverly planted to look good from an aerial perspective – and the wide blue expanse of Mount's Bay are astonishing, and there's much to see inside the castle, too. Parts of the Benedictine monastery that was built here in the 12th century have been incorporated into the castle; the monks' refectory, now known as the Chevy Chase room, has a remarkable 15th-century ceiling and plaster frieze depicting hunting scenes and the Lady Chapel was converted into a drawing room during the 18th century. Much of the Victorian building work was designed by J P St Aubyn, the architect responsible for so much heavy-handed church restoration, though at home he seems to have had a lighter touch. And there's a model made of the Mount and castle, sculpted from hundreds of champagne corks by a butler who clearly had far too much time on his hands.

It's hard not to find yourself wondering what it would be like to live here in one of the National Trust cottages. I saw children's bikes and wellies and the amphibious boat trundling down the shore on 'the mum's run' to the local mainland primary school. What an idyllic existence, perhaps. 'It's not for everyone,' said the boatman on the way back. 'When the black flag is run up the flagpole, that means the weather's too bad for the boats and we're cut off then. Not everyone can endure that for very long.' I heard too, how the island continues to release its hidden secrets every now and then. In July 2009, for example, Darren Little, an amateur archaeologist and volunteer gardener who lives on the island, was cutting back some long grass when he put his hand under a hedge and pulled out a smallish lump of metal. Another person might have tossed it aside, but Darren's curiosity was aroused. It turned out to be just the first piece in a hoard of 47 items – ranging from buckles to axe heads – thought to be a smith's 'scrap heap', dating from the late Bronze Age (1500–800BC). Having been authenticated by the British Museum, the find is now on display in the castle.

The Greek geographer, Pytheas, toured the south coast of Britain, early in the 4th century BC and described an island called Ictis, accessible from the mainland at low tide. Wagon-loads of tin, he wrote, were brought to the island, where lively commerce with Mediterranean traders had resulted in a 'civilised manner of life'. It's a pity that Pytheas (or Diodorus who more or less copied Pytheas's lost account 300 years later) doesn't mention the great forest that is thought to lie submerged beneath Mount's Bay and would have provided fuel for the smelting houses on the coast from the Bronze Age until the Dark Ages, when the sea bed must have sunk dramatically for the story to be believed. But the old name for the island in Cornish is Carrek Luz en Cuz, 'the rock in the wood' and I'm sure I'm not the only person who has peered into the water from the side of a dinghy, hoping for a glimpse of a tree stump, far below.

James and Mary St Aubyn who live in the castle, showed me the gardens, begun in the 18th century and added to over the centuries by previous generations of St Aubyns including four sisters who created three terraces of narrow walled gardens under the south face of the rock, whose pink brick walls give shelter to a colourful and tenderly exotic range of plants, a respite from the brutal granite and spiky succulents that bake on the exposed rock outside. 'The rock acts as a kind of giant night-storage heater,' explains Alan Cook, the head gardener. 'People ask how we can get away with planting such tender things in such an exposed place, but the rock creates its own microclimate.'

In May 2011, a vast chunk of rock, perched above the terraced gardens on the south side of the island, split away from the mother rock and fell at the feet of a couple of astonished German visitors. Months were spent assessing how to prevent further damage; the solution has been a series of long steel pins, bolted and cemented into the rock at its most vulnerable points like wall-ties – you can see them if you look up from the eastern terraces, but it's more likely that your gaze will be seized by the jewel-like succulents at your feet, that look like a coral reef when seen from the battlements.

The St Michael's Way

I think most people make up their own version of the route, using the OS Explorer map 102, as the published guide appears to be out of print and there are all sorts of route-shortening options. My own version is to start at the train station in **Carbis Bay**, and aim for **Trencrom Hill** via any one of the footpaths on the far side of the A3074, which soon link up with a scallop-shell waymarker, which indicates you are on the St Michael's Way. Just west of Ludgvan, an impressive new sculpture garden lies right next to the footpath. **Tremenheere** (*www.tremeheere.co.uk*) is making the headlines for many reasons: the sensitively placed collection of rare, sub-tropical trees and ferns, collected by local GP Neil Armstrong, rate amongst the best Cornwall has to offer, and a Skyspace by Slow Artist, James Turrell, is simply awesome. Camera obscuras above and below ground also encourage visitors to slow down to take in the garden and landscape from unexpected angles. A fabulous café and shop at the entrance are a destination in themselves. Do go.

In **Ludgvan**, the White Hart is just the kind of village pub that a thirsty or hungry walker likes to see, and a good place to decide which route to take next. The options are to head southeast across the RSPB reserve at Marazion Marsh to **St Michael's Mount** (there are buses back to Carbis Bay from Marazion) or to head southwest, across farmland to Penzance (where either train or bus will take you back). Penzance to Marazion is a three-mile walk along the beach.

Food and drink

There's no better place from which to soak up the view of the Mount and the beach than the terrace of the **Godolphin Arms** in Marazion. Just two miles further east, however, in Perranuthnoe there are two very special pitstops, perfect for Slow explorers.

Peppercorn Kitchen Lynfield Yard, Perranuthnoe TR20 9NE ℗ 01736 719584 Ⓦ www.peppercornkitchen.co.uk. On the lane down to the beach, beside the Cowshed gallery, Jenni and Lisa produce a small, daily menu of homemade lunches and teas, popular all year with local families. In winter there's a cosy logburner indoors and in summer there are picnic tables outside on the grass. Something Mediterranean, north African or Middle Eastern is always on the daily menu and Jenni's cakes have acquired a cult following.

Victoria Inn Perranuthnoe TR20 9NP ℗ 01736 710309 Ⓦ www.victoriainn-penzance.co.uk. Eye-catchingly pink and claiming to be 'Cornwall's oldest pub', the Victoria is one of the top eating places in west Cornwall, and has acquired shedloads of accolades and awards in the past few years. It's more of a restaurant with a bar than a pub, but the local ales are well kept and include Sharp's Doom Bar and Skinner's Heligan Honey.

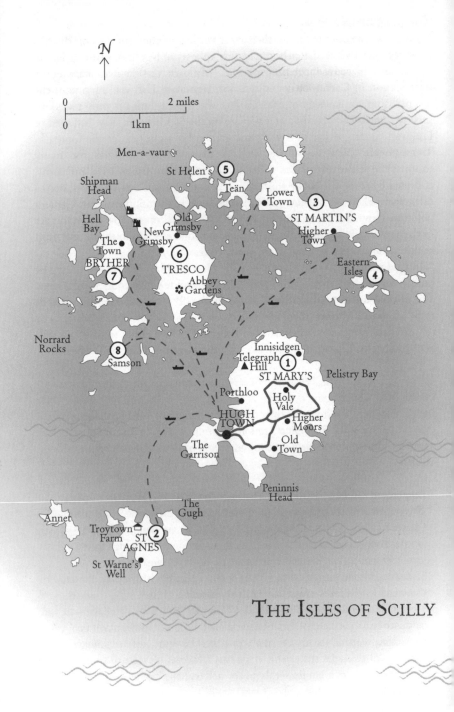

THE ISLES OF SCILLY

10. THE ISLES OF SCILLY

In many ways, life on the Isles of Scilly is an unselfconscious example of what the Slow concept is all about. Local culture and tradition, landscape, seascape, history and natural history are given affectionate respect here; people take time to enjoy what makes their islands so special. Traffic jams, chain stores and fast-food outlets belong to another world; everyone seems to have time to pause for a chat, leaning on the garden gate or over the shop counter. Children are able to roam and explore freely and safely, while wrinklier visitors remark that 'this is what life used to be like, 50 years ago'. And everywhere you go, you sense an enviably easy and relaxed sense of community among the 2,000 residents and a willingness to share their good-natured, rat-racelessness with visitors, too.

Five inhabited islands, 51 uninhabited islands and dozens of jagged rocks and deadly reefs make up the Scilly archipelago, 28 miles southwest of Land's End. But what you see are merely the hilltops of a submerged landmass, lost to an encroaching sea around a thousand years ago. Ancient field boundaries and Bronze Age settlements lie beneath the translucent waters that separate Bryher, Samson, Tresco, St Martin's and St Mary's (a deep channel has always set St Agnes apart) and, for a brief period during the extreme low tides of the spring equinox, it's possible still to paddle between some islands.

The islands are startlingly beautiful, with beaches that have an almost tropical quality – a turquoise sea, crystal clear and cool as jade washes into shallow bays of sparkling white sand; spiky, succulent, showy subtropical plants flourish casually in gardens and waysides. And yet, on shores where the Atlantic crashes into the archipelago, the rock-strewn seascape is more Hebridean than Caribbean. Evidence of human occupation is not overwhelming – there are no big hotels or holiday villages – houses and cottages appear randomly among the lush vegetation or cluster around the curve of a harbour. Above the shoreline, chains of drystone walls coated in hairy lichen form a jigsaw of tiny fields, scattered across the sheltered, leeward slopes. Many, since the near-collapse of flower and potato farming, are abandoned to drifts of wild flowers, though some are still lined with sweet-scented narcissi or vegetables; elsewhere you might chance upon a couple of cows or a goat.

On higher, exposed ground, it's all granite and gorse and cushions of heather and ling. Permissive footpaths thread across and around the islands – and while it's not difficult to get momentarily disorientated, it's impossible to get seriously lost. Walking on Scilly is quite unlike walking on the mainland: maps aren't really needed and in any case (with Tresco being a notable exception), waymarked routes and signs bearing place names don't exist. The fun lies in exploring, rather than notching up miles of path, in discovering the distinctive character of each island and in enjoying the pauses for the heart-stopping views across the misty recessions of the archipelago.

St Mary's, the largest of the inhabited islands, is the hub for all these adventures: flights from the mainland arrive here and the ferry from Penzance ties up at Town Quay, next to the busy inter-island boats. It's the only island with anything resembling a town, and most of the residential and holiday accommodation is to be found here. There's a variety of holiday accommodation to be found on the **Off Islands** – as the four other inhabited islands are known – each containing a loosely linked hamlet or two, where populations dwindle to a weather-beaten core in the winter. The uninhabited islands, many little more than a fist or spike of granite rising above the water, others with beaches and relics of past human occupation, are home to countless breeding populations of seabirds and seals.

Each of the five inhabited islands has its own very distinct character, and it's funny how so many visitors end up with a partisan feeling for one island in particular. 'It was always St Martin's for me,' says the island's baker; 'the people, the beaches, the starry night skies.' An elderly passenger on the ferry sighed, 'Bryher. For the solitude and the birds. I have to go every year, even if just for a day.' His wife chips in, 'St Mary's isn't appreciated enough outside Hugh Town: I love walking Up Country through the nature reserves to Pelistry Bay.' A giggling six year old says, 'I love camping at Troytown Farm (on St Agnes) because it's next to the beach and there are cows and ice-cream.' And, 'We're third generation Tresco', I overheard one woman say with pride – she was a holiday visitor, not a resident.

Getting there

It's a bit of an adventure getting to Scilly, whatever the means of travel. By ferry there's always the chance of seeing dolphins and the slow revelation of the Cornish coast from Penzance to Land's End and arrival in the sheltering embrace of St Mary's harbour is unforgettable. From the air, the islands appear as scattered fragments of a stained-glass window: sapphire blue and pale jade sea surrounding cut-out pieces of land that are green and gold with daffodils and Bermuda buttercups in spring or russet red with dying bracken in autumn.

However, this is mere romantic twaddle to the islanders for there's no more vexed issue at the time of writing than the **Scilly Link**. Plans for the replacement of the passenger ferry, the *Scillonian III*, and improvements to the harbour and ferry terminal in Penzance have foundered upon reefs of politicised in-fighting. Despite the uncertain future, the Isles of Scilly Steamship Company, which has run the vital service from Penzance to St Mary's since 1926, and is still largely owned by islanders, remains optimistic that government help will be forthcoming and that while the debate continues, the 34-year-old *Scillonian III* will continue to transport passengers and some freight from late March until late October each year until she is decommissioned in 2014.

Out of season, the company's freight vessel, *Gry Maritha* (dubbed locally *The Grim Reaper* on account of her flat-bottomed and therefore stomach-churningly slow and rolling performance), takes the occasional (and it must be said, somewhat desperate) passenger, so all but the hardiest take to the sky routes during the winter months. **Helicopters** fly from Penzance to St Mary's and there's a direct service to Tresco as well. However, since the agreed sale of the Penzance heliport to Sainsbury's, British International, who operate the helicopter service, have yet to secure a suitable alternative site.

At present, the only route to Scilly with an unclouded future is the **Skybus service**, also owned by the Isles of Scilly Steamship Company, which operates a fleet of six small aircraft (so small that if you lean forward your chin is on the pilot's shoulder) from the tiny airport at Land's End, as well as offering flights from Newquay, Bristol and Southampton airports during the summer months.

Note that there are no flights or ferry services on a Sunday.

Transport

British International Helicopters Eastern Green, Penzance ℗ 01736 363871 ⓦ www.islesofscillyhelicopter.com. Helicopter flights to St Mary's and Tresco.
Isles of Scilly Travel Centre Quay St, Penzance ℗ 0845 710 5555 or 01736 334220 ⓦ www.ios-travel.co.uk. Covers ferry and Skybus travel to Scilly.

Getting around

For visitors, there is no option but to leave the car behind on the mainland; island taxis, golf buggies or tractors are there to transport the newly arrived and/or their baggage to campsites or hotels if needed, but thereafter getting around the islands on foot, or perhaps bike – and between them by boat – is what it's all about.

Inter-island boats

ⓦ www.scillyboating.co.uk

Weather and tides permitting, there are boat trips from St Mary's to the Off Islands every day. The Off Islands run their own daily ferry services too, and there's also a fast water-taxi, taking up to 12 passengers.

Those who like to plan these trips ahead can do so at the ticket kiosk on the quay or the tourist information centre in Hugh Town. If you prefer a more serendipitous approach, the answer is to wander down to the quay, consult the chalked-up departure list, hop aboard and pay *en route*. If one boat is full, another is laid on, so there's never any stress about getting tickets in advance.

Often the boatmen will add an optional seal- and bird-spotting trip around a group of uninhabited islands to one of the regular routes.

Walk Scilly

Scilly businessman, Euan Rodger, came up with the idea of a walking festival (*www.walkscilly.co.uk*) to kick start the pre-Easter holiday season. A relatively small affair when it started in 2006, there are now over 50 guided walks throughout the week across the five inhabited islands, and the regular island guides are joined by specialists from the mainland, such as Penzance-based Rachel Lambert, who leads foraging walks, followed by cook-ups in the evening and photographer Robert Sanger, from Truro, who offers tips on coastal photography.

The week concludes with the Scilly Ten – a ten-mile run (or walk) around St Mary's, to raise funds for charity.

Buses

You can tour St Mary's in a very handsome vintage cream and blue St Trinian's-style bus, starting and finishing at Holgate's Green in Hugh Town. Island Rovers (*01732 422131*) chalk up times of departure outside the tourist information centre.

Cycling

Bikes are a great way to get around on St Mary's and Tresco, and useful if you are staying 'Up Country' and see yourself wanting to cycle in and out of Hugh Town each day. But with only nine miles of tarmac road on the islands, and all the interesting, sandy paths technically reserved for those on foot, you might regret the cost of taking your own bike on the *Scillonian* (£12 each way), and choose to hire a bike for a morning or day instead.

Cycle hire

Book a Bike Beverley Hills, Pilots Retreat, St Mary's ① 01720 422786 Ⓦ www.bookabikeonscilly.co.uk. Mountain bikes delivered to and collected from your accommodation

St Mary's Bike Hire The Strand (opposite Holgates Green), Hugh Town, St Mary's ① 07796 638506 Ⓦ www.stmarysbikehire.co.uk. With a £15 deposit, you can hire a bike for a half-day, a whole day or a week. Child seats are available too.

Tresco Bike Hire Island Office, New Grimsby ① 01720 422849 Ⓦ www.tresco.co.uk. Adult and children's bikes, as well as all-terrain pushchairs and wheelchairs available for hire by the day.

Sea kayaking

The first thing that hits you is the silence: getting around the islands by motor launch is practical and fun, but nothing beats the quiet enjoyment of moving silently through the water, and this is the way to get up close to nesting seabirds and sunbathing seals. Very calm seas and some previous paddling experience are necessary before you can venture out to the uninhabited rocks and islands, but even novices can enjoy pottering in shallow waters off the inward-facing beaches of the archipelago on stable, sit-on-top kayaks offered by the hire companies listed below.

Sea kayak hire

Bryher, Tresco and St Martin's Bennett Boatyard Annkea Quay, Bryher ℗ 07979 393206 ⓦ www.bennettboatyard.com. Hires kayaks by the day or half-day. Paddling is restricted to the safe waters between Bryher, Tresco and St Martin's. Deliveries and pick-ups can also be organised from St Martin's (they have a base by the campsite) or Tresco.

St Mary's Chris Peat ℗ 0789 999 6493 ⓦ www.kayakscilly.com. Offers coaching for novices and excursions in small groups. Experienced paddlers can hire single or double kayaks and take off for the day.

Tresco Ravensporth Sailing Base ℗ 01720 424419 ⓦ www.sailingscilly.com. Sit- on single and double kayaks; pottering close to the beach is encouraged, unless very experienced and sea very calm.

Accommodation

A comprehensive list of accommodation from campsites to upmarket hotels can be found at www.simplyscilly.co.uk. By far the greatest number of **B&Bs and self-catering cottages** are to be found on St Mary's; there are very few on St Agnes, Bryher and St Martin's. The tourist information centre has a finger on the pulse of all availabilities, late deals and out of season offers. If looking for a cottage rental on Tresco, you can contact the island office directly on 01720 422849.

Unless you're heading to Tresco or one of the small handful of smart hotels and holiday lets scattered across the islands, it's best not to expect mainland standards in your accommodation. Wi-Fi is not guaranteed, nor are cotton sheets and décor may raise nostalgic memories of the 1970s. But for the many who come back to Scilly year after year, generation after generation, that cosy and unchanging familiarity is precious, if a little outdated to fresh eyes.

There are only four **campsites** spread across the islands – one each on St Mary's (*01720 422670; www.garrisonholidays.com; ted@garrisonholidays. com*), St Agnes (Troytown Farm; see below), Bryher (*01720 422559; www. bryhercampsite.co.uk; relax@bryhercampsite.co.uk*) and St Martin's (*01720 422888; www.stmartinscampsite.co.uk*). Reserving a pitch is essential, especially during the school holidays. Note that during the pilot gig championships in May, every single bed and tent pitch is reserved, months in advance.

Atlantic Hotel Hugh St, Hugh Town, St Mary's TR21 0PL ① 01720 422417 Open Feb–Nov. Ⓦ www.atlantichotelscilly.co.uk Ⓔ atlantichotel@staustellbrewery.co.uk. A small, friendly hotel, overlooking the harbour, with a beamy (and occasionally noisy) pub downstairs. Prices reflect lots of effort put into bringing rooms up to mainland standards: new 'vi-sprung' mattresses, cotton sheets and fresh decoration.

Bylet Guest House Church Rd, Hugh Town, St Mary's TR21 0NA ①01720 422479 Ⓦ www.byletholidays.com Ⓔ thebylet@bushinternet.com; open Mar–Oct; reasonable rates. Close to the centre of Hugh Town, two cosy first-floor apartments each have twin beds, shower room, kitchen and living space.

Isles of Scilly Country Guesthouse Sage House, High Lanes, St Mary's TR21 0NW Ⓦ www.scillyguesthouse.co.uk ① 01720 422440 Ⓔ scillyguesthouse@hotmail. co.uk. About 30 minutes' walk from Hugh Town, a B&B run on green principles by lively, thoughtful Sabine, who moved to Scilly from Germany in 2003. Breakfasts, served in the sunny conservatory, are superb and make the most of Scillonian eggs, bacon and sausages. There is a small kitchen for residents wanting to cook for themselves in the evening, though Sabine prepares evening meals too, with a bit of notice. Simply furnished, very comfortable rooms (including several singles on the ground floor) at reasonable prices. Cycle hire might come in useful if staying here.

Pier House Hugh Town, St Mary's TR21 0HY ① 07769 151617 or 01720 423061 Ⓦ www.pier-house.co.uk Ⓔ tanyaandpetereynolds@btinternet.com. Next to the Mermaid Inn and the harbour pier, so couldn't be handier for inter-island boats and mainland ferry. An old pilchard house with bags of character; rooms have exposed stone walls, great views over the harbour and Off Islands. Tariff average; breakfasts hearty.

South Tinks Holy Vale, St Mary's TR21 0NT ① 01720 423523 Ⓦ www.come2scilly. com Ⓔ enquiries@come2scilly.com. Self-catering accommodation for two in a small but luxuriously kitted-out single-storey building. Pretty garden and idyllic, sheltered position in a wooded hamlet, 15 minutes' walk from Hugh Town. Average prices. The website lists a number of other self-catering properties on the island.

Troytown Farm St Agnes ① 01720 422360 Ⓦ www.troytown.co.uk Ⓔ enquiries@troytown.co.uk. Three self-catering lets on the farm which sells its own dairy produce, bacon, sausages and seasonal veg. The Cottage sleeps four, The Croft sleeps five – both are superb for families with children. The Flat sleeps two. All very nicely done up in a contemporary style and great value. The campsite just below the farm next to the beach is dinky, but gets booked up very quickly.

Tourist information centre

Hugh Town (St Mary's) Hugh St ① 01720 424031. The IoS Steamship Company office is attached to the same building, making it handy for travel enquiries and bookings too.

① St Mary's

Each morning there's what passes for a rush hour in **Hugh Town** as newspapers that have come in on the early flights are delivered to the shops, children hare off to school on bikes, dogs are walked and everyone stops whatever it is they're doing to discuss the weather. An hour or so later, there's a second rush hour as visitors emerge from the hotels and guesthouses and descend on the harbour to consult the boards and decide which of the Off Islands to explore that day. Later, towards the end of the afternoon, the ferries return, disgorge their passengers and the streets fill up with people making plans for the evening. In the summer this might mean a moonlit boat ride to another island for dinner, fish and chips on the beach, folk music in one of the pubs or taking in one of the frequent evening talks, given by local experts on Scillonian history or wildlife.

Tempting though it is to hop on an inter-island boat, there's lots to be said for spending a Slow day on St Mary's, pottering, chatting, walking or just soaking up the views. You might start by wandering through the **Garrison gate** (turn left in front of the chemist's in Hugh Town) and climb the steep hill to enjoy the views from the **Star Castle** – now a rather splendid hotel – built in 1595 within moated fortifications constructed in the shape of an eight-pointed star. From this wonderful vantage point you can look north across the wide blue waters to the twin peaks of barren Samson, the tree-fringed shores of Tresco and the white beaches of St Martin's. On Wednesday and Friday evenings in summer, you'll see the island gig crews at the oars, cheered on by a flotilla of small boats. Turn southwest and there's St Agnes, rising quietly to one side of the main archipelago and further still, beyond the seabird sanctuary of Annet and the Western Rocks, the lonely column of the Bishop Rock lighthouse.

A mile of level footpath runs around the coastline of the Garrison promontory, passing historic fortifications and cannon positions representing centuries of hostilities with the French, Dutch and Spanish. Circumnavigating the Garrison is an easy stroll, and on warm summer evenings it's almost a ritual pre-dinner promenade. On a winter's afternoon, in sharp slanting light, and with only seabirds for company, there's a different feeling altogether.

There's a good account of the Civil War siege of the Garrison in the superb **Isles of Scilly Museum** (*Church St, Hugh Town; 01720 422 337; www.iosmuseum. org*). No dusty collections here – there's a real sense of active participation by island residents, and curiosity when something new is dredged up from the sea bed or soil, such as the fine Bronze Age iron sword in its scabbard that was dug up by a Bryher farmer in 1999 or the recent recovery of timberwork from the 1798 wreck of the *Colossus*.

There are a number of art and craft galleries in Hugh Town, but it would be easy to miss the **Phoenix Craft workshops**, just beyond St Mary's Church, on the Porthmellon Industrial Estate. Here you'll see the work of artist Oriel Hicks (*01720 422900; www.phoenixstainedglass.co.uk*), who has produced new stained-glass windows in all the islands' churches. They are immediately recognisable, letting in more light than their Victorian or Edwardian counterparts, and filled with the colours, birds and plants of the Scillonian landscape. (Some of the finest examples of her work, showing puffins, kestrels, diving seals, arum lilies and shoreline flowers, are in Bryher church.)

Less than a mile away on the far side of the hill dominated by the solid grey cylinder of **Buzza Tower** (originally built as a windmill, but now used as a landmark by boatmen entering the harbour from Tresco) is the former 'capital' of St Mary's, **Old Town**. The deep, snug bay still has the ragged remains of its granite harbour wall, a cluster of houses and, standing alone on the western shore of the bay, a little granite church, surrounded by a steeply tiered churchyard and elm trees. There was once a Norman castle on the slopes overlooking the harbour, but the whole town simply shifted its emphasis to the Hugh Town side of of the hill, when the principal defences against the threat of invasion by the Spanish and French – the Star Castle and the Garrison ramparts – were built on the westernmost promontory of the island in the 16th century.

Up Country

Walk away from Hugh Town or Old Town, and within a few minutes you're in another world (referred to locally as 'Up Country'), where rural life goes on unperturbed by the busy comings and goings of the harbour or the grassy airport and helipad on the hill above Old Town. In fact, there are moments in the centre of the island where you lose sight and sound of the sea altogether. **Holy Vale**, a hamlet buried deep in a stream-fed valley, is picturesquely unspoilt, but it's the avenues and woods of mature elm (Dutch elm disease bypassed the islands) that really make you feel the clock has been turned back 50 years. That, and the sight of thrushes, hopping tamely about the undergrowth, or an old red tractor in a sea of white-flowered three-cornered leeks. In the small but fragrant daffodil fields, the flowers are picked and bunched by farmers and their families, who pause to chat and straighten their backs. (On mainland Cornwall, it's not unusual to see up to 40 eastern European migrant workers harvesting a field of daffs at lightning, robotic speeds.)

There's a garden close to Holy Vale, called **Carreg Dhu**: an acre or two of exotic-looking shrubs and trees, semi-tender succulents and perennials, a thicket of towering camellias, broad grassy paths and a scattering of benches. It's open all year, and by the box for donations there's a list of jobs that need doing and a canvas bag of hand tools, for anyone to use who feels like a spot of weeding or dead-heading.

Historic and prehistoric sites

You could also spend a day exploring the relics of Bronze Age settlements and burial chambers that lie dotted about the island. Information and maps are in the TIC, museum and local newsagent and bookshop, but this being Scilly, it's just as easy to wander along the coast path (most Bronze Age sites are close to the sea) and stumble across the old stones at **Halangy Down** and **Innisidgen** along the way. One of the most impressive chambered barrows is close to **Porth Hellick** (there are signposts from the hamlet called Normandy), the wild and rock-strewn bay where **Sir Cloudsley Shovell**, Admiral of the Fleet, was washed ashore, either dead or dying in 1707; four ships in his fleet were wrecked on rocks off St Agnes and nearly 2,000 sailors also perished as a result of a miscalculation in navigation. A rough stone marks the spot where his body was found. Locals seem to enjoy the story that an arrogant Shovell disregarded the warning of a Scillonian sailor who recognised the dangerous reef and hanged the man for his

The war with the Netherlands

From 1649 to 1651 the Royalist Governor of Scilly, John Grenville, directed a fleet of privateers in a series of plundering attacks on Dutch (and English) merchant ships in order to raise money for Charles II and his exiled court in Scotland. Not surprisingly, the Dutch were a little annoyed. With 13 ships to back him up, the Dutch admiral, Maarten Harpertszoon Tromp, landed on the islands demanding the release of all Dutch ships, crews and cargoes. Grenville, who was only 23 at the time, handed over the prisoners, but admitted (with what was perceived as youthful arrogance) that the ships and their cargoes had already been sold. An infuriated Tromp declared war on Scilly, but diplomatically left the fighting to the Roundhead army, which was already assembled on ships close to the islands. After fighting on Tresco and retreat to the Garrison on St Mary's, where he was besieged, Grenville and his men were forced to surrender (the terms were extraordinarily generous), but nobody remembered to sign a peace treaty with the Netherlands.

Until 1986 that is – when the chairman of the Isles of Scilly Council, Roy Duncan, decided enough was enough and wrote to the Dutch Embassy, asking for the continuing state of war to be brought to an end. Ambassador Huydecoper, recognising the gravity of the situation, leaped into action and on 17 April 1986 presented the islanders with a scroll, declaring an end to the hostilities. 'It must have been awful to know we could have attacked you at any moment,' he told the assembled Scillonians.

troubles. Perhaps that makes the storytellers happier to recount the equally unsubstantiated tale of the old lady who confessed on her deathbed that she had found the Admiral still alive on the beach, stolen his ring and bopped him on the head. It spoils the story, perhaps, to remember that Shovell was as brave and talented a sailor as Nelson, and worked his way up from humble cabin boy to Admiral of the Fleet on merit alone.

Food and drink

You have superb opportunities on the islands to eat fish caught in Scilly's clear and unpolluted waters and potatoes, asparagus or salads pulled from the sandy, seaweed-enriched soil just minutes before they arrive at the table. High Tide on St Agnes or Adam's fish and chips on St Martin's won't break the bank, either. On all the islands you find garden or farm gate stalls, accompanied by an honesty box, selling eggs, honey, vegetables and fruit as the seasons dictate; and there's plenty of wild food too if you know what you're looking for: you might see chefs foraging for salty samphire or leafy alexanders to go with a freshly caught crab or lobster. And that's not all: Bryher fudge and ice cream from the small dairy herd on St Agnes are second to none – and the bakery on St Martin's has an almost cult following.

However, local food and drink is not as plentiful, straightforward to produce or easy to come by as you might imagine. Take **meat**, for example. There's beef from Tresco and pork and bacon from St Agnes on many of the islands' better menus, and a new flock of Jacob's ewes has arrived on St Mary's – but there's been no abattoir on the islands since the post-CJD regulations came into force in the 1990s, and a proposal to build a new one has recently been rejected. Animals are therefore transported to the mainland for slaughter, which is not much fun for them, increases the food miles and makes Scillonian meat expensive to buy.

Fish, you might think, are easier to put on the menu – but 90% of the Scilly catch goes straight to the mainland, partly because demand on the islands is limited and variable – and partly to avoid the loss of the single handling premium. As one resident involved in Scillonian catering put it (sounding somewhat surreal), 'Most fish come from the mainland.' This is particularly frustrating as Scilly fishermen, operating in small boats and often turning to other jobs in the winter months come about as close to the ideal of sustainable, inshore, mixed-species fishing as you can get.

The near-collapse of flower growing on Scilly has led to a lot of abandoned small fields, but thankfully, a number of small **organic growers**, such as Jonathan Smith on St Martin's, have taken up the challenge to supply the islands with fresh greens and there's a farmers' market in Hugh Town on the first Thursday of every month, and a Cornish deli (*Hugh St; 01720 422734*) in the town centre , but the Co-op is still everybody's first port of call, it seems. Tresco's small supermarket (waggishly known as Trescos) is well stocked with Cornish produce and decent home-baked bread, while the smaller islands make do with a post-office-cum-shop that sells indispensable items such as tinned mushroom soup and Kit-Kats.

Local beers come from Ales of Scilly, brewed on St Mary's (*01720 422419*). Mark Praeger produces various strengths of ale, starting with Maiden Voyage and rising to the appropriately named Scuppered at 4.8%, which you'll see is the pint of choice for locals. He's a one-man band, but always happy, if not busy or delivering, to show visitors round the brewery.

Juliet's Garden Seaways Flower Farm, TR21 0NF ℗ 01720 422228. Everybody I've spoken to recommends this lovely spot, overlooking Porthloo Beach, about 20 minutes' walk from Hugh Town. You can go just for a coffee or cream tea or eat fish caught in the morning. If the restaurant is closed at lunchtime, it's because fishing is still in progress.

Kaffeehaus Salbei Isles of Scilly Country Guesthouse, Sage House, High Lanes, St Mary's TR21 0NW ℗ 01720 422535; open all year. Just when you least expect it, on a quiet lane 'Up Country', a wonderful café pops up, run by Sabine, an expert Bavarian cook, serving strudel, cake and rye bread and excellent coffees and teas.

Tolman Café Old Town TR21 0NJ ℗ 01720 423060. Overlooking the old harbour, an unpretentious little café serving homemade soups and cakes, full breakfasts and bistro-style lunches. Sit outside and sparrows and thrushes come flocking instantly to your table.

The Off Islands

Each of the four inhabited Off Islands lie within a 20-minute boat journey from St Mary's and ferry times are arranged so that you can spend the best part of the day on an island, and later boats in summer allow for an evening meal. Four or five hours is long enough to get a feel for the character of each island, stretch your legs and find a deserted beach for a picnic, a swim – or enjoy a pub lunch. It's only when you've visited them all that you can be absolutely sure which one has claimed your heart.

② St Agnes

Lying to the southwest, or 'round the back' of St Mary's, from which it is separated by deep water, St Agnes feels cut off and remote from the other inhabited islands which appear to face each other in a friendly kind of circle. But those who love St Agnes and live there, value it for this very isolation, the continuity of its native families who fish and farm and the rare sculptural beauty of its granite-stacked shores and moorland. 'It's how Scilly used to be,' you'll hear. 'Not much changes on St Agnes.'

Arriving in the little harbour below the Turk's Head, the island's only pub, you can see the sandbar which connects the island at low tide to the Gugh, a gorse-smothered crest of rock where Bronze Age burial mounds are still discernable and a lonely standing stone, set aslant like the gnomon of a sundial, points towards the west. The only two houses on Gugh face the sandbar, their oddly curving roofs designed to withstand the winter gales. The rest of St Agnes's houses lie clustered close to or around the lighthouse (disused since the light was lit on Bishop's Rock) and much-loved church, less than half a mile from the harbour. The odd golf buggy or tractor shuttles up and down the tiny lane ferrying bags and camping gear – pursue the lane to the end and you arrive at the western end of the island, where Troytown Farm has a miniature campsite just a drystone wall away from the beach.

Follow the coast east from Troytown and the pretty white beaches, piled with smooth round rocks and pebbles of the western shores, give way to spectacular coves and jutting cliffs of stacked granite. St Warna (the patron saint of shipwrecks) gives her name to the most dramatic of these and to a Holy Well close by. A sevenfold-labyrinth laid out in stones on the turf by a lighthouse-keeper has been here since 1729, though it's possible he was retracing the lines of a much older pattern. The eastern side of the island is all wild moor and the happily named Wingletang Down could be a giant's primitive sculture garden. The level, heathery landscape is dotted with huge, sculptural crags and piles of granite that take little imagination to be transformed into faces, beasts or abstractions of the natural world.

The moor runs down to the arc of Beady pool, a glittering white beach where shiny ochre, black and white beads can still be found, washed ashore from the wreck of a 17th-century merchant ship. If you're unsure what to search for, have a look first in the museum in Hugh Town on St Mary's, where there's quite a collection.

Food and drink

The **post office shop** is good for basics as well as being an outlet for local, organic produce.

Coastguards Café ① 01720 422197 and **High Tide Seafood Restaurant** ① 01720 423869. Tristan Hick rustles up fresh produce from the family farm for cream teas, lunches and packed picnics in a wooden building at the back of the coastguard cottages. In the evenings, Mark Eberlein takes over and transforms it into a candlelit, licensed restaurant, serving fish caught in the morning, wild food harvested from the hedges and shoreline and fresh ingredients from local farms.
Troytown Farm Shop ① 01720 422360 ⓦ www.troytown.co.uk. Sells fresh milk, cream, butter and wonderful ice creams from its own small dairy herd. Sausages and bacon from home-reared pigs and seasonal veg from the polytunnels are also available.
Turk's Head ① 01720 422434. Britain's most southwesterly pub is cosy and welcoming inside and the garden in front has views over the harbour and the Gugh; on a sunny day it's the place to sit and wait for the passenger ferry to come in. Food is simple – soups, pasties, sandwiches and locally caught fish when available – and everything, including the bread, is homemade and delicious, too. Ales are from St Austell and Skinner's.

Round the rugged rocks: Annet and the Western Rocks

West of St Agnes the green-topped island is **Annet**, home to colonies of puffins and shearwaters, among thousands of other seabirds. Boats from St Agnes and St Mary's offer birdwatching trips around the islands, though landing is prohibited as Annet is a bird sanctuary. Sadly, the puffins find no sanctuary from black-backed gulls, who predate viciously on the vulnerable chicks at breeding time.

The boatmen will take you in as close as possible to the jagged rocks on the westernmost fringes of the archipelago, the **Western Rocks**, which have wrecked scores of ships over the centuries, in order to see seals who bask on the leeward shores. Among the screaming birds on barren, lonely **Rosevear**, you'll see a sobering sight: the ruins of stone huts, built as shelters for the men constructing the **Bishop Rock lighthouse**.

The original construction was designed by James Walker, the chief engineer to Trinity House, in 1847. His plan was to raise the tower on cast-iron legs, so that the sea could pass through. But it was swept away in 1850, before the paraffin lantern could be lit, revealing the extreme challenge of building a tower that could survive the full force of the Atlantic. Undeterred, Walker started again, raising a granite tower, 120 feet high, built to a similar specification as the Eddystone lighthouse, which was finally lit in 1858. But the waves dashed over it in stormy weather – lifting the 550-pound fog bell from the top during one memorable storm – and the granite blocks started to crack, so Walker's successor, James Douglass, raised the tower by a further 55 feet and sheathed it all in a protective layer of concrete. It's the tallest of all pillar lighthouses around the British coast, and in gales the light at the top sways – by as much as six feet. It's a comfort to think that since 1992 it has been operated remotely from Trinity House headquarters in Harwich.

③ St Martin's

From St Mary's, the long gleam of white beach across the glittering sea to the north identifies St Martin's, as surely as the red and white, bullet-shaped daymark identifies the island to shipping arriving from the east. The ferry deposits passengers at Higher Town quay, and a narrow concrete lane winds between the straggle of houses that dot the south-facing slopes of the island, the occasional groupings of buildings called Higher Town, Middle Town and Lower Town. Flower farms, market gardens and even a vineyard flourish on the southern slopes, hidden behind high hedges of salt-tolerant griselina and pittosporum.

When people tell you why St Martin's is their favourite island, they usually mention two things: the empty, white beaches and the concentration of wonderful, simple food produced here from the land and the sea.

A Slow day on St Martin might start with a stroll to the St Martin's Bakery to scoop up a few picnic ingredients and a walk along Par Beach or along the gorse-covered inland ridge to Chapel Down, the easternmost rump of the island, less than a mile from Higher Town. The red and white nose of the daymark is a constant presence on the northern headland and the coastal path eventually runs past it. Looking west, beyond the daymark you suddenly realise why there's so much talk of St Martin's perfect beaches: at your feet lies the horseshoe-shaped Bread and Cheese Cove, and around the headland the long, sparkling white sweep of Great Bay. (The sand is partly composed of tiny particles of quartz, which is why it appears to sparkle.) The sea is that particular shade of turquoise blue and jade green peculiar to Scilly. On a clear blue March day, I walked the length of both beaches without seeing a soul, but residents tell me that's it's rare to find more than a handful of families on either beach as most visitors opt for the instantly accessible splendour of the south coast sands of Lawrence's Bay and Par Beach. If the tide is out, White Island can be reached across a stony bar at the furthest tip of Great Bay. There are old kelp-burning pits ahead as you cross onto the island and the empty Atlantic to the north.

Following the coast path round the western headlands to Lower Town is an easy half-hour; it doesn't take more than a couple of hours to circumnavigate the whole island. Allow much longer if you're easily distracted by beachcombing and rockpooling or unable to refrain from pausing to gape at the undiluted beauty of the land and sea and sky.

The sheltered south coast is where Jonathan Smith grows an astonishing crop of organic vegetables at **Scilly Organics** (*www.scillyorganics.com*); there's a terrific display on sale at the farm gate from May to October and a helpfully signed route around the small fields for those keen to explore his six acres that run down to Lawrence's Bay. Further east, above Higher Town Bay, Little Arthur Farm and Café (see Food and drink below) are also big on organic veg and the St Martin's Vineyard and winery is open to visitors (*01720 423418*) too.

〜〜〜〜

Food and drink

Adam's Fish and Chips Higher Town ① 01720 423082. Adam Morton goes fishing for pollock in the morning, digs his spuds in the afternoon and produces superb fish and chips in the evening. That's how he started, and not much has changed, except that Adam has been able to build a wooden hut with seating for 50, overlooking Par Beach, beneath Little Arthur Farm, where he grew up. It's proved so successful that he has enlisted the help of another Scilly fisherman and his brother, James, is growing the potatoes. Booking essential if you want a table, but it's just as nice sitting on the beach.

Little Arthur Café Higher Town ① 01720 422779. The Morton family's organic smallholding has a small café where you can munch sandwiches filled with crab or lobster, homemade mackerel pâté or salads and eggs from the hens in the garden.

Gig racing
Ⓦ www.worldgigs.co.uk.

There's always been excitement and competition when gigs are launched. In the past, crews raced to be first to put a pilot on board ships entering Scilly's treacherous navigational passages; not for fun, but for the fee that was a vital source of income. There was no cash for coming second. Islanders would spring to the oars too, when a ship went down, racing to save lives and salvage cargo. Motorised pilot boats eventually replaced the gigs, but during the 1960s a few surviving elm-built gigs were revived for racing. The *Shah*, built in 1873, is still the pride of the St Agnes gig racers and in April 2011, she carried the coffin of Osbert 'Obbie' Hicks from St Mary's to the little island churchyard on St Agnes, where he had lived all his life. As a youngster, back in the 1930s, Obbie accompanied his father Jack on pilotage jobs – in fact, Jack was the last recorded pilot to be shipped by gig when was put on board the SS *Foremost* in December 1938 by the gig *Gipsy*. Sadly, *Gipsy* was left to rot, but when gig racing started up, *Shah* was fit for action and so was Obbie; Jack stepped back into the old boat he knew so well as coxwain. If you find yourself on Scilly at the time of the World Gig Championships in the first week of May, look out for Jack Hicks's great-grandchildren, still at the oars of the *Shah* today.

Keep an eye out too, for Tresco and Bryher's flagship gig, *Czar*, a gig with a history behind her. Peter Martin completed her restoration in 2008 at his workshop on St Mary's, but she had originally been built in 1879 by the best-known gig builder of his day, William Peters of St Mawes. Peters had already built a fast pilot gig for Bryher and designed the slightly longer *Czar* with a place for a seventh oar, reckoning that was the only way she could outrun her rival. *Czar* was delivered just ahead of a wild and stormy night during which two ships were wrecked. Immediately launched as a rescue and salvage vessel, she paid for herself on that first night in service.

St Martin's Bakery Moo Green, Higher Town Ⓣ 01720 423444. Toby Tobin-Dougan's handmade loaves, rolls, pasties and pies have won awards and a devoted following. The bakery closes in the winter and Toby runs courses in bread- and pastry-making which sound like a lot of fun (*www.scillyonline.co.uk/stmbakery*).

St Martin's Hotel Lower Town Ⓣ 01720 422090. Built in 1989 to resemble a row of granite cottages, the hotel is the island's smartest place to stay and eat. (It was even awarded a Michelin star in 2007.) Special evening boats from Bryher, Tresco and St Mary's are laid on for dinners here in the summer.

Seven Stones Lower Town ☎ 01720 423505. A big, roomy pub with a friendly atmosphere, local ales and flowers on the bar. Lots of outdoor seating in front of the pub, which can get very busy at lunchtimes, with views over the harbour to Tresco and St Mary's. Sunday roasts are a winter treat on the island.

④ The Eastern Isles

Frequent boat trips tour around the craggy islands, but no landings are made as they are sanctuaries for breeding colonies of seals and seabirds. Even the boatman was surprised by the quantity of seals we discovered on a sheltered beach of Great Ganilly, when I visited in March. Upwards of 100 seals lay flopped on the beach or appeared close to the boat, heads bobbing with dog-like curiosity. Kayaking is a wonderful way to get even closer to the seals and birds (see page 254), but you can get closer still with a snorkel and flippers. The St Martin's Dive School (*01720 422848; www.scillydiving.com*) equips you, gives instruction and leads swimmers (minimum age eight) into the seal-filled waters.

⑤ Teän and St Helen's

Lying off the west coast of St Martin's, these two islands and their third, smaller neighbour, **Round Island**, are uninhabited, but often visited by private boats and specialist tour groups in the summer. On **St Helen's** the remains of a Celtic oratory, overlaid with those of a medieval church, maintained by the

Wildlife on Scilly

In 1985, the newly created Isles of Scilly Wildlife Trust (*www.ios-wildlifetrust. org.uk*) took on the mighty responsibility of leasing from the Duchy all the untenanted land in Scilly in order to safeguard the extraordinary biodiversity on the islands, which includes some home-grown specialities, such as the snouty little Scilly shrew and the chestnut-coloured Scilly bee. Many visitors to Scilly come specifically for the wildlife (including a few who come to volunteer their services to the Trust) and hordes of birdwatchers will descend on the islands whenever a rare migrant, such as a hoopoe or golden oriole which has been blown off-course, is spotted. I was impressed by the casual appearance of a ring ouzel during my first amble round St Mary's one April, and even more impressed by the boatman who gently drew his boat in close to the rocky shore of Great Arthur in the Eastern Isles, where he had spotted a pair of diminutive purple sandpipers. But even non-birdwatchers will be astonished at the local blackbirds, which have distinctively reddish-orange – as opposed to yellow – beaks and at the tameness (let alone the quantity) of the sparrows and thrushes on the islands. I can't think when I last saw a thrush on mainland Cornwall.

The local bird expert is Will Wagstaff; his guided walks and evening talks are advertised on the quay in St Mary's.

monks of Tavistock until the 15th century, a priest's house and small field system are still visible, and on the south shore of the island are the ruins of an 18th-century Pest House, intended – but scarcely used – for quarantining plague victims on ships headed for west coast English ports.

Once a year, early in August, a pilgrimage to the island is led by the vicar of Scilly, who holds a service in the chapel ruins, followed by a picnic on the beach.

From St Martin's Hotel on the western tip of St Martin's, it looks as though you could swim to **Teän**, but the water's deep and the current in the narrow sound strong. Private boat trips are available or you can join a guided tour of the tiny island, which has a rich archaeological history. Worked flints are still found on the beach, there are Bronze Age burial mounds and medieval graves beside the ruins of St Theona's Chapel. The most visible traces of human existence on the island are the remains of the house where the Nance family lived in the 17th and 18th centuries; the Nances introduced Scillonians to the foul-smelling but profitable business of burning dried-out kelp seaweed to make soda ash, which was sent to Bristol, where it was used in the manufacture of glass. The Scilly kelp-burners lost a vital part of their income when a similar product from Spain, called barilla, became cheaply available after the Napoleonic Wars ended in 1815.

⑥ Tresco

Tresco is as different from the other inhabited islands as Padstow is from Newlyn. The other islands give the impression of having grown haphazardly, with buildings casually strewn along the sandy sheltered shores and miniature fields sprouting long-abandoned varieties of narcissus. On Tresco, things look more organised, less dictated to by weather and tide and unfavourable economies. It looks as though the National Trust has stepped in and smartened things up in a tasteful way. Signposts give timings for the walks to the New Inn or to Pentle Bay, recycling bins are thoughtfully provided, polite notices explain which areas are private, and tarmac lanes are filled with smiling families on bicycles and Prince Harry lookalikes in sailing gear. There's no campsite and only a very limited number of bed and breakfast rooms, but timeshare flats are promoted, in a conscious effort to create a sort of extended 'Tresco family' – people who will come back year after year and regard it as a (second) home, rather than treat it as a holiday commodity for a week.

At the midpoint of the island, **New Grimsby** could not be further removed in appearance from its mainland namesake. Estate cottages, offices, the Tresco Stores and Flying Boat Club huddle at one end of the shallow bay; while at the harbour end stand an art and craft gallery and the New Inn. It's just a step from here to St Nicholas's Church, built in 1878 to the design of Thomas Dorrien-Smith, (the nephew of Augustus) and over the hill lie the spectacular white beaches of Old Grimsby and Pentle Bay. A circular walk, taking in both the Grimsbys, an Elizabethan defensive fort known as the Blockhouse, and the east coast beaches, with wonderful views over the Eastern Rocks, as well as the lakeside approach to the Abbey takes a gentle hour.

It's only when you get to the rugged, northernmost acres of the island covered in bracken and gorse that you find yourself reminded of the other islands. The remains of two defensive **fortresses** look across the western shore to Bryher. The higher of the two, which is just a ruin, is known as King Charles's Castle, though it was built long before his day by Henry VIII, in case of attack by the French. Some poor military architect's head must have rolled, for the building was placed too high. There's a fine view over any ship attempting to enter the narrow sound below, but as soon as you point a cannon at it, gravity takes command of the cannonball before it can be fired. Oops.

In consequence, Henry ensured the second fort was built lower down, just above the high-tide mark (renamed Cromwell's Castle after the Civil War) and added a third fort for good measure (the **Blockhouse**) on the seaward-facing shore at the south point of Old Grimsby Bay. But neither saw any real action until 1651, when Parliamentarian troops under Admiral Blake fought the Royalist governor of Scilly, John Grenville, back to St Mary's. Cromwell's Castle was rebuilt as a solid tower and gun platform and a garrison of Roundheads was installed within. Some of the grafitti scratched on the stone walls is thought to have been left by soldiers manning the garrison.

The Abbey Garden

① 01720 424105 ⓦ www.tresco.co.uk.

At the south end of the island, given shelter by a thick fringe of trees and a natural rise in the land to the north, the world-class gardens play a major part in drawing visitors to the island. What makes the gardens so special is the enormous range of plants from around the globe that flourish here, without glass or any kind of protection except the band of Monterey pines and cypresses and monumental hedges of evergreen oak that encircle the south-facing terraces. There are all the established favourites – exotics you see growing all over Scilly – such as giant blue Echiums (known as Cornish foxgloves on the mainland), glossy purple-black aeoniums, fat, spiky aloes and a profusion of Watsonias. But there's so much more: enough to make seasoned curators of botanic gardens go weak at the knees and render the most senior garden writers speechless with wonder. The local microclimates within the 17 acres allow not only subtropical plants to be grown, but also New Zealand Pohutukawa trees with massive spreading branches, often smothered in crimson flowers, Australian banksias and South African proteas, Madeiran clethras and dozens of sweet, yellow-flowered mimosas.

Mike Nelhams, the curator, who came here as head gardener at the tender age of 27 after working at High Beeches in Sussex, stresses however, that it's not a botanic garden; 'every plant here has to be garden worthy, fantastic to look at and play its part in the local and overall display. We're not into collecting rare plants just because we can grow them and make a collection.'

The islands, the Duchy and the Smiths

It's surprising how many people think that Scilly is a part of Cornwall, but it's not. It's a unitary authority (the smallest in the UK) in its own right. True, the islanders are represented in Parliament by the MP for St Ives and some areas of local government, such as Health and Local Enterprise Partnerships, are shared with Cornwall Council. But for many on the islands, the complex relationship with the mainland revolves mainly around the Duchy of Cornwall, from whom all buildings and land are leased. This goes back to 1337, when Edward III creatively rearranged an old earldom, incorporating choice bits of southwest England to form the Duchy of Cornwall, in order to provide an income for his eldest son, the Prince of Wales. It's fair to add that while the Isles of Scilly may look like a jewel in the Duchy crown, it's hardly a financial asset: overall, I was told, the Duchy spends more on the islands than it receives.

The entire island of Tresco is leased from the Duchy by the Dorrien-Smith family, which explains why it has such a strong and separate identity. This began in 1834, when Augustus Smith, a Hertfordshire banker, was granted the lease – and governorship – of not just Tresco, but all the islands. He seems to have been a benevolent kind of dictator, making sure that retired or disabled islanders were spared from poverty, building schools and creatively encouraging attendance, by charging the children a penny a day if they went and a twopenny fine if they didn't. But his attempts to reform the economic and moral dereliction he perceived (which included waging war on smuggling and sending the unemployed and unemployable back to the mainland), did not endear him to everyone. Tresco alone now remains in the hands of his great-great-great nephew, Robert Dorrien-Smith, who continues the tradition of benevolent stewardship and personal investment in the island community. All 160 permanent residents on the smartly maintained island are employed and housed (a perk which continues after retirement) by the 'Boss'.

The impression as you enter is of lush scents, textures and flowers, but it's the sense of volume that draws you in. Like a classical Italian garden, there is height and structure, long vistas contained within high hedges; steps crowned with sculptures and the ruins of an ancient place of worship. It's a bit wild, too, just like a Tuscan garden, and plants are encouraged to self-seed and give each other support and shelter. Gardeners grow here too. Mike encourages the team of nine, taking them to visit the best subtropical and Mediterranean gardens around Europe, organising international exchanges of plants and students, and recently, arranging for Tresco to be twinned with the famous Hanbury gardens at La Mortola in Italy.

In a quiet corner of the gardens, the **Valhalla Museum** exhibits a collection of ships' figureheads, salvaged from wrecks around the islands' treacherous coast.

The private Utopia of Augustus Smith

What kind of man would want to leave his life as a successful merchant banker with a comfortable estate in Hertfordshire, and take on the lease and responsibility for five islands existing on the brink of extreme poverty? The complex, wealthy and socially imaginative Augustus Smith saw his opportunity to create a model society, founded on what he recognised as sound economic and moral principles. As an MP, Smith had already fought against the enclosure of Berkhamsted Common and improved access to education for the poor, but clearly this was just the start of a utopian vision that rapidly took shape when he bought the lease from the Duchy in 1834. In between restructuring the economy and population of the islands, Smith found time to start planting a magnificent garden, realising that he could grow just about anything the world had to offer. It's tempting to see it as a private Eden, but one in which Smith played the role of God, not Adam.

Food and drink

Tresco's upmarket aspirations are reflected in the food and drink on the island and prices reflect the quality of what's on offer here. Budget-conscious visitors might want to bring a picnic.

Abbey Gardens Café ⓣ 01720 424105. Similar in presentation to a National Trust café: good coffee, cakes and sandwiches and interesting specials board at lunchtime.

New Inn ⓣ 01720 422844. Indoors, the bar is made from reclaimed driftwood; outdoors, in a sheltered courtyard and garden are tables and chairs overlooking the harbour. The menu is designed to please foodies; Scillonian and Cornish ales are on tap.

Tresco Stores ⓣ 01720 422806. Not unlike Waitrose, this is more of a giant deli than a supermarket, with the emphasis firmly on Cornish produce. St Agnes's Troytown dairy ice cream and milk can be found here and Tresco's delicious beef.

⑦ Bryher

The smallest of the inhabited islands has a simple, barefoot beauty, that many feared would be lost when the Tresco estate took over the Hell Bay Hotel and gave it an upmarket eco-makeover in 1999. Those fears turned out to be unfounded, for Bryher remains far from gentrified, and that feeling of wild remoteness remains unchanged, its beauty reflected in the extraordinary stained-glass windows in the little church, close to the quay, made by Oriel Hicks, whose workshops are on St Mary's and can be visited (see page 258). Nevertheless, changes are afoot. There's been a recent influx of younger residents, families with young children too, and their energy is revitalising the small community.

The north and south faces of the island couldn't be more different: Rushy Bay at the south end is pristine white sand and translucent jade and turquoise water. Shipman Head Down, to the north has a wild, Hebridean look to it, and yet they are separated by just a mile of sandy tracks and paths. Similarly, the east coast turns a neighbourly face across a narrow stretch of water to Tresco while the west coast faces the onslaught of the Atlantic (Hell Bay did not acquire its name by chance) and sunsets that reduce everyone to silence. Bryher was my first introduction to the Isles of Scilly and the diversity of its beauty took my breath away. Like so many people arriving on Scilly for the first time, I found it hard to believe I was still in England, just a few minutes' flight from the mainland.

Katherine Sawyer, Scilly's resident archaeologist, who regularly leads guided walks around the islands (*01720 423326*), made the visit even more enjoyable. I could have scrunched my way quite happily alone up the granite-strewn slope to enjoy the views from Shipman Head Down on Bryher, while little white-rumped birds sprang from the heather all round, but with Katherine guiding, our four-strong group discovered that some of the underfoot scrunch was flint, deposited on the northern points of the islands 20,000 years ago by south-bound glaciers crashing to a halt. Some of the granite boulders transpired to be remnants of Bronze Age ramparts, or a primitive customs barrier. The birds turned out to be wheatears, breaking the long journey from tropical Africa to more northerly parts of Europe. And the cushiony quilt of ling and bell heather, more properly known as 'maritime waved heathland', sculpted by wind and salt spray, is grazed by ponies and cattle, as part of a land conservation scheme on Bryher. I was glad also, to be quietly informed on my first day that islanders don't like it when people say 'Scilly Isles': it's always 'The Isles of Scilly' or just 'Scilly'. Information, especially when delivered by a friendly native, with a dry sense of humour, is bliss.

Food and drink

Home-grown produce, eggs, jam, flowers and fudge plus an honesty box at the garden gate is not an uncommon sight on the island. Fresh fish, crab and lobster can be found at Dawn Vue (close to Anneka Quay) or ① 01720 422975 to see what's available.

Fraggle Rock Bar and Café ① 01720 422222. A café-cum-pub at the north end of the island; convivial fish and chip nights on Fri; decent pub grub and Cornish ales on tap at other times.

Hell Bay Hotel ① 01720 422947. Hell Bay is a little further to the north; the hotel overlooks Great Porth Beach; a superb spot for a morning coffee or afternoon tea. The upmarket bar menu is available at lunchtime, but you'll need reservations for evening meals if not staying at the hotel.

Vine Café ① 01720 423168. Close to the post office and shop, this offers a menu of homemade thick soups, hearty sandwiches and cakes, books on the shelves and friendly chat.

⑧ Samson

The twin, barren peaks of Samson make it one of the more easily recognisable landmarks of the Scilly archipelago. Boats stop here *en route* for Bryher and drop adventurous passengers in the shallow water on the beach and pick them up again a few hours later. There are no loos, no shelter from sun or rain, nor are there any cafés on the island – just empty beaches, birds and the sad ruins of cottages last inhabited during the 1850s and the crumbling walls of the park, where deer were briefly kept by Augustus Smith, until they escaped. There is much evidence of older populations that lived here when Samson was part of a single land mass: groups of open-mouthed, Bronze Age burial cists and graves are dotted about the island and low tides may reveal remnants of stone-edged medieval field boundaries. Waiting for the boat to return to the beach, with your back to a sand-dune, looking out at the islands, the sea, the birds and the sky – and not counting the minutes as they pass – has to be one of the most authentic Slow experiences of the many to be enjoyed on Scilly.

Index

Main entries in **bold**, map pages in *italics*.